PSAT/NMSQT*
FOR
DUMMIES®

by Geraldine Woods with Kristin Josephson

WILEY

John Wiley & Sons, Inc.

PSAT/NMSQT* For Dummies®

Published by
John Wiley & Sons, Inc.
111 River St.
Hoboken, NJ 07030-5774
www.wiley.com

Copyright © 2013 by John Wiley & Sons, Inc., Hoboken, New Jersey

Published by John Wiley & Sons, Inc., Hoboken, New Jersey

Published simultaneously in Canada

No part of this publication may be reproduced, stored in a retrieval system or transmitted in any form or by any means, electronic, mechanical, photocopying, recording, scanning or otherwise, except as permitted under Sections 107 or 108 of the 1976 United States Copyright Act, without the prior written permission of the Publisher. Requests to the Publisher for permission should be addressed to the Permissions Department, John Wiley & Sons, Inc., 111 River Street, Hoboken, NJ 07030, (201) 748-6011, fax (201) 748-6008, or online at http://www.wiley.com/go/permissions.

Trademarks: Wiley, the Wiley logo, For Dummies, the Dummies Man logo, A Reference for the Rest of Us!, The Dummies Way, Dummies Daily, The Fun and Easy Way, Dummies.com, Making Everything Easier, and related trade dress are trademarks or registered trademarks of John Wiley & Sons, Inc., and/or its affiliates in the United States and other countries, and may not be used without written permission. PSAT/NMSQT is a registered trademark of the College Board and the National Merit Scholarship Corporation, which were not involved in the production of, and do not endorse, this product. All other trademarks are the property of their respective owners. John Wiley & Sons, Inc., is not associated with any product or vendor mentioned in this book.

LIMIT OF LIABILITY/DISCLAIMER OF WARRANTY: THE PUBLISHER AND THE AUTHOR MAKE NO REPRESENTATIONS OR WARRANTIES WITH RESPECT TO THE ACCURACY OR COMPLETENESS OF THE CONTENTS OF THIS WORK AND SPECIFICALLY DISCLAIM ALL WARRANTIES, INCLUDING WITHOUT LIMITATION WARRANTIES OF FITNESS FOR A PARTICULAR PURPOSE. NO WARRANTY MAY BE CREATED OR EXTENDED BY SALES OR PROMOTIONAL MATERIALS. THE ADVICE AND STRATEGIES CONTAINED HEREIN MAY NOT BE SUITABLE FOR EVERY SITUATION. THIS WORK IS SOLD WITH THE UNDERSTANDING THAT THE PUBLISHER IS NOT ENGAGED IN RENDERING LEGAL, ACCOUNTING, OR OTHER PROFESSIONAL SERVICES. IF PROFESSIONAL ASSISTANCE IS REQUIRED, THE SERVICES OF A COMPETENT PROFESSIONAL PERSON SHOULD BE SOUGHT. NEITHER THE PUBLISHER NOR THE AUTHOR SHALL BE LIABLE FOR DAMAGES ARISING HEREFROM. THE FACT THAT AN ORGANIZATION OR WEBSITE IS REFERRED TO IN THIS WORK AS A CITATION AND/OR A POTENTIAL SOURCE OF FURTHER INFORMATION DOES NOT MEAN THAT THE AUTHOR OR THE PUBLISHER ENDORSES THE INFORMATION THE ORGANIZATION OR WEBSITE MAY PROVIDE OR RECOMMENDATIONS IT MAY MAKE. FURTHER, READERS SHOULD BE AWARE THAT INTERNET WEBSITES LISTED IN THIS WORK MAY HAVE CHANGED OR DISAPPEARED BETWEEN WHEN THIS WORK WAS WRITTEN AND WHEN IT IS READ.

For general information on our other products and services, please contact our Customer Care Department within the U.S. at 877-762-2974, outside the U.S. at 317-572-3993, or fax 317-572-4002.

For technical support, please visit www.wiley.com/techsupport.

Wiley publishes in a variety of print and electronic formats and by print-on-demand. Some material included with standard print versions of this book may not be included in e-books or in print-on-demand. If this book refers to media such as a CD or DVD that is not included in the version you purchased, you may download this material at http://booksupport.wiley.com. For more information about Wiley products, visit www.wiley.com.

Library of Congress Control Number: 2012956408

ISBN 978-1-118-42429-2 (pbk); ISBN 978-1-118-42433-9 (ebk); ISBN 978-1-118-42431-5 (ebk); ISBN 978-1-118-42434-6 (ebk)

Manufactured in the United States of America

10 9 8 7 6 5 4 3 2 1

WILEY

About the Authors

Geraldine Woods has prepared students for the PSAT/NMSQT, both academically and emotionally, for the past three decades. She is the author of more than 50 books, including *SAT For Dummies, English Grammar For Dummies, English Grammar Workbook For Dummies, Research Papers For Dummies,* and *College Admission Essays For Dummies,* all published by Wiley. She lives in New York City with her husband and two parakeets.

Kristin Josephson survived the college admission process only to drop out of the Massachusetts Institute of Technology 16 months later to attend circus school in San Francisco. While there, she studied flying trapeze, trampoline, and acrobatics. Kristin discovered her passion for teaching while she was tutoring in the Bay Area, a passion that led her to complete her degree at Colorado College. Kristin eventually became a teacher at a private school in New York City, where she has been teaching high school mathematics since 2007.

Dedication

From Gerri: For P and LG, together forever, and growing all the time.

Author's Acknowledgments

From Gerri: I appreciate the efforts of Alissa Schwipps, Todd Lothery, and Lindsay Lefevere of Wiley, as well as those of my agent, Lisa Queen. I am grateful for the close attention of my technical editors, Karen Berlin Ishii and Gail Lewis.

Publisher's Acknowledgments

We're proud of this book; please send us your comments at http://dummies.custhelp.com. For other comments, please contact our Customer Care Department within the U.S. at 877-762-2974, outside the U.S. at 317-572-3993, or fax 317-572-4002.

Some of the people who helped bring this book to market include the following:

Acquisitions, Editorial, and Vertical Websites

Senior Project Editor: Alissa Schwipps

Executive Editor: Lindsay Sandman Lefevere

Copy Editor: Todd Lothery

Assistant Editor: David Lutton

Editorial Program Coordinator: Joe Niesen

Technical Editors: Karen Berlin Ishii, Gail Lewis

Editorial Manager: Christine Meloy Beck

Editorial Assistants: Rachelle S. Amick, Alexa Koschier

Cover Photos: © Kostyantin Pankin/iStockphoto.com

Cartoons: Rich Tennant (www.the5thwave.com)

Composition Services

Project Coordinator: Patrick Redmond

Layout and Graphics: Carrie A. Cesavice, Erin Zeltner

Proofreaders: Jessica Kramer, Lisa Young Stiers

Indexer: BIM Indexing & Proofreading Services

Special Help
Christina Guthrie

Publishing and Editorial for Consumer Dummies

Kathleen Nebenhaus, Vice President and Executive Publisher

David Palmer, Associate Publisher

Kristin Ferguson-Wagstaffe, Product Development Director

Publishing for Technology Dummies

Andy Cummings, Vice President and Publisher

Composition Services

Debbie Stailey, Director of Composition Services

Contents at a Glance

Table of Contents

Introduction

*P*SAT/NMSQT. Say that three times fast, and you sound like you're inhaling a particularly tangled strand of spaghetti. But no matter how you pronounce it, the PSAT/NMSQT is actually a key to your future, because it's an exam that can open doors to college admissions and scholarships.

The word *preliminary* (the P in PSAT) hints at one important reason to take this test: You take the PSAT/NMSQT before the SAT, so when you hit the SAT, you've already sampled the test-taking experience. Knowing what to expect makes you more confident. Plus, the College Board (the organization that administers both tests) reports that students who take the PSAT/NMSQT on average score 146 points higher on the SAT than those who skip the preliminary exam. Because the top score on the SAT is 2400, 146 points is a significant chunk and can make a difference in your college application.

Another advantage of the PSAT/NMSQT is financial. When you take the test as a high-school junior, you're automatically entered into a number of scholarship competitions that the National Merit Scholarship Corporation runs. (If you take the test before junior year, you can't be considered for a scholarship, but you can retake the exam when you're eligible. The extra practice will most likely raise your score.) Besides its own National Merit Scholarships, the corporation awards National Achievement Scholarships to top-scoring African-American students. The same exam also gives test-takers a chance to enroll in the National Hispanic Recognition Program, which identifies outstanding Hispanic/Latino students and sends their names to colleges, boosting the odds that they'll be offered scholarships funded by these institutions. And — as they say in TV infomercials — that's not all! The PSAT/NMSQT is a gateway to other juicy scholarships financed by corporations, unions, and other organizations. How juicy? Awards range from a few hundred to many thousands of dollars.

All in all, you can gain a lot from the PSAT/NMSQT. But as the slogan says, "No pain, no gain." In the case of the PSAT/NMSQT, though, the pain is minimal. Sacrifice a few hours of your life to preparation — and a little more than two hours taking the exam — and you boost your chances of attending your favorite college, perhaps with scholarship aid. Definitely worth the effort!

About This Book

Whether or not you're hoping for a scholarship, you've already demonstrated your brilliance by purchasing *PSAT/NMSQT For Dummies* (she commented modestly). But brilliance isn't enough when it comes to standardized tests. Every exam has little quirks — favorite question topics, common traps that may ensnare you, timing issues, and so forth. Never fear. In *PSAT/NMSQT For Dummies,* I review the most common topics that appear on the reading, writing, and math sections of the exam. I show you how to decode the language the College Board favors for its questions. (*Hint:* No real person talks that way.) I also provide some long-term strategies for sharpening your skills and explain when, how, and where to sign up. For students needing accommodations (extra time, large type, and so forth), I tell you how to proceed (and persuade), so that the College Board meets your needs.

Theory is fine, but you can't master the PSAT/NMSQT without actually taking an exam. I start off small. In each chapter devoted to a question type (sentence completions or algebra, for example), I include practice problems. Then I hit the big time, giving you four complete exams, each accompanied by an answer key that tells you *why* a particular answer is correct and why another attractive answer doesn't make the grade. The scoring guide in the appendix tells you how you did, so you can measure your improvement. Don't do all the exams at once. (If you do, your eyeballs will fall out. Your brain, too.) Instead, take one, score it, return to it for extra review, and then take another. On exam day, you'll be ready to ace the PSAT/NMSQT.

Also, like other *For Dummies* books, this book is **modular** (made up of units that can be arranged in many ways), meaning you don't have to read it from start to finish but can instead dip into it in whatever order you like. Start with Part I for the details of the exam's logistics, delve into Parts II and III for practice and review, or head straight to Part IV to get started on a practice test. It's up to you.

Conventions Used in This Book

In this book, I describe the Fly-Fishing Convention and the Butter Churners of America Convention. Oops. Not really. The **conventions** (practices or procedures) I do use are fairly simple to grasp:

- ✔ When I tell you about a website, I use `monofont`, which looks like this: `www.college board.com` or `www.nationalmerit.org`.

- ✔ **Bold** text highlights important points and the action parts of numbered steps or processes.

- ✔ Keep your eye out for this *font* (typestyle), which indicates a good addition to your PSAT/NMSQT vocabulary. I define any word written this way immediately, so you can strengthen your vocabulary painlessly as you read. (Did you notice this font at the beginning of the section? It signals one definition for *convention*.) Although the exam has no section labeled *vocabulary,* the critical reading passages and sentence completions often feature tough words, the kind that English teachers and test-writers love. Instead of asking you to memorize a lengthy list — an inefficient and ineffective method, in my view — I slide new words into your brain gradually, so they stay there, ready to help you on test day and beyond.

By the way, I choose to name the exam by its first four letters — the "pee ess eh tee." Feel free to refer to it as "messy spaghetti" or whatever appeals to you. You can even latch onto the official name: The Preliminary SAT/National Merit Scholarship Qualifying Test. (What does *SAT* stand for? You had to ask! It used to represent *Scholastic Aptitude Test.* Now the College Board, which creates and administers the exam, says that "SAT means SAT." Whatever. They call the shots!)

What You're Not to Read

I was the kind of kid who fell down the stairs because I couldn't stop reading long enough to look at the steps. I'm still that way, actually. So it's tough to tell you *not* to pay attention to every single word in this book. However, I also know that life in the 21st century doesn't give you many extra minutes. Here's what to drop:

✔ **Stuff you already know:** In this book I cover *everything* that's on the test, but you probably don't need to review everything. If your math teacher occasionally goes out for coffee and lets you teach the class, you can probably skip some math review chapters in Part III. If you never met a reading passage that stumped you, just dip a toe into Chapter 4. You can always return to that chapter later if you find yourself making errors on the passage-based reading questions.

✔ **Explanations of technical terms:** A chapter of answers and explanations follows each practice test. In the explanations, I sometimes explain things in two different ways — once in ordinary language and then again in more technical terms that you may have learned in English or math class. (In the writing section, for example, I may say that a sentence is wrong because it doesn't express a complete thought and also explain that grammarians call a complete thought an *independent clause*.) If you answered correctly, feel free to skip the technical terms.

✔ **Practical information about the test, unless you need it:** In many high schools, the administration does pretty much everything for you. Nameless, overworked, and underpaid employees order the exams, arrange accommodations for those with special needs, and sign you up for the most helpful sort of score report. My school even supplies sharpened number two pencils! In that kind of situation, your role is limited to paying for the exam, signing statements about the accommodations you need, and showing up. Oh, and you also have to take the test. If I just described your high school, skip the logistical information in Chapter 2. If you're in a less helpful environment, take what you need from Chapter 2 and leave the rest alone.

Foolish Assumptions

Whenever I mention *For Dummies* books, most people enthusiastically tell me how books in the series helped them learn French, wallpaper a kitchen, or write a will. But every so often I hear a comment like, *"I* don't read *For Dummies* books because *I'm* not a dummy." My answer is always the same. I assume that my readers are *not* dummies. They just want useful information presented in a lighthearted, easy-to-understand way. To me, that indicates that my readers are *smarties*. Here are a few other assumptions I made about you, the reader:

✔ You plan to take the PSAT/NMSQT this year or next, and you want to ace the test.

✔ You're busy, and you have no patience for anyone who wastes your time.

✔ You want to learn strategy and techniques for the PSAT/NMSQT, so your test score accurately reflects your abilities.

✔ You've studied two years of high-school math already, but you can benefit from a refresher of some basic concepts as they appear on the exam. (If math really puzzles you, you may want to check out more in-depth *For Dummies* titles on this subject, including *Algebra I For Dummies,* by Mary Jane Sterling, or *Geometry For Dummies,* by Mark Ryan, both published by Wiley.)

✔ You don't have a nervous breakdown when you face a reading passage, but you could use some help with PSAT-style comprehension questions.

✔ You know a fair amount of English grammar. (If grammar isn't your friend, take a look at another of my *For Dummies* books — either *English Grammar For Dummies,* 2nd Edition, or *English Grammar Workbook For Dummies,* 2nd Edition, both published by Wiley. The first reviews the essentials of grammar, and the second gives you a chance to practice proper English, including concepts that are frequent flyers on the PSAT/NMSQT.)

How This Book Is Organized

First up in *PSAT/NMSQT For Dummies* is a quick tour of the exam, so you know what you're taking, how much time you have, how to sign up, where your scores go, and how thin your wallet will be when you're finished. After a review of the content you're expected to know for the test, I provide the best strategy for each type of question, along with some practice. Finally, I offer four whole PSAT/NMSQT exams, complete with answers, explanations, and scoring guides, so you can gauge how you're doing. Now for the details.

Part I: Soaring Over the PSAT/NMSQT

When you get to the test center on the big day, you don't want surprises. This part covers the practical stuff: when and where to go, what to bring (including the kind of calculator you're allowed), and what you'll probably see on the exam. I also explain what to expect after the exam (when your scores will arrive, for example). If you have special needs, in this part you can find out how to arrange for extra time, large print, fee waivers, and the like. Here I also explain the application process for National Merit Scholarships, National Achievement Scholarships (for African-American students), and the National Hispanic Recognition Program (for Hispanic/Latino students). Finally, this part provides strategies for long-range, short-range, and "it's tomorrow? really?" preparation.

Part II: Word Up!: The Critical Reading and Writing Sections

Word up, in case you aren't familiar with this slang expression, means "I agree." Whether or not you *do* agree with standardized tests as an accurate measure of your reading and writing skills, you have to complete one writing and two reading sections on the PSAT/NMSQT. In this part, I start you off with sentence completions and then move on to passage-based questions, the two **components** (elements or ingredients) of the exam's reading sections. Then I tell you how to crack the writing section, in which, oddly enough, you do no writing whatsoever. Instead, you answer multiple-choice questions about improving sentences or paragraphs and spotting errors. In each chapter I illustrate the types of questions the PSAT/NMSQT throws at you and explain the best approach so you won't fumble when you see them. I also tuck some practice into each chapter. By the time you finish this part, your reading and writing skills will be sharp.

Part III: Assembling a Math Tool Kit

Numbers and operations, algebra, geometry, statistics, and probability. What could be more fun? (Don't answer that.) Whether you love or hate math, you need to know quite a bit for the PSAT/NMSQT. In this part I review the basics, show you some amazing techniques (plugging-in and backsolving, for example), and give you sample problems for every topic.

Part IV: Practice Makes Perfect: Practice Exams

Before you murder a little more than two completely innocent hours taking the PSAT/NMSQT, you should take a practice test under real exam conditions. (Okay, *almost* real. The timing and number two pencil are the same, but you won't have to block out sniffles from the kid in the next row who forgot his handkerchief.) Four practice tests, plus answers, explanations, and some additional tips, make up this part. ***Note:*** Honesty ***compels*** (forces) me to admit that I wrote these exams, not the College Board. However, these exams are just like the official versions and will prepare you well for what you face on test day.

Part V: The Part of Tens

No *For Dummies* book would be complete without the Part of Tens. Here you find ten ways to sharpen your PSAT/NMSQT skills and ten mistakes you can easily avoid. I also provide an appendix with tables that help you convert your raw test scores to the 20–80 scale that the PSAT/NMSQT favors.

Icons Used in This Book

Apart from royalty checks, these little drawings are my favorite part of every *For Dummies* book. Each alerts you to something special that will help you achieve the highest score possible.

Imagine an experienced test-taker, someone who's picked apart and analyzed the PSAT/NMSQT, leaning over your shoulder and whispering in your ear. Well, I *have* picked apart and analyzed the PSAT/NMSQT. This icon is my whisper telling you, "Here's a technique that will help!"

If you see this icon, a danger ***lurks*** (lies waiting, ready to ambush). No fear for you, though, because when you know where the trap is, you can avoid it.

On test day you face real questions, just like the ones identified with this icon.

This book is packed with ideas. As standardized tests approach, your brain may overflow. Make sure anything marked with this icon doesn't spill out because it shows you the most ***crucial*** (significant, important) elements, the information you want at your fingertips.

Where to Go from Here

Go shopping. Go bowling. Go to the Fly-Fishing Convention. Nope: I was just kidding. But if you've read the whole introduction, you really should take a break. Text a friend, go for a run, or watch a silly TV show — *The Real Vampires of Beverly Hills* or something similar.

Are you back? Good. Now take inventory. What do you know about the PSAT/NMSQT? If the answer is "very little," hit Chapters 1 and 2. If you know a lot about the test, skip Part I and turn the magnifying glass on yourself. What are your strengths and weaknesses? Okay, I know you don't actually have any weaknesses, but your skills in some areas may not be quite as strong. After you've taken inventory of your academic abilities, hit the chapters that cover material you're unsure about.

Can't diagnose yourself? No problem. Try a practice test (you need about two and a quarter hours, allowing for one break). Score it (there goes another half hour) and take a close look at the type of question that stumped you (one more half hour). Now hit Parts II or III for review. Rest and catch up on your usual life activities. Then it's time for another practice exam. Keep going until the PSAT/NMSQT is as familiar as your face in the mirror. That face will be smiling on test day, because you'll be ready.

Part I
Soaring Over the PSAT/NMSQT

In this part . . .

As I write this, two parakeets are flying over my head. I can only imagine what they see. Dust balls behind the sofa? The jade ring I lost two months ago? They have an advantage, their broad view of the entire living room.

This part gives you the same advantage, despite your lack of wings. Chapter 1 tells you what's on the test and shows you typical questions. In the same chapter you find out which scholarships you can win by doing well on the PSAT/NMSQT. Chapter 2 is devoted to practical stuff: how to sign up, when and where to show up, and how to create a study plan. In Chapter 2 you also learn some basic strategy, such as when to guess and when to skip a question.

Chapter 1

Introducing the Exam

*N*umber two pencils are probably rolling around in your backpack right now. (Why is it always number two, anyway? Doesn't anyone like number three pencils? Or number ones?) If you survived elementary and middle school, you've probably become good friends with these writing *implements* (tools) because you've already taken *multitudinous* (very many) standardized tests. The PSAT/NMSQT is just another one of those exams. It's not easy, but it's not as hard as you may imagine either. On the PSAT/NMSQT, you don't have to know what year some guy you never heard of invaded a country that doesn't exist anymore. Nor do you have to recite the periodic table or remember the rhyme scheme of a sonnet. In fact, you don't need much factual information at all. What you do need is reading, writing, and math skills. You've been working on those every day since you started school. So the good news is that you're halfway to success on the PSAT/NMSQT by the time you locate a number two pencil and sit down to work.

In this chapter, I explain the structure and timing of the PSAT/NMSQT. I also discuss the scholarships that high-scorers *contend* (compete) for, so you can determine whether the bucks you spend on the exam are likely to multiply and return to your wallet in the form of tuition aid.

One Letter Makes a Difference: The PSAT and the SAT

The PSAT/NMSQT is intended to *precede* (go before) the SAT. That's why the College Board, which creates the test, says that the "P" stands for "preliminary." Think of the PSAT/NMSQT as a mini-SAT. If the SAT is an ocean, the PSAT/NMSQT is where you dip your toes into the surf. Even at the shoreline, though, you can take a splash in the eye. Because to be *forewarned* (told of danger in advance) is to be *forearmed* (prepared), you'll do better on the SAT if you take the PSAT first.

Many colleges require or encourage their applicants to take the SAT, and about 3 million people do so every year. Most students take the exam in the spring of junior year and then again in the autumn or winter of senior year. The SAT has ten sections, but only nine count toward your score. The tenth section, which isn't identified, lets the test-writers evaluate new questions. In other words, you pay to take a test and they use your work to *refine* (improve) their product. Nice of them, right?

Like the PSAT/NMSQT, the SAT tests critical reading, writing, and math. The question types and level of difficulty are the same on both exams, with two exceptions. The SAT includes some math typically taught in the third year of high school; the PSAT/NMSQT stops at the two-year level. On the SAT you also write a short essay (with a pencil! practically medieval!), but the PSAT is essay-free. Both tests require you to answer a ton of multiple-choice questions and a handful of math grid-ins. (See Chapter 6 for more on grid-ins.) Each area of the SAT (reading, writing, and math) is scored on a 200–800 point scale, similar to the 20–80 scale of the PSAT/NMSQT, but with an extra zero. Basically, you get 200 just for showing up, and 800 if you're a genius.

One other important factor distinguishes the SAT from the PSAT/NMSQT: The PSAT/NMSQT serves as a screening tool for several important scholarships, including the National Merit Scholarship program. (Check out "Bubbling for Dollars: National Merit and Other Scholarships" later in this chapter for more information.)

Familiarity Breeds Content (ment): Surveying the PSAT/NMSQT

Picture your smile when you get an acceptance letter from Really-Wanna-Go-There University. Imagine your joy when the Foundation to Assist Tired Test-Takers offers you tuition aid. Doing well on the PSAT/NMSQT makes these *scenarios* (outlines of expected events) more likely. Colleges often recruit top scorers on the PSAT/NMSQT, and the exam screens students for many scholarships.

When you take the PSAT/NMSQT, the best way to feel *content* (which means "happy" when the accent's on the last syllable) is to know the exam's *content* (which means "what's inside" when the accent's on the first syllable). You face five sections, always in the same order:

Section 1	Critical Reading	25 minutes	8 sentence completions
			16 multiple-choice, passage-based questions
Section 2	Mathematics	25 minutes	20 multiple-choice questions
Section 3	Critical Reading	25 minutes	5 sentence completions
			19 multiple-choice, passage-based questions
Section 4	Mathematics	25 minutes	8 multiple-choice questions
			10 grid-ins
Section 5	Writing	30 minutes	20 sentence-improvement questions
			14 error-recognition questions
			5 paragraph-improvement questions

You get some breaks — five minutes between Sections 2 and 3, and a minute after Section 4. Not much, true, but enough to stretch tight muscles and ready yourself for the next question *barrage* (concentrated burst of enemy fire). For details on the types of questions you face, read on.

Critical Reading

Wouldn't it be fun if the "critical" portion of this section's name meant that you could review the exam on the Internet? ("No stars. The first passage was boring, and the sentence completions were the verbal equivalent of a sleeping pill.") Unfortunately, in this context "critical" means that you have to dig into the sentences and passages, paying attention to what they say as well as what they *imply* (hint at).

Sentence completions

Given a sentence with one or two words left out, you have to figure out which word or pair of words fits the meaning of the sentence. For example, you may see a question like this:

The proctor required students to wear _____ badges before she admitted them to the testing room.

(A) humiliating

(B) identifying

(C) obscure

(D) stolen

(E) colossal

Common sense, as well as some knowledge of vocabulary, helps you with this one. What sort of badges would you need in a testing room? The kind that assures the authorities that you haven't paid your genius cousin to take the test for you — in other words, *identifying* badges, Choice (B). (By the way, you don't need a badge for the real exam. If you take the test in a school you don't attend, though, bring a photo ID with you. More on this topic appears in Chapter 2.) Before you move ahead, take a second to learn some vocabulary words. *Humiliating* means "embarrassing," *obscure* is "little known," and *colossal* is a fancy word for "huge."

Each PSAT/NMSQT has 13 of these questions, and those are 13 points you don't want to lose. Turn to Chapter 3 for sentence-completion techniques and practice questions.

Passage-based questions

These are standard reading-comprehension questions: factual information, inference (determining what the passage implies but doesn't state), vocabulary-in-context, main idea, tone, and so forth. Each reading section contains two short passages (100 to 150 words each). Next up are long passages — anywhere from 600 to 850 words. Somewhere in every exam is a pair of passages, either short or long, written by different authors about the same topic. In a paired-passage section, you find a few questions on each and then some questions that compare or contrast the two.

Many passages come from modern works, but generally some older material (19th or early 20th century) shows up. The College Board tends to ask easier questions about passages that are hard to read and harder questions about passages that are easy to read. (In other words, they get you one way or another!) Expect to see passages about science and history, usually a memoir, and even some fiction. Here's a sample PSAT/NMSQT passage-based question:

Line   With great ceremony, I pour a glass of milk and place a cookie on a napkin for Santa, along with an apple for the reindeer. When Tommy is asleep, I drink most of the milk and eat the cookie. I take a bite out of the apple. When Tommy wakes, he runs to check. "Santa was here!" he shouts. A few months later, having been told the facts of life by a classmate, he
(05)   asks me whether Santa is real. I am ready for the Santa issue, because I long ago decided to tell the truth in response to direct questions. "No," I reply sadly. "Dad and I are Santa."

Tommy's crushed for a moment and then says, "You're wrong. He ate the cookie. The reindeer ate the apple." I leave it alone, but the following Christmas when I ask him to put the food out, he looks at me scornfully. "I'm not a baby," he says. "There is no Santa." A piece of (10) his childhood — and my heart — hits the floor with a thud.

In the context of this passage, the most likely meaning of the "facts of life" (Line 4) is that

(A) childhood must end

(B) the narrator ate Santa's snacks

(C) the Santa Claus story is an old tradition

(D) family customs evolve

(E) Santa doesn't exist

The passage describes the way that Tommy, like all children, learns that a childhood myth isn't true. (Oops. You still believe? Then I was just kidding. The real answer for *you* is (B). Please stop crying!) Back to the nonbelievers: Choices (A) and (D) are ***plausible*** (seemingly true or acceptable), but they're too general. Choice (B) doesn't work because the classmate wouldn't have any way of knowing who ***ingested*** (ate) the snacks, and Choice (C) is wrong because the passage says nothing about Santa's history. This, by the way, is an example of critical, as opposed to casual, reading. The passage doesn't define "the facts of life," but you can figure out its meaning by putting together clues from what the passage *does* say. The answer is Choice (E).

Not too hard, right? But that's just the tip of the PSAT/NMSQT reading-comprehension iceberg. For much more information and practice, check out Chapter 4.

Mathematics

Expect to see math problems from four different areas:

- ✔ **Numbers and operations:** In this sort of question, you add, subtract, divide, multiply, calculate percents, and deal with ratios. You also have to know different types of numbers, such as prime, even, odd, integer, and so forth. The test-makers also ask you about sets, sequences, and series. Some questions are all numbers, and others are word problems in which you have to figure out stuff like how long it takes to drive to Aunt Matilda's house if your car goes 10 miles an hour for a third of the way and 100 miles an hour for the rest of the journey, not counting the time you spend in traffic court for speeding. If you panicked while reading this bullet, calm down. I go over all these topics in Chapter 7.

- ✔ **Algebra and functions:** In these problems, little x's and y's show up, along with or inside equations and functions. You deal with direct and inverse variation, radicals and exponents, and factoring. Not friends with algebra or functions? No worries. Chapter 8 tells you what you need to know.

- ✔ **Geometry:** Squares, polygons, circles, and lots and lots of triangles fall into this category, as do solids such as cubes or cylinders. For a ton of information and practice, spend some quality time in Chapter 9.

- ✔ **Probability, statistics, and data interpretation:** If 15 other students are taking the PSAT/NMSQT in your classroom, and 10 of them have colds, what is the probability that someone will sneeze on your answer sheet? You have to answer this kind of question (well, not *exactly* this kind — the test-writers have no sense of humor whatsoever). You also have to read charts and graphs and use the information to answer word problems. Chapter 10 gives you the lowdown on this branch of math.

Most of the math questions on the PSAT/NMSQT are multiple choice, but ten questions in Section 4 are open-ended, the *grid-ins*. You figure out the answer and bubble in the numbers. For more on the **peculiarities** (odd characteristics) of grid-ins, read Chapter 6. The same chapter also explains what kind of calculator you're allowed to use during the exam, as well as when a calculator helps and when it just slows you down.

Here's a sample multiple-choice question, followed by a grid-in:

After the PSAT/NMSQT, 7 friends participated in a thumb-wrestling contest. Each thumb-wrestler played 2 matches against each of the other participants. What was the total number of thumb-wrestling matches?

(A) 10

(B) 20

(C) 21

(D) 42

(E) 44

You can make a little chart to solve this one, listing all of friend #1's matches (1-2, 1-3, 1-4, 1-5, 1-6, and 1-7), then all of #2's matches that aren't already listed (2-3, 2-4, 2-5, 2-6, 2-7), and so forth. If you do so, you find 21 possible combinations. Notice that 21 is an answer choice. However, the question states that every exhausted test-taker played *two* matches with each of the other participants, so the real answer is 21 × 2, or 42, Choice (D).

In one school, 200 students took the PSAT/NMSQT in 2012. If the number of students taking the test increased by 10% each year for the next two years, how many students took the PSAT/NMSQT in 2014?

The number of students dying of boredom (sorry, I meant "taking the test") increased by 10%, so in 2013, 20 more students were bubbling in answers, for a total of 220. The following year, 22 more students took the exam, for a grand total of 242 brain-emptied, weary kids.

Writing

To my **dismay** (sadness mixed with disappointment), you don't have to write anything on the writing section of the PSAT/NMSQT. Why? My guess is that the College Board doesn't want to pay English teachers like me to read essays. Scanning machines are cheaper and don't require caffeinated beverages. Three types of questions appear in Section 5. I discuss them in the following sections.

Improving sentences

Faced with five versions of the same sentence, can you select the best? That's what the PSAT/NMSQT tries to find out. You see a sentence with an underlined portion or, rarely, with everything underlined. Choice (A) repeats the sentence as is. The next four choices change things, perhaps for the better. Sometimes the original sentence isn't grammatically correct. Sometimes it's written in proper English, but its style is awkward. Here's a sample sentence-improvement question:

<u>Irregardless of the fact that the borrowed sweater</u> was dotted with ketchup stains, Eloise claimed that she hadn't eaten anything while wearing it.

(A) Irregardless of the fact that the borrowed sweater

(B) Despite the fact that the borrowed sweater

(C) Being a fact that the borrowed sweater

(D) Not having been that the borrowed sweater, which

(E) Without regard to the borrowed sweater, it

"Irregardless" isn't a real word in proper English, so Choice (A), the original, is out. Choice (B) does the job quickly and cleanly, so it's the best answer. The other choices add extra words or change the meaning slightly.

When you work on improving-sentence questions, look for **fluid** (smooth), **concise** (no extra words), grammatical writing.

Error recognition

I confess: I love error-recognition questions. I mean, who doesn't enjoy pointing out someone else's mistakes? This type of question gives you a sentence with four underlined portions, each labeled (A), (B), (C), or (D). After the sentence you see Choice (E), which is "no error." You have to determine which part of the sentence must be changed, if any, in order to achieve proper English. Check out this sample:

<u>Having thrown</u> spitballs at his sister for three hours, <u>Kevin took</u> a <u>break, he went for a run</u>
      A   B   C

and returned <u>ready to continue</u> the battle. <u>No error.</u>
               D   E

The original, as written, is a run-on sentence. Two complete thoughts are joined only by a comma. The first is "Having thrown spitballs at his sister for three hours, Kevin took a break." The second complete thought is "he went for a run and returned ready to continue the battle." You commit a grammatical felony if you attempt to unite these two with a **puny** (weak, lacking size or strength) comma. The correct answer is Choice (C) because that's the part of the sentence that you'd have to change to correct it. You could exchange the comma for a semicolon or place a period after "break" and capitalize "he." No matter. In this kind of question, you don't need to correct the sentence. You just have to spot the error. To ace this portion of the exam, check out Chapter 5.

Paragraph improvement

As an experienced writer and writing teacher, I can tell you that no writer *ever* produces a clean first draft. Go back to that "perfect" paper you wrote a few weeks ago, and I bet you find a mistake or a paragraph that lacks **coherence** (logical arrangement of parts to form a whole). The PSAT/NMSQT recognizes this fact and gives you a two- or three-paragraph essay that represents a typical student's first draft. The essay is followed by five questions. You may be asked about grammatical errors in specific sentences, or you may have to identify what's missing or unnecessary in a particular paragraph. Sometimes you're asked whether you should move a sentence to another position. Take a peek at this sample:

[1] A butcher in a small, English village was threatened with a lawsuit. [2] The Olympics have become too commercialized. [3] The butcher's crime was to arrange sausages into five rings to celebrate the London Olympics. [4] The rings were supposed to represent the Olympic rings, which are part of the Olympic "brand." [5] The butcher needed permission and he had to pay a fee if he wanted to use this symbol.

Which change, if any, would most improve Paragraph 1 (Sentences 1–5)?

(A) No change

(B) Delete Sentence 2.

(C) Move Sentence 2 to the end of the paragraph.

(D) Delete Sentence 5.

(E) Combine Sentences 1 and 2.

Sentence 2 is the topic sentence, the one that unifies the paragraph. The **anecdote** (short report of something that happened) illustrates the writer's view that the Olympics have become commercialized. (The butcher story, by the way, is true.) You can place Sentence 2 at the beginning of the paragraph, so the reader is prepared for the story. However, none of the answer choices allow that option. The other good spot for Sentence 2 is at the end of the paragraph, where it serves to explain why the writer is talking about sausages. So the answer is Choice (C).

I've shown you only one paragraph, but I give you some full-sized paragraph-improvement questions in Chapter 5.

Understanding Your Scores — and More

About two months after you wipe the sweat off your tired face and hand in your exam, your scores arrive at your school, where you can retrieve them from the principal or guidance counselor or whoever else was responsible for administering the exam. If you're home-schooled, your scores land in your mailbox. The score sheet contains a lot of information that can help you prepare for future exams (the SAT, for example):

- ✔ **A score from 20 to 80 for critical reading, mathematics, and writing:** Along with this base score, you'll see a range of 8 points. In other words, if your math score is 50, you may see a range of 46 to 54. The range shows scores you may receive if you took the exam again at your current skill level and allows for the fact that sometimes a student is lucky — or unlucky — on a particular test day.

- ✔ **A "selection index":** This is the sum of your critical reading, mathematics, and writing scores. The selection index also tells you how you measure up when you're compared to other students of the same age. If you took the test as a junior and you're in the 50th percentile, for example, you did better than half of all juniors who took the exam when you did.

- ✔ **Scholarship eligibility:** This little box on the score sheet tells you whether you're still in the running for scholarships that use this exam as a qualifying test. (Check out the next section for more info.)

- ✔ **Skill breakdown:** Three boxes, one for each division of the exam (critical reading, writing, and mathematics), provide details about your correct and incorrect answers. For example, you may see that you answered 4 out of 5 algebra questions correctly or that you nailed 8 geometry questions but left 2 blank.

- ✔ **Your answers:** All the questions are listed, along with the correct answer — Choice (D), for instance — and your answer. Each question is labeled easy, medium, or hard. Explanations for the answers are available online at www.collegeboard.org.

In addition to your score report, you also get your test booklet, so you can relive those three wonderful hours, question by question. Just kidding! Use the test booklet to refine your skills as you move on to the wonderful world of the SAT or ACT, two gateway exams that play a significant role in college admissions.

Bubbling for Dollars: National Merit and Other Scholarships

Do you have serious brain power? If so, the PSAT/NMSQT may open the door for you to compete for a **N**ational **M**erit **S**cholarship (the NMS in this book's title). Perhaps you'll **q**ualify (the Q in the book's title) for a scholarship by doing well on this **t**est (and there's the T in the book's title). The PSAT/NMSQT is a gateway to other scholarships also.

You don't have to fill out a separate application to enter these scholarship competitions. If you take the PSAT/NMSQT in the third year of a traditional high school (in other words, as a junior), you're automatically a candidate for a National Merit Scholarship when you sign up for the test. If you take the test before junior year, you won't be considered for a scholarship. You can, however, retake the test when you're older and the scholarship competition is open to you.

 If you're in a three-year or nontraditional high-school program, you still have a shot at winning a scholarship. You may take the test in your last year of high-school study, finish the application process while in college, and receive an award for the last three years of your college career. For more information, check the website of the National Merit Scholarship Corporation (www. nationalmerit.org). If you don't have access to the Internet, call or write:

> National Merit Scholarship Corporation
> 1560 Sherman Avenue
> Suite 200
> Evanston, Illinois 60201-4897
> Telephone: 847- 866-5100

You can use this contact information to find out about all the scholarships that the PSAT/NMSQT administers.

National Merit Scholarships

About 1.5 million students take the PSAT/NMSQT every year. The top 50,000 scorers who are eligible for scholarships are invited to participate in the College Plans Reporting Service. If you're invited to this party, say yes! You name two colleges, and the National Merit Scholarship Corporation sends them information about you. Because you've done well, you may receive other scholarships or offers of financial aid from your selected schools.

About 34,000 students of the top 50,000 become *commended students*. If you're one, you receive a very nice letter complimenting you on your achievements. Needless to say, being a commended student is a very good line on your resume. The other 16,000 students in the top scoring group move on to semifinalist status. If you get this far, you have to fill out an application, and your name is given to colleges and media. Your mailbox will fill with offers to visit schools that hope to *entice* (tempt) you to apply. Semifinalists are spread around the country, in proportion to the number of students living there. If a state has 5 percent of the nation's graduating seniors, for example, it will have 5 percent of the semifinalists also.

About 90 percent of semifinalists become finalists after supplying still more information to the National Merit Scholarship Corporation. You have to write an essay about yourself, and your school sends a transcript and a description of its curriculum and grading system. You also have to take the SAT and score in the upper ranks, to prove that your high PSAT/NMSQT score wasn't a *fluke* (a chance occurrence).

More than 9,600 students win scholarships that can be used at accredited colleges and universities anywhere in the United States, but not at service academies (West Point, for example) or virtual colleges, which grant degrees for online studies. Most winners are finalists, but some scholarships financed by corporations, colleges, unions, and other groups go to students who did very well on the PSAT/NMSQT but not quite high enough to qualify as finalists. These awards may be for children of employees, perhaps, or students who have expressed a strong commitment to attending a specific college.

For a list of sponsored scholarships, check the National Merit Scholarship Corporation's website (www.nationalmerit.org), or use the phone number or address in the preceding section. Who knows? Perhaps your Uncle Leo's company grants scholarships to finalists who are nieces or nephews of its workers. Then all those boring Thanksgiving dinners will pay off!

National Achievement Scholarships

National Achievement Scholarships recognize outstanding African-American students. If you're African American and want to be considered for one of these awards, bubble in Section 14 of the answer sheet. By completing this section, which is optional, you enter the competition for one of these *prestigious* (celebrated, high-status) awards. Some are financed by the National Achievement Program itself; corporations and other organizations fund other awards. As in the National Merit Scholarship program, a scholarship funded by an organization may carry extra requirements (children of employees, for instance). For more information about sponsored National Achievement Scholarships, go to the website (www.nationalmerit.org) and click the National Achievement Scholarship tab or use the address or phone number for the National Merit Scholarship Corporation earlier in the chapter.

Trying for a National Achievement Scholarship doesn't take you out of the race for a National Merit Scholarship. You can win both and end up with two impressive award certificates to display on your wall. However, you get only one chunk of money. No double dipping in the National Merit/National Achievement financial aid pool!

What are your odds of winning? Well, out of 160,000 entrants, about 1,600 become semifinalists, and 1,300 of those gain finalist status after completing additional requirements (essays, information about your grades and courses, and so forth). About 800 terrific students win. Even if you're not one of those 800, you still may benefit from the National Achievement Scholarship program. A list of 3,000 or so of the highest-scoring applicants is sent to colleges and universities around the country. If you're one of these *outstanding participants*, you can expect some interesting letters from schools, inviting you to apply. They may offer you their own scholarships.

African-American students may also be interested in another organization, the National Scholarship Service. Open to all African-American students who take the PSAT/NMSQT in junior year, the National Scholarship Service doesn't grant awards. With your permission, the National Scholarship Service sends your name, contact information, and scores to schools throughout the country. You can contact this organization, which is *not* part of the National Merit Scholarship program or the College Board, by writing to the National Scholarship Service, 980 Martin Luther King Drive, SW, PO Box 11409, Atlanta, Georgia 30310.

National Hispanic Recognition Program

If the roots of your family tree extend to a Spanish-speaking country, you may be eligible for the National Hispanic Recognition Program simply by taking the PSAT/NMSQT and indicating that you're Hispanic/Latino. Winners don't receive scholarships from this College Board program or the National Merit Scholarship Corporation (which is not involved in this program), but their names are sent to colleges and universities around the country that are, according to the College Board, "particularly interested in communicating with exceptional Hispanic/Latino students." Those institutions may invite winners to apply, perhaps sweetening the invitation by offering their own scholarships.

To qualify for this competition, you must

- ✔ Be at least one quarter Hispanic/Latino
- ✔ Take the PSAT/NMSQT in your third year of high school
- ✔ Score in the top *tier* (rank) on the exam
- ✔ Maintain a 3.0 grade point average
- ✔ Be a United States citizen or legal permanent resident or have an I-551 stamp on your passport

Each year about 235,000 students enter the competition, and 5,000 win. For more information, go to the College Board website (www.collegeboard.org), call 877-358-6777, or write to the College Board, National Hispanic Recognition Program, 11955 Democracy Drive, Reston, Virginia 20190.

Telluride Scholarships

For more than a century, the Telluride Association has sponsored free summer programs for students from around the world who have, in the association's words, "a passion for learning." Participants attend seminars led by college professors, which last six weeks and are held on college campuses in Michigan and New York. Although participants don't receive college credit, they essentially take a college-level course — including many hours of reading and writing homework. Top-scoring students on the PSAT/NMSQT may apply for a Telluride spot, and those with financial need may receive transportation grants. For more information, check the website (www.tellurideassociation.org), call 607-273-5011, or write to the Telluride Association, 217 West Avenue, Ithaca, NY 14850.

Putting yourself out there: Student Search Service

One section of the PSAT/NMSQT answer sheet asks you whether you want to participate in the Student Search Service. If you say "yes," you give the College Board permission to provide information about you to 1,100 colleges and universities in the United States. Specifically, the College Board reports your name, address, gender, date of birth, high school, expected graduation date, and — if you choose to answer these questions — your ethnic background, possible college major, and e-mail address. The service is free. Participants in the Student Search Service receive a lot of mail, both electronic and paper. Colleges send information packets or links, hoping to attract applicants.

Chapter 2

Getting Practical: PSAT/NMSQT Logistics

In This Chapter

▶ Registering for the exam

▶ Knowing what to expect on test day

▶ Studying for the exam and designing an effective test strategy

*O*ld-time journalists always followed the "five-W one-H" rule, answering "who? what? when? where? why? and how?" in the first paragraph of a news story. In this chapter I'm an old-time journalist. You already know three Ws: The *who* is you, the *what* is the PSAT/NMSQT, and the *why* is college admission and scholarships. In this chapter I answer the remaining questions, so you know the exam's *logistics* (practical details). If you have special needs — large type, extended time, and so on — this chapter is important for you, because in it I explain the College Board's procedure for granting accommodations. Last, but definitely not least, I tell you how to create a test-prep schedule and how to handle test-day nerves.

Signing and Showing Up: When, Where, and How to Take the PSAT/NMSQT

If your school is supplied with a support staff that anticipates your every need, skip this section. Just stop by the guidance office to find out what, if anything, you have to do. If your school isn't particularly efficient or if you're home-schooled, everything you need to know is in this section.

Signing up for the test

Most students in a traditional, four-year high school take the PSAT/NMSQT in their third year, as juniors. An increasing number of students **opt for** (choose) an earlier exam, as sophomores or even younger students. Taking the test early can be helpful because you'll probably improve your scores on **subsequent** (later) exams. If you're in a nontraditional high-school program, take some time to think about what's best for you. In a three-year high school, you can take the exam in the October preceding your graduation, followed by the SAT in December or January. If you're likely to spend five years in high school, go for the second-to-last October for the PSAT/NMSQT and the SAT in the autumn or winter of your last year before graduation. Home-schoolers, use these guidelines and work backward from the date you expect to complete the high-school curriculum.

If you're *vying* (competing) for a National Merit or National Achievement Scholarship, you may not be eligible for an award if you take the exam at the wrong time. Check out the section on scholarships in Chapter 1 for more information.

The exam is offered only in mid- to late October, on either a Wednesday or a Saturday of the same week. Each school offering the PSAT/NMSQT chooses one of those two days. You sign up through your high school in early September and pay your fee. Take this opportunity to pick up a student guide, a booklet from the College Board describing the exam.

You can also find a downloadable student bulletin on the College Board's website (www. collegeboard.org). Click the PSAT/NMSQT button at the top of the screen.

The College Board charges about $14 for each PSAT/NMSQT given in the United States, but schools may tack on a couple of bucks to cover administrative costs, and the College Board adds a few dollars for overseas exams. Your school can request fee waivers (a free test) for any junior in financial need. If you're in that category, talk to your school officials as soon as possible — ideally, during the spring preceding the test.

Many schools order exams for every 11th grader, but just to be sure you're on the list, check with a school official. If you plan to take the exam in 9th or 10th grade, inform your school by the end of the school year before the test, if possible. If your high school doesn't offer the test or if you're home-schooled, call a local school. Still can't find a testing center? Check the College Board website (www.collegeboard.org/psat) or call the College Board (609-771-7070) for the names of schools near you that offer the exam. Don't wait! Some schools offer test spots to guests, but many have limited seating and operate on a first-come, first-served basis. By mid-September of the year you want to take the test, you should know where you're going on test day.

Meeting special needs

If you qualify for accommodations in your school exams, you may be eligible for accommodations on the PSAT/NMSQT also. By accommodations I mean large type or Braille exams, extended time (50 percent or 100 percent more than the usual amount), a reader for the questions or a writer to record your answers, extra breaks, and other adjustments that allow all students a fair shot at showing what they know.

Your school may apply for accommodations for you, or you can apply yourself. If your school is doing all the work, alert the person in charge of testing — usually your guidance counselor, the college counseling office, or the principal — that you're planning to take the test. Ask about forms you must fill out. You have to supply a consent form signed by a parent or guardian; the school needs permission before releasing any information about you to the College Board. If you're doing all the work, download a Student Eligibility Form from the College Board's website (www.collegeboard.org) or call the College Board's Services for Students with Disabilities to request one (609-771-7137). You may be asked for documentation (a form filled out by a doctor, for example). The College Board will probably ask for information about you from your school also.

If you've qualified for accommodations on any College Board test (an AP, for example), you may not have to reapply. Check with your school or call 609-771-7137 for more information.

Certifying that you need accommodations takes time — at least seven weeks. Don't **procrastinate.** (I should explain what "procrastinate" means, but first I have to . . . okay, you get the joke! "Procrastinate" means "delay.")

If you break your wrist or suffer anything that the College Board calls a "temporary medical condition," talk to a school official or call the College Board right away. You *may* be granted extra time (so you can bubble answers using your non-dominant hand — your left hand if you're a righty, and vice versa) or some other help. However, it's just as likely that the College Board will say, "Better luck next year," written in more polite and official language, of course.

If you're granted accommodations, the College Board sends you an *eligibility letter* and informs the school. It also assigns you an *SSD eligibility code* that you'll need on the exam. Bring the eligibility letter with you to the test.

My general approach to life is "whatever can go wrong, will go wrong." Even though the school where you're taking the exam *should* receive notification about your accommodations and prepare accordingly, it never hurts to check ahead of time. Bring a copy of your eligibility letter to the school administrator to be sure that everything is in place for you.

Showing up: What to expect on test day

Filmmaker Woody Allen once told *The New York Times* that "showing up is 80 percent of life." I don't know whether Woody's right or wrong, but I do know that simply showing up isn't enough to do well on the PSAT/NMSQT. You also need to know what to expect. (You also need to show up in good shape — calm and ready to take the exam. For advice on soothing your nerves, check out Chapter 19.)

What to bring with you

The PSAT/NMSQT rules are quite strict and don't allow you to bring much with you to the test. You have to leave your book bag, snack, favorite stuffed animal, and tons of other things in your locker or in a designated area. You should have these items with you:

- ✔ **A couple of number two pencils and at least one good eraser:** Don't go crazy with the sharpener. You don't want the pencil point to break the minute you put pressure on it! Also, be sure the eraser is clean — no initials, "I love Herman," or anything else.

- ✔ **A watch, in case you can't see the room clock:** The watch can't have a timer and it must be quiet. If it beeps, the proctor is allowed to throw you out.

- ✔ **An approved calculator:** You don't absolutely have to have a calculator, but sometimes it speeds you through a math problem. See Chapter 6 to find out which calculators are "legal" on the PSAT/NMSQT.

- ✔ **Your eligibility letter, if you have one:** If you've been granted accommodations (see the earlier "Meeting special needs" section), bring the letter saying so.

- ✔ **Photo ID and school code:** You don't actually need a photo ID, but if you're taking the exam in a school you don't attend, having a photo ID is a good idea. Similarly, the proctor announces only the code of the school where the exam is given. If you're in alien territory, you should know your school's number, which you must bubble in on the answer sheet. If you don't, your scores will be reported to the testing site. True, you can call or stop by to retrieve them, but when you enter your own school's code, your scores are sent there.

  Home-schoolers have their own code. Before test day, check the College Board website or student guide and memorize the number. Your scores and test booklets will be sent to your home address.

- ✔ **E-mail address:** This is also optional, but useful. The College Board and the National Merit Scholarship Corporation may send you information by e-mail if you write your address on the answer sheet.

✔ **Your Social Security number or student ID number:** These numbers are optional, but they may come in handy. One spot on the answer sheet asks for your student ID number (if your school uses such a system). If you don't have an ID number, you can substitute your Social Security number. These numbers *facilitate* (make easier) the return of your question booklet after the exam has been scored. Getting your booklet back is important because you can prepare for the SAT by analyzing your PSAT/NMSQT work (for example, calculations you did next to a math problem).

What to do when you get there

Turn around and run away. Just kidding! You're prepped and ready, so *stride* (walk with long, quick steps) into the school with confidence. Here's what you do next:

✔ **Dump everything you aren't allowed to have with you.** If you're taking the exam at your own high school, drop your stuff into your locker. If you're in an unfamiliar school, ask where you can leave extra items.

To minimize opportunities to cheat, the College Board bans pretty much everything but the items listed in the preceding section. On test day, travel light! Also, remember to turn off your phone. If it's in a book bag under your desk when Uncle George calls to wish you luck, the proctor *won't* be amused. You'll be booted from the room and your scores will be canceled.

✔ **Go to the test room.** The proctor will probably keep everyone in the hall until it's time to begin. Unless the proctor knows you, you may have to show some identification on the way in.

Try to find a quiet spot, and stay away from anyone talking about the test. In fact, make a pact with your friends to avoid the subject. Why? Because *inevitably* (surely) you'll hear a comment that will fire up your nervous system, such as, "I hear 90 percent of the math section is advanced geometry," or, "I memorized two thirds of the dictionary." First, some of the comments you hear are wrong. (Only 25 to 30 percent of the math is geometry, and much of it is easy.) Second, it doesn't matter what anyone else has done to prepare. You're doing exactly what you need to do, right now — learning about the test and practicing for it.

✔ **Follow the proctor's directions.** In some schools, you fill out the identification part of the answer sheet a day or so before the test. (Great idea! You save a half hour on test day.) In most schools, on the morning of the exam you bubble in your name, address, and other information. Listen carefully to the proctor, and don't jump ahead. You may also choose to answer some optional questions about race, religion, possible college major, and so forth. This information is sent, only with your permission, to colleges interested in contacting prospective students. For example, a school *affiliated* (closely or officially connected) with a particular religion may send information to test-takers of the same faith.

Don't skip Sections 13 and 14 of the answer sheet if you want to be considered for a National Merit Scholarship or a National Achievement Scholarship. Turn to Chapter 1 for more information on these awards.

✔ **Start the test.** Of course, you turn to a section only when the proctor announces that you should do so. During the five-minute break between Sections 2 and 3, stretch your muscles, roll your neck around, and think happy thoughts. If you need to use the restroom, ask the proctor. And smile: You're almost done!

As you exit the exam room, clear your mind of everything related to the PSAT/NMSQT. Remember that you aren't allowed to talk, tweet, or communicate anything about the questions. (That's one of the promises you make when you sign your name.) Plus, you can't do anything about the results until you see your scores in December. At that point you can make a battle plan for the SAT, or, if you plan to take the PSAT/NMSQT again, for that test.

Receiving your scores

About two months after you take the PSAT/NMSQT, your scores are ready. You can pick them up at the same office where you signed up for the exam. Along with a number from 20 (you showed up and did nothing) to 80 (you're perfect!) for critical reading, writing, and mathematics, you also find out how you did in comparison with other test-takers in the same year of school. This last bit is expressed as a ***percentile*** (number in relation to 100 percent of the test-takers in your category). The score report indicates the level of difficulty of each question (easy, medium, or hard) and tells you exactly which questions you got wrong. Your test booklet is also returned, so you can ***reminisce*** (think about the past) about that lovely day in October when your brain fried. The scores are *not* reported to colleges, but they do go to the National Merit Scholarship Corporation. (See Chapter 1 for information on scholarships.)

Creating an Exam Strategy

Don't you hate clothing labels that claim "one size fits all"? Some people pop a seam, and others can invite friends into the same T-shirt for an ***impromptu*** (unplanned, spur of the moment) party. When it comes to the PSAT/NMSQT, though, one size fits *most* test-takers. In this section I explain some general strategy. Later in this chapter I tell you when to guess and when to cut your losses and move on. (You may skip a question, but *don't* skip "Guessing games: Scoring on test day" later in this chapter. A guessing strategy is essential, and you can't make it up during the test.) In Parts II and III of *PSAT/NMSQT For Dummies,* I give you more tricks and techniques for each type of question.

Now for your general strategy. Before you walk into the exam room, consider the following questions:

- ✔ **How fast do you read?** If you resemble a snail when it comes to reading speed, you probably won't get to every question in Sections 1, 3, and 5 (critical reading and writing). Spend some quality time in Part II of this book, and carefully evaluate your strengths and weaknesses. Accept that you probably won't get to every question. Play to your strengths, as I explain in "Guessing games: Scoring on test day" later in this chapter.

- ✔ **Which areas of math are easy for you?** Sections 2 and 4 feature many different types of problems. You may get to all of them, but you don't need to work through them in order. Look for geometry problems if you love graphs and polygons. If algebra makes you break out in a rash, hit those questions last.

  If you skip around, be extra careful to enter your answer on the correct line. Say (in your head, not aloud) "the answer to Question 4 is B" as you look at Line 4 and bubble in the oval labeled "B."

- ✔ **Do you have test anxiety?** Some people have nerves of steel, and others sweat all over their answer sheets. If you're in the first group, congratulations. You can move on to the next section. Still here? Okay, the key for you is to channel your anxiety. A recent study showed that stress can actually improve your performance on an exam. When you feel your palms turn to water or your heart race, picture a pleasant experience — the moment your team wins a game or a romantic partner stops by to chat. The same physical symptoms show up then, also. Now tell yourself that you won the game (and the girl or guy), just as you will win on the PSAT/NMSQT.

✔ **How focused are you?** Some athletes claim that they never notice the cheering crowd until after the game. Other people hop from one thing to another — taking note of the applause, checking the scoreboard, planning the next play — never giving full attention to anything. But focus is important on the PSAT/NMSQT. True, sometimes you should survey a section so you can select the questions you're most likely to answer correctly. However, working on one question while thinking about another is never good.

If focus is hard for you, try this trick: Place one hand over the questions that precede the one you're working on. Cover questions that follow with the answer sheet. Now only one question is visible, and your attention is pinned there.

Answering these questions helps you approach the exam in a way that suits your personality and skills. After you take the practice tests in Part IV, you'll have more information that will help you review difficult concepts and perfect your test strategy.

Early birds and late bloomers: Making a study plan

You just mastered finger-painting and got comfortable in kindergarten, right? NO? You're starting PSAT/NMSQT prep in *high school?* Way too late! Just kidding. Start breathing again: No matter when the exam is — next year, next month, or tomorrow — you can still find ways to improve your performance.

Starting early

If you plan to take the PSAT/NMSQT 6 to 12 months from now, you have time for these steps:

✔ **Work on your vocabulary.** The exam has no section devoted specifically to vocabulary, but every question in the critical reading sections assumes that you know a hefty chunk of the dictionary. In this book, words that often appear on the exam are identified with a *special font.* Slow down when you see one, say the word once or twice, and think about how you'd use it in a sentence of your own. When you're reading homework material for school — science, math, history, and of course English — take note of unfamiliar words. Figure out the meaning from context if you can. If not, grab a handy adult or check the dictionary. Consider making a list of these words, along with the definition and the sentence you found the word in. In other words, create a little dictionary of your own. From time to time, read over the words, gradually making them part of your working vocabulary.

✔ **Read more.** Yes, you have soccer practice all afternoon and an English essay that's due tomorrow. Plus, you have to memorize your part in the school play. I get it: Your life is crammed with activities. But if you can devote a short time each day to reading something you like, you'll improve your comprehension skills. Of course, some reading material gives you more to chew on. You won't learn much from tweets or instant messages! Hit the newspaper, a novel, a biography, and similar sources to get the most out of the time you invest. As a bonus, your writing skills will improve because reading good literature *imprints* (places firmly in your mind) proper grammar.

✔ **Save your math notes.** Even if they're covered with chocolate stains or *illicit* (illegal) notes to friends, the notes you take in math class are a great way to review for the PSAT/NMSQT. Part III of this book helps also, of course!

✔ **Take tough courses.** Most high schools offer a range of courses, and most students know which ones require serious brainpower. Choose those classes and give them your best effort. The skills you develop will serve you well when you take any standardized test, including the PSAT/NMSQT.

✔ **Do some practice tests.** You have four in this book. Don't take all of them in the same week. Complete one, check your answers, and read the explanations. Then analyze your performance. Review the appropriate material in Parts II and III before you hit the next practice test.

One last thing: As the real PSAT/NMSQT approaches, smile. You've done everything you can to ensure a good result.

Steering a middle course

If your PSAT/NMSQT is just a few months in the future, you can relax, but not too much. You have time to ready yourself for the Big Moment. Try these tactics:

✔ **Brush up on vocabulary.** In the preceding section I explain how to *incorporate* (add in) new words to your vocabulary as you read this book. You just picked up one meaning of "incorporate" with no effort! You can do the same thing in every chapter. Also, you have time to make a personal dictionary, as I describe in the preceding section.

✔ **Talk about what you read.** In the preceding section I recommend reading for pleasure, and that's a good plan for you, too. To *extract* (pull out) maximum meaning, talk about what you're reading with friends or family. You may find that you understand what you've read more fully. And no, you don't have to join Nerds Anonymous if you follow this suggestion. Lots of people like to read. Even popular people!

✔ **Get a study buddy for math.** If you and a friend do your homework together (as long as your math teacher knows and approves), you may learn more. Don't look for someone who knows everything; I'm not talking about a tutoring situation. As you and your friend talk about how to solve a problem, you find yourself explaining the underlying concepts in terms you understand. The result? Both of you learn the logical basis of math, a key component of the PSAT/NMSQT.

Studying with a friend works for writing and critical reading also. Think about it for a second. When you read silently, you use one portion of your brain. When you speak, you use more of your brain. Talking adds even more brainpower. However, be sure to check with your teachers before you *collaborate* (work together). Some may interpret your actions as cheating.

✔ **Take a couple of practice tests.** Four is a good number, and *coincidentally* (by chance), that's the number of practice exams in Part IV of this book. If you can manage only two, you're still ahead of the game. Don't skimp on the after-test activity, though. Read every explanation I provide in the answer chapters, so you can get the same sort of question right the next time you see one.

Working late

Your PSAT/NMSQT is only a month or (gasp) a week away? Oh boy. Time to get serious. Try these steps:

✔ **Read Chapter 1.** There I go over the basic question types. At least you know what to expect.

✔ **Read the bullets in Chapters 3, 4, 5, and 6.** In those chapters I highlight techniques that you can apply to critical reading (Chapters 3 and 4), writing (Chapter 5), and math (Chapter 6).

✔ **Take at least one practice test.** Score your test and read the explanations. Think about *why* you answered incorrectly. Was it a vocabulary issue? Did you misunderstand the task? Did you run out of time? Now you know what to work on. For example, suppose you lost several points in the error-recognition questions in the writing section. After reading the explanations, you see that subject-verb agreement was the problem. Now dig up your English text and review the rules.

No matter how desperate you are, don't **stint** (restrict to a tiny amount) on sleep. You have to rest to bring your brain to maximum efficiency. Eight hours of last-minute study and one hour of sleep is a recipe for disaster.

Guessing games: Scoring on test day

Hamlet was wrong. The real question is not "to be or not to be?" but rather "to guess or to leave blank?" While taking the test, you can't **devise** (plan, invent) a guessing strategy. So do it now, get comfortable with it, and follow your strategy faithfully. Here are the essential facts:

- Many test-takers don't have enough time to answer every question.
- The PSAT/NMSQT gives you one point for every correct answer.
- You receive no points for questions you leave blank.
- You lose a quarter point for every wrong answer to a multiple-choice question.
- You lose no points for an incorrect grid-in response.

With these facts in mind, your strategy is clear:

- **Answer all the questions you know.** As you work through a section, some questions pop up, wave their hands, and scream, "Answer me! You know me! I'm your friend!" Be sure to pace yourself so that you **garner** (gather) all those points.

- **Mark any questions that stump you.** In the margin, circle the question number or write a check mark (✓) or some other symbol. Consider using two check marks (✓✓) or a special symbol for extra-tough questions.

- **If you have time, return to the questions you skipped.** Avoid the really hard questions unless you're well supplied with extra minutes.

- **Eliminate any multiple-choice options that are clearly wrong.** Think of this step as a process of elimination.

- **Guess if you've eliminated one or more choices.** Do the math: If you cross off one multiple-choice answer, you have four left, which gives you a one-in-four chance of guessing correctly. Because you lose a quarter point for a wrong answer, you have even odds of guessing correctly. If you can eliminate two answers, your odds of guessing correctly are better still.

- **Don't skip grid-ins.** Because you don't lose points for incorrect grid-in answers, try to answer every one of them, unless you're totally clueless about the problem and you need extra minutes for questions you *may* know something about.

Based on statistical evidence — how average test-takers do on a particular question — the test-makers place sentence completions, writing, and math questions in order of difficulty. (The critical reading passage-based questions are different; there, the questions follow the order of the passage itself.) In the order-of-difficulty sections, the easier stuff is at the beginning, so you should try to answer everything that shows up early in a section — the first ten questions, perhaps. That said, everyone's mind works differently. You may find Question 24 painless but be stumped by Question 12. If you think you know an answer, bubble it in. But if you see something confusing at the end of a section and you're running out of time, you may do better if you return to the beginning of the section and fill in answers you skipped the first time through rather than grapple with a super-tough problem you're unlikely to answer correctly.

Part II
Word Up!: The Critical Reading and Writing Sections

The 5th Wave   By Rich Tennant

"I went around to all the businesses in town collecting new words for the critical reading sections of the PSAT. I learned a lot of new words related to not being annoying."

In this part . . .

In college — the long-term goal that's driving you toward the PSAT/NMSQT — each semester you have to read 20 pounds of textbooks (or the electronic equivalent) and write maybe 10,000 words in proper English. To determine your ability to handle that much reading and writing, the PSAT/NMSQT asks you to read for a total of 50 minutes and write for 0 minutes. (No, that's not a typo. All the "writing" questions on the exam are multiple-choice responses. The only thing you actually write is your name.)

In this section I guide you through each type of critical reading and writing question and help you **formulate** (invent) a strategy that works. I also provide plenty of sample questions, so you can apply and perfect your techniques.

Chapter 3

Blanking Out on the PSAT: Sentence Completions

The number 13 is supposed to be unlucky, but it's a great number of points to aim for when you answer PSAT/NMSQT sentence-completion questions. Each critical reading section leads off with sentence completions, eight in Section 1 and five in Section 3. Sentence-completion questions are relatively easy to answer, especially if you've built a strong vocabulary. If you haven't and the test is *not* tomorrow, turn to Chapter 2 for some suggestions for improving your **store** (stockpile) of words. (The test *is* tomorrow? Don't panic. Follow the guidelines for last-minute preparation in Chapter 2, and after you've recovered from the PSAT/NMSQT, use the vocabulary-building plan in the same chapter to prepare yourself for the SAT.)

A few key techniques go a long way toward a successful **bout** (contest or match) with this type of question, and in this chapter I lay out a route that helps you **amass** (collect) as many of the 13 points as possible.

Missing Links: Surveying Sentence Completions

Sentence-completion questions come in two varieties: chocolate and vanilla. Sorry, I meant to say *one blank* and *two blanks*. The test-writers give you a sentence with — you guessed it! — one or two blanks, and you have to choose words to fill those blanks from five multiple-choice answers. The sentences contain clues to help you figure out what's missing.

Sentences with complicated **syntax** (grammatical structure) often feature simple words, as in this example:

The governor decided to keep the restrictions in place but also agreed to open the hearings to those who had _____ them.

(A) supported

(B) considered

(C) opposed

(D) approved

(E) judged

The answer is Choice (C). The word *but* signals a change in direction, so you know that the second action in the sentence has to contrast with the first, *to keep the restrictions in place.* What contrasts with keeping the **status quo** (existing condition, things as they are)? Listening to views from *those who had opposed* the restrictions. There you go: Choice (C) is the answer.

Two-blank sentences may have an even more **intricate** (complex) syntax. Check out this example:

Although he was not _____ by nature, Stan couldn't resist making _____ comments about the reviewer, who was less than pleased with Stan's new play.

(A) unfeeling . . . positive

(B) charitable . . . unfavorable

(C) cruel . . . favorable

(D) generous . . . critical

(E) unkind . . . sarcastic

The answer is Choice (E). The answer choices are common words, and I bet you use all of them in everyday conversation. The sentence, however, has a few twists and turns. You start with *although,* a word that signals something happening despite another action or condition. Then you hit a negative statement: talking about what's *not* in Stan's nature. Next up is another negative: Stan *couldn't resist,* which tells you that you're looking for something Stan actually did after he read a review of his play. Another complication: The reviewer was *less than pleased,* a roundabout way of saying that the reviewer hated the play. If you follow each of these clues, you know that you have to figure out Stan's nature and an action that goes against that nature. Choice (E) fits perfectly. Stan wasn't *unkind.* Therefore, you'd expect him to be *kind* to the reviewer. However, Stan gave in to temptation and wrote *sarcastic* comments.

Not all two-blank questions are more difficult than single-blank sentences. Don't skip a question without reading it! Some two-blank sentences are actually easier because they're long enough to provide several clues.

Sentences with high-level vocabulary words tend to be written in a straightforward manner, like this one:

After she had eaten the last doughnut, Eve hurried to the grocery to _____ her supply of snacks before the children returned from school.

(A) deplete

(B) replenish

(C) confiscate

(D) retain

(E) depreciate

The answer is Choice (B). The meaning of the sentence is simple: Eve pigged out, and her kids will starve to death if she doesn't restock. The answer choices, though, are tough. Choice (A), **deplete,** means "reduce." Choice (B), **replenish,** means "restock." **Confiscate,** Choice (C), is what I do when one of my students brings a cellphone to class: I take it away, using my authority as the teacher. Choice (D), **retain,** means "keep," and Choice (E), **depreciate,** means "decrease in value." If your vocabulary is up to the task, the answer is clear: Choice (B).

Of course, not every sentence on the PSAT/NMSQT fits these patterns perfectly. Sometimes the test-writers hit you with double trouble: a complicated sentence with vocabulary that only dictionary fans know. You may also find medium-level vocabulary and slightly complicated syntax. Luckily, you don't have to categorize the questions; you just have to answer them.

Filling in the Blanks: Strategies for Success

When you see a sentence completion, the last thing you want to do is blank out. In this section, I first explain a general approach to sentence completions, and then I go into more detail on word clues and sentence types, so you can identify the correct answer quickly.

Gearing up for battle: General strategy

The PSAT/NMSQT is the academic equivalent of war. Here's your overall battle plan for approaching a sentence-completion problem:

- ✔ **First, glance at the answer choices.** If you don't know *any* of the answer words, the question probably isn't worth your time. Move on to the next sentence. When you reach the end of the section, you can go back if you have time. The techniques for decoding unknown words discussed later in this section may lead you to the answer. If you're familiar with one or two answer choices, stick around.

  Remember the guessing rule: If you can eliminate one or more answer choices because you're sure they're wrong, go for it. (For more on guessing, turn to Chapter 2.)

- ✔ **Read the entire sentence.** I can hear you saying, "Duh! What else would I do?" But a surprising number of test-takers begin the sentence, assume they know where it's going, and zip to an answer choice. Naturally, the test-writers have placed a trap for the ***unwary*** (not cautious) students who behave this way. Especially in two-blank questions, expect at least one answer to fit the first blank perfectly and bomb on the second blank. Read the whole thing!

- ✔ **If you can, fill in the blank(s) with your own words.** Not every sentence reveals its meaning without the missing words. But if you do know what the sentence is expressing, finish it yourself, using your own words in place of the blanks, without worrying about the answer choices. In the first section of this chapter, for example, you see a sentence about Eve snarfing down doughnuts before her kids come home from school. You might mentally insert *refill* or something similar in the blank. Now you know that you need a ***synonym*** (word with the same meaning) for *refill*.

- ✔ **Check the answer choices again.** Cross off any that don't do the job and examine what's left. Mentally insert them into the blank(s). In the question booklet, put a check mark next to any answer choice that may work.

  In two-blank questions, sometimes the second blank is easier to fill than the first. Work backwards if you spot an answer choice that fits!

- ✔ **Choose the best answer.** Sometimes more than one answer makes sense. In this situation, though, one choice probably matches the sentence more closely than the others. That's the one you want.

On PSAT/NMSQT critical reading questions, you're looking for the *best* answer, not just a workable solution.

Refining your approach

The general strategy I outline in the preceding section works well, but knowing a few more specific techniques improves your chances of success. Think of these approaches as weapons in your campaign to conquer sentence completions.

Identifying signal words and phrases

Only three letters separate these two statements, but the meanings they express may as well be on opposite sides of the Grand Canyon:

> "I've seen your essay, and I'm giving you an A."

> "I've seen your essay, but I'm giving you an A."

The first statement implies that the essay was great. The second statement gives you the idea that the essay didn't deserve an A. For some reason — perhaps class participation or the apple you left on his desk every morning — the teacher awarded the top grade anyway. The *and* signals continuation; the *but* alerts you to a change in direction. Not all signal words are short, and some signals contain several words. Regardless, when you run into a signal word or phrase in a sentence completion, circle it so that it stays in your mind.

Here are some common signal words and phrases, grouped by theme, along with an explanation of how they function in a sentence:

- ✔ **Cause and effect:** *Because, therefore, so, accordingly, thus, hence, consequently, as a result, as a consequence of, if/then, so that.* The sentence sets up two situations or events, in which one causes the other.

- ✔ **Change or contrast:** *Not, on the other hand, but, otherwise, yet, however, nevertheless, still, nonetheless, although, though, despite, regardless.* These words whip the sentence around and send the meaning in the opposite direction.

- ✔ **Comparison:** *More, less, than, equal, equally, same.* Two or more elements are measured against others described in the sentence.

- ✔ **Continuation:** *And, also, in addition to, as well as, moreover, along with, besides, likewise, not only/but also.* The pattern of ideas already established keeps going.

- ✔ **Example:** *For example, for instance, not the only, in other words, that is, such as, as in, like, similarly, similar to.* Some sort of category has been created, and these words send you to illustrations of that category.

On the PSAT/NMSQT, the example structure may offer a definition of the missing word, as in this sentence:

Carlota was thrilled to meet the _____, the absolute ruler whose reign has been compared to Emperor Constantine's.

Among the answer choices for the preceding sentence, you'll find something like *dictator* or **potentate** (a synonym for *dictator*).

- ✔ **Time:** *After, then, subsequently, while, earlier, later, next, previously, preceding, once, finally, last, since, originally, at the beginning, at the end, before.* These words establish a time frame for a series of events or a process.

Verb tense also alerts you to time. Check the main verbs and **participles** (verb forms that may be used as descriptions).

Try your hand at sentence-completion Questions 1 through 5. Zero in on the signal words!

1. Having performed poorly in the _____, Zachary gradually improved and was pleased to win a medal later in the competition.

    (A) playoffs

    (B) conclusion

    (C) finale

    (D) preliminaries

    (E) tournament

2. Because enemy forces were about to attack, the sentries were especially _____ and scanned the horizon _____.

    (A) vigilant . . . ceaselessly

    (B) cooperative . . . incessantly

    (C) tenacious . . . infrequently

    (D) attentive . . . rarely

    (E) dubious . . . consistently

3. Although the percentage of students requesting financial aid is high, the college maintains that the tuition is not _____.

    (A) transient

    (B) burdensome

    (C) troublesome

    (D) modest

    (E) diminished

4. In addition to chronic lateness, several clients of the firm mentioned his _____ when they were asked to comment on the employee's performance.

    (A) discretion

    (B) gentility

    (C) incompetence

    (D) candor

    (E) acumen

5. The chef's cooking was _____, following the traditional French methods exactly.

    (A) orthodox

    (B) heretical

    (C) mainstream

    (D) deviant

    (E) innovative

1. **D.** The sentence contains several time clues: *gradually* and *later* create a timeline, and the introductory verb form (a participle) places the action of performing farther in the past from the present moment than the main verb in the sentence, *improved.* Therefore, you know that you need something that happened earlier in the timeline than Zachary's medal, which was awarded *later.* Choice (D) is perfect because the *preliminaries* take place *before* the rest of the contest.

2. **A.** The first word of the sentence is *because,* so you know you're dealing with a cause-and-effect situation. What happens when the enemy is on the move? Sentries watch until their eyeballs fall out. Therefore, Choices (A) and (D) work for the first blank. (**Vigilant** means "watchful.") If you leapt at Choice (D), you fell into a trap. Sentries on high alert don't scan the horizon *rarely,* the second word in Choice (D). Instead, sentries scan **ceaselessly** (without stopping).

3. **B.** When those **gargantuan** (giant) tuition bills arrive, what adjective will you assign to them? (Please! This is a family-friendly book!) Back to the sentence: The clue here is *although,* which signals that something doesn't add up (in addition to your tuition bills). The sentence tells you that many students request aid, so you expect the college to say, "Yes, we charge too much." But *although* tells you that what you expect is wrong. Therefore, the school likely **maintains** (declares) that the tuition is just fine, or not *burdensome,* as Choice (B) states. Quick vocab lesson: **transient** means "brief, passing, not permanent."

4. **C.** You start off with *in addition to,* so you know that you're matching something to *chronic lateness.* Most clients aren't too happy when their ten o'clock appointment strolls in at eleven on a regular basis. Therefore, it's a good bet that you should fill the blank with a negative word. Now turn to the vocabulary file in your head. **Discretion** is "prudent, responsible conduct," and **gentility** is "proper behavior." **Incompetence** means "inability to do the job," and **candor** is "open, honest speech." One left: **acumen** is "mental quickness and accuracy." Only Choice (C) works with *chronic lateness,* so that's your answer.

5. **A.** Every word following the comma **comprises** (is part of, makes up) a definition of *orthodox,* Choice (A). I can't resist injecting a couple of vocabulary words into your brain: **heretical** is the opposite of "orthodox," and **deviant** means "differing from the norm" — the opposite of Choice (C), *mainstream.* Choice (E), **innovative,** means "inventive, tending to create something new."

Gaining information from punctuation

Punctuation is your friend when you're trying to crack a sentence completion because punctuation adds meaning to written expression. On the PSAT/NMSQT, you get the most mileage out of three punctuation marks: the semicolon, the colon, and quotation marks.

Paying attention to punctuation pays off when you hit the passage-based questions, too. (Check out Chapter 4 to practice some passage-based questions.)

A *semicolon* (a dot atop a comma) is like the bench that you sit on for a moment while hiking, according to one writer. You rest there and then continue the journey. If you see a semicolon, you probably *won't* see a change in meaning. Instead, the second portion of the sentence (the part that follows the semicolon) is an extension of the first portion. The relation may be implied cause-and-effect or an additional fact. Take a look at these examples:

> The committee chair must take attendance; the meeting can't be held if too many members are absent.

> Efforts to locate the puppy were unsuccessful; the searchers vowed to continue the next morning.

In the first sentence, the semicolon indicates *why* the committee chair has to take attendance — a cause-and-effect relationship. In the second example, the semicolon moves the action forward in time. The searchers failed, but they will be back.

A *colon* (one dot atop another) may introduce a list, and it may also join two complete sentences when the second sentence explains the meaning of the first. Here are colons in action:

> The exhibit contains many controversial artworks: a decaying basket of fruit, a mirror that distorts viewers' faces, and a defaced portrait of a popular film star.

> *Timon of Athens* was never performed during Shakespeare's lifetime: The play was unfinished when he died.

The colon introduces the list of artworks in the first example. In the second sentence, the colon offers a reason why the play wasn't produced.

Quotation marks generally indicate that someone is speaking, but on the PSAT/NMSQT you may also see *sanitizing quotation marks,* which distance the writer from what she is saying, as in this sentence:

> Mark's mother insisted that we listen attentively to his "music."

The quotation marks tell you that the sounds Mark produces (squeaky hinges, garbage can lids hitting one another, whatever) aren't truly music, in the writer's view.

Keep your eye on the punctuation in Questions 6 and 7.

6. That variety of plant is _____; however, the berries on the other bush are nutritious and easily digested.

   (A) unattractive

   (B) inedible

   (C) dominant

   (D) widespread

   (E) perennial

7. The children were under strict orders to be _____: They were to mingle with the guests and help everyone feel at home.

   (A) amenable

   (B) stern

   (C) hospitable

   (D) petulant

   (E) magnanimous

Now check your answers:

6. **B.** The semicolon signals that the second half of the sentence continues the topic of the first half. Because the second half is about berries and their value as a food source, the first half has to be about food also. The word *however* tells you that the sentence, while still on topic, changes direction, so *inedible* (can't be eaten) works perfectly.

7. **C.** Everything following the colon is a definition of what precedes the colon — the orders the children received. They're supposed to *mingle* (mix in socially) and make the guests comfortable, so *hospitable* (welcoming) is perfect. Before you go, take a moment to learn some vocabulary: *amenable* is "open to, willing to go along with," and *stern* is "strict." *Petulant* is "irritable," and *magnanimous* is "generous."

Applying real world experience

Every sentence-completion question on the PSAT/NMSQT can be answered with the information that's right there, in the sentence. Nevertheless, sometimes your experience in the real world gives you a little extra help. By the way, when I say "the real world," I'm *not* talking about reality television, which is about as far from reality as you can get.

Suppose you see this sentence:

> Relying on _____ answers, Molly truthfully answered her mother's questions about the broken window and yet escaped without punishment.

You may not know Molly, but you probably know what happens when a child tries to avoid being grounded while submitting to her mom's *interrogation* (questioning). Apart from lying, the most effective method is to give answers that may be interpreted more than one way. For example, Molly's mom may have asked, "Did you see who broke the window?" Molly can truthfully say no, unless she was looking in a mirror when she practiced her curve ball. So if one of the answer choices is *vague* or *evasive* (intentionally unclear), your life experience takes you to the correct response.

The real world takes you only so far on the PSAT/NMSQT. No matter what your experience, look at each sentence very carefully. The clues are there. Your job is to find the answer choice that best matches them.

Try your hand at applying real-life experience as you answer Questions 8 and 9:

8. _____ the atmosphere of the library, Oliver's voice was _____ in the farthest corner of the room.

   (A) Enhancing . . . distinguishable

   (B) Compounding . . . faint

   (C) Complementing . . . undefined

   (D) Disturbing . . . audible

   (E) Irritating . . . unnecessary

9. Because neither Jean nor her opponents were willing to _____ that point, the discussion continued for several more hours.

   (A) recede

   (B) concede

   (C) combat

   (D) convey

   (E) communicate

Now check your answers:

8. **D.** Have you been in a library lately? I wrote this question sitting in one. Everyone, including me, was reading or taking silent notes. One idiot, unfortunately, was making dinner plans on his cellphone. With 20 people glaring at him, he ended the call. However, libraries are usually quiet, so start with that assumption. The first blank probably refers to something that either keeps the atmosphere the same or ruins it. Now look at the pairs. If Oliver's voice was ***audible,*** everyone could hear him, so he was *disturbing* the atmosphere.

9. **B.** Have you ever attended a meeting or family gathering with opposing sides? You know, then, that one way to end the discussion is ***compromise*** (each side giving in a little until the middle ground is reached). Another way to get out of the meeting before everyone's hair turns gray is for one of the sides to give in. The answer choices don't provide a synonym for *compromise,* but you do see ***concede*** (reluctantly accept an idea or proposal). Vocab time: ***recede*** means to move backward *physically,* so that answer doesn't work in this sentence. ***Convey,*** in this context, is a synonym for Choice (E), *communicate.*

Dealing with difficult vocabulary

If the words on the PSAT/NMSQT were baseball players, a fair number of them would be in the Major Leagues, and a few would be all-stars. Your best bet is to ***accumulate*** (gather) and know the definitions of a large fund of PSAT/NMSQT favorites.

No matter how many words you know, however, chances are you'll still run into a few strangers when you take the test. You should apply the guessing rules, of course. (See Chapter 2 for details on when to guess and when to skip.) But if you have time, you may be able to crack open the meaning of an unfamiliar word by analyzing its parts. Try these techniques:

✔ **Look for a similar word.** You know that *mistake* means "to do something wrong." You can probably figure out that *misdiagnosis* refers to a doctor's errors and that to *mischaracterize* is "to give a faulty description or impression." (***Characterize*** means "to describe, to list the qualities of.")

✔ **Apply your knowledge of prefixes, suffixes, and roots.** This trick is a slight variation of the preceding bullet point. In whatever time you have before the exam, memorize a few common *prefixes* (letters or syllables at the beginning of a word), *suffixes* (letters or syllables at the end of a word), and *roots* (the middle!). For example, *anti* is a prefix meaning "against," and *path* is a root meaning "feeling." Knowing these facts, you can figure out the definition of ***antipathy*** (strong feeling *against* someone or something). Bonus: If you see ***apathy*** on the exam, you may conclude, correctly, that the word has something to do with feeling, even without knowing that the prefix *a* means "without or not." (I would tell you the definition of *apathy,* but I don't care. Just kidding: *apathy* means "without feeling or caring.")

Because so much of English comes from Greek and Latin, you can find lists of word parts ***derived*** (originating) from those languages. A quick search on the Internet turns up plenty of great reference sites. Don't attempt to memorize a huge list; aiming for a thousand word parts is likely to result in confusion. Instead, pick a realistic number and glue them to your brain.

Take note of prefixes, suffixes, and roots in Questions 10 through 12.

10. Although the most efficient design for that instrument resembles a dentist's drill, customers prefer _____ robots, probably because people look for reflections of themselves.

    (A) anthropomorphic

    (B) temperate

    (C) idyllic

    (D) philanthropic

    (E) prolific

11. The new dam _____ water from its natural path, to the dismay of farmers who depend on the river to irrigate their crops.

    (A) converts

    (B) diverts

    (C) separates

    (D) disburses

    (E) allocates

12. The nation welcomed _____ aid but denied entry to weapons inspectors.

    (A) unselfish

    (B) geocentric

    (C) alternative

    (D) cautionary

    (E) humanitarian

Now check your answers:

10. **A.** The root *anthrop* refers to human beings, so Choices (A) and (D) are possibilities. The prefix *phil,* however, means "loving." The definition of ***philanthropic*** is "loving humankind" and is generally applied to those who donate or work for good causes. Choice (A) is a better answer because another root contained in the word, *morph,* means "form or shape." Therefore, ***anthropomorphic*** means "shaped like a human being."

11. **B.** The root *vert* means "turn." Choices (A) and (B) are possible at first glance because the river has been moved away from where it used to flow. Now look at the prefixes: *con* means "with," and *di* means "apart, in different directions." Clearly, Choice (B) is better because the river has been turned in a different direction. Two more things to add to your vocabulary file: ***burse*** is an old word for *purse,* where you carry money and valuable things. To ***disburse*** is "to pay out" (and the *bursar* is the college official who'll collect your money someday). The root *loc* means "place"; you see it in *locate, location,* and Choice (E) ***allocate***, which means "to set something aside — in a place! — for a specific purpose."

12. **E.** You don't have to be a mega-brain to realize that ***humanitarian*** refers to human beings. The word itself may be defined as "concerned with saving human lives" and works perfectly in this sentence. Were you fooled by Choice (B)? The prefix *geo* means "earth," and the root *centr* is "centered." There you go: ***geocentric*** means "centered on the earth."

Chapter 4

Exploring the Secret Passage: Reading Comprehension Questions

Thirty-five delightful questions in the critical reading sections of the PSAT/NMSQT are based on passages, which is test-speak for a few paragraphs, usually sliced from a longer work, that are dropped into an exam so you can answer reading-comprehension questions about them. Okay, I was kidding about "delightful." Nothing about the PSAT/NMSQT falls into that category, but at least with this sort of question you get to read something. And as you may *infer* (conclude based on evidence), I agree with Abraham Lincoln, who said that his best friend is "the man who'll get me a book I ain't read."

Reading for fun and reading to score points are somewhat different, of course, but you can minimize the pain and maximize the gain on passage-based questions if you approach them properly. In this chapter, I show you how to do just that and give you a chance to practice.

Taking a Look at Passage-Based Questions

Because the PSAT/NMSQT is the *precursor* (forerunner) of the SAT, the exam you take in order to convince schools that you're ready for college-level work, the passages reflect the variety and reading level of typical college freshmen courses. (Notice I said *courses,* not postings on social media or instant messages between roommates. Those are a lot easier to read!) Here's what to expect:

- **Passages ranging from 100 to 850 words.** Generally you find two short passages, 100 to 150 words long, in each of the two critical reading sections. Short passages show up right after the sentence completions (see Chapter 3 for more information) and may be separate or paired. Either way, the short passages merit a total of four questions. Longer passages may also be paired or appear solo. Expect six to twelve questions for longer passages.

- **Content from many disciplines.** In this context, a *discipline* is a branch of learning, not the branch a cranky teacher would like to thwack on the heads of *unruly* (disorderly) students. You may run across science, social science, history, autobiography, biography, and fiction. Expect mostly modern writing, but generally each PSAT/NMSQT includes at least one and often a couple of older works from the 19th or early 20th century.

- ✔ **Varied purposes and styles.** Some passages make an argument for a specific point of view, some tell a story, and others simply give information. The style may be flowery, *terse* (using as few words as possible to make a point), *pompous* (emphasizing the writer's importance), or something else.

- ✔ **Questions that follow the order of the passage.** In every other section of the test, questions appear in order of difficulty — the easiest first and the hardest last. Passage-based questions, however, move along from line to line. The first question asks about something at the beginning of the passage, and later questions concern material appearing towards the end. Questions that apply to the whole passage (tone or purpose, for example) pop up anywhere.

The questions are the usual, standardized-test *fare* (diet). The test-writers quiz you on the facts, what is implied but not stated, the meaning of words in the context of the passage, the author's purpose and attitude, and so forth. The questions aren't the kind you ask in real life, when you say something like "Why didn't George mow the lawn?" when George parks the lawnmower and turns on the television. Instead, PSAT/NMSQT questions are fancied up for the academic crowd, so that a normal *query* (question) becomes

George's abandonment of the lawnmower may best be interpreted as which of the following?

(A) a strategy for avoiding manual labor

(B) a statement about human existence

(C) a plea for help

(D) a character flaw

(E) a rebellion against societal norms

Because I'm illustrating terminology and not working off a real passage, I won't attempt to answer this question. My experience with human nature pushes me toward Choice (A) — which brings me to an important point. Life experience is great, but on the PSAT/NMSQT, stick with the passage. Everything you need to know is there, and no answer is correct *unless* you find evidence for it in the passage.

I show you examples of common PSAT/NMSQT questions and explain how to answer them in "Assembling a Tool Kit for Every Question Type" later in this chapter.

Planning Your Approach to Passages

Former Secretary of State Colin Powell once advised, "Always focus on the front windshield and not the rearview mirror." In this section you can look ahead at passage-based questions and map the way to your goal, a high score in critical reading. Follow these steps:

- ✔ **Work on the passages in order.** Don't waste time flipping through the whole section. Start with the first passage and continue to the end. However, you may find that some passages are harder for you than others. If you run into a passage that may as well be written in Lithuanian (unless, of course, you *know* Lithuanian), skip it. You can always go back to the passage, time permitting.

- ✔ **For pairs, work on each passage separately and then on comparison/contrast questions.** Generally, paired-passage questions divide into three parts: (1) questions about the first passage; (2) questions about the second passage; and (3) questions that compare or contrast the passages. Treat these as three distinct tasks.

✔ **Read the introduction first.** A few sentences precede each passage or pair of passages. The test-writers always include directions that say something like "read the passage and answer Questions 9 through 12." (What do they think you're going to do? Shred Questions 9 through 12?) But look at those sentences anyway, because sometimes you find a golden nugget — identification of the source material. Occasionally, that information tips the scales toward one answer and away from another.

✔ **Read the questions.** Don't waste time glancing at the answer choices. Just look at the question *stem,* the part that sits above the A, B, C, D, and E choices. As you read, underline key words. Check out these questions, with the important words underlined:

> In the context of Line 4, what is the best definition of "play"?

> The tone of the passage may be characterized as . . .

In the next section of this chapter, "Assembling a Tool Kit for Every Question Type," I provide examples of each question and show you which words to underline.

✔ **Read and annotate the passage.** Yes, I know, some people (and some other test-prep books) advise you to read only a few lines here and there, just enough to find an answer. But on the PSAT/NMSQT, *an* answer isn't good enough. You must bubble in *the* answer, and for that task, spotty reading doesn't **suffice** (meet your needs). As you read, keep the questions in mind. When you run across something important, underline it. Working from the example in the preceding bullet point, underline "play" so you can find it quickly when you're ready to answer the question about its meaning. Also underline and write a marginal note near any words that indicate the author's tone. Don't write much — maybe a quick "t" for "tone."

Underlining too many words is as useless as underlining none at all. The goal is to guide yourself to important ideas. Use your pencil **sparingly** (in a limited way).

✔ **Return to the questions and read the answer choices.** Some answers leap out at you, especially if you've annotated the passage properly. For example, you may have underlined words that reveal irritation and opposition. When you see *antagonistic* as an answer choice in a tone question, you can confidently bubble it in.

✔ **Return to the passage as needed.** Not every answer is obvious at first glance. Fortunately, the test-writers frequently direct you to a line or set of lines. Reread to find the answer.

✔ **Use the process of elimination.** Of the five answer choices, you may see one or two that flash a neon "WRONG!" sign in your brain. Put a slash through those answers and concentrate on what's left.

✔ **Look for specifics.** Most PSAT/NMSQT questions provide two answers that *could* be correct. Your job is to go for the *best* answer, which is frequently the more specific.

The answer to every passage-based question must be supported by something stated or implied in the passage. Think of yourself as a detective; without evidence, you're sunk.

✔ **Keep an eye on the clock.** With only a few minutes left, hit the questions that can be answered fast — vocabulary in context, a factual question attached to a specific line, and the like. Be sure to get to those questions before the proctor calls time.

✔ **Guess appropriately.** In Chapter 2, I explain how to beat the odds by guessing.

The preceding bullet points outline a good, all-purpose approach — the test-prep equivalent of a suit from a department store. A little tailoring, though, may be a good idea. Think about your skills and academic habits. Are you a slow reader? Do you tend to agonize over particular types of questions (main idea or inference, perhaps)? **Alter** (change) the steps above until you achieve a good fit. Every time you score a practice test from Part IV, revisit these steps and adjust them accordingly.

Getting a ticket to speed reading

Are you a snail or a racehorse when it comes to reading? Most people fall somewhere in the middle, but with a little practice, anyone can learn to pick up the pace without sacrificing comprehension. Speed reading is an **asset** (valuable quality) not only on a timed test such as the PSAT/NMSQT but in other situations as well. How happy would you be to finish your homework reading in half the time?

Here's the secret: Reading speed improves with practice. When you're plodding through Chapter 4 of *Boring Ideas and Facts* or a similar textbook, set a timer for two minutes. Force yourself to read a little more quickly than usual during that period. When the timer goes off, stop. Think about what you just read. Did you understand it? If the answer is no, you went a bit too fast. Try again, more slowly this time. If you did understand, also try again. This time, read faster still.

Repeat this exercise at least once a day. Each time, check yourself. Gradually the faster pace will feel normal.

Assembling a Tool Kit for Every Question Type

Army officers distinguish between strategy and tactics. Strategy refers to the overall plan. Tactics get to the nitty-gritty level: how many soldiers to send where, with which weapons. In the preceding section I discuss a general strategy for passage-based questions. In this section I tackle tactics.

Getting the facts straight

How many balloons did the clown pop during the performance? Do dust mites relocate after you vacuum? Does Einstein's theory of relativity take into account Uncle Charles's tendency to snore? These questions, like a fair number on the PSAT/NMSQT, should be answered only with facts *specifically stated* in the passage. To answer a fact question, do the following:

- ✔ **Underline key words.** In the first question of this section, for example, the key words are "how many balloons."

- ✔ **Check the lines you're being asked about.** You may see a line reference in the question. Or, you may have underlined the answer as you read through the passage.

  Passage-based questions follow the passage from top to bottom. If you don't see a line reference, check the question above and below the one you're trying to answer. Chances are the evidence you need is somewhere between those two. For example, suppose you're on Question 21. Number 20 references Line 30, and Number 22 references Line 40. Look for your answer to Question 21 in Lines 30 to 40.

- ✔ **With a "rule out" question, use the process of elimination.** Some fact questions give you three statements and ask you to identify the true one(s). You may also see a five-choice question that asks you to pluck out the false statement. Put a check mark next to the true statements. Then choose your answer.

Try your hand at fact Questions 1 and 2, based on an excerpt from *Residential Design for Aging in Place*, by Drue Lawlor and Michael A. Thomas (Wiley).

Line At its completion in the early 1950s, Levittown included 17,400 homes. The new development was now a major suburban community that included 82,000 husbands and wives and their children. In a second wave of development and construction in 1951, the Levitt family created an additional Levittown community of 17,000 homes in Bucks County, Pennsylvania,
(05) near Philadelphia. The suburban sprawl had begun. Families would fill them quickly. The growing popularity and availability of automobiles also encouraged the flight to get out of big cities. The National Highway Program of 1956 built highways and interstate roads connecting rural areas to metropolitan areas, contributing to a flurry of even more suburban development.

1. According to the passage, which of the following statements are true?

    I. Private companies may build towns.

    II. The growth of the American automobile industry paralleled the rise of suburbs.

    III. Levittown homes could not be purchased by single people.

    (A) I only

    (B) II only

    (C) I and II

    (D) II and III

    (E) all of the above

2. According to the passage, the establishment of suburbs

    (A) affected family size

    (B) was dependent on public transportation

    (C) began during the 19th century

    (D) took place mainly in Pennsylvania

    (E) was a national phenomenon

Now check your answers:

1. **C.** The passage tells you that "the Levitt family created" (Lines 3–4) Levittown, so you know that I is true. Lines 6–7 refer to the "growing popularity and availability of automobiles" that "encouraged the flight . . . out of big cities." Therefore, II is true. Although the passage mentions families, you aren't told whether Levittown houses were restricted to families or open to singles. Because you can't prove III, you must assume it is false. Choice (C) is the answer.

2. **E.** The passage refers to the "National Highway Program" (Line 7) and "interstate roads" (Line 7) and links both to "suburban development" (Lines 8–9). Therefore, Choice (E) is correct. Were you fooled by Choice (D)? True, the passage mentions Bucks Country, Pennsylvania, but only as the location of *one* suburb, not all suburbs.

As in the preceding question, the test-writers often try to catch you with an answer that's too narrow. Read carefully to be sure that your answer is justified by all the information in the passage.

Deducing the answer to inference questions

The fictional detective Sherlock Holmes specialized in **shrewd** (perceptive) observations that led him to logical conclusions. When you run across an inference question on the PSAT/NMSQT, channel your inner Sherlock Holmes. Look at what the passage says, and extend the meaning of those clues to a probable answer. For example, the passage may describe an actor who's constantly glancing around between scenes, checking the director's reaction. A description of the actor's dressing room mentions a copy of a show business publication with circled help-wanted ads, along with some newspapers open to the reviews of the actor's show. What do you infer from these clues? The actor is insecure about his job or talent (or both!). The passage doesn't *tell* you that he is insecure; you figured it out from the information supplied. Approach inference questions this way:

- ✔ **Identify inference questions.** In the section "Planning Your Approach to Passages" earlier in this chapter, I tell you to read the question *stems* first. Most inferences include some form of the words *imply, suggest, likely,* or *probably.* (A few non-inference questions use those words too. Check that the question requires you to extend your knowledge beyond what appears in the passage.)

- ✔ **As you read the passage, put a check in the margin next to every clue.** For example, suppose the question stem says, "What is the most likely reason for Alan's refusal to speak to Rosa?" As you read, you discover that Rosa and Alan were once good friends. Check! Then you see that Rosa complained to her supervisor about Alan's work on a project. Check! Consequently, Alan was fired. Check!

- ✔ **Use logic to extend what you know.** Now that you have clues, look for an answer that logically flows from them. Continuing the example of Alan and Rosa from the preceding bullet point, you want an answer choice that mentions Alan's anger at Rosa's actions.

Inference questions sometimes extend beyond the passage. You may be asked to identify a statement with which the author would agree, for example. No problem! Simply think about what's in the passage and the beliefs implied. Then look for a statement that matches those views.

Take a shot at inference Questions 3 and 4, based on an excerpt from *The Recipe Writer's Handbook,* by Barbara Gibbs Ostmann and Jane Baker (Wiley).

Line   An experienced reporter who was assigned to work on a newspaper food section did not
        know the difference in recipe writing between a lowercase *t* and an uppercase *T* (teaspoon
        and tablespoon, respectively). Needless to say, he didn't last long on the food beat. The
        point is that the reporter's level of knowledge may be typical. One woman called a cooking
(05)   hotline to say that she had a new oven. She wanted to know whether it was preheated.
        Another woman called to complain that her cake had turned out gritty. It turns out that she
        had used whole eggs — shells and all. Another caller had driven all over town looking for
        powdered sherry. She was furious that a recipe ingredient wasn't available. The recipe had
        called for "dry sherry." Other callers inquired how far to drop "drop cookies," where to get
(10)   a soup can of water, and how to tell whether a pan is 9 inches.

3. The reporter mentioned in Line 1 was transferred from the food section of a newspaper probably because he

   (A) lacked basic information about cooking

   (B) couldn't follow grammar rules

   (C) had a background in general reporting

   (D) was not a leading expert on food

   (E) did not know how to use ingredients properly

4. The authors most likely describe these particular phone calls to the food hotline (Lines 4–10) because they believe that

   (A) recipes should be written more clearly

   (B) more hotlines are needed

   (C) the average person needs better culinary education

   (D) cooking errors may be dangerous

   (E) only advanced chefs can follow recipes

Now check your answers:

3. **A.** The passage tells you that the reporter was experienced (check!) but confused two common recipe abbreviations (check!). The authors throw in "needless to say" (Line 3, and another check!). Okay, Sherlock Holmes, what do you conclude? The reporter probably knows grammar (he or she is "experienced") but not the *conventions* (rules) of recipe writing. Those two facts point you to Choices (A) and (D). Your third clue, "needless to say," makes Choice (A) the better answer, because that phrase is the equivalent of "everybody knows you have to understand the difference between *t* and *T* to read a recipe."

4. **C.** Right before the phone call descriptions, the passage says that "the reporter's level of knowledge may be typical" (Line 4). In the explanation for Question 3, I show three clues that lead you to believe that the reporter lacked basic knowledge. Continuing with the phone calls, you see a bunch of dumb questioners, including one who threw egg shells into batter and another who didn't know how to measure a pan. That last clue is the kicker. Even if calling the local restaurant for reservations is the limit of your *culinary* (cooking-related) experience, you can probably measure a pan. Therefore, Choice (C) is the logical inference.

Saying the magic word: Vocabulary questions

All the vocabulary questions on the PSAT/NMSQT are "in context": that is, you have to find a definition that fits the way the word is used in the sentence. The test-makers often camouflage the answer by surrounding it with other meanings of the word. No worries! A simple method leads you to the right response:

✔ **Reread the sentences surrounding the word they're asking about.** Sometimes, you can get away with one sentence, but if you have time, a sentence before and after may provide a clue.

✔ **Restate the sentence, inserting your own word(s).** Don't worry about the answer choices at this point. Just find a word or a phrase that makes sense.

✔ **Locate an answer choice that fits your definition.** Suppose you came up with *decorate* for this step. In the five answer choices, you see *beautify,* which matches your definition well enough.

✔ **Insert your answer choice into the sentence.** If it fits, you're done. If not, try another word.

Vocabulary-in-context questions are among the easiest on the PSAT/NMSQT. Try to answer all of them, unless you're really stuck. In that case, skip the question. Most of the time, you can eliminate some wrong answers and take a guess.

Answer Questions 5 and 6 by referring to the passage about Levittown in the "Getting the facts straight" section earlier in this chapter.

5. What is the meaning of "development" in the context of Line 1?

   (A) change

   (B) gradual process

   (C) housing

   (D) fund raising

   (E) improvement

6. In the context of Line 8, which of the following is the best definition of "flurry"?

   (A) snowstorm

   (B) sudden burst of activity

   (C) gust of wind

   (D) shower

   (E) trend

Now check your answers:

5. **C.** The "new development" is "a major suburban community" (Lines 1 and 2), so your own definition may be "town" or "new homes." When you check the answer choices (all of which are definitions of "development"), only Choice (C) works. There's your answer! By the way, Choice (A) is a runner-up because "change" fits the sentence in some ways. But so does "housing," which is a more specific — and therefore better — answer.

6. **B.** The passage refers to "a flurry" of suburban development, right after discussing the connection of rural areas to metropolitan areas — prime territory for suburbs. The passage also mentions that families would move into suburbs "quickly" (Line 5). Therefore, your own definition might be something like "quick increase" or "spike in." Choice (B) matches those definitions and works nicely when inserted into the sentence.

Figuring out figurative language

When language leaves the real world and enters the *realm* (kingdom) of imagination, English teachers call it *figurative* and refer to the phrases it appears in as *figures of speech*. You're probably most familiar with **metaphors** and **similes** (when something is described by comparing it to something else), and you may employ **hyperbole** (exaggeration) or understatement to make a joke. **Symbolism** — when something carries extra meaning — has probably popped up in one or two of your English classes also. On the PSAT/NMSQT, you may see a question asking you to identify one of these literary techniques. More commonly, you're asked about the phrase itself: its effect on the meaning of the passage, perhaps. Here's how to proceed:

✔ **Reread the phrase.** Figure out what the phrase is doing. Does it make a comparison? Do you see *like* or *as* in the phrase? A comparison without *like* or *as* is a metaphor. With those words, you have a simile. When reading question stems, watch out for these terms and others in the bold type in the preceding paragraph.

✔ **Check the question.** If you're supposed to identify the figure of speech (and you know what the figure of speech is), you're done. Make a match and move on. If they ask how the expression affects meaning, read the next bullet point.

✔ **Create a mental image.** For example, suppose you see "eyes shining like a pond at noon." Picture the sun shining on water. Or perhaps the phrase is "eyes shining like nuggets of coal." Now "see" little black lumps of coal.

✔ **Match the image to an answer choice.** Using the example in the preceding bullet point, the first simile is soft and fluid. The second is cold and hard. One answer choice probably expresses that information, and that's your answer.

Try your hand at interpreting figurative language with Questions 7 and 8. The following passage is excerpted from Virginia Woolf's novel, *Jacob's Room*.

Line   Tears made all the flowers in her garden move in red waves and spangled the kitchen with bright knives, and made Mrs. Jarvis, the rector's wife, think at church — while the hymn-tune played and Mrs. Flanders bent low over her little boys' heads — that marriage is a fortress and widows stray solitary in the open fields, picking up stones, gleaning a few golden

(05)   straws, lonely, unprotected, poor creatures. Mrs. Flanders had been a widow for these two years.

7. The reference to "bright knives" (Line 2) serves to

  (A) associate domestic life with Mrs. Jarvis

  (B) show that cooking is important to Mrs. Flanders

  (C) illustrate the nature of the relationship between Mrs. Jarvis and Mrs. Flanders

  (D) emphasize the widow's pain

  (E) give information about Mrs. Jarvis's approach to life

8. The dominant literary technique in this passage is

  (A) hyperbole

  (B) metaphor

  (C) understatement

  (D) simile

  (E) symbolism

Now check your answers:

7. **D.** The "bright knives" are a metaphorical description of "tears," which flow from Mrs. Flanders' eyes. The passage tells you that Mrs. Flanders "had been a widow for these two years" (Lines 5–6), and as such she must "stray solitary . . . picking up stones" (Line 4). Clearly, Mrs. Flanders is in pain, and the metaphor underlines that fact.

8. **B.** This passage is chock full of metaphors: tears are "bright knives" (Line 2), marriage is a "fortress" (Lines 3–4), and a widow's joys are "a few golden straws" (Lines 4–5). Yup, Choice (B) is the answer.

Toning Your Reading Muscles

Tone is the way the author's voice sounds in your head, as in "Don't take that tone with me, young lady" (one of my mother's favorite sayings). You can "hear" the passage correctly if you follow these steps:

✔ **Notice diction.** *Diction* is an English-teacher term for word choice. The difference between a *silly* and a *stupid* trick, for example, is huge. The first hints at "isn't she cute," and the other leans toward the "you could've been killed!" direction. As you read, underline unusual words and those that create a strong impression. They indicate tone.

✔ **Pay attention to syntax.** Another English-teacher term! *Syntax* is the way in which parts of the sentence fit together grammatically. Don't panic; you don't have to identify parts of speech or label clauses. Just *listen* to the voice in your head as you read the passage. Are the sentences long and complicated? Short and punchy? Do they give orders or simply lay out information? Answering these questions gives you other clues about the tone of a passage.

✔ **Don't ignore content.** If the passage explains how rare elements are crucial to building cell phones and computers, you're getting information. If you see statements of opinion or *recollections* (memories), you know that the author has written an argument or a memoir. Still more clues to tone!

✔ **Put everything together and choose an answer.** After you've nailed diction, syntax, and content, you should be ready to pick an answer. Look for something that fits. A passage that *recounts* (tells) happy memories may be nostalgic; one that complains may be *antagonistic* (opposing strongly) or bitter.

Tone questions sometimes are the easiest in the pack, because you may recognize the tone on the first read-through. Don't spend too much time on a tone question if you're really puzzled or if the answer choices are words you don't understand. Follow the guessing rule: if you can cross one off, take a guess.

In the interest of space, I'm cheating a little here, because the PSAT/NMSQT always hands you a full passage when it asks about tone. Instead of giving you a lengthy excerpt, in this practice I supply just a sentence or two from three different works, along with five possible words to characterize the tone of the sentence(s). Get your reading muscles in shape with Questions 9 through 11:

9. Identify the tone of this sentence:

   The stagnant thinking of those committee members is reflected in the lack of originality in their proposal.

   (A) reflective

   (B) didactic

   (C) informative

   (D) sympathetic

   (E) critical

10. Identify the tone of this passage:

    On hot summer nights his family drove to the local ice cream stand, where, for just a few minutes, nothing mattered but the cold, sweet treat. No dessert, before or since, was as delicious as a double-dip cone eaten while he balanced on a log behind the parking lot.

    (A) nostalgic

    (B) biting

    (C) irreverent

    (D) cynical

    (E) satirical

11. Identify the tone in this passage:

   All registered cyclists have passed an examination covering traffic rules and safety. Those interested in the new BikeShare Program must register their bicycles and provide a major credit card to ensure payment. Call 555-1212 for more information.

   (A) argumentative

   (B) sentimental

   (C) idealistic

   (D) informative

   (E) caustic

Now check your answers:

9. **E.** A good vocabulary is the key to this question. Something that's **stagnant** never moves or changes, and no one ever wants to be accused of "stagnant thinking" or a "lack of originality." Therefore, Choice (E) works perfectly. A bit of vocabulary: **reflective** is the "I'm thinking" tone, and a **didactic** tone is what you hear from people, especially teachers, who sometimes sound as if they know it all.

10. **A.** You're strolling down a memory lane here, with no potholes in sight. Therefore, **nostalgic** (yearning for a happy moment in the past) is your answer. Take a second for vocabulary: a **biting** tone cuts and hurts, an **irreverent** one mocks something considered holy, and a **cynical** tone is distrustful and bitter. You've probably seen **satirical** comedy shows that specialize in ridicule.

11. **D.** The passage is straightforward, giving you information without evaluating the content. Choice (D) is a perfect fit. Do you know the meaning of Choice (E)? A **caustic** tone drips acid all over the reader. You may hear a caustic tone during some arguments.

Relating Structure and Style to Content

A few PSAT/NMSQT questions ask you to relate *how* a passage is written — its structure or style — to *what* the passage says. I address the aspects of structure and style you're most likely to be quizzed about in "Figuring out figurative language" and "Toning Your Reading Muscles" earlier in this chapter. Here I hit a couple of topics that make only cameo appearances on the exam. (A **cameo** occurs when a mega-star shows up for one scene in a film.) Possible exam questions include these:

   The examples in Paragraph 2 serve to . . .

   The author describes Mary's room (Lines 6–8) in order to . . .

   In contrast to the first paragraph (Lines 1–5), the second paragraph . . .

   The question "How many roads lie before me?" (Line 3) is intended to . . .

When you hit a question about style or structure, two techniques help:

✔ **If possible, state in your own words what the author accomplishes in that sentence or paragraph.** If you see a list or examples, you may say, "She's proving the point she made in the first sentence." After reading a description, you may think, "She wants me to see how poor Ellen's family is." After you have that statement in your mind, the answer choice is probably clear. If not, try the next bullet point.

✔ **Mentally delete or change the indicated sentence or paragraph.** Suppose they're asking about a list of examples. Okay, glance over the passage. Without those examples, would the author's case be weaker? Or, imagine that the author made a statement ("I create my own destiny") instead of asking a question ("Do I create my own destiny?"). How does your reaction change? If the question concerns the relationship between two paragraphs, flip them around or imagine the passage without one of them. The effect of a deletion or change points you toward the significance of the original version. After you decide the role of the original sentence or paragraph, all you have to do is select an answer choice that matches your idea.

Get to work! Take a look at another excerpt from *The Recipe Writer's Handbook,* by Barbara Gibbs Ostmann and Jane Baker (Wiley), and answer Questions 12 and 13 that follow.

Line   It's not surprising that several recent studies by national food companies have shown that an overwhelming number of today's recipe users are cooking illiterates — that is, they haven't learned to cook alongside their mothers or grandmothers, and they lack knowledge of what many food professionals consider basic food terminology and skills. These young
(05)   adults, aged 25 to 30 years, are often called "the lost generation" in the kitchen.

A national food literacy survey, conducted in late 1990 by the National Family Opinion Research Center, Inc. on behalf of the National Pork Producers Council, revealed some startling results. Although 90 percent of the 735 adults (aged 25 to 54) considered themselves to be good to excellent cooks, almost three fourths of them flunked a basic 20-point cooking
(10)   quiz. Only one person out of the 735 people surveyed received a perfect score on the multiple-choice, true-false test, which included questions about how many ounces are in one cup and equivalent in cups of one stick of margarine. A staggering 45 percent of respondents didn't know how many teaspoons are in one tablespoon.

Most of the respondents expressed a desire to cook, but they cited lack of time and lack of
(15)   basic cooking knowledge as the reasons they didn't. However, 51 percent said they try a new recipe at least once a month, and 30 percent said they try a new recipe at least two or three times a month. When looking for recipes and cooking information, one third of the respondents reach for a cookbook.

12. Which phrase best describes the relationship between Paragraph 1 (Lines 1–5) and Paragraph 2 (Lines 6–13)?

   (A) specific to general

   (B) question and answer

   (C) assertion and proof

   (D) opposing views

   (E) problem and solution

13. Information about the number of people trying new recipes is included in order to

   (A) define the market for cookbooks

   (B) contradict the findings of the National Pork Producers Study

   (C) emphasize the importance of innovation in cooking

   (D) promote convenience foods

   (E) explain how cookbooks should be written

Now check your answers:

12. **C.** Everything in paragraph one is general. The authors ask you to believe them when they define "the lost generation" (Line 5) as "cooking illiterates" (Line 2). Paragraph two, however, is all fact. The fact that three out of four people flunked a cooking quiz backs up the **assertion** (claim) in the first paragraph.

13. **A.** Nobody knows how to cook, but a lot of people keep trying anyway, and a third of them turn to cookbooks. That's how I restate the ideas in the third paragraph (Lines 14–18). Add in the information from the introduction (which you should *always* read) and you know that the authors believe in recipes. After all, they wrote a handbook for recipe writers! Put these two ideas together and you arrive at Choice (A). You can get to Choice (A) by another route also. How would the passage be different without the "trying-something-new" information? You'd think that the world is doomed to terrible cooking, and cookbook writers need a career change. There you go: Choice (A) makes sense.

Reading with attitude and purpose

Questions about the author's attitude and purpose are closely related to tone. (Check out the section earlier in this chapter, "Toning Your Reading Muscles," for more information on tone.) Imagine that your PSAT/NMSQT has a passage about a polluted river. The tone is angry: Polluters are pouring **toxic** (poisonous) chemicals into the water, and officials can't be bothered to stop them. Depending upon the content of the rest of the passage, the author's attitude may be characterized as pro-environment or anti-government or both. The author's purpose may be to persuade citizens to take action (boycott the company that's polluting the river or protest at city hall, perhaps). To discover attitude and purpose, follow these guidelines:

✔ **Look for statements of opinion.** Not every opinion begins with "I think" or "in my opinion." As a matter of fact, I cross out those words when I see them in my students' essays because if a writer declares something, he or she believes it (unless, of course, the passage is humorous and the writer is poking fun or pretending).

✔ **Consider what's missing.** Studies show that people tend to cite studies proving their ideas and ignore studies challenging them. In other words, people pick and choose evidence to suit their purpose. Suppose, for example, that the imaginary polluted-river passage I discuss at the beginning of this section contains a paragraph about technology that **renders** (makes) pollutants harmless. Great, you think. The river can be cleaned up easily. But wait, what's the cost? If the passage never discusses the downside, the author's attitude is more extreme. Similarly, if the passage omits any mention of law enforcement and focuses only on politicians, the author's purpose may be to overturn elected officials and install a new slate.

✔ **Don't forget diction.** *Diction* — word choice —affects meaning. If the river is "toxic," people may die. If it's "muddy," the situation sounds less dangerous. Diction alone can't give you the answer to an attitude or purpose question, but it may help!

Attitude and purpose questions frequently pop up when you're dealing with paired passages. The question may ask you the difference between the two authors' attitudes or may say something like, "in contrast to the author of Passage I, the author of Passage II is more. . . ." No worries! Just determine the attitude of each author and compare them.

Take a crack at practice Questions 14 and 15, based on a pair of passages. The first is adapted from a biography of Frederick Douglass, a former slave and important **abolitionist** (opponent of slavery). The second is an excerpt from a letter written by Douglass to his publisher, in which Douglass agrees to write an autobiography.

Passage 1

Line By the slave code it was unlawful for a slave to go beyond the limits of his own neighborhood
without written permission from his master. Douglass could write a pass himself if he knew
how. His master kept a shipyard, and in this and neighboring establishments of the same
kind the boy spent much of his time. He noticed that the carpenters, after dressing pieces of
(05) timber, marked them with certain letters to indicate their positions in the vessel. By asking
questions of the workmen he learned the names of these letters and their significance. In
time he learned to write, and thus again demonstrated the power of the mind to overleap
the bounds that men set for it.

Passage 11

Any facts, either from slaves, slaveholders, or bystanders, calculated to enlighten the public
(10) mind by revealing the true nature of the slave system, can scarcely be withheld. I see, too,
that there are special reasons why I should write my own biography, in preference to
employing another to do it. Not only is slavery on trial, but unfortunately, the enslaved
people are also on trial. It is alleged that they are naturally inferior; that they are *so low* in
the scale of humanity and so utterly stupid that they are unconscious of their wrongs and
(15) do not apprehend their rights. Looking, then, at your request from this standpoint and
wishing everything of which you think me capable to go to the benefit of my afflicted
people, I part with my doubts and hesitation.

14. The purpose of Passage I is to

   (A) prove that anyone can learn to read

   (B) reveal information about Douglass's childhood

   (C) criticize slavery

   (D) inspire the reader

   (E) illustrate Douglass's determination

15. In Passage II, Douglass's attitude may best be described as

   (A) humble

   (B) arrogant

   (C) condescending

   (D) proud

   (E) combative

Now check your answers:

14. **E.** Purpose questions usually come in three sizes: too narrow, too broad, and just right.
The answer choices here illustrate all three varieties. Choices (A) and (B) are too narrow,
because how Douglass learned to read isn't the point of the story. It's just one example of
Douglass's determination and ***ingenuity*** (cleverness). Choices (C) and (D) are too broad;
yes, the author criticizes slavery and the story is inspiring. However, those answers say
nothing about Douglass. Go for Choice (E), which is just right.

15. **A.** Douglass doesn't brag about his achievements, even though he has every right to do so.
(I recommend that you read his autobiography; it's a real-life thriller.) Instead, he agrees to
write about himself only to disprove those who attempt to justify slavery and also for the
"benefit of my afflicted people" (Lines 16–17). Therefore, Choice (A) fits perfectly.

Snapping the big picture: Main idea

I attended a wedding recently at which the mother of the bride herded every single family member (including third cousins) into one spot so the photographer could snap a picture. The photographer had one second to get it right. Too narrow a focus and he'd miss Aunt Matilda. Too wide, and the faces would be little blobs on the landscape. You're a wedding photographer when you answer a main-idea question. Your choice should include the whole passage but not extend into a neighboring universe.

Main-idea questions may come with a straightforward label ("What is the main idea of this passage?") or pop up disguised as title questions ("Which of the following is the best title for this passage?").

Either way, turn to the process of elimination for this sort of question. The test-makers often place way-too-general answers alongside answers that are too narrow. Cross off these obviously wrong answer choices first. Then look at the remaining possibilities. If you're deciding between two, go for the more specific if you're sure it includes all the subtopics of the passage.

The main idea of a paragraph is often expressed in one sentence, known as the *topic sentence,* that sums up the point. The topic sentence can be anywhere: top, bottom, or mid-passage. As you read, underline the topic sentence of each paragraph. At the end of the passage, reread everything you underlined. You have a skeleton of the passage and are ready to find an answer that covers those points. Of course, if you're working on a short passage with only one paragraph, once you find the topic sentence, you're done!

No time like the present to go main-idea hunting. Read this passage, which is an excerpt from *Landscapes in History: Design and Planning in the Eastern and Western Traditions,* by Philip Pregill and Nancy Vokman (Wiley). Answer Question 16 that follows.

Line   In early America there was space on which to experiment, and a corresponding psychological need to fill that space with "civilized" uses. The capture and management of plants and space was one way to assert control over an environment which was, at once, seen as both fruitful and hostile. Americans were less attuned to and less adept at urban planning and
(05)   urban design. The American Revolution created a demand for an urban design that would manifest the ideals of a democratic republic. As a result of this demand, the first planned city of the "enlightened" age in North America was created as the new national capital, Washington.

16. Which of the following is the best title for this passage?

   (A) Urban Planning and Urban Design

   (B) Managing Plants and Space in Early America

   (C) The Meaning of Planned Cities

   (D) Design and Democratic Ideals in Early America

   (E) Washington, the Planned Capital

Now check your answer:

16. **D.** Three categories occur in this short passage: too broad, too narrow, and just right. In the "too broad" category you have Choices (A) and (C). Those titles could refer to New York, Singapore, and, well, *any* city that has a plan. Next up, too narrow: Choices (B) and (E). The passage mentions managing plants and space, but it also talks about urban planning, which includes buildings and streets. Also, Washington is the topic of only one sentence, the last. In the just right category is Choice (D), because it captures everything discussed in the passage.

Getting It Together: One More Practice Passage

My first bike had training wheels. Those handy gadgets stabilized me until balancing on two wheels became second nature. This section gives you a reading-comprehension passage with training wheels. Unlike the real exam, here I label each question, providing a small sample of what you may see on the real exam. Work through it, following the general steps I describe in "Planning Your Approach to Passages." As you answer Questions 17 through 22, flip back to look at the specific steps for vocabulary-in-context, attitude, inference, and other types of questions. Last, check your answers and read the explanations. When you get to the practice exams in Part IV, the training wheels are off, but you'll be ready to hit the road — and not with your nose or knees!

Line Mrs. Hutch seldom succeeded in collecting the full amount of the rents from her tenants. I suppose that made the bookkeeping complicated, which must have been wearing on her nerves and hence her temper. We lived on Dover Street, in fear of her temper. Saturday had a distinct quality about it, derived from the imminence of Mrs. Hutch's visit. Of course I

(05) awoke on Saturday morning with the no-school feeling; but the grim thing that leaped to its feet and glowered down on me, while the rest of my consciousness was still yawning on its back, was the Mrs-Hutch-is-coming-and-there's-no-rent feeling.

It is hard, if you are a young girl, full of life and inclined to be glad, to go to sleep in anxiety and awake in fear. Poverty is apt to interfere with the circulation and happiness of the

(10) young, which is damaging to the complexion of the soul. It is certain to breed gray hairs and a premature longing for death. It is pitiful, if you are the home-keeping mother of an impoverished family, to drop into bed at night and awake unstrengthened in the early morning. The haunting consciousness of poverty is unhealthy for a woman who still bears. It has been known to cause physical and spiritual malformations in the babies she nurses.

(15) It did require strength to lift the burden of life, in the gray morning on Dover Street and especially on Saturday morning. Perhaps my mother's pack was the heaviest to lift. To the man of the house, poverty is a bulky dragon with gripping claws and a poisonous breath; but he bellows in the open, and it is possible to give him knightly battle, with the full swing of the angry arm that cuts the enemy. To the housewife, want is a creature that crawls in

(20) the dark. The woman has an endless, inglorious struggle with the pest; her triumphs are too petty for applause, her failures too small for notice.

Mrs. Hutch, of course, was only one symptom of the disease of poverty, but there were times when she seemed to me the sharpest pain. Saturday evening brought Mrs. Hutch. The landlady climbed the stairs with determination and landed at the top with emphasis. Her

(25) knock on the door was clear and strong; it was impossible to pretend not to hear it. Invariably she asked for my father, and almost invariably he was not at home because he was out looking for work. Had he left her the rent? My mother's gentle "No, ma'am" was the signal for the storm.

I do not want to repeat what Mrs. Hutch said. It would be hard on her, and hard on me. She

(30) grew red in the face; her voice grew shriller with every word. My poor mother hung her head where she stood; the children stared from their corners; the frightened baby cried. The angry landlady rehearsed our sins like a prophet foretelling doom. We owed so many weeks' rent; we were too lazy to work; we never intended to pay; we lived on others; we deserved to be put out without warning. She reproached my mother for having too many

(35) children; she blamed us all for coming to America.

17. **Fact:** The "grim thing that leaped to its feet" (Line 5) may best be defined as

    (A) Mrs. Hutch's temper

    (B) Mrs. Hutch's visit to collect rent the family cannot pay

    (C) the narrator's fear of other tenants

    (D) the narrator's realization that her father is absent

    (E) the fact that the school is closed

18. **Vocabulary-in-context:** Which of the following is the best definition of "bears" (Line 13)?

    (A) withstands

    (B) dangerous animals

    (C) tolerates

    (D) gives birth to

    (E) supports

19. **Inference:** The narrator of this passage would probably agree with which of the following statements?

    (A) Male and female roles in the family differ.

    (B) Landlords face many problems.

    (C) Unhealthy living conditions cannot easily be changed.

    (D) Children always understand their parents' feelings.

    (E) Poverty is more challenging for children than for adults.

20. **Structure and style:** The details about Mrs. Hutch in Paragraph 4 (Lines 22–28) are intended to

    (A) humanize her character

    (B) contrast Mrs. Hutch with the mother

    (C) emphasize Mrs. Hutch's power

    (D) justify the family's nonpayment of rent

    (E) show the difficulties Mrs. Hutch faces

21. **Tone:** Which of the following best characterizes the tone of this passage?

    (A) regretful

    (B) nostalgic

    (C) indifferent

    (D) critical

    (E) antagonistic

22. **Main idea:** Which of the following best expresses the main idea of this passage?

    (A) Eliminating Poverty in America

    (B) A Family's Struggle

    (C) Facing Problems

    (D) When the Rent Is Due

    (E) Mrs. Hutch and Me

Now check your answers:

17. **B.** At first you may have thought this question called for interpretation, but the answer is right there in Paragraph one, buried (as fact questions sometimes are) in a long sentence. The narrator says that "the grim thing . . . was the Mrs.-Hutch-is-coming-and-there's-no-rent feeling" (Line 7). Once you yank out the distractions, the answer is clearly Choice (B).

18. **D.** All the answer choices are definitions of "bears," but only Choice (D) makes sense. The sentence following "bears" refers to "the babies she nurses" (Line 14), so you know you're in child-bearing territory.

19. **A.** You have an interesting set of statements in the answer choices. I bet you agree with several. Your job, though, isn't to express your ideas but to infer which statement the narrator believes. And for that task, you need clues. Reread paragraph three: You see that men fight poverty openly, in a "knightly battle" (Line 18), and women are engaged in "an endless, inglorious struggle" (Line 20). Also, the father is out "looking for work" (Line 27) while the mother minds the kids and faces Mrs. Hutch. Yup, all clues point to Choice (A).

20. **C.** Mrs. Hutch "climbed the stairs with determination and landed at the top with emphasis" (Line 24). You can't avoid her "clear and strong" knock (Line 25). When she hears that the rent won't be paid, she causes a "storm" (Line 28). Just as important is what you don't find out: her age, what she wears, or her background. By hitting these details and omitting others, the author shows a powerful person, one who causes the "sharpest pain" (Line 23).

21. **D.** The passage *depicts* (shows) poverty as a terrible state, one that saps the life out of those who suffer from it. In the last paragraph, the author lists several inaccurate remarks made about the poor: Mrs. Hutch says that the family "never intended to pay" (Line 33) and "were too lazy to work" (Line 33) — while the father is out "looking for work" (Line 27). Therefore, the author's tone is critical. Were you fooled by Choice (B)? Yes, the narrator remembers her childhood, but she exhibits no desire to return to the good old days, a feeling present in nostalgia.

22. **D.** The first paragraph ends with a statement about "Mrs. Hutch-is-coming-and-there's-no-rent" (Line 7), and the last two paragraphs describe the awful conversation between the mother and Mrs. Hutch when the rent is due. Granted, the second and third paragraphs discuss poverty more generally, but they don't discuss ways to eliminate poverty. Choice (D) is the best answer here. Choice (A) has no support in the passage, and Choices (B) and (C) are too broad. Choice (E) is too narrow, because the mother and father *and* the narrator must deal with Mrs. Hutch. The passage says little about the narrator's relationship with Mrs. Hutch, other than the fear that her visits *engender* (cause).

Chapter 5

As Easy as ABC and D and E: Writing

*W*riting, I've always thought, involves scribbling one word after another on a page and then polishing my sentences until I'm satisfied that they say what I mean. Writing on the PSAT/NMSQT, on the other hand, involves bubbling in A, B, C, D, or E. To be fair, the test format and my vision of writing overlap in one area. The exam asks you to improve sentences, spot errors, and revise paragraphs. That's what I do when I polish my work, and I imagine you do the same. On the exam, though, you have to match your vision of a better sentence or paragraph with a multiple-choice answer. In this chapter I explain how to do so efficiently, so you can "write" your way to a great score. First I take you through each of the three types of writing questions, with plenty of examples for practice. Then I discuss budgeting your time for this section because you don't have a lot of it — just 30 minutes to answer 39 questions. Finally, I review grammar concepts that the PSAT/NMSQT *loves* to test. (If you need a complete grammar review, take a look at *English Grammar For Dummies,* 2nd Edition, or *English Grammar Workbook For Dummies,* 2nd Edition, both published by Wiley and written by yours truly.)

Scanning the PSAT/NMSQT Writing Section

Scanning (reading carefully) is the opposite of *skimming,* which is what you do when you run your eyes quickly across a page. You'll do better on the PSAT/NMSQT if you scan this section, in which I discuss the three types of writing questions that *comprise* (make up) the writing section and outline the best approach to each.

Sentence improvement

The first 20 questions in the writing section hand you a fairly long sentence that resembles what you might read in a textbook or write in an essay or research paper. A portion of the sentence — or, rarely, the whole thing — is underlined. You have to select the best version of the underlined material from five possibilities. Choice (A) is always the original wording, and the other four choices change the original in different ways. However, nothing in the non-underlined portion of the sentence ever changes. Therefore, whatever you choose *must* fit with the rest of the sentence. If you swap out the underlined portion and insert your answer choice, the sentence has to make sense as a whole. Here's a sample sentence-improvement question, with a dash of *For Dummies* humor that you definitely *won't* find on the real exam:

Having bubbled in answers for two hours, Hannah <u>didn't want nothing more than to break</u> her pencil in half and throw the pieces at the proctor.

(A) didn't want nothing more than to break

(B) she didn't want nothing more than to break

(C) wanted nothing more than that she would break

(D) wanted nothing more than to break

(E) wanted to break more than anything

The original sentence, Choice (A), contains a double negative ("didn't want nothing"), as does Choice (B). Double negatives are big no-nos in proper English, so right away you can cross out Choices (A) and (B). Choice (C) throws in an unnecessary clause ("that she would break"), and Choice (E) sounds awkward. Choice (D) gets the point across in proper English and without **_superfluous_** (unnecessary) words.

Sentence-improvement questions evaluate your knowledge of proper English grammar, but style is a factor also. Sometimes more than one answer is technically correct, but one may be wordy or awkward and another more mature-sounding. As always on the PSAT/NMSQT, you're in search of the *best* possible answer. With these questions, your choice should always create a grammatically correct, smooth, and concise sentence.

Here's your approach to sentence-improvement questions:

- ✔ **Read every word of the original sentence.** Too obvious to mention, right? But you'd be surprised how many test-takers look at the underlined material and ignore the rest of the sentence. Bad idea! Because nothing in the non-underlined portion of the sentence may be changed, your answer *must* work when the whole sentence is considered.

- ✔ **If you find a grammar mistake in the original, turn to the answer choices immediately.** Find every answer that corrects the error, and cross off the others. Check whether anything still in the running contains a different grammar error. If so, toss that answer, too. Now look at whatever is left. One choice is probably smoother and more concise than another. That's your answer.

- ✔ **If no obvious error appears, determine what varies in the answer choices.** If you see one choice with "would have said" and one with "had said," zero in on the verbs. Where you see variation, you may find a clue to the problem in the sentence.

- ✔ **If no grammar error appears, revise the underlined material.** Don't write anything down. Simply "hear" the sentence in your head and rewrite it mentally. Now check for a match, rejecting any choice that contains nonstandard English. Also, be aware that no matter how good your writing skills, chances are no answer choice will match your rewording exactly. You may find something close, though. Go for that answer.

Anything is fair game for sentence-improvement questions, but a few grammar and style issues are frequent flyers. (I review these concepts in "Training Your Grammar Muscles: A Review of Common Grammar Errors" later in this chapter.) Here's what to look for:

- ✔ **Verb tense:** Grammarians talk about *sequence of tenses* — how one action is placed earlier in the past than another, for example. The answer choices for sentence-improvement questions often vary only in verb tense, a good reason to check that issue carefully.

- ✔ **Complete sentences:** Sometimes the "sentence" is really a fragment, and sometimes two sentences are joined improperly, creating a run-on sentence. You have to locate an answer that creates a complete, properly punctuated sentence.

✔ **Extra words:** Frequently, the original sentence expresses an idea in ten words when six will *suffice* (be enough). Be on the alert for wordiness and repetition.

✔ **Nonstandard expressions:** Words or expressions that make your English teachers frown (*irregardless, John and myself, being that,* and others) often show up in sentence improvements. Look for an answer choice that takes them out.

✔ **Agreement:** In Grammarland, singular goes with singular and plural with plural. This rule applies to subject-verb pairs, pronouns and the words they refer to, and nouns (logical consistency, so you don't end up saying something like, "Mary and Helen are a doctor").

✔ **Passive voice:** "Martin broke the window" is better than "a window was broken by Martin" because active voice, in which the subject does the action, gives more information than passive voice, in which the subject is acted upon. Of course, sometimes you need passive verbs, but if you're down to two choices and active voice is possible, go for that answer.

Practice questions are a chance to train your eyes, so you can spot the best answer quickly. Try Questions 1 through 5:

1. The clerk, encouraged by his supervisor's <u>praise and frightened by</u> the recent lag in sales, the result of a poor economy.

   (A) praise and frightened by

   (B) praise, was frightened by

   (C) praise, frightening him by

   (D) praise that frightened him with

   (E) praise; he was frightened by

2. Knowing the bell would soon ring, <u>their essays were completed by the students as quickly as possible.</u>

   (A) their essays were completed by the students as quickly as possible

   (B) their essays were completed as quickly as possible by the students

   (C) the students completed their essays as quickly as possible

   (D) as quick as possible, the students completed their essays

   (E) the students completed his or her essays as quickly as possible

3. According to ancient Greek myths, Antigone defied the <u>king, and her life was lost</u> as a result.

   (A) king, and her life was lost

   (B) king, which was how her life was lost

   (C) king, but her life was lost

   (D) king and lost her life

   (E) king, she lost her life

4. <u>Because he draws from life,</u> Charles often sketches people in the park.

   (A) Because he draws from life,

   (B) Being as he draws from life,

   (C) Being that he draws from life

   (D) As it is true that he draws from life

   (E) The fact that he draws from life is the reason that

5. <u>If Norma would not have understood Japanese</u>, she would not have offered to translate the document.

   (A) If Norma would not have understood Japanese

   (B) Not understanding Japanese

   (C) If it was true that Norma didn't understand

   (D) If Norma didn't understand

   (E) If Norma had not understood

Now check your answers:

1. **B.** The original isn't a complete sentence because no verb matches the subject, "clerk." In Choice (B), the verb "was" pairs up with "clerk," and the sentence is complete. No other choice creates a complete sentence except Choice (E), which adds an unnecessary pronoun, "he."

2. **C.** In the original sentence, the description "knowing the bell would soon ring" describes "their essays." However, the essays don't know the bell is going to ring; the students do. Choices (C), (D), and (E) make "students" the subject of the sentence. But Choice (D) incorrectly changes the adverb "quickly" to an adjective, "quick." And Choice (E) is wrong because the plural noun "students" must be paired with the plural pronoun "their," not with the singular "his or her."

3. **D.** The original sentence is grammatically correct, but it shifts from an active verb ("defied") to a passive verb ("was lost"). Choice (D) expresses the same information more concisely and smoothly, staying in active voice.

4. **A.** The original sentence, Choice (A), is effective and grammatically correct. The other answer choices have problems. Choices (B) and (C) begin with nonstandard expressions, "being as" and "being that." Choices (D) and (E) are wordy.

5. **E.** In a sentence expressing a *hypothetical* (true in theory only) situation, the "if" portion of the sentence *never* contains the helping verb "would." Instead, the verb there must be subjunctive. Don't worry about the grammar terminology; just pull out the "would" and insert "had." (In a sentence without an action verb, use "were" in the "if" part of the sentence.) Choice (E) is your answer.

Error identification

Section 5 of the PSAT/NMSQT always includes 14 error-recognition problems. Each question is a fairly long sentence, with four portions underlined and labeled A, B, C, or D. Choice (E), no error, appears after each sentence. You have to find the section of the sentence that *must* be changed in order to correct a mistake in grammar, punctuation, or standard English expression. If you can't locate an error, your answer is Choice (E). Here's an example:

<u>The proctor, who was</u> both bored and <u>she was preoccupied</u> by the parking ticket
      A   B

<u>she received</u> on the way to school, <u>never noticed</u> Hannah. <u>No error.</u>
   C   D   E

This sentence has a parallelism problem. In Grammarland, a sentence is *parallel* if elements performing the same function have the same grammatical identity. Conjunction pairs such as "both/and" and "either/or" must join parallel elements, but in this sentence, "both" links "bored," an adjective, to "she was preoccupied," a complete thought containing a subject and a verb. In case you're a fan of grammar terminology, "she was preoccupied" is a clause. Choice (B) is the answer because that's where the mistake is.

You can correct some sentences in more than one way. For example, to correct a misplaced description you can move the description *or* the word described. In such a situation, only one of the possible spots for correction is underlined.

Tackling error-recognition problems is easy if you follow these steps:

✔ **Read the whole sentence.** Even if you think the mistake is in the very first word in the sentence, keep reading. Although the directions tell you confidently that "no sentence contains more than one error," you may see two problems in one sentence. A veteran test-maker, I can **attest** (testify) to the fact that no matter how hard a writer works to ensure only one possible mistake, sometimes a second creeps in. In that situation, you may discover that one error is minor — a scraped knee — and one is major — a broken leg. Go for the broken leg and leave the scraped knee alone.

✔ **Check each underlined section, in order.** Don't forget about punctuation; a punctuation error, very often a misplaced comma, may be tucked into a five-word section.

✔ **Select your answer.** The toughest answer to identify, by the way, is Choice (E). For some reason test-takers *really* want to find a mistake and too often mistrust the "no error" option. Sometimes, though, the sentence is correct, and Choice (E) is the answer.

Keep an eye out for these mistakes, which appear often in error-recognition questions, and turn to "Training Your Grammar Muscles: A Review of Common Grammar Errors" later in this chapter if you need additional review:

✔ **Pronoun problems:** Check for "he/him" and other case mix-ups, a "-self" pronoun (*myself, himself, ourselves,* and so on) where one shouldn't be, and possessive pronouns. Also be sure that the pronoun agrees with the word it represents — singular with singular, plural with plural. Be sure that the pronoun isn't vague ("she" in a sentence discussing two females, for example).

✔ **Parallelism:** The example at the beginning of this section concerns parallelism. Look for nonparallel elements in lists or compounds (pairs or triplets).

✔ **Punctuation:** You may find a comma where a semicolon is required or an unnecessary or missing comma. Don't worry about other punctuation marks; they're unlikely to be an issue on the PSAT/NMSQT.

✔ **Verb tense:** Take note of every verb. Be sure each expresses the correct time frame, based on the content of the sentence.

✔ **Unnecessary shifts:** If you're talking about "a person," don't shift to "you" or "they." Don't change verb tense without a reason.

✔ **Nonstandard expressions:** Words and expressions that people use in everyday language aren't always correct when you're in test territory. Look for such expressions as "set yourself down," "can't hardly," and so forth.

✔ **Illogical or improper comparisons:** Look for doubles ("more prettier" instead of "prettier") and illogical content ("Washington was more popular than any president," a statement implying that Washington wasn't a president).

Give Questions 6 through 10 your best shot.

6. <u>Beeping</u> his horn, the truck driver <u>warned</u> <u>Ellen and I</u> to move <u>out of</u> the intersection.
     A   B   C   D
   <u>No error.</u>
    E

7. The <u>brightly painted</u> rocking chair <u>was</u> neither purchased <u>nor was it noticed</u> in <u>the busiest</u>
         A   B   C   D
   shop in the antiques district. <u>No error.</u>
                                  E

8. <u>Careful by nature</u>, John had revised his estimate <u>for heating and air-conditioning</u>
        A   B

  <u>at least five times</u> before he <u>had felt ready</u> to present his proposal to the construction
        C   D

  manager. <u>No error.</u>
          E

9. Everyone in that school <u>is required</u> <u>to attend</u> physical education classes <u>at least</u> four times
                   A   B   C

  a week because <u>you benefit from</u> an active life. <u>No error.</u>
                 D   E

10. <u>Between you and I</u>, the smell <u>coming from</u> that corner of the room <u>is</u> <u>offensive, and</u> the
     A   B   C   D

  janitor should be fired. <u>No error.</u>
                  E

Now check your answers:

6. **C.** The pronoun "I" is for subjects only, but in this sentence, it's functioning as an object of the verb "warned." The proper expression is "Ellen and me," Choice (C), because "me" is the appropriate pronoun for objects.

7. **C.** This sentence contains a pair of conjunctions, "neither/nor." Whatever these conjunctions join must be parallel. That is, whatever follows these words must have the same grammatical identity. In this sentence, though, "neither" is followed by "purchased," and "nor" is followed by a subject-verb combo, "was it noticed." One of these elements has to change. "Purchased" isn't underlined, so your answer is Choice (C). How would the correct sentence sound? Something like this: "The brightly painted rocking chair was neither purchased nor noticed in the busiest shop in the antiques district."

8. **D.** The helping verb "had" places an action earlier in the past than another action. The revisions precede the moment when John "felt ready," not "had felt ready." Choice (D) is your answer.

9. **D.** The sentence begins by talking *about* people ("everyone") and then shifts by talking *to* people, represented by the pronoun "you." Because you have no good reason for the shift, the "you benefit" should be "everyone benefits" or something similar, so Choice (D) is correct.

10. **A.** The preposition "between" takes an object pronoun ("me"), not a subject pronoun ("I"). Yes, I know you hear "between you and I" all the time. The test-writers also hear that expression; that's why they put it on the test fairly often. The test-writers and I (and you too, now) know that "between you and I," Choice (A), is wrong!

Paragraph improvement

The life story of a first lady, the role of pop culture in modern life, censorship, and a ***host*** (large number) of other topics show up in the paragraph-improvement section. The "Improving Paragraphs" section of the PSAT/NMSQT features about 15 sentences on one topic, divided into three or four paragraphs. The paragraphs are supposed to represent a student's typical first draft of a report or essay. The sentences are numbered, and the whole thing is accompanied by five questions, which may ask you about the best way to combine two sentences or which sentence should be deleted or moved. The goal here is to see that you can think about structure (how the ideas are organized, where transitions are needed, and so forth) and style (combining or varying sentence patterns).

Grammar errors show up in this section, but in general, paragraph-improvement steps back from the micro-level to look at the larger picture. You have the usual five options;

sometimes one option is to leave everything the same, but not always. Hit paragraph-improvement questions this way:

- **Skim read all the paragraphs.** Get an overview first. Don't read the questions until you've gone through all the sentences.

- **Think about the underlying logic.** You should be able to see the path from one idea to the next. Each paragraph should be unified, revolving around one main idea.

- **Consider how you'd improve the paragraphs.** If this were your report or essay, would you change anything before handing it in? Don't get to the sentence level yet; think about the whole thing. Jot down a few notes in the margin.

- **Now survey the questions.** Depending on how much time you have, you may decide to do all five questions, or you may pick the easiest — those that deal with combining two sentences or fixing a grammar mistake. Although paragraph-improvement questions stay mostly on the larger level, some address issues in individual sentences. If you're short on time, go to those questions first.

Paragraph-improvement questions differ from sentence-improvement and error-recognition problems in that many questions address the passage as a whole. You can't forget about grammar, though, because English teachers write this part of the exam, and grammar is as appealing as ice cream to them. Here's what to look for:

- **Vague statements or missing arguments:** You may find a question about what's missing. Look for overly general sentences that could be cut or specific details that should be added.

- **Misplaced sentences:** Check each paragraph for unity. Does every sentence concern the same topic? If not, the off-topic sentence should be cut or deleted.

- **Missing transitions:** When you move from one paragraph to another, can the reader follow your logic? If not, a sentence linking the two paragraphs — a transition — is needed.

- **Faulty conclusions:** Does the essay stop dead, or do you detect a sense of closure? The reader should feel that the facts or arguments are complete at the end of the last paragraph.

- **Choppy sentences:** Typically, two short sentences appear next to each other. One question may ask you whether the sentences should be combined into one, and if so, how the new sentence reads. In general, you should *always* combine short sentences on the same topic. Look for a smooth way to glue them together, without losing meaning.

- **Run-on sentences or fragments:** Check for two complete thoughts linked only by a comma (a run-on, in other words) or a "sentence" that never gets to the point because it's just a fragment. One question probably asks you how to revise the run-on or fragment.

Here's one paragraph-improvement "essay" and practice Questions 11 through 15. Good luck!

[1] Historic preservationists argue that buildings constructed many decades ago should be preserved and not torn down. [2] They also want to save newer buildings that are unique. [3] The buildings have interesting features, or an important event took place in them. [4] One building was where a famous poet lived.

[5] The Committee to Save the Collerton Hotel has raised money for a campaign to save the hotel from developers. [6] The developers bought the old building a year ago. [7] The roof leaks, paint is peeling from the walls. [8] The developers plan to level the site. [9] They want to build 15 houses there. [10] The houses will bring new families to town, they say, spurring economic development.

[11] Preservationists and developers will probably never agree. [12] The developers make a good case for a more prosperous town. [13] The preservationists argue that history is important. [14] The town council will soon vote. [15] At that time one side will win, though no decision can please everyone.

11. Which of the following, if any, would improve Paragraph 1?

    (A) No change.

    (B) Delete Sentence 2.

    (C) Delete Sentence 3.

    (D) Add information about the poet mentioned in Sentence 4.

    (E) Delete Sentence 4 and add information about the Collerton Hotel.

12. Which change, if any, would most improve Sentence 7?

    (A) No change.

    (B) The roof leaks, and paint is peeling from the walls.

    (C) With the roof leaking, paint also peels from the walls.

    (D) The roof leaks though paint is peeling from the walls.

    (E) There is a leaky roof and peeling paint.

13. How may Sentences 8 and 9 best be combined?

    (A) The developers plan to level the site and build 15 houses there.

    (B) Wanting to build 15 houses there, the developers plan to level the site.

    (C) The site having been leveled, the developers want to build 15 houses.

    (D) After having been leveled, the developers want to build 15 houses.

    (E) The developers will level the site, and building 15 houses.

14. What change, if any, would improve Paragraph 2?

    (A) No change.

    (B) Delete Sentence 5.

    (C) Add the arguments made by the Committee to Save the Collerton Hotel.

    (D) Delete Sentence 10.

    (E) Add more information on the cost of the developers' project.

15. What, if any, is the best revision of Paragraph 3?

    (A) No change.

    (B) Add the writer's own opinion.

    (C) Add information on the town council's procedures.

    (D) Add quotations from council members.

    (E) Delete Sentence 15.

    Now check your answers. (Turn to "Training Your Grammar Muscles: A Review of Common Grammar Errors" later in this chapter if you need additional information about any grammar errors mentioned in these explanations.)

11. **E.** Because the essay discusses one particular fight — whether to *raze* (knock down, level) a hotel — that issue should come up in the first paragraph. Right now, the paragraph is too general. Sentence 4 is way too vague and adds nothing to the essay, so Choice (E) is your answer.

12. **B.** The original sentence is a run-on, with two complete thoughts glued together only by a comma. Nope! Choice (B) adds a conjunction and corrects the grammar error. Choices (C) and (D) are grammatically correct, but they introduce ideas outside the frame of logic. Choice (E) has a grammar error: The subject is plural ("roof *and* paint"), so the verb must be plural also. In other words, the sentence should begin with "there are," not "there is."

13. **A.** Smooth and short: that's your goal in combining sentences. Of course, you also have to keep the meaning and use correct grammar. Choice (A) is correct. Choices (B) and (C) are the only other correct sentences, but both are unnecessarily long.

14. **C.** Paragraph 2 gives some specific information on the developers' plans but says nothing about what the committee wants to do or why members feel the hotel should be saved. The reader can't be involved in an argument if only one side makes a case. Choice (C) is the answer.

15. **E.** The last sentence is glaringly obvious and contributes nothing to the essay. Dump it by picking Choice (E).

Budgeting Your Time

Spend a moment thinking about time. The writing section comes last, after you've *endured* (suffered through) two critical reading and two math sections. Writing is the longest section of the exam, both in minutes (30) and number of questions (39). With less than a minute per question, many test-takers hear the proctor yell, "Stop!" before they've finished. Your strategy must include time management, according to these guidelines:

- ✔ **Not all questions require the same amount of time.** The exam opens with 20 sentence-improvement questions, then 14 error-recognition questions, and finally 5 paragraph-improvement questions. Most people can zoom through the error-recognition questions quickly. Paragraph improvement typically gobbles up the most minutes, with sentence improvement somewhere in between. Of course, your reaction time to each type of question may be completely different. Check out the third bullet for advice on tailoring your time budget so that it emphasizes your strengths and minimizes any weaknesses.

- ✔ **"Order of difficulty" is less clear in the writing section.** In most sections of the exam, the questions appear in order of difficulty, from easiest to hardest. Therefore, you're probably used to answering everything at the beginning of a section. The writing section, though, covers a very wide range of topics — every possible way to *mangle* (crush, twist, deform) the language. You can't easily rely on order of difficulty in sentence improvements, and error recognition is only slightly better. Paragraph-improvement questions follow the order of the sentences in the selection. Best tactic: Forget about order of difficulty. Do what's easiest for you, and hit the hard problems later.

- ✔ **Measure yourself.** In the preceding bullet I speak about "most people," but you're not most people. You're *unique* (one of a kind). As you practice each type of question, time yourself. How long do you typically take to answer a sentence-improvement question? Are you fast or slow when it comes to paragraph improvement? How many minutes do you need for error recognition? Make a profile and update it as you become more familiar with PSAT/NMSQT writing. Remember, you don't have to answer the questions in order. Start with your strongest section, move on to your next strongest, and then finish up with the hardest type of question. Your score will be higher if you get all the paragraph-improvement questions right, even if you have to skip a couple of sentence-improvement problems.

✔ **Don't hesitate to guess.** With so few minutes, you may have to guess or skip some questions entirely. Turn to the guessing guidelines in Chapter 2 for more information.

By the end of the exam, you'll be **enervated** (exhausted). A question that takes you 10 seconds to answer when you're fresh and **vigorous** (energetic) may require 30 seconds later in the morning. Budget your time with this fact in mind.

Training Your Grammar Muscles: A Review of Common Grammar Errors

Perhaps you've heard of the Hall of Fame — the ultimate honor for athletes of various sports. English teachers have created the **antithesis** (opposite): a list of common errors that make up the Grammar Hall of Shame. You won't be ashamed of your PSAT/NMSQT score, though, if you review the basic concepts in this section.

Agreement

Grammarians love agreement, which is why so many agreement problems appear on the PSAT/NMSQT. This grammar principle matches singular with singular and plural with plural. Specifically, check for agreement in these areas:

✔ **Subjects and verbs:** You probably know the easy ones ("Matt has a cold," not "Matt have a cold"), but you may be less sure about the proper verb when the subject and verb are separated by other words. Ignore interrupters such as "as well as," "in addition to," and "along with." These phrases appear to make the subject plural, but they're just camouflage. Cross them out and check the true subject/verb pair. Also ignore descriptions that come between a subject and its verb. For example, when you see "a box of baby clothes and toys was hidden in the closet," mentally cross out "of baby clothes and toys" and check that the singular subject, "box," matches the singular verb, "was hidden."

✔ **Pronouns and antecedents:** Don't panic. **Antecedent** is just a fancy term for the word a pronoun refers to, which may be a noun or another pronoun. Most people have little trouble matching a noun with its pronoun ("boys" and "them," for example). However, errors pop up with pronoun/pronoun pairs. All these pronouns are singular: *everyone, everybody, everything, someone, somebody, something, anyone, anybody, anything, no one, nobody, nothing, either, neither, each,* and *every.* When you refer to one of these pronouns, use *his, him, it,* or *her,* not *their* or *them.* In other words, "everyone handed in his or her test," not "their test."

Case

Case is the grammar term for the difference between *I* and *me* and *mine.* The first is a subject pronoun, the second an object pronoun, and the last a possessive pronoun. Here's what you need to know about each type:

✔ **Subject pronouns may function as the subject of a sentence.** Subject pronouns also show up after verbs that express a state of being, but don't worry about those situations; the PSAT/NMSQT doesn't throw those sentences at you. Subject pronouns include *I, you, he, she, it, we, they, whoever,* and *who*.

✔ **Object pronouns function as objects.** Grammarians aren't terribly original in their terminology, right? You need object pronouns after verbs, verbals (words that resemble verbs but act as nouns or descriptions in a sentence), and prepositions (words that express relationships, such as *by, for, from, to, about, on,* and so forth). Object pronouns include the following: *me, you, him, her, it, us, them, whomever,* and *whom*.

✔ **Possessive pronouns express ownership.** Possessive pronouns include *my, mine, yours, his, her, hers, its, our, ours, their, theirs,* and *whose*. Possessive pronouns don't need apostrophes to show ownership, and the test-makers may check to see that you understand the difference between *whose* (possessive) and *who's* (a contraction of "who is").

If a pronoun is part of a list, you may not realize what case you need. Isolating the pronoun sometimes helps you "hear" the correct case. For example, suppose the sentence reads, "The proctor slapped Agnes and I because he thought we were having too much fun taking the PSAT." Isolate the pronoun by placing your finger over "Agnes and." What sounds better, "slapped I" or "slapped me"? The correct choice is "me."

Verb tense

English has six tenses, but most cause little difficulty. On the PSAT/NMSQT, three verb tense situations may stump you:

✔ **Present perfect tense:** This tense uses *has* or *have* with another verb (*has fallen, have written, has been,* and so on). Present perfect tense links the past and present. If I tell you that "I have lived there for 89 years," I'm still living there, and I lived there in the past also. The simple past tense ("I lived there for 89 years") implies that I live somewhere else now.

✔ **Past perfect tense:** Tack a *had* onto another verb and you've got past perfect tense, which moves an event in the past to a point that is earlier than another past-tense event. For example, "Judy had bubbled in three answers before the proctor threw her out." The bubbling occurred before the throwing out.

✔ **Unnecessary shifts:** You may run across a sentence that begins in one tense and then shifts to another. If you need to show a change, fine: "Yesterday Henry was tired, but tomorrow he will be full of energy." In this example, the verb *was* is past tense because that part of the sentence discusses *yesterday;* the verb *will be* is in future tense, which is appropriate for the part of the sentence discussing *tomorrow.* Don't change without a good reason: "Henry went into the store, and then he buys ten bags of candy!" In this example, the tense makes no sense because the sentence doesn't signal a time change between past and present.

You may run into one more verb problem in an "if" sentence expressing a situation that isn't true. Strictly speaking, this type of sentence doesn't have a tense problem, but you need to pay attention to the verb anyway. Suppose you see this sentence: "If I would have known about the exam, I wouldn't have scheduled an orchestra rehearsal in the next room." Nope! Incorrect! The "if" portion of the sentence, which isn't true, *never* contains the word "would." Here's the correction: "If I had known about the exam, I wouldn't have scheduled an orchestra rehearsal in the next room." One more example, also correct: "If I were Queen of Testing, I would eliminate the PSAT/NMSQT and give everyone a perfect score." Notice that "were," which usually pairs with plural subjects, here matches the singular pronoun "I." The odd pairing is allowed only in "if" sentences that express a condition that is contrary to fact. (Curious about the grammar term? "Were" is subjunctive. Happy now?)

Complete sentences

English teachers hate *run-ons* (two sentences improperly run together) and *fragments* (a bunch of words that don't add up to a complete sentence). What's a complete sentence? I thought you'd never ask! Look for a subject/verb pair and a complete thought. Check out these examples of a complete sentence, a fragment, and a run-on:

Complete sentence: Daisy cried with joy after receiving a high test score. (The subject/verb pair is "Daisy cried." The sentence expresses a complete thought.)

Fragment: Having studied so much, Daisy, screaming about her high scores. (This statement lacks a subject/verb pair. One possible correction: Having studied so much, Daisy screamed about her high scores.)

Run-on: Daisy ran to show her scores to Uncle Oscar, he had promised her a reward. (Each half of this statement is a complete sentence, but only a comma joins the two parts. Penalty box! Use a semicolon or add *because* before the second statement.)

Watch out for *however, consequently, therefore,* and *then.* These words can't legally join one complete sentence to another.

Parallelism

Proper English values balance, so if you see a list or paired conjunctions (*either/or, neither/nor,* or *not only/but also,* for example), check for parallelism. The rule is simple: Everything performing the same job in the sentence must have the same grammatical identity. Check out these incorrect and correct examples:

Incorrect: Bob wants to go shopping, to buy a new *For Dummies* book, and having fun reading it. (The last item on the list doesn't match.)

Correct: Bob wants to go shopping, to buy a new *For Dummies* book, and to have fun reading it. (Now everything matches.)

Incorrect: Bob will either ace the PSAT or he will pay his sister to take the test. (Forget about grammar for a moment. Don't even think about cheating! Okay, back to grammar. After the first conjunction, "either," you have a verb ("ace"), but not a subject. After the second conjunction, "or," you have a subject ("he") and a verb ("will pay"). Not parallel!

Correct: Bob will either ace the PSAT or pay his sister to take the test. (Now both conjunctions are followed by verbs, "ace" and "pay.")

Part III

Assembling a Math Tool Kit

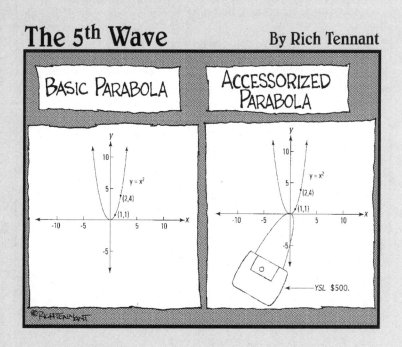

The 5th Wave   By Rich Tennant

BASIC PARABOLA   ACCESSORIZED PARABOLA

← YSL $500.

In this part . . .

A math teacher I know used to wear a carpenter's apron to class. In it he stashed colored pencils, calculators, erasers, and other handy tools of the mathematician's trade. I like to think that more than gadgets were in that apron, though. Perhaps he had a Pythagorean theorem or a probability formula in one of the canvas pockets and a way to calculate square roots in another. Wouldn't those tools be helpful?

In this part, I help you assemble your own tool kit so that you can solve every problem you're likely to find on the PSAT/NMSQT. Chapter 6 starts you off with some excellent techniques (plugging-in, backsolving, and others) that work with all sorts of questions. In Chapter 6, you also find information on how to conquer grid-ins, a special type of math problem presented without multiple-choice answers. Chapters 7 through 10 take you into numbers and operations, algebra, geometry, probability, statistics, and data interpretation. In each chapter, you find some practice problems and explanations, as well as general information you need for each topic. If you work through these chapters carefully, your tool kit will be in great shape for the exam, with one exception: You have to provide your own pencils and calculator!

Chapter 6

When 2 + 4 = 1 Great Score: Preparing for PSAT Math

In This Chapter

▶ Getting comfortable with multiple-choice problems and grid-ins

▶ Knowing the rules about using your calculator

▶ Choosing the best strategy for each type of math question

Sections 2 and 4 on the PSAT/NMSQT are devoted to math — everything from basic arithmetic to geometry to statistics. Depending on how you feel about math (and in my experience, few people are lukewarm), you're either jumping for joy or gulping in panic at the prospect of answering 38 math questions (20 in Section 2 and 18 in Section 4). This chapter has something for everyone: those who can't help calculating the angle of the hockey stick while scoring the winning goal and those who hide under the table to avoid figuring out the 18 percent tip on a restaurant check.

Math is, well, always math, but PSAT/NMSQT math has some special quirks. If you learn the techniques in this chapter and apply them when you're being tortured — sorry, I mean *tested* — your score will climb. (Figure out the percent of increase after you read Chapter 8.)

No Compass Required: Decoding the Directions

Because you're reading this book, I know that your motto, like the Boy Scouts', is "be prepared." So you should walk into the testing room on PSAT/NMSQT day well acquainted, or even best friends, with the exam directions, especially for the math sections. Pressed for time, you don't want to scan anything but the problems themselves on test day. (Did you know that *scan* means "read carefully"? Many people confuse scan with *skim,* which is what you do when you zoom through reading material without thinking much.)

Multiple-choice math questions

The multiple-choice math directions are fairly standard. You have to choose the correct answer from five possibilities. You're allowed to use a calculator (read more about calculators in "Armed and Ready: Using Your Calculator" later in this chapter). The directions also state that all figures are on a *plane* (a two-dimensional, flat surface) unless otherwise stated. Diagrams are drawn to scale except when clearly labeled *NOT drawn to scale.*

However, the directions do more than simply tell you what to do. The College Board is very generous (except when it's collecting your testing fees). You don't necessarily have to memorize any math formulas before you take the PSAT/NMSQT, because tucked into the directions at the start of each math section is a little box of goodies: formulas for the area and circumference of a circle, the area of a rectangle and triangle, the volume of a cube and cylinder, and the angles of triangles. Still, it's best to know these formulas ahead so you don't spend valuable time looking them up. Here's what you see:

Notes:

✔ You may use a calculator.

✔ All numbers used in this exam are real numbers.

✔ All figures lie in a plane.

✔ You may assume that all figures are to scale unless the problem specifically indicates otherwise.

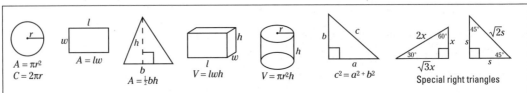

There are 360 degrees of arc in a circle.

There are 180 degrees in a straight line.

There are 180 degrees in the sum of the interior angles of a triangle.

Grid-ins

The last ten problems of the second math section are *grid-ins*. On your answer sheet you see ten boxes, each with four columns stacked with the numbers 0–9 and decimal points. Two of the columns have slanted fraction lines. Here's a blank grid-in box:

For grid-in questions, first come up with an answer. Then follow these guidelines:

✔ **Write your answer in the little squares at the top of the grid.** Now you know what you have to bubble in. (In the context of the PSAT/NMSQT, to *bubble* means to "darken an oval with pencil.") Remember that the little boxes are there to guide you. They are *not* scored.

✔ **Darken the appropriate ovals.** Bubble only one symbol or number per column.

✔ **Start wherever you want.** As long as your answer fits, don't worry about which column you start in. If you want to bubble 59, for example, you can begin in the first, second, or third column. (You can't begin in the fourth because you run out of room for the second digit, the 9.)

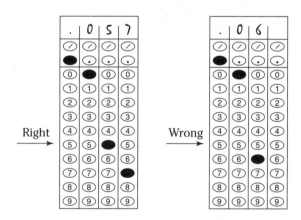

✔ **Don't place a zero before a decimal point, unless it's the last digit in a longer number.** In other words, 50.3 is fine, but 0.53 isn't. Go for .53 instead.

✔ **Don't round off a number unless it extends beyond the grid. When you *do* round off, be sure to use all four boxes.** Suppose your solution is ⁷⁄₁₂₃. You don't have enough boxes for four digits and a slash, so you need a decimal. Your calculator tells you that the decimal equivalent of ⁷⁄₁₂₃ is a very big bunch of numbers, beginning with .0569105. (I won't bother typing in the next 20 or so digits.) You can round off to .057 (using all four boxes) but *not* to .06, because then you'd have one empty box. The PSAT/NMSQT counts that sort of rounding off as wrong because your answer is less specific than it should be.

Right → Wrong →

✔ **Don't worry about negative numbers.** No answer is negative; you have no bubble for a minus sign.

✔ **If you come up with more than one solution, bubble only one answer.** If your answer may be expressed as either a decimal or a fraction, choose *one* of those forms. Don't try to squeeze in both. Also, sometimes a PSAT/NMSQT math question has more than one possible solution. A prime number less than 10, for example, may be 2, 3, 5, or 7. Any of these answers would be graded as correct.

✔ **Mixed numbers are a no-no.** You can bubble in a fraction (⅝, for example), but you can't record a mixed number. If you bubble in 5½, the computer reads your answer as ⁵¹⁄₂. If you end up with a mixed number (such as 5½), record it as ¹¹⁄₂ (an improper fraction) or as a decimal (5.5).

The multiple-choice and grid-in directions aren't exactly rocket science, but they *are* important. When you take the practice exams in this book, check your gridding as well as your mathematical ability, because both are necessary for success.

Armed and Ready: Using Your Calculator

Educators tend to frown on technological *innovations* (new things or ideas). When chalk replaced memorization and typewriters gave way to computers, the tsk-tsk-tsking in the nation's faculty lounges was louder than the fourth grade at recess. But the College Board is a little more in touch with reality than the average teacher, so you're allowed to bring a calculator to the PSAT/NMSQT.

The test-makers tell you, accurately, that you can solve every problem on the test without a calculator. But why would you want to add and divide when you have a machine to do the arithmetic for you? The key factor is to use the calculator efficiently and accurately. Sometimes the calculator bogs you down in a string of numbers that a formula can slice through instantly. At other times, the calculator takes the place of simple but time-consuming arithmetic (long division, for example). In the practice tests, I tell you when a calculator would help and when it would *hinder* (act as an obstacle). Be sure you know the difference, and use your calculator only when it will help you.

Don't have a calculator? The College Board doesn't include one with your testing fee, but your math teacher may have one you can borrow. Home-schoolers, call your local high school to see whether a loaner is available.

The College Board has several rules about calculator use during the PSAT/NMSQT:

- ✔ Your calculator may not have a raised keyboard or the ability to connect to the Internet. In other words, no mini-computers or smartphones.

- ✔ Battery power is fine; power cords aren't. (Proctors don't want to worry about outlets or too-short cords.) If your batteries die during the exam, too bad. The proctor won't sell you any AAAs, and you're not allowed to run out to a convenience store.

- ✔ The best calculator for this test is a scientific calculator, which can handle the basics (adding, subtracting, multiplying, dividing) and more advanced calculations such as square roots, fractions, and exponents.

Be sure that you know how to operate your calculator *before* you take the test. If you've bought or borrowed one recently, use it as needed when you work through the math problems in this book. By the time you complete the fourth practice test (you're going to do all the exams, right?), you should know how to calculate at the speed of light. And on the PSAT/NMSQT, every second counts.

No matter how well you know your calculator, it works only if you enter the correct numbers. Say (in your head, not aloud) every step you take, as in *5 divided by 7 plus the square root of 9*. Keep your eyes glued to the little screen to be sure that it shows $5/7 + \sqrt{9}$ and not $5 + 7 - \sqrt{2}$. After you complete a problem, hit "clear" so that you begin with a clean slate for the next one.

Creating a Battle Plan for PSAT/NMSQT Math

Right now, look in the mirror and say to that smart student staring back: "You don't have to finish every math problem on the test." Okay, how do you feel? Relieved? You should be, because two things are true: (1) On the PSAT/NMSQT, you can achieve a high score even if you leave some answers blank; (2) You're supposed to complete a total of 38 problems in 50 minutes. Math genius that you are, I'm sure you've already calculated the amount of time you have for each question: 1.315789 minutes, give or take a nanosecond. But here's the catch: Not all math questions are equally hard, even though each is worth the same — one point. Therefore, clever strategy maximizes your score.

The test-makers put the easier questions first and the harder questions later. Within each category of math (geometry or probability, for example), the questions also move from easy to hard. You want to move *as quickly as possible,* then, through the first six or seven questions in each math section. Why am I making a big deal out of *as quickly as possible?* Because if you go too fast, you may miss a key word in the question or mess up some simple arithmetic. You'll arrive at the hard questions with plenty of time, but you won't have raked in all those "may as well be free" points from the beginning of the section.

The grid-ins form a mini-section. The first couple of grid-ins are easy, the next couple a bit more difficult, and the last problems harder still. If the last few multiple-choice problems stump you, skip them and move to the grid-ins. Return to those questions later, if time permits.

You lose a quarter point for each wrong multiple-choice answer. You receive no points for an incorrect grid-in, but the scorers make no additional deduction for a wrong answer in that type of question. You may end up with a lower score if you answer every multiple-choice question but make a bunch of errors. (See Chapter 2 for more information on scoring, including when you should guess and when you should leave a question blank.)

Words such as *hard* and *easy* are **subjective** (personal to each individual). You may gobble up a triangle question that your classmate sweats over and then struggle with an equation that is totally obvious to someone else. Luckily, the practice problems in this part help you identify your own strengths and weaknesses. When you take the practice exams in Part IV, notice how quickly you can correctly complete the problems that are your **forte** (area of excellence).

Here's your strategy:

- ✔ **Answer all the easy, early questions.** Read the question, decide how to do it, and then answer it.

- ✔ **With an eye on the clock, answer all or most of the medium-difficulty questions.** These are the seven or eight middle questions. If you *encounter* (meet) a tough question in the middle of a section, circle it and go back to it if you have time.

  If you skip a question, be sure that you skip the answer line also. A good technique is to say (in your head only, not aloud) something like "the answer to number 12 is C" as you darken the oval. Keep track of where you are!

- ✔ **Hit the last four or five questions in each math section only if time permits.** Even there, in the "hard question zone," you may find something that's easy — for you. Solve what you can.

- ✔ **After you've seen all the questions, go back to anything you skipped.** Zero in on the type of question in which you excel. Try those problems again, and keep going until time runs out.

- ✔ **Try not to skip a grid-in.** You aren't penalized for wrong answers in this type of question, so if you have time, put *something* in, even if you're stumped. However, don't waste too much time on a grid-in if you have absolutely no idea how to do the problem. Spend the extra minute working on a problem you skipped that *may* earn you a point.

Building a Math Tool Kit

One of the first things that every do-it-yourselfer learns is that the proper tool makes all the difference. You don't need a saw or a screwdriver on the PSAT/NMSQT, but a couple of special techniques help you nail the math questions. What techniques? Read on.

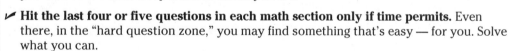

Plugging in

Plugging in is a great technique for solving lots of PSAT/NMSQT problems, especially those involving percents and variables. To plug in, pick a number — almost any number — and work through the problem with that number. Here's what I mean. Imagine a problem involving percents, such as this one:

A tasteful, orange-and-purple shirt is marked down 40%, but somehow it fails to sell. The store owner lowers the price by an additional 10%. What is the total discount on this fashion-forward item?

(A) 25%

(B) 30%

(C) 35%

(D) 46%

(E) 50%

The answer is Choice (D). The question doesn't explain how much the shirt cost originally (or who chose the colors). No worries: Just choose a number. For percent problems, 100 is always a good bet. Now work through the problem. The original price is $100. The first discount is $40, so the new price is $60. The next discount is 10% of $60, or $6. Subtract $6 from $60, and the new price is $54. The original price was $100, so the discount is $100 – $54, or $46. That means that the total discount is 46%, also known as Choice (D).

Here's another example:

During the hours marked on Jeannie's calendar as "PSAT/NMSQT Prep," Jeannie actually spends ½ her time watching reality TV shows. She devotes ⅔ of the remaining prep time to shredding old love letters. During what proportion of the time Jeannie claims to be studying is she actually preparing for the PSAT/NMSQT?

(A) ⅙

(B) ⅓

(C) ½

(D) ⅔

(E) ⅚

The answer is Choice (A). You can solve this problem with algebra, naming the time studying as *x*. However, you can also plug in. You don't know how much time Jeannie *said* she was studying. Her mom checks her calendar, so chances are it's a respectable amount. Plug in a number. Because you're dealing with ½ and ⅔, you probably want those denominators to be factors of the number you select. How about 12? Jeannie said she would study for 12 hours, but she watched TV for 6 hours. Subtract 6 from 12, and you have 6 hours left for study. Jeannie shreds her letters for ⅔ of the remaining time, or 4 hours. She has 2 hours for study remaining. Go back to your plug-in number, 12, and you see that Jeannie spent 2/12, or ⅙, of her time studying. Your answer is Choice (A).

Backsolving

A variation of plugging in, which I describe in the preceding section, is *backsolving*. This technique is great for simple equations or arithmetic problems. When you backsolve, you plug in the answer choices to see which one works.

Generally, the answer choices are listed in size order — from the smallest to the largest number. Start with Choice (C), which falls in the middle. When you try that answer, you may realize that Choice (C) is too big, and then you know you have to try Choices (A) and (B). Or, you may discover that Choice (C) is too small, and then you can check Choices (D) and (E).

Take a look at these example problems, each answered by backsolving:

A number is tripled, increased by 4, and then halved. If the result is 8, what was the number?

(A) 2

(B) 4

(C) 8

(D) 12

(E) 16

The answer is Choice (B). You *could* solve with algebra, letting x represent the original number. However, backsolving works just fine. Try Choice (C), 8, as the original number and see what happens: 8 tripled is 24, which becomes 28 when increased by 4, and then 14 when halved. Fourteen is too big, so try an answer that's smaller than Choice (C); Choice (B) is a good next try. If the original number is 4, it becomes 12 when tripled, 16 when increased by 4, and then 8 when halved — the result you want! The correct answer is Choice (B).

If $f(x) = x^2 - 3x - 2$, what value of x results in $f(x) = 2$?

(A) 1

(B) 2

(C) 3

(D) 4

(E) 5

The answer is Choice (D). You can answer this question by creating a quadratic equation and then factoring, but it may be easier for you to backsolve. As usual, start with Choice (C) and go from there. If x is 3, you get $f(3) = (3)^2 - 3(3) - 2 = 9 - 9 - 2 = -2$. Uh-oh, –2 is too small. Try a larger answer, Choice (D). If x is 4, you get $f(4) = (4)^2 - 3(4) - 2 = 16 - 12 - 2 = 2$, the answer you're looking for!

Sketching a diagram

You know those annoying problems where one friend is driving west and the other is on a train heading east, both moving at different speeds? (Why doesn't everyone just stay home? But back to math.) You may find that a little sketch allows you to "see" the answer or at least the route to the answer. Here's an example:

Stan and Evan leave school to bicycle home. Both boys ride at a rate of 15 miles per hour. Evan rides directly east for 12 minutes to get home, and Stan rides directly south for 16 minutes to get to his home. How many miles apart are Evan's and Stan's homes?

(A) 4

(B) 5

(C) 10

(D) 15

(E) 20

The answer is Choice (B). Diagram time! Make sure you label your diagram so you get a good sense of what's going on in the problem. But first, determine how far each of the boys live from school. To get home, Evan rides for 12 minutes, or $\frac{1}{5}$ of an hour, meaning that he travels (15 miles per hour) $\times$ ($\frac{1}{5}$ hour) = 3 miles. The formula is (rate) $\times$ (time) = distance. (For more information on rate/time/distance problems, see Chapter 8.) Stan rides for $\frac{16}{60}$ of an hour, so his distance is (15 miles per hour) $\times$ ($\frac{16}{60}$ hour) = 4 miles.

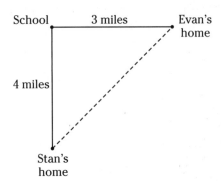

Hopefully you noticed that you have a right triangle, which means that you can use the Pythagorean theorem. Recall that $a^2 + b^2 = c^2$, where a and b are the legs of the triangle and c is the hypotenuse. In this case, $3^2 + 4^2 = 5^2$, so Stan and Evan live 5 miles apart, Choice (B).

Keeping it real

The PSAT/NMSQT doesn't always give you real-world problems (not counting its role in ruining your life), but sometimes you can use your knowledge of how the world works to help you on the exam. If you're solving a problem involving decreasing prices, you know that you're never going to get more than a 100 percent reduction. No store pays you to haul the stuff away! Nor will you find that 110 students are studying Spanish if the problem tells you that the school has only 50 kids. Keep your eye on reality. If your answer doesn't fit, go back and try again.

Using the booklet

Only your answer sheet is graded, but your question booklet is actually a valuable tool for PSAT/NMSQT math. As you read each question, circle key ideas (*integers, largest, less than,* and other such words). The little circles help you focus on the question's important elements. Also, use the blank space around each question to jot down the calculations you're doing to arrive at an answer. If you come up with –12 and none of the answer choices matches that number, you can check your steps to see if you wrote a 2, for example, when you intended to write 4.

If you've spent more than a minute on one problem, even if you aren't done with finding the answer, you should probably move on to the next. If you have time, you can return to that problem. Having the steps written in your booklet helps you jump in where you left off.

Chapter 7

Counting Down and Adding Up: Numbers and Operations

. . . .

In This Chapter

▶ Choosing the best approach to numbers and operations questions

▶ Solving percent and ratio problems

▶ Tackling rate/time/distance questions

▶ Handling sequences and sets

. . . .

*W*hen I hear *numbers and operations,* I think about how much a little appendectomy costs in a typical hospital: about as much as a week in Paris, in a first-class hotel with a four-star restaurant! But on the PSAT/NMSQT, *numbers and operations* have nothing to do with surgery, unless you need to have your brain reimplanted in your skull after more than two hours of mind-numbing test questions.

In this chapter I explain the numbers and operations questions you have to answer, such as ratios, percents, rate/time/distance, sets, and other fun activities. The good news is that you've probably been solving this sort of problem for years. More good news: A couple of tricks, which I describe in Chapter 6, help you solve these questions with a minimum of effort.

You've Got Their Number: Basic Numbers and Operations Questions

The arithmetic you learned in elementary and middle school serves you well when you're working on numbers and operations questions. Some of the questions you face on the exam are just simple calculations. However, the PSAT/NMSQT makes you perform those four operations with many types of numbers, not just the ones you learned by finger- and toe-counting. To make things even more confusing, the letter *n* sometimes replaces the word *number.* The test-makers also throw several combinations at you, so the order in which you do things (the *order of operations,* in math-speak) matters a lot.

Climbing the number family tree

When you solve a problem on the PSAT/NMSQT, you may run into something like one of these phrases:

> Three *prime* numbers added to . . .

> The greatest *positive number* is . . .

> A *negative integer* multiplied by . . .

You can't do the problem if you don't know what type of numbers you're dealing with. Fortunately, the test-makers usually confine themselves to a few key terms.

✔ An ***integer*** may be either *positive* (greater than zero) or *negative* (less than zero). Zero is also an integer, but it's neither positive nor negative; like me, it's in a class by itself. Integers are never decimals or fractions.

✔ A ***whole number*** is a positive number that never includes fractions or decimals. Whole numbers are *even* (divisible by 2) or *odd* (not evenly divisible by 2). Zero is also a whole number.

✔ A ***prime number*** has only two factors; it can't be divided by anything other than itself and 1. (In case you're wondering, 1 and 0 are *not* prime numbers.)

✔ A ***factor*** of a number is any number that divides neatly into another, larger number without leaving a remainder. For example, 3 is a factor of 21, because when you divide 21 by 3, you get 7 and no remainder.

✔ One more essential vocabulary word is ***consecutive*** (following one after another, with no interruption, as in "8, 9, 10").

When you read a numbers and operations question, get in the habit of underlining the kind of number you're searching for. Keep the type of number in your mind as you work through the problem and select an answer.

Check out these sample questions.

1. The product of three consecutive odd numbers is 315. What is the smallest of these integers?

    (A) 3

    (B) 5

    (C) 7

    (D) 9

    (E) 11

2. Three prime numbers are multiplied together. Which of the following statements, if any, must be true?

    I. The product must be odd.

    II. The product must be prime.

    III. The product must have exactly 5 factors.

    (A) I only

    (B) II only

    (C) III only

    (D) I and III only

    (E) none of the above

3. What is the sum of the integers in the set {–5, –2.7, 0, ⅔, $\sqrt{7}$, 10}

    (A) –7.7

    (B) –5

    (C) 3.3

    (D) 5

    (E) 10

Now check your answers:

1. **B.** *Plugging in* is a great way to solve this problem. Remember, you want to try Choice (C) first. If 7 is the smallest number, then 9 and 11 are the other two numbers. Multiply those three together and you get 693 — much too big. Try Choice (B): $5 \times 7 \times 9 = 315$, and you've found your answer!

   Underlining key terms in the question is a great way to focus your attention on important details. In Question 1, you might underline "consecutive," "odd," "smallest," and "integers."

2. **E.** How well do you know your prime numbers? Remember that 2 is the only even prime number, so if you multiply 2 by two other primes, the result is even. Therefore, Option I isn't necessarily true. If you're multiplying three numbers together to get your product, then each of those numbers is a factor of the product, so the product can't be prime. Therefore, Option II is out. And Option III is a trick! Pick three prime numbers to see what happens: 2, 3, and 5 will work, and their product is 30. You know that 2, 3, and 5 are all factors, but so is the product of any two of them: 6, 10, and 15. Also, remember that 30 and 1 are factors. Your answer is Choice (E).

3. **D.** You know that integers are positive or negative whole numbers, or 0. The integers in the set are –5, 0, and 10. When you add them together, the sum is 5, Choice (D).

Meeting Aunt Sally: Order of operations

Please Excuse My Dear Aunt Sally (PEMDAS) is a **mnemonic** (memory aid) that helps you remember which operation comes first, which comes second, and so forth. The order matters because if you ignore Aunt Sally, you end up with the wrong answer. And you can be sure that the testers plant wrong answers among the choices that look very appealing to anyone who forgets the proper order of operations.

You may have heard of Aunt Sally in a slightly different way, as GEMDAS. In that case think of GEMDAS as a plea to our first president: *George, Excuse My Dear Aunt Sally.*

Every time you see a question that requires several steps, invite Aunt Sally to the party. Here's what each letter means, *in order:*

1. *P* **is for** *parentheses.*

   Do everything in parentheses first. (If you're working with the GEMDAS memory aid, the *G* stands for *grouping.* Whatever is in parentheses is a grouping.)

2. *E* **stands for** *exponents.*

   Your second step is to calculate or simplify exponents (squares, cubes, and so on).

3. *M* **means** *multiply,* **and** *D* **is** *divide.*

   Work from left to right, multiplying and dividing as you go.

   Make sure you don't multiply everything before dividing — left to right is the key!

4. *A* **stands for** *add,* **and** *S* **means** *subtract.*

   Again, work from left to right, adding and subtracting as needed.

Some calculators have PEMDAS programmed in. Before you rely on your calculator to remember Aunt Sally, check it out. The manual that came with the calculator or the website of the manufacturer may tell you, or you can try a few sample problems to see whether PEMDAS is automatic or not. If it isn't, enter each calculation separately.

Take a look at PEMDAS in action. Suppose you have to figure out the value of this:

$$551 - (220 \div 4 \times 8) + 5^3$$

Keeping Aunt Sally in mind, begin with the **P**arenthesis: $220 \div 4 \times 8$. Work from left to right: $220 \div 4 = 55$. Multiply 55 by 8 and you get 440. Now hit the **E**xponent. When you cube 5 $(5 \times 5 \times 5)$ you get 125. Here's what you have so far:

$$551 - 440 + 125$$

Go from left to right, and you have $551 - 440 = 111$. Now you have $111 + 125$, which gives you 236.

By the way, PEMDAS also works for questions in which you find a **_variable_** (a letter, such as n or x, that represents a number).

Aunt Sally loves company. Invite her to these practice problems.

4. Simplify: $1 + (2 - 4)^2 + 10 \div 2$

   (A) −9

   (B) −4.5

   (C) 4.5

   (D) 5.5

   (E) 10

5. The expression $10 - 2(2 - 3^2) - 9 \div 3 \times 2$ is equal to

   (A) −18

   (B) −9

   (C) 2

   (D) 18

   (E) 25.5

6. Simplify $-172 - (3^2 - 90 \div 9)$

   (A) −181

   (B) −173

   (C) −172

   (D) −171

   (E) −163

Now check your answers:

4. **E.** Parentheses first: $(2 - 4) = (-2)$. Exponents next: $(-2)^2 = 4$. Now you have $1 + 4 + 10 \div 2$. The problem has no multiplication, but you should divide the last two terms before you worry about addition or subtraction. $10 \div 2 = 5$, so $1 + 4 + 5 = 10$, Choice (E).

5. **D.** Deal with the parentheses first: $(2 - 3^2)$, so you apply PEMDAS to the expression within the parentheses. Exponents first: $3^2 = 9$, so $2 - 3^2$ then becomes $2 - 9 = -7$. Rewrite the original expression: $10 - 2(-7) - 9 \div 3 \times 2$. Now multiply and divide from left to right: $2(-7) = -14$, and $9 \div 3 \times 2 = 3 \times 2 = 6$. That big nasty expression you started with now looks like $10 - (-14) - 6 = 10 + 14 - 6$. Add from left to right and you end up with 18, Choice (D).

6. **D.** You want to handle the parentheses first, but they include some other operations, so you need to simplify the math inside of the parentheses. In there, deal with the exponent first: $3^2 = 9$, so you have $9 - 90 \div 9$. Remember that division comes before subtraction, so simplify to $9 - 10$, which is -1. The whole expression is now $-172 - (-1)$, or $-172 + 1$, which equals -171, Choice (D).

Working with radicals and absolute value

When you apply PEMDAS (the order of operations I describe in the preceding section), you may run across a radical. A ***radical*** is a square root, the number that, multiplied by itself, gives you the number under the radical. The $\sqrt{64}$ is 8, because $8 \times 8 = 64$. You may also find an ***absolute value*** (a number placed inside two parallel lines, which represents either the positive or the negative form of the number). Remember these rules when you hit a radical or absolute value:

- ✔ **You can multiply and divide radicals.** So $\sqrt{7} \times \sqrt{15} = \sqrt{105}$, and $\sqrt{99} \div \sqrt{3} = \sqrt{33}$. The numbers don't change, just because they have that cute little tent-like symbol over them.

- ✔ **You can add or subtract radicals only when they match.** It's legal to subtract $3\sqrt{3}$ from $10\sqrt{3}$. (The answer is $7\sqrt{3}$.)

- ✔ **To add or subtract unlike radicals, factor out a perfect square so that the radicals match.** Let's say you're trying to add $\sqrt{45}$ and $\sqrt{20}$. Mismatch! But $\sqrt{45}$ can be factored into $\sqrt{9} \times \sqrt{5}$, which equals $3\sqrt{5}$. In the same way, you can factor $\sqrt{20}$ into $\sqrt{4} \times \sqrt{5}$, which equals $2\sqrt{5}$. Okay, now you're adding $3\sqrt{5}$ and $2\sqrt{5}$, which comes to $5\sqrt{5}$.

  Don't forget that when two negative numbers are multiplied, the result is positive. That means, for example, that 3^2 and $(-3)^2$ both equal 9.

- ✔ **Treat radicals like parentheses, in the order of operations.** Simplify anything inside of the radical, deal with the radical, and then move on.

- ✔ **Treat absolute values like parentheses, in the order of operations.** In other words, compute the absolute value before you work the rest of the problem. You can recognize absolute value because the number appears to be lying between two train tracks, like this: $|11|$. You can have a few things inside the train tracks, like this: $|2-5|$. If you can simplify an absolute value, do so before doing anything else. So change $|2-5|$ to $|-3|$. After you simplify, change whatever's on the train tracks to positive 3.

Don't change the absolute value to positive until you've simplified it. Do the math *inside* the train tracks first, and then change the answer to positive.

Here's a radical suggestion: Try these practice problems.

7. Simplify: $\sqrt{5+2^2} - |2-7| + 4$

   (A) -2

   (B) 2

   (C) 6

   (D) 12

   (E) 16

8. The expression $4\sqrt{9+|2-5|}$ is equivalent to

   (A) 8

   (B) $4\sqrt{6}$

   (C) $8\sqrt{3}$

   (D) $12+4\sqrt{3}$

   (E) $16\sqrt{3}$

9. Simplify the following expression: $\sqrt{8^2-3^2-1}$

   (A) $2\sqrt{14}$

   (B) $3\sqrt{6}$

   (C) $4\sqrt{14}$

   (D) $6\sqrt{3}$

   (E) $9\sqrt{6}$

   Now check your answers:

7. **B.** Deal with the radical first: $5+2^2$ requires you to square 2 before adding it to 5, so you get $5+4=9$, which becomes 3 when you apply the square root. Your expression now looks like $3-|2-7|+4$; time to tackle the absolute value part. You know that $2-7=-5$, but the absolute value sign turns that into a positive 5. Your expression is now $3-5+4$, or 2, Choice (B).

8. **C.** Absolute value inside of a radical?! Take it one step at a time. The absolute value needs to be handled before you can even think about the radical, so start there. $|2-5|=|-3|=3$, so you can rewrite the expression as $4\sqrt{9+3}=4\sqrt{12}$ when you simplify inside of the radical. Unfortunately, 12 isn't a perfect square, but it does have 4 as a factor. You can rewrite: $4\sqrt{12}=4\sqrt{4}\sqrt{3}=8\sqrt{3}$, Choice (C).

9. **B.** Simplify everything inside of the radical first, beginning with exponents: $8^2-3^2-1=64-9-1=54$. Now, see if you can split 54 up so that it is the product of a perfect square and another number: $54=9\times6$. Put that back inside of the radical, and you find that $\sqrt{54}=\sqrt{9\times6}=\sqrt{9}\sqrt{6}=3\sqrt{6}$, Choice (B).

Scoring 100% on Percentage Problems

Thomas Edison, who invented the light bulb and thus proved that he had some serious brain power, once said, "We don't know a millionth of one percent about anything." Edison may have been right when it comes to knowledge in general, but when you take the PSAT/NMSQT, you can easily find the right answer to 100% of the questions involving percents. A percent is nothing more than a useful way to represent how much of 100 you're talking about. Because 100% of anything is the whole thing, 50% is half, 25% is a quarter, and so forth. You see percents expressed with the word *of,* as in *66% of.* The *of* is a stand-in for multiplication. Here's how to approach percent problems:

✔ **Use your calculator if it has a % button.** Some do; some don't. If you have a % button on your calculator and you need to find 13% of 189, you can simply enter "13% × 189" to see that the answer is 24.57. No percent button? Just convert the percent to a decimal by moving the decimal point two spaces to the left. In that case you'd enter "0.13 × 189" for the same result. You can also change a percent to a fraction (13% = 13/100).

✔ **Consider plugging in.** This PSAT/NMSQT trick, plugging in, is tailor-made for percent problems. Plug in 100 and you're all set. (Not sure how to plug in? Turn to Chapter 6 for a complete explanation.)

✔ **Remember the "is-of" formula.** In this formula, you have

$$\frac{is}{of} = \frac{\%}{100}$$

so if you're asked, "80% of what number is 8," you can see that

$$\frac{8}{x} = \frac{80}{100}$$

Now cross multiply: $80x = 800$. Divide by 80 and you get $x = 10$.

✔ **Pay special attention to problems asking for the percent of increase or decrease.** Plugging in helps here also, or you can use this formula:

$$\frac{\text{amount of change}}{\text{original amount}} = \frac{\%}{100}$$

✔ **Don't forget that percentages may be more than 100.** You'd probably like your allowance to increase by 300% (so you'd pocket 4 times as much money), but it's more likely that your college tuition will rise 500% by the time you graduate.

Ready for some percent problems? Give these your best shot.

10. Jane goes to get her hair cut and tells the person cutting her hair that she would like her hair to be 25% shorter than it currently is. After the haircut, Jane's hair is 12 inches long. How many inches long was Jane's hair before the haircut?

(A) 9

(B) 12

(C) 14

(D) 16

(E) 18

11. A bookstore sells books for 20% more than it buys them for. During a sale, a customer buys a book with a 25% discount coupon. What percent of the price that the store paid did the book sell for?

(A) 60%

(B) 75%

(C) 90%

(D) 100%

(E) 110%

12. Forty percent of the seats at a baseball stadium are in the shade at 4 p.m. If the stadium has 25,000 seats, how many seats are in the sun at 4 p.m.?

(A) 5,000

(B) 10,000

(C) 12,500

(D) 15,000

(E) 20,000

Now check your answers:

10. **D.** Plugging in is a great strategy for solving this problem. If Jane began with 14 inches of hair — Choice (C) — then after the haircut she'll still have 75% of that length: 14(0.75) = 10.5 inches. Jane has more hair left than that, so pick a longer starting length. If Jane began with 16 inches of hair, Choice (D), then she'd have 16(0.75) = 12 inches of hair after the cut — the answer you're looking for!

11. **C.** As usual, you want to use 100 as your initial amount in a percent problem, even if it sounds silly for a book to cost $100. That means that the customers saw the price as 20% or $20 higher: $120. A 25% discount is the same as paying 75% of the price, so the sale price is 120(0.75) = $90. $90 is 90% of $100, so Choice (C) is the one you want.

12. **D.** If 40% of the seats are in the shade, then 60% of them are in the sun. To find out how many seats are in the sun, you want to know what number is 60% of 25,000. Using the formula $\frac{is}{of} = \frac{\%}{100}$ and letting x be the number you're looking for: $\frac{x}{25,000} = \frac{60}{100}$. Cross-multiply and simplify, and you see that $x = 15,000$, Choice (D).

Listening to the Ratio

Percents, which I explain in the preceding section, are all about the relationship between a part and the whole. **Ratios** express the relationship *between* parts. You hear references to ratios all the time when people say things like, "last season that pitcher delivered seven strikeouts for every nine walks," or, "the ratio of peas to carrots in the average box is eight to one." Notice that in these comments you *aren't* given the total number of batters the pitcher faced or the amount of chopped-up veggies you may have for dinner. Again, ratios are about parts, not wholes.

Ratios are usually written with a *colon* (one dot atop another), this way:

> The ratio of slurps to burps is 12:5.

When you read that sentence aloud, the colon becomes "to," as in, "the ratio of slurps to burps is 12 to 5."

On the PSAT/NMSQT, you may be asked about *possible* totals. The sum of the parts is a possible total, but so are all the multiples of that sum. So if the ratio of biology majors to French majors is 4 to 3, the total number of French and biology majors may be 7, 14, 21, 28 . . . you get the idea! If you're asked to say what *is* or *must be* the total, the answer is *cannot be determined,* because any multiple of 7 is possible, based on the sum of the ratio parts.

Backsolving, a trick I explain in detail in Chapter 6, helps with ratios. If you're asked about a possible total, look for an answer choice that's a multiple of the sum of the parts.

Sometimes the test-makers give you the total and the ratio and ask you to figure out how many are in each part, as in this question:

> George gobbles 2 jelly beans for every 3 gummy worms. If George has 75 pieces of candy, how many jelly beans does he have?

George will have a major stomachache, but no worries for you, because you simply follow these steps:

1. Add the parts.

You know George's sweet stash contains jelly beans and gummy worms in a 2:3 ratio, and 2 + 3 = 5.

2. Divide the total by the sum you calculated.

Okay, 75 divided by 5 gives you a *quotient* (what you get when you divide) of 15.

3. Multiply each part of the ratio by the quotient.

So you have 2×15, which equals 30 jelly beans, and 3×15, which equals 45 gummy worms.

4. Check your work by adding the parts.

Your total should be 75, and 30 + 45 does indeed equal 75.

Gobble up a gummy-whatever and turn your attention to these questions.

13. The ratio of children to adults in a movie theater is 2:5. If the theater has 175 people, how many of them are children?

   (A) 2

   (B) 50

   (C) 100

   (D) 125

   (E) 150

14. A bag contains marbles and dice. If the ratio of marbles to dice in the bag is 4:5, what is one possible total number of marbles and dice in the bag?

   (A) 27

   (B) 28

   (C) 29

   (D) 30

   (E) 31

15. Chester Middle School's chess team has a winning to losing ratio of 9:4. If the team won 99 of the chess games that they played, how many games did they play altogether?

   (A) 140

   (B) 141

   (C) 142

   (D) 143

   (E) 144

Now check your answers:

13. **B.** If the ratio of children to adults is 2:5, then children make up $\frac{2}{2+5} = \frac{2}{7}$ of the audience. Now just multiply the proportion of children by the total number of people: $\frac{2}{7}(175) = 50$ children in the audience, Choice (B).

14. **A.** You know that for every 4 marbles there are 5 dice, so your total number of marbles and dice must be a multiple of 4 + 5 = 9. Choice (A) is the only one that's a multiple of 9, so it's the one you're looking for!

15. **D.** To get from the winning ratio to the winning number of games, you just need to multiply by 11 (because $99 = 9 \times 11$), so the number of games lost must also be the ratio of games lost multiplied by 11, or 44 games. Add together 99 winning and 44 losing games, and you have a total of 143 chess games. Checkmate with Choice (D)!

Just Stay Home! Rate, Time, and Distance Problems

Don't you hate questions in which one guy is driving east at 40 miles an hour and a friend is moving west doing 65? You're supposed to figure out where they meet and ignore the fact that in real life they can just call each other and explain where they are. But if you get one of these problems on the PSAT/NMSQT, at least you can solve it fairly easily. Just remember this formula: **R**ate × **T**ime = **D**istance (RTD).

A little sketch or a chart often helps you with rate/time/distance questions.

Here's an example. Your robot toddles along at a rate of 3 feet per minute for 30 minutes. MegaBrain's robot zooms at 30 feet per second for 10 minutes. How much farther will MegaBrain's robot travel than your robot?

To solve this one, try a chart. The headings match the terms of the formula, Rate × Time = Distance. Before you fill in the boxes, though, be sure that everything matches. MegaBrain's robot travels 30 feet per second. (Watch out for these tricky changes in units!) Because a minute has 60 seconds, MegaBrain's speed is 1800 feet per minute. Now you can fill in the chart. Start with what you know:

	Rate	Time	Distance
Your robot	3 feet per minute	30 minutes	
MegaBrain's robot	1800 feet per minute	10 minutes	

Now fill in the empty squares. Your robot goes 3 × 30 or 90 feet. MegaBrain's robot travels 1800 × 10 or 18,000 feet.

	Rate	Time	Distance
Your robot	3 feet per minute	30 minutes	90
MegaBrain's robot	1800 feet per minute	10 minutes	18,000

MegaBrain's robot travels 18,000 – 90 feet, or 17,910 feet farther than yours.

You may be asked how far apart they are. If so, note whether they're traveling in the same direction or in the opposite direction. In the same direction, you subtract, as I did in the preceding example. In the opposite direction, you add. (Sketch it out and you'll see.)

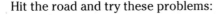

Hit the road and try these problems:

16. James and Kat are standing at opposite ends of a football field, 300 feet away from each other. If Kat walks at a rate of 12 feet per second, James walks at a rate of 8 feet per second, and they walk toward each other, how long will it take for them to meet up?

(A) 15 seconds

(B) 75 seconds

(C) 2 minutes

(D) 3 minutes

(E) 15 minutes

17. Two boats meet up in a lake, and after the captains share sandwiches, head off in different directions. The motorboat heads directly east at a rate of 36 miles per hour, and the sailboat goes north at a rate of 15 miles per hour. If both boats continue traveling in straight lines, how far apart will they be in 2 hours?

   (A) 21 miles

   (B) 39 miles

   (C) 51 miles

   (D) 78 miles

   (E) 100 miles

18. Alexis walked at a rate of 3 miles per hour for 20 minutes and then stopped to talk on the phone for 16 minutes. After her phone conversation, Alexis walked at a rate of 5 miles per hour for the remainder of the hour. What was Alexis's average speed over the hour?

   (A) 2 mph

   (B) 2.5 mph

   (C) 3 mph

   (D) 3.5 mph

   (E) 4 mph

   Now check your answers:

16. **A.** You know that both James and Kat are walking for the same length of time, and you want to know what that time is, so for the moment, just call it t. James will walk (8 feet/second) $\times t$ feet (rate $\times$ time), and Kat will walk (12 feet/second) $\times t$ feet. Together, they walk 300 feet, so you know that $8t + 12t = 300$. Add together like terms and you get $20t = 300$, and when you divide you see that $t = 15$. You can think about units by remembering that you're dividing 300 feet by 20 feet/second, which works out to 15 seconds. Choice (A) is your answer.

17. **D.** RTD and right triangles? You can do it! Draw yourself a picture first.

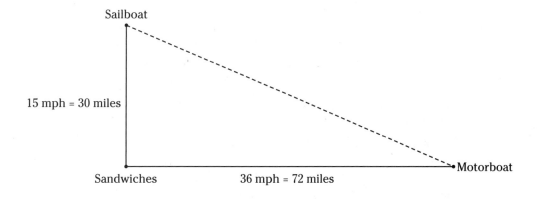

   You know that each boat is traveling for 2 hours, so you can use RTD to determine how far each has traveled: 30 miles for the sailboat and 72 miles for the motorboat. Now all you need to do is apply the Pythagorean theorem to figure out how far apart the boats are: $30^2 + 72^2 = d^2$; $900 + 5184 = d^2$; $d = 78$ miles apart, Choice (D).

18. **C.** To find Alexis's average speed, you first need to find the total distance she traveled and the total time that she was traveling (these both include the time that she was stopped!). For the first part of her trip, Alexis traveled for 20 minutes, or $\frac{1}{3}$ of an hour, at a rate of 3 miles per hour. Using RTD, you can see that she traveled 1 mile during those first 20 minutes. Alexis didn't make forward progress during her phone conversation, so you know that she spent the first 36 minutes going 1 mile. In the remaining 24 minutes ($60 - 36 = 24$ minutes) of the hour, Alexis walked at a rate of 5 miles per hour. 24 minutes out of 60 is the same as $\frac{2}{5}$ of an hour. Using RTD, $(\frac{2}{5}) \times 5 = 2$ miles of travel during the last 24 minutes, for a total of 3 miles in 60 minutes. This makes Alexis's average speed 3 miles per hour, Choice (C).

Knowing What Comes Next: Sequences

Math meets fortunetelling in **sequences** (numbers arranged in a fixed order). The PSAT/NMSQT lords provide a set of numbers (each number is called a **term**) and ask you to identify another term in the sequence. They may want the next term or a term many steps along. Sequences show up in two varieties on the PSAT/NMSQT: arithmetic (when the terms occur because of adding or subtracting) and geometric (when you multiply or divide to move from one term to another). Here are two examples of each type of sequence:

Arithmetic: 2, 10, 18, 26 . . . (add 8 to arrive at the next term)

Arithmetic: 16, 9, 2, –5 . . . (subtract 7 to arrive at the next term)

Geometric: 2, 30, 450 . . . (multiply by 15 to arrive at the next term)

Geometric: 350, 70, 14, 2.8 . . . (divide by 5 to arrive at the next term)

If you're asked for the fourth term beyond the numbers presented, you can just calculate your way to the correct answer. If they want the 41st term in the sequence, your time will run out if you take the time to calculate all those intermediate steps. Formulas to the rescue! You can use these shortcuts to find any term in a sequence:

- ✔ **Call the term you're seeking the nth term.** The number of steps to get from the first term to the term you want is $n - 1$. So to go from the first term to, say, the 25th term, you need 24 steps.

- ✔ **In an arithmetic sequence, calculate the difference between terms in the sequence.** In the first example, the difference (also known as d) is 8.

- ✔ **Apply this formula to find the nth term in an arithmetic sequence:**

  n^{th} term = the first term + $(n - 1)d$

  So in the first arithmetic sequence, the 20th term would be $2 + (20 - 1)8$. When you figure it out, you get 154.

- ✔ **In a geometric sequence, figure out the ratio of one term to the next.** Before you faint, the ratio in a geometric sequence, abbreviated as r, is just the number you're multiplying or dividing by. In the first geometric sequence, $r = 15$.

- ✔ **Apply the formula for a geometric sequence:**

  n^{th} term = the first term $\times r^{(n-1)}$

  Okay, take another look at the first geometric sequence example, and use the formula to find the fifth term: 5th term = $2 \times 15^{(5-1)}$, which gives you 2×15^4, which gives you $2 \times 50,625$, which gives you 101,250. (That's a big number, but geometric sequences grow large *fast*.)

On the PSAT/NMSQT you may find a sequence problem that's all numbers, but sometimes sequences are tucked into word problems, like this one:

> After your mother discovers that you cut a class on Monday, she takes away your phone for 3 days. She tells you that for every additional cut, you'll lose the phone for 3 extra days. If you cut class every day for the rest of the week, for how many days will your connection to the outside world be suspended? And will your friends *ever* speak with you again?

You can just add up the numbers (3 days as of Monday, 6 days as of Tuesday, 9 as of Wednesday, 12 as of Thursday, with a grand total of 15 when you add 3 for Friday). Or, you can apply the earlier arithmetic formula. No matter which method you use, your social life is toast.

The sequence of events goes like this: I explain something, and then you do the problems. I did my part. Now it's your turn. Try these:

19. In the following sequence, determine the value of the 17th term.

    15, 11, 7, 3, . . .

    (A) 0

    (B) –41

    (C) –45

    (D) –49

    (E) –53

20. Jose checks the population of his ant farm once per week. When he checks during the first week, he has 160 ants. During week 2, he has 240 ants; week 3 has a count of 360 ants; and week 4 has a count of 540 ants. If the ant population continues to grow like this, how many ants do you expect Jose to count during week 6?

    (A) 810

    (B) 1,000

    (C) 1,200

    (D) 1,215

    (E) 1,230

21. In a certain geometric sequence, each term is half as large as the preceding term. If the first term has a value of 64, which term has a value of ¼?

    (A) 8th term

    (B) 9th term

    (C) 10th term

    (D) 14th term

    (E) 16th term

Now check your answers:

19. **D.** You're looking for a specific term in an arithmetic sequence, so you want to use the formula n^{th} term = the first term + $(n-1)d$. You want the 17th term, so n will be 17. The first term is 15, and the constant difference is –4 (each term is 4 less than the previous term). Plugging these numbers into the formula: 17th term = 15 + (17 – 1)(–4) = 15 + (16)(–4) = 15 – 64 = –49, Choice (D).

20. **D.** A geometric sequence! Did you see that each week Jose has ⅔ as many ants as he had the week before? You could use the formula for this one, but it's probably easier to just calculate directly to the 6th week. Week 5 = 540 × ⅔ = 810 ants. Week 6 = 810 × ⅔ = 1,215 ants, Choice (D).

21. **B.** You could always solve this problem by simply writing out the terms and counting to see which one equals ¼ (64, 32, 16, 8, 4, 2, . . .), but in this case flex your new geometric sequence muscles and try to solve this problem algebraically. Your key equation: n^{th} term = the first term × $r^{(n-1)}$. You don't know what n is yet, but you know that the first term is 64, r is ½ (because you always multiply by ½ to get the next term), and the nth term is ¼. Plug all this into the equation and you get: $\frac{1}{4} = 64\left(\frac{1}{2}\right)^{n-1}$. Divide both sides by 64: $\frac{1}{256} = \left(\frac{1}{2}\right)^{n-1}$. How many times do you need to multiply 2 by itself to get 256? Eight times, meaning that $n - 1$ is 8, so n is 9, Choice (B).

Setting the Stage with Mathematical Sets

Do you collect stamps, bottle caps, or tissues sneezed in by famous people? If so, your collection is a ***set.*** The PSAT/NMSQT doesn't care about the stuff you display on your wall (though a mental health professional may want to know more about your interest in tissues). The exam evaluates how well you deal with mathematical sets. No worries — all you need to remember are a few facts:

✔ The elements of a set are enclosed by brackets:{–2, –1, 0, 1, 4, 6, 7}

✔ If the set continues on, you see three dots after the last element: {2, 4, 6, 8 . . .}

✔ A set with nothing in it — not even one element — is called an ***empty set*** and may be represented by brackets with nothing between them: { }. An empty set is usually represented by a crossed-out zero: ∅.

✔ To find the ***union*** of two sets, put them together and then cross out any elements that show up more than once. For example, the union of {5, 5.5, 6, 6.5} and {6, 7, 8} is {5, 5.5, 6, 6.5, 7, 8}.

✔ To find the ***intersection*** of two sets, see which elements they have in common. In the preceding bullet, the intersection of the two sets is {6}, because that's the only common element. If two sets have no common elements, the intersection is an empty set.

If all the PSAT/NMSQT asked you to do was to look at lists of numbers, set questions would be no-brainers. However, they favor questions like "what is the intersection of the set of two-digit prime numbers less than 19 and the set of odd numbers from 11 to 35?" The answer, by the way, is {11, 13, 17}.

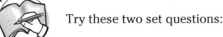

Try these two set questions:

22. How many elements are the intersection of the sets {E, G, I, R} and {I, K, R, S, T}?

(A) 1

(B) 2

(C) 4

(D) 5

(E) 7

23. Set A = {1, 2, 3, 4, 5}, set B = {2, 4, 6, 8}, and set C = {2, 3, 5, 7}. Which element is not in the union of sets A and C?

    (A) 2

    (B) 3

    (C) 4

    (D) 5

    (E) 6

Now check your answers:

22. **B.** The intersection of two sets is the elements in common. Both sets have the letters I and R, so these two sets have 2 elements in the intersection, Choice (B).

23. **E.** The easiest way to do this problem is to simply figure out what the union of sets A and C is, and then look for the answer choice that doesn't fit. A is {1, 2, 3, 4, 5}, and set C adds only the number 7 into the mix (recall that the union of two sets is the inclusive one — the operation that includes all the numbers in either set). So, the union of A and C is {1, 2, 3, 4, 5, 7}. Among the answer choices, Choice (E) is the only one that doesn't belong.

Chapter 8

Mastering the *X* Factor: Algebra and Functions

. . . .

In This Chapter

▶ Applying effective techniques to algebra and function problems

▶ Dealing with exponents and variables

▶ Figuring out factors and functions

▶ Using tools to solve equations

▶ Solving direct and inverse variation problems

. . . .

*T*he word *algebra* comes from an Arabic word meaning "the reunion of broken parts." You may be looking forward to some "algebra" after the PSAT/NMSQT, though I imagine the parts you plan to reunite have more to do with your sanity than with numbers and variables. In this chapter I ignore your mental state and concentrate on the algebra questions you'll see on the exam. Fortunately, PSAT/NMSQT algebra is pretty easy, and you can rack up many points if you master a few key concepts. You have to know how to deal with *x*'s and *y*'s and other **variables,** which are stand-ins for numbers. Variables, well, *vary* or change, but the basic rules governing them don't. This chapter covers the basic rules that the PSAT/NMSQT writers **deem** (consider) most important and gives you a chance to take those rules for a *test*-drive. (Sorry, I couldn't resist the pun.) I also explain how to master **functions,** a fancy word for the relationship between one number (say, how many hours you spend doing your math homework) and another (your PSAT/NMSQT score).

In this chapter (and in the book as a whole), × is a multiplication sign in questions without variables. Whenever a problem includes a variable (an *x,* for example), a raised dot is the symbol that tells you to multiply.

Selecting Tools for Algebra and Function Problems

Your math tool kit — techniques that allow you to cut through problems like a hot knife through butter — contains some tricks that are especially useful for algebra and function questions. Read on:

▮ ✔ **Be sure you know what the symbols mean.** Algebra often deals with equations (the equal sign is a dead giveaway), but you may also see these little signs:

  • ≠ (does not equal)

  • < or > (less than or greater than — the open side is next to the larger amount)

- ≤ or ≥ (less than or equal to, or greater than or equal to — the open side is next to the larger amount)

- + or – (positive or negative)

- ± (plus or minus)

- $\sqrt{\ }$ or $\sqrt[3]{\ }$ (square root or cube root)

- $|\ |$ (absolute value, when a number is inside)

✔ **Don't forget your calculator when you're solving algebra and function problems.** These questions often force you to deal with exponents and square roots, which most calculators can handle easily.

✔ **Try plugging in.** Pick a likely number, but not just any number, and plug it in where you see a variable. Doing so should give you an idea of the answer or allow you to check an answer you've already figured out. (For more on plugging in, see Chapter 6.)

✔ **Use backsolving.** Take one of the answers — Choice (C) is often a good place to start — and substitute that answer in the equation. Then check to see which answer works. (For more on backsolving, turn to Chapter 6.)

✔ **In equations, isolate what you need to solve.** After you know what you're supposed to find (the value of x perhaps), isolate that variable on one side of the equation. By definition, each side of an equation is equal, so if the variable is all alone on one side, the other side represents its value.

In the sections that follow, I tell you which of these techniques are best for each type of problem.

Appealing to a Higher Power: Exponents and Radicals

Many of the algebra and function questions you're up against on the PSAT/NMSQT contain *exponents,* raised numbers or letters. The number or letter *not* raised is called the *base.* When mathematicians talk about exponents, they call them *powers,* as in "six to the eighth power." The second power is referred to as a *square,* and the third power is a *cube.* If you have a number in front of the base, it's called a *numerical coefficient. Radicals* appear here and there on the PSAT/NMSQT. You may know radicals as square roots, written under this sign: $\sqrt{\ }$. Some examples:

✔ The base is 2 and the exponent is 3: 2^3 (also called *two cubed*)

✔ The base is y and the exponent is 4: y^4 (read as *y to the fourth power*)

✔ The numerical coefficient is 5, the base is a, and the exponent is 2: $5a^2$ (read as *five a squared*)

✔ The square root of 25 is 5: $\sqrt{25} = 5$. (Why 5? Because $5 \times 5 = 25$.)

The vocabulary doesn't matter, but what you do with the base, exponents, and coefficients is important. Keep these rules in mind when you're solving a PSAT/NMSQT problem with exponents or radicals:

✔ **A base with an exponent of zero equals 1.** Another, more usual way to express this is *base to the zero power.* So $6^0 = 1$, as does x^0.

✔ **A base with an exponent of 1 equals the base.** Most of the time, the 1 is simply omitted, but strictly speaking, $7^1 = 7$ and $x^1 = x$.

✔ **An exponent tells you how many times the base is multiplied.** Therefore, a base to the second power is the base multiplied by itself. (The second power is better known as *squared*.) So $5^2 = 5 \times 5 = 25$. Moving on, $5^4 = 5 \times 5 \times 5 \times 5 = 625$.

✔ **When you're finding a square root, look at the number under the radical and decide what was multiplied by itself to arrive at that number.** If you see $\sqrt{49}$, you know that $7 \times 7 = 49$, so 7 is the square root of 49.

The exponent tells you how many times you have to multiply the base by itself, but the exponent isn't what you multiply. If you see 4^3, you multiply $4 \times 4 \times 4$ to get 64. You *don't* multiply 4×3 to get 12.

✔ **Exponents can be negative numbers or fractions.** A negative exponent flips the base by creating a ***reciprocal***, 1 over the base. So x^{-3} is the reciprocal of x^3, which you can write as $\frac{1}{x^3}$. In fractional exponents, the fraction's denominator tells you which root or radical to apply to the base. So $81^{1/2}$ is asking for the square root of 81, or 9. Another example: $8^{1/3}$ is 2 because you're finding the cube root of 8.

Your calculator is a good friend when you're working with powers. Use either the y^x button or the $\wedge$ button. Just type the base, then the exponent, then the equal-sign button and you're done! Most calculators can also handle fractional powers. Enter $\wedge$ before the fraction, and then enter the fraction. Be sure to place the fraction in parenthesis! If you forget the parenthesis, you get the wrong answer. On some calculators, you press the second function key to find a root in this form: $\sqrt[x]{y}$.

✔ **To multiply like bases, add the exponents.** To divide like bases, subtract the exponents. So $y^5 \cdot y^4 = y^9$ and $y^5 \div y^2 = y^3$.

Don't even *think* about applying the preceding rule to unlike bases. Nope. Never. Not gonna happen! You have to factor it out or deal with it as it is. (For more on factoring, read the next section, "Getting It Together and Falling Apart: FOIL and Factoring.")

✔ **For an exponent inside and outside a parenthesis, multiply the exponents.** So $\left(5^3\right)^2 = 5^6$ and $\left(7^x\right)^5 = 7^{5x}$.

✔ **To add or subtract, both the bases and the exponents must match.** You can't add 6^2 and 8^3, nor can you subtract $2x^4$ from $4x^3$. However, you can deal with addition and subtraction if the bases and powers match. When everything matches, all you have to do is add or subtract the coefficients (the numbers in front of the base). Here's a legal problem and solution: $2x^2 + 5x^2 = 7x^2$. One more example, this time with subtraction: $9y^3 - y^3 = 8y^3$. Did you notice that I subtracted 1 from 9, even though no 1 appears in the question? The 1 in front of the y^3 is understood because 1 of anything is itself.

Power to the people! Now that your head is filled with exponent rules, try these problems.

1. Simplify: $\left(x^2\right)^3 x^3$

   (A) x^3

   (B) x^8

   (C) x^9

   (D) x^{12}

   (E) x^{18}

2. The expression 2^a3^a can be written as

    (A) 5^a

    (B) 5^{2a}

    (C) 6^a

    (D) 6^{2a}

    (E) 6^{a^2}

3. Simplify: $8^{\frac{1}{3}}2^2(25)^{\frac{1}{2}}$

    (A) 5

    (B) 40

    (C) $20\sqrt{8}$

    (D) $\sqrt[3]{400}$

    (E) 400

Now check your answers:

1. **C.** PEMDAS to the rescue once again! First you want to cube x^2, so you get x^6x^3, and then you add the exponents together now that you have the same base: x^9, or Choice (C).

2. **C.** In this case you have a copies of 2 and a copies of 3, so you can think of each copy of 2 matching up with a copy of 3 and multiplying to make 6. You end up with a copies of 6, or Choice (C).

3. **B.** Take each term by itself, simplify it, and then multiply everything together. First, $8^{\frac{1}{3}} = \sqrt[3]{8} = 2$. Next, $2^2 = 4$, no problem. Finally, $(25)^{\frac{1}{2}} = \sqrt{25} = 5$. Now, just multiply the three results together: $2 \times 4 \times 5 = 40$. Choice (B) it is!

Getting It Together and Falling Apart: FOIL and Factoring

I live in New York City, and on pretty much every block someone is either building something new — combining concrete, bricks, and all sorts of interesting things — or tearing something down. This section is the algebraic equivalent of all those construction (or deconstruction) projects. First I explain how to multiply algebraic expressions, and then I tell you how to factor them.

FOIL: Multiplying algebraic terms

FOIL is a ***mnemonic*** (a memory aid) that helps you remember how to multiply in Algebra Land. In the preceding section, I explain how to multiply one term by another term when exponents are involved. Here I concentrate on multiple terms, with and without exponents. Before I get to FOIL, I should explain the easy stuff:

  ✔ **To multiply two or more terms by one term, use the distributive property.** What, you forgot the distributive property? Not to worry: It's simple. Just multiply the single term by each of the terms in the parenthesis. Then recombine everything. Here's a sample: Imagine that you have to multiply $4x^2(6x^2 - 2)$. First, multiply $4x^2$ by $6x^2$, which gives you $24x^4$. Now multiply $4x^2$ by -2, which gives you $-8x^2$. Put it all together and you have $24x^4 - 8x^2$.

✔ **To multiple two terms by two other terms, use FOIL.** The letters of FOIL stand for First, Outer, Inner, Last. When you multiply two terms by two terms, you work in FOIL order. Take a look at this problem:

$(a - 2)(a - 8)$

- Run for **First** by multiplying $a \cdot a$, which gives you a^2.
- Go to the **Outer** limits and multiply $a \cdot -8$, which gives you $-8a$.
- Work your way to the **Inner** layer by multiplying $-2 \cdot a$, which gives you $-2a$.
- Take the (almost) **Last** step and multiply -2×-8, which gives you 16.
- Now put it together and you have $a^2 - 8a - 2a + 16$.
- Combine like terms $(-8a - 2a)$ and you get $-10a$. Replace the separate terms $(-8a$ and $-2a)$ with $-10a$.
- There you go: Your answer is $a^2 - 10a + 16$.

The PSAT/NMSQT writers (and I) recommend that you memorize two FOIL problems that pop up all over the place. So memorize them!

- $(a + b)(a - b) = a^2 - b^2$. This shortcut works only when you're multiplying terms that are exactly alike, except for their signs. You can use it for $(b + 3)(b - 3)$, which equals $b^2 - 9$. You can't use it for $(b + 3)(a - 15)$. This FOIL problem is known as _the difference of two squares_.

- $(a + b)^2 = (a + b)(a + b) = a^2 + 2ab + b^2$. This is FOIL, plain and simple, already worked out for you. If you see a problem that looks like this, try backsolving for a and b.

See if you can FOIL all by yourself:

4. Simplify: $(2a + 3)(a - 4)$

    (A) $a^2 - a - 12$

    (B) $2a^2 - 11a - 12$

    (C) $2a^2 - 5a - 12$

    (D) $2a^2 - a - 12$

    (E) $2a^2 + 5a - 12$

5. The expression $(x + y)(2x - 3y)$ is equivalent to

    (A) $x^2 - 3y^2$

    (B) $x^2 - xy - 3y^2$

    (C) $2x^2 - 3y^2$

    (D) $2x^2 - xy - 3y^2$

    (E) $2x^2 + xy - 3y^2$

Now check your answers:

4. **C.** FOIL! First: $(2a)(a) = 2a^2$. Outer: $(2a)(-4) = -8a$. Inner: $(3)(a) = 3a$. Last: $(3)(-4) = -12$. Add all those terms up and combine like terms: $2a^2 - 8a + 3a - 12 = 2a^2 - 5a - 12$, or Choice (C).

5. **D.** FOIL again! First: $(x)(2x) = 2x^2$. Outer: $(x)(-3y) = -3xy$. Inner: $(y)(2x) = 2xy$. Last: $(y)(-3y) = -3y^2$. Now combine the terms: $2x^2 - 3xy + 2xy - 3y^2 = 2x^2 - xy - 3y^2$, or Choice (D).

Factoring

In the preceding section you put things together; now you take them apart. When you factor, you break down an expression into the original terms that were (or could have been) multiplied to get that expression. Factoring is basically FOIL backwards (LIOF? Doesn't sound as good as FOIL!). When you take the PSAT/NMSQT, the factoring you have to do is pretty basic. You'll likely see an expression with three terms that were calculated using FOIL. For example, you may have to factor $x^2 + 10x + 24$ or something similar.

Here are the steps for factoring the example ($x^2 + 10x + 24$):

- ✔ **Draw two sets of parentheses.** Now you have a "home" ready for two factors.

- ✔ **Look at the first term and decide how you get there.** The first term is x^2, so you must have multiplied x by x. Place those values in the First spot in each parenthesis:

  $(x\ )(x\ )$.

- ✔ **Examine the last term and decide how you get there.** The last term is 24. To arrive at 24, you may have multiplied 24 by 1, 12 by 2, 8 by 3, or 6 by 4. Even two negative numbers work, because when you multiply two negatives, you get a positive number. Because you can't tell, for the moment leave the Last spot in each parenthesis open.

- ✔ **Look at the middle term.** The numbers that you're looking for to put into the parentheses along with the x's need to add up to the value of the middle term. Of the aforementioned pairs, 24 and 1 give you 25 (too big), 12 and 2 give you 14 (too big), 8 and 3 give you 11 (still too big), and 6 and 4 give you 10 (perfect!). Now you know that you need 6 and 4 in the spots: $x^2 + 10x + 24 = (x+6)(x+4)$. Keep in mind that if the numbers in the parentheses are negative, adding up may actually mean subtracting!

Memorize the two FOIL equations earlier in this section, because when you see the result, you already know the factors. Every second you save gives you more time to work on another problem.

Just for practice, try this question:

6. The expression $x^2 - 2x - 15$ is equivalent to

 (A) $x(x-2)$

 (B) $(x-2)(x-15)$

 (C) $(x+3)(x-5)$

 (D) $(x-3)(x+5)$

 (E) $(x+15)(x-1)$

Now check your answer:

6. **C.** You know that the first term is x^2, so you may as well set up your parentheses for anti-FOILing with x's in them: $(x+?)(x+?)$. You know that the last term is –15, so the second numbers in the parentheses must multiply to –15. Your choices are 1 and –15, –1 and 15, 3 and –5, or –3 and 5. Already, Choices (A) and (B) are out of contention. You can quickly check the outer and inner terms of the remaining choices to determine the answer or look at the middle term (–2x) and see that the two numbers you're looking for must add to –2. The only numbers that fit that condition are 3 and –5, so Choice (C) is the answer!

Balancing Act: Solving Equations

An equation is a balancing act. Think of the equal sign as the support for a seesaw. When you work on an equation, you want to keep the sides of the seesaw balanced. So whatever you do to one side of the equation, you have to do to the other side also. Here's what I mean. Suppose you open Section 2 of the PSAT/NMSQT and see this question:

If $5\left(\dfrac{x}{y}\right) + 5 = 45$, what is the value of $\dfrac{x}{y}$?

(A) 2

(B) 4

(C) 6

(D) 8

(E) 10

That equation may look big and nasty, but it isn't. You know that the side to the right of the equal sign is 45, so the other side must also be 45. The left side of the equation is just written differently. You can solve this problem in a few ways:

✔ **Backsolving:** Take one of the answers — Choice (C) is often a good place to start — and substitute that answer in the equation. So place 6 into the spot where $\left(\dfrac{x}{y}\right)$ appears. Okay, $5 \times 6 = 30$. Add 5 and you have 35 — too little. Try something bigger, such as Choice (D). Now you have 5×8, which gives you 40. Add 5 and you have 45. You're there! The answer is Choice (D). (For more on backsolving, check out Chapter 6.)

✔ **Plugging in:** Suppose this problem is a grid-in, with no multiple-choice answers. No worries! Pick a likely number. You can't go too high, because you have to multiply by 5 and then add 5. How about 4? No, $5 \times 4 = 20$, and when you add 5 more, you're only at 25. You need something bigger. How about 7? Now you have 5×7, which is 35, but adding 5 takes you only to 40. The next number up, 8, is what you want. (For more on plugging in, see Chapter 6.)

✔ **Isolate what you need to solve:** In this question, you're supposed to find the value of $\left(\dfrac{x}{y}\right)$, so your goal is to isolate it on one side of the equation. Remember, you have to do the same thing to each side. First, subtract 5 from each side. Now you have $5\left(\dfrac{x}{y}\right) = 45 - 5$, or 40. Now divide each side by 5, and you get $\left(\dfrac{x}{y}\right) = 8$, which is your answer.

Notice that you never have to deal with the fact that the element you're asked to find is a fraction. The test-makers like to throw some extra information at you to see whether you can focus on the real question.

On the PSAT/NMSQT, expect to see equations with absolute value, exponents, and square roots in them. I explain absolute value in Chapter 7. For more information about exponents and square roots (radicals), see "Appealing to a Higher Power: Exponents and Radicals" earlier in this chapter.

Toughen up your equation-solving muscles with these problems:

7. Solve for x. $2x^2 + 6 = 38$

(A) ± 4

(B) $\pm\sqrt{13}$

(C) $\pm\sqrt{22}$

(D) ± 22

(E) ± 32

8. Solve for x. $|x + 5| = 2x + 5$

(A) $-\frac{10}{3}$ only

(B) 0 only

(C) 5 only

(D) 0 or $-\frac{10}{3}$

(E) 0 or 5

9. If $9 = \sqrt{x - 3}$, then $x =$

(A) 0

(B) 6

(C) 18

(D) 78

(E) 84

10. Solve the equation for $\frac{a}{b}$: $6x + \frac{3a}{b} = 12$

(A) $4 - 2x$

(B) $4 - 6x$

(C) 6

(D) $6 - 3x$

(E) $12 - 6x$

Now check your answers:

7. **A.** Don't let the x^2 make you nervous; just isolate it from the rest of the equation, and then worry about it. First, subtract 6 from both sides: $2x^2 = 32$. Then divide both sides by 2: $x^2 = 16$. You can see that x needs to be 4 or –4 to become 16 when squared. Choice (A) is your answer. Remember, you can always choose to backsolve with questions like these!

8. **B.** Backsolving is a great idea here. You have only three numbers to try! Plug in 0 first. That gives you 5 = 5, so you know that 0 must be a possible answer. You can eliminate Choices (A) and (C). Now plug in 5, and you get 10 = 15. Nope! Eliminate Choice (E). If you plug in $-\frac{10}{3}$, you get $\frac{5}{3} = -\frac{5}{3}$, which is clearly wrong. Choice (B) is the answer.

9. **E.** Your first step should be to square both sides so that the square root goes away. After squaring, your equation is $81 = x - 3$, so you add 3 to both sides, and voilà! Choice (E), 84, is your answer!

10. **A.** The goal here is to isolate $\frac{a}{b}$, so first subtract $6x$ from each side of the equation. Now you have $3\frac{a}{b} = 12 - 6x$. Now divide each side by 3, which gives you $\frac{a}{b} = 4 - 2x$, also known as Choice (A).

The Spice of Life: Direct and Inverse Variation

Not every algebra problem on the PSAT/NMSQT is an equation. You may need to find out what happens to one quantity when it *varies directly* or *inversely* in relation to another quantity. No sweat. You already know how to solve these problems.

Direct variation questions are just ratios in disguise. (I discuss ratios in detail in Chapter 7.) To solve a problem in which two quantities (say, a and b) vary directly, remember that the ratio of a to b is a constant. (Which constant? That's probably what the question wants you to find out.) Set up a ratio with the original values of a and b marked with the subscript 1 and the new values marked with a 2:

$$\frac{a_1}{b_1} = \frac{a_2}{b_2}$$

Now you can cross-multiply and solve. Here's the ratio for this question: At my last party, the number of balloons inflated (12) varied directly with the number of balloons popped before the party even began (8). How many balloons will pop before my next party if I inflate 36 balloons? Okay, call the balloons inflated a_1 and the balloons popped b_1. So a_1 is 12 and b_1 is 8. Your ratio is then

$$\frac{12}{8} = \frac{36}{b_2}$$

When you cross-multiply, you get

$$288 = 12b_2$$

Now divide each side of the equation by 12, and you get $24 = b_2$. Your answer is 24 deflated, garbage-ready balloons.

Notice that when one variable increases, the other variable does too. You can eliminate some choices quickly if you remember this fact about direct variation.

Now for inverse variation. Here the product of the two variables (say, a and b) is always the same number, or **constant.** So if $a = 7$ and $b = 9$, the constant is 7×9 or 63. So if a is 3, b must be 21, because $3 \times 21 = 63$. If the number of balloons destroyed by ripping or puncturing before the party varies inversely, I may lose 7 to rips and 9 to punctures, or 3 to rips and 21 to punctures. Either way my party will be lacking in decorations.

I can't let you go without a little practice. Try these!

11. The number of word problems a math teacher assigns varies directly with the number of questions she is asked during class. She assigned 6 word problems on Monday after 15 questions were asked. If 20 questions were asked on Wednesday, how many word problems did she assign?

    (A) 4

    (B) 6

    (C) 8

    (D) 10

    (E) 15

12. The values of p and q vary inversely. When p has a value of 8, q has a value of 10. What is the value of p when q is 4?

    (A) 2

    (B) 5

    (C) 10

    (D) 20

    (E) 40

    Now check your answers:

11. **C.** Remember, direct variation means that the ratio is constant, so set up an equation: $\frac{6}{15} = \frac{?}{20}$. You can either cross-multiply to solve or see that the first fraction reduces down to $\frac{2}{5}$, meaning that for every 5 questions, the teacher assigns 2 word problems. This means that when the teacher hears 20 questions (4×5), she'll assign $4 \times 2 = 8$ word problems, Choice (C).

12. **D.** When you're dealing with variables that vary inversely, always remember that multiplication is the key. No matter what p and q are, they should always multiply to the same value. The given values, 8 and 10, multiply to 80, so all p-q pairs should multiply to 80. When q is 4, p must be $(80 \div 4) = 20$, Choice (D).

Function (al) Literacy

Functions are like computers. You input something, x, and something else comes out. The variable, x, can change. (That's why it's called a variable!) Every time x changes, so does the result. You can express functions in different ways. You start with a long, graceful f. Then you have something in parenthesis, usually x. This expression reads as *eff of ex*. Some functions look like equations:

$$f(x) = -3x + 8$$

The difference between this function and another equation is that you can plug anything into the variable spot and end up with another correct answer. In other words, the numbers in functions come in pairs. Which brings me to another way that functions are written: charts. Here's a chart of some values of the preceding function:

x	*f(x)*
1	5
2	2
3	−1

I could continue, plopping in negative numbers and all sorts of things, but I won't bore you. Instead, I'll move on to another way that a function may appear: as a graph. Here's a graph of the preceding function:

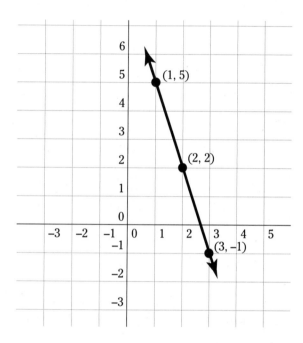

For the PSAT/NMSQT, you need to get up close and personal with *linear* and *quadratic* functions. You've probably drawn a zillion linear functions when you created graphs. The linear function you're most likely to run into on the exam is $f(x) = mx + b$. In graphs, *m* is the slope of the line — the amount that the line moves forward and either up or down. The *b* is where the line cuts across, or *intersects,* the *y*-axis. Here's a typical PSAT/NMSQT question about linear functions:

Which of the following charts represents a linear function?

(A)			(B)			(C)			(D)			(E)	
x	*y*		*x*	*y*		*x*	*y*		*x*	*y*		*x*	*y*
−2	−2		−2	3		−2	10		−2	1		−2	1
−1	−4		−1	0		−1	8		−1	3		−1	2
1	4		1	0		1	4		1	5		1	1
2	2		2	3		2	2		2	7		2	2
4	1		4	15		4	−2		4	9		4	1

First, remember that *linear function* really just means that the function is a straight line when you graph it, which means that it has a constant slope. One way to solve this problem is to think about the slope between each pair of points in each chart. In Choice (A), the first two points are (–2, –2) and (–1, –4). You can think of slope as *rise over run* or as *change in y over change in x*. In this case, when x gets 1 bigger (from –2 to –1), y gets 2 smaller (from –2 to –4), meaning that the slope is $\frac{-2}{1} = -2$. Now compare the next two points, (–1, –4) and (1, 4). In this case, x gets 2 bigger and y gets 8 bigger, making a slope of $\frac{8}{2} = 4$. Different slope, so these three points don't make a line. Onward to Choice (B)! The first two points, (–2, 3) and (–1, 0), have a slope of –3, and the next two points, (–1, 0) and (1, 0), have a slope of 0. Now check out Choice (C): The slope between (–2, 10) and (–1, 8) is –2 and between (–1, 8) and (1, 4) is also –2. Ooh! Keep going to see whether –2 is the slope for the next points as well: (1, 4) and (2, 2) have a slope of –2, and (2, 2) and (4, –2) also have a slope of –2. Success! Choice (C) is the right one.

Linear functions appear in the world, too, not just on the exam. For example, the fare you pay to travel on a train may vary depending on the distance you go. In a particular city, your subway fare depends on how many stops you travel. You pay 50 cents for any ride and then an additional 25 cents for each stop that you travel. You can model the cost of a subway ride as $c = 0.50 + 0.25x$, where c is the cost of the ride, and x is the number of stops that you travel.

Ready to try some function questions? Here you go:

13. If $y = -\frac{1}{2}x + 3$, which of these points lies on the line?

   (A) (–1, 5)

   (B) (0, 2)

   (C) (1, 3)

   (D) (2, 2)

   (E) (4, 2)

14. What is the equation of the line passing through the points (1, 5) and (3, 6)?

   (A) $y = -\frac{1}{2}x + 3$

   (B) $y = \frac{1}{2}x + 4$

   (C) $y = \frac{1}{2}x + \frac{9}{2}$

   (D) $y = 2x + 4$

   (E) $y = 2x + \frac{9}{2}$

Now check your answers:

13. **D.** For each ordered pair, just plug the x-value into the x in the equation and see whether the y-value that pops out matches the y-value in the ordered pair. If it does, you found your answer! One trick here is to see that x will be divided by 2, so any odd x-value won't have a whole number y-value paired with it, which eliminates Choices (A) and (C). Testing Choice (B) is easy — plug in x = 0 and you get y = 3, not the y-value in the answer. In Choice (D), you plug in x = 2 and get y = 2 as the output — exactly what you're hoping for! Choice (D) it is.

14. **C.** Your first step should be to find the slope of the line: $\frac{\text{change in } y}{\text{change in } x} = \frac{6-5}{3-1} = \frac{1}{2}$, which narrows your answers down to Choice (B) or (C). To determine which answer it is, plug 1 in for x and check whether the y value that pops out is 5. Checking Choice (B): $\frac{1}{2}(1) + 4 = \frac{9}{2}$, wrong answer. Check Choice (C): $\frac{1}{2}(1) + \frac{9}{2} = \frac{10}{2} = 5$, the number you want!

Quadratic functions show up as *y* = *ax*² + *bx* + *c* or *f(x)* = *ax*² + *bx* + *c*. You don't have to do much with quadratic functions, just interpret graphs. (They look like the nose of an airplane, looking down from above.)

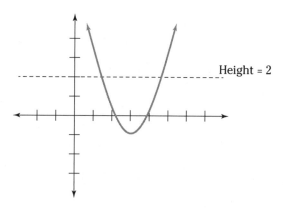

When you're dealing with a quadratic function, remember these rules:

✔ The **roots** or **zeros** of a function are the points where the graph crosses the *x*-axis (the horizontal line). At those spots, *f(x)* = 0.

✔ You may be asked about how often a function equals a specific value — say, where *f(x)* = *a*. The letter *a* stands for the height of the line that is passing through the graph. In the sample graph, the function reaches a height of 2 above the *x*-axis in two places, so the equation *f(x)* = 2 has two solutions.

✔ If you add a number to a function, you move the graph up. So if your function is *f(x)* + 10, the graph moves up 10 units. Subtracting a number moves the graph down. So *f(x)* – 10 moves the graph down 10 units. Notice that the addition or subtraction is *to* the function, not *in* the function.

✔ If you add to *x* (now you're *inside* the little parenthesis that follows the function sign), the graph moves that many units to the left. So *f(x* + 10) goes left 10 units. If you subtract from *x* (again, you're *inside* the parenthesis following the function sign), you move right. So *f(x* – 10) goes 10 units to the right.

You want to be perfect, right? Well, practice with these questions:

15. In the graph of *f(x)* shown here, what are the solutions to *f(x)* = –2?

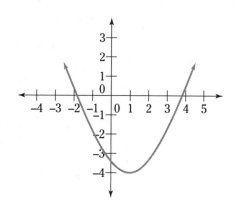

(A) –4

(B) –2.5 and 4.5

(C) –2 and 4

(D) –1 and 3

(E) 1

16. How does the graph of $f(x) - 2$ compare to the graph of $f(x)$?

(A) The graphs look the same.

(B) $f(x) - 2$ looks like $f(x)$ shifted down by 2.

(C) $f(x) - 2$ looks like $f(x)$ shifted left by 2.

(D) $f(x) - 2$ looks like $f(x)$ shifted right by 2.

(E) $f(x) - 2$ looks like $f(x)$ stretched vertically by a factor of 2.

17. In the graph of $f(x)$ shown here, which answer choice best represents the graph of $f(x - 3)$?

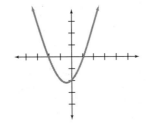

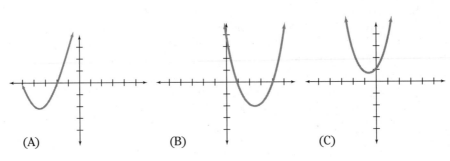

(A)   (B)   (C)

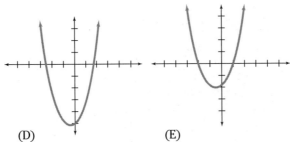

(D)   (E)

Now check your answers:

15. **D.** Look to see where the *y*-value of the graph is –2. It may help to sketch a horizontal line onto the page at *y* = –2 and then see where the horizontal line crosses the original graph:

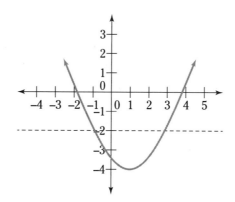

After you have that line drawn in, it's much easier to see that the *x*-coordinates of those points of intersection are at –1 and 3, Choice (D).

16. **B.** This question is all about understanding *transformations* (movements and stretches) of graphs. Remember: *f(x)* always represents the *y*-coordinate of a point, so you can rewrite any point *(x, y)* as *(x, f(x))*. This means that *f(x)* – 2 is subtracting 2 units from the *y*-value of the original graph; in other words, moving it down. Choice (B) is the one you want.

17. **B.** Remember: When you add to or subtract from *x* (inside the parentheses of the function), you move the function left or right. In this case, 3 is subtracted from *x*, meaning that the new graph is 3 units to the right, looking like Choice (B).

One more thing about graphing questions: Sometimes the PSAT/NMSQT doesn't give you a graph to look at. Instead, you're given two points and asked about the graph that would connect them. To solve these problems, you have to know three formulas:

✔ The slope of the line connecting points (x_1, y_1) and (x_2, y_2) is $\frac{y_2 - y_1}{x_2 - x_1}$.

✔ The distance between points (x_1, y_1) and (x_2, y_2) is $\sqrt{(x_2 - x_1)^2 + (y_2 - y_1)^2}$.

✔ The midpoint of the line that connects (x_1, y_1) and (x_2, y_2) is $\left(\frac{x_2 + x_1}{2}, \frac{y_2 + y_1}{2} \right)$.

Try these formulas with the points (–2, 4) and (4, –8):

✔ Slope = $\frac{-8 - 4}{4 - (-2)} = \frac{-12}{6} = -2$

✔ Distance = $\sqrt{(4 - (-2))^2 + (-8 - 4)^2} = \sqrt{36 + 144} = \sqrt{180} = \sqrt{9 \cdot 4 \cdot 5} = 6\sqrt{5}$

✔ Midpoint = $\left(\frac{4 + (-2)}{2}, \frac{-8 + 4}{2} \right) = \left(\frac{2}{2}, \frac{-4}{2} \right) = (1, -2)$

Are you still functioning? Good. Then you can solve these problems:

18. What is the slope of the line passing through the origin and the point (6, –3)?

(A) –3

(B) –2

(C) $-\frac{1}{2}$

(D) $\frac{1}{2}$

(E) 2

19. What is the distance between the *y*-intercept of the line $y = \frac{2}{3}x + 2$ and the point (–3, –2)?

(A) 2

(B) 3

(C) 4

(D) 5

(E) 6

20. Determine the midpoint of $(a, -b)$ and $(3a, 3b)$.

(A) $(a, -2b)$

(B) $(a, -b)$

(C) (a, b)

(D) $(2a, b)$

(E) $(2a, 2b)$

Now check your answers:

18. **B.** First, make sure that you remember that the coordinates of the origin are (0, 0), and then use the slope formula! $\frac{y_2 - y_1}{x_2 - x_1} = \frac{6 - 0}{-3 - 0} = \frac{6}{-3} = -2$. Choice (B) is your answer.

19. **D.** Hopefully you remember that when a line is in $y = mx + b$ form, it's really easy to find the *y*-intercept — it's just the value of *b*! That means that the *y*-intercept of the line given in the equation is 2, or the point (0, 2). Now that you know the point's coordinates, you can plug everything into the distance formula: $\sqrt{(-3-0)^2 + (-2-2)^2}$, $\sqrt{9+16} = 5$, or Choice (D).

20. **D.** Midpoint formula to the rescue! $\left(\frac{3a+a}{2}, \frac{3b+(-b)}{2}\right) = \left(\frac{4a}{2}, \frac{2b}{2}\right) = (2a, b)$; your answer is Choice (D).

Heading into Weirdness: Symbols

Because the test-makers want to be sure that you understand the principles of math, they throw in some strange symbols that they made up. With an only-for-the-test symbol, you can't use a formula that you've memorized. You have to tap into the underlying logic of mathematical operations. These symbols show up in functions, as in this question:

If $\%(a) = a^2 - 3$, then what is the value of $\%(-2)$?

(A) -7

(B) -5

(C) -3

(D) -1

(E) 1

Choice (E) is the one you want. Don't let these symbol problems make you nervous; they're all about substitution. To determine the value of $\%(-2)$, just plug -2 into the original equation wherever you see a: $\%(-2) = (-2)^2 - 3 = 4 - 3 = 1$.

I can't let you go without hitting you with some symbol practice:

21. Let $\langle a, b \rangle = \frac{1}{2}a + b^2$. Which of the following is equal to $\langle -2, -1 \rangle$?

(A) $\langle -8, 2 \rangle$

(B) $\langle -4, 2 \rangle$

(C) $\langle 0, 2 \rangle$

(D) $\langle 1, 1 \rangle$

(E) $\langle 2, -2 \rangle$

22. If $*x = 2x - x^2$, what is the value of $*4$?

(A) -14

(B) -8

(C) 0

(D) 4

(E) 8

Now check your answers:

21. **A.** Your first step should be to calculate the value of $\langle -2, -1 \rangle$, which you can do using substitution: $\langle -2, -1 \rangle = \frac{1}{2}(-2) + (-1)^2 = -1 + 1 = 0$. From there you can either try out each of the answer choices or cleverly notice that the answer that works will have a negative a value that's twice as big as the square of the b value. Choice (A) is the one that works. You can check it: $\langle -8, 2 \rangle = \frac{1}{2}(-8) + 2^2 = -4 + 4 = 0$.

22. **B.** Substitution, yet again, is the key. Wherever you see an x in the original equation, replace it with a 4: $*4 = 2(4) - (4)^2 = 8 - 16 = -8$, Choice (B).

Chapter 9

Getting in Shape for Geometry Questions

In This Chapter

▶ Employing the best techniques for geometry questions

▶ Dealing with triangles, squares, rectangles, and other shapes

▶ Answering questions about circles

▶ Calculating volume and surface area

*B*etween 25 percent and 30 percent of PSAT/NMSQT math concerns geometry, but you don't have to state theorems or write proofs, as you probably do in your math class. (Did I just hear a sign of relief?) Instead, the test-makers hit you with simpler material, such as figuring out the value of angles and calculating area, perimeter, or volume. Never fear: If you read this chapter carefully and work through the sample problems, you'll be well prepared for PSAT/NMSQT geometry.

Technically, graphing falls under the category of geometry, but graphs overlap with data interpretation. If your graph-reading skills need a touch-up, turn to Chapter 10.

Back to the Drawing Board: Approaching Geometry Problems

This chapter is about math, not art, but you should pretend you're Rembrandt when you hit a geometry question on the PSAT/NMSQT. Why? Because geometry concerns shapes and lines, and if you can see them, you can understand them better. Follow these steps:

✔ **Examine the diagram, if the question has one.** The little drawings on the exam are a good starting place. Look at the information they provide and notice every number and variable (45°, 2 feet, *x,* and so forth).

The drawings on the PSAT/NMSQT are as accurate as possible, but they can deceive you. Something may look like a right angle, for instance, but not actually be one. Check the question; it may state that *ABD* is a right angle or include a little square drawn in the angle. You may also see one of these right-angle symbols: ⊥, ∟. But don't assume anything! Rely on the information given and your knowledge of math, not on an estimate.

Some diagrams are labeled *not drawn to scale.* If you see that phrase, be extra careful. The drawings *don't* give you an idea of relative length or size.

✔ **If no diagram appears, sketch one in the test booklet.** Don't take time for museum-ready quality. Just be sure that you have everything in the right place.

✔ **Read the information supplied by the question, calculate if necessary, and add everything you can to the diagram.** If the question tells you that one angle is twice as large as another and the smaller angle is labeled 30°, label the bigger angle 60°.

✔ **Search for basic shapes hidden inside more complicated diagrams.** You may see a triangle with one side extended like a flagpole, for example. So? It's still a triangle! Everything you know about triangles still applies. Plus, the "flagpole" may supply extra information, such as the measurement of an angle *outside* the triangle. Because straight lines always equal 180°, you can sometimes figure out the angle *inside* the triangle by looking at the angle *outside* the triangle.

✔ **Reread the question and identify what the test-makers want to know.** Are you looking for the length of side *b* or trying to find out what number can't possibly represent the length of side *b?* If you answer the wrong question, your math skills won't matter.

As you read the question, underline key words that indicate what you have to figure out. In the preceding bullet, for example, you might underline "can't" and "length of side *b*." The underlining focuses your attention on your goal.

✔ **Use the formula box only as a reminder.** Because they have kind hearts and aren't *actually* trying to torture you, the question-writers provide a little box of information at the beginning of each math section. (A copy of the information box appears in Chapter 6.) The box tells you the number of degrees in a circle, straight line, and triangle. It also supplies formulas for area and volume, the Pythagorean theorem, and the measurements of special right triangles. If you're nervous, peek at the box to check on these basics. However, you may be pressed for time, and turning back to find formulas can eat up precious seconds. Your goal, which you can reach by working through this chapter, is to know this information *before* you receive the test booklet.

Mathematicians love specialized terms almost as much as grammarians do. (Trust me. I'm a grammarian, and I *know*.) The good news is that you don't need to know many terms to solve PSAT/NMSQT geometry problems. A few basic words, which I define in this chapter, will get you through. So even though your math teacher throws around words such as *scalene triangle,* you don't have to memorize the fact that a scalene triangle has three unequal sides.

Playing Every Angle

When two lines meet, they go out for dinner and . . . oops, that's life, not math. Let me try again: When two lines meet they form an angle. Angles are measured in degrees. On the PSAT/NMSQT, you won't find any negative or zero angles, and you probably won't have to deal with fractional angles either (no 45.9°, for example). You do have to know these basic facts:

✔ **A right angle measures 90°.** Right angles are a *very* big deal because they show up in a lot of formulas. If you see one, pay attention.

✔ **The sum of angles around a point is 360°.** Think of the lines forming a circle around a center point. *Note:* This fact appears in the information box on the exam.

✔ **A straight-line angle equals 180°.** Earlier I said that an angle is formed when two lines meet. When those lines meet head-on, they create a *straight-line angle,* which just sits there looking like a straight line. If a line cuts through a straight line, the two angles formed are **supplementary** or **supplemental,** math terms that mean the two angles add up to 180°.

✔ **Angles opposite each other are equal.** These angles are also called **vertical angles.** In this diagram, *x* and *y* are vertical angles.

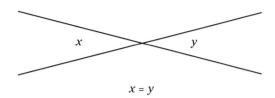

$x = y$

You may see the phrase *vertical angles* in a test question. Don't assume that vertical angles are standing up just because in other contexts *vertical* means *upright.* Vertical angles are opposite each other, regardless of whether they're up and down or side by side.

✔ **If a line cuts through parallel lines, the small angles at one intersection measure the same as the small angles at the other intersection.** Similarly, the big angles at one intersection equal the big angles at the other intersection. Take a look at this sketch:

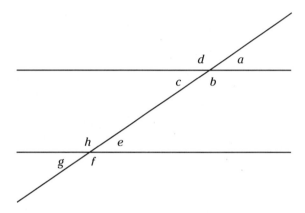

The small angles at the first intersection are *a* and *c,* and the small angles at the second intersection are *e* and *g.* All these angles are equal. So are the bigger angles: *b* and *d* and *f* and *h.* By the way, equal angles are called ***congruent*** in math-speak.

You won't be quizzed on this information, but you may have to use it in a problem. Take a look at this question:

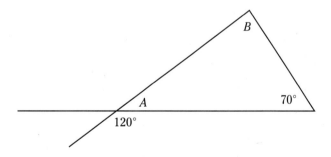

Suppose you're asked to find *B.* A straight line equals 180°, so you can find *A* by subtracting 120° from 180°, which gives you 60°. You also know that the three angles of a triangle add up to 180°, so 60° + 70° + *B* = 180°. Therefore, *B* = 50°.

Your turn. Try these problems:

1. In the following figure, lines *l* and *m* are parallel. Determine the value of *x*.

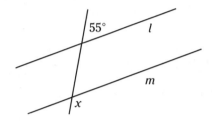

(A) 55°

(B) 75°

(C) 95°

(D) 125°

(E) 155°

2. Determine the measure of angle *a*.

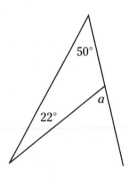

(A) 22°

(B) 33°

(C) 50°

(D) 72°

(E) 108°

3. Find the value of *x* in the following figure.

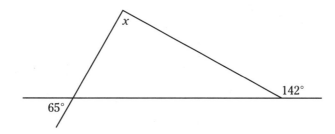

(A) 65°

(B) 77°

(C) 90°

(D) 103°

(E) 142°

Now check your answers.

1. **D.** Remember that lines cutting parallel lines form a whole bunch of equal angles. The small angles that the cut forms are all equal (in this problem, each is 55°), and all the large angles are also equal (in this problem, they equal *x*). You can see that the 55° angle is supplementary to a large angle, so the two angles must add up to 180°. Subtract: 180° – 55° = 125°, so all the large angles, including *x*, must measure 125°, Choice (D).

2. **D.** You know that there are 180° in a triangle, so you can find the third angle in the triangle using subtraction: 180° – 50° – 22° = 108°. Now that you know that, you can see that 108° is supplemental to *a*, so *a* = 180° – 108° = 72°, or Choice (D).

3. **B.** Yet again, the key to this problem is knowing that there are 180° in a triangle. You know that the angle on the bottom left of the triangle measures 65° because it's a vertical angle with the angle labeled 65°. You know that the angle on the bottom right of the triangle measures 38° because it's supplementary to the 142° angle that's labeled. To find *x*, simply subtract those numbers from 180°: 180° – 65° – 38° = 77°, Choice (B).

Conquering the Eternal Triangle

The PSAT/NMSQT *loves* triangles, so you need to develop a little affection for them also. Fortunately, triangles are easy to love. In the following section I deal with triangle basics. Then, in the section "Taking a closer look at right triangles," I pay extra attention to right triangles because they appear frequently on the exam.

Brushing up on triangle basics

Here are the facts about triangles:

- ✔ **The angles inside a triangle add up to 180°.** If you know two angles, you can figure out the third. *Note:* This fact appears in the information box on the exam.

- ✔ **The largest angle is opposite the longest side of the triangle.** Can you guess what else is true? The smallest angle is opposite the smallest side of the triangle.

- ✔ **Sides of equal length are opposite equal angles.** So if you have two sides, each of which is x in length, and opposite one of those sides is an angle that measures 45°, then the angle opposite the other side (that's also x in length) will measure 45° as well.

- ✔ **The sum of two sides must be greater than the length of the third side.** If two sides of the triangle measure 4 and 6, the third side must be less than 10. This is the *triangle inequality rule*.

- ✔ **The sides of similar triangles are in proportion.** If you see a question referring to similar triangles, use your ratio skills to figure out the length of a side. (For more information on ratios, turn to Chapter 7.) For example, suppose two similar triangles are in a ratio of 3:4, with the longest side of the smaller triangle measuring 30 meters. The longest side of the larger triangle is therefore 40 meters. The heights and bases of similar triangles are also in proportion.

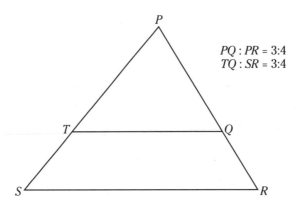

$PQ : PR = 3{:}4$
$TQ : SR = 3{:}4$

- ✔ **The ratio of the area of similar triangles equals the square of the ratio of their sides.** If each side of triangle *ABC* is ½ the length of each side of triangle *DEF*, the area of triangle *ABC* is ¼ of the area of triangle *DEF*, because $(\frac{1}{2})^2 = \frac{1}{4}$.

This section is about triangles, but the rules for similarity work for other shapes also, as long as their angles are equal and their sides are in proportion (angle to angle, side to side).

Remember that the diagrams on the PSAT/NMSQT can fool you. Unless the question *says* that the shapes are similar or you see that the triangles share angles, assume that the shapes you see *aren't* similar.

- ✔ **The area of a triangle = ½ base × the height.** *Note:* This formula is in the information box on the exam. The height of a triangle (also known as the **altitude**) may be a side (in a right triangle, as I explain in the next section) or it may be a line drawn **perpendicular** (at right angles) to the base of the triangle from the angle opposite the base. Or, in extremely rare and strange problems, the height may be outside the triangle, in which case it's drawn as a broken line. In the following figure, h is the height of each triangle. Notice the little square that indicates a right angle.

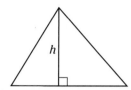 

Time to road-test these ideas. Try these four problems, all dealing with triangles.

4. In the following figure, triangle *BCD* is similar to triangle *ACE,* and the ratio of the length of *AB* to *BC* is 1:2. If the area of triangle *BCD* is 8, then what is the area of triangle *ACE?*

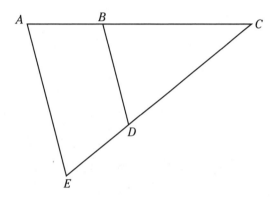

(A) 10

(B) 12

(C) 14

(D) 16

(E) 18

5. Two sides of a triangle are 3 and 5 units long. Which of the following *can't* be the length of the third side?

(A) 2

(B) 3

(C) 4

(D) 5

(E) 6

6. What is the perimeter of triangle *ABC*?

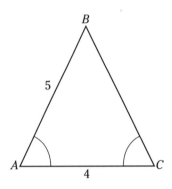

(A) 7

(B) $2\sqrt{21}$

(C) 14

(D) $4\sqrt{12}$

(E) 21

7. If the area of triangle *ACD* is 12, and the length of side *AC* is 6, what is the length of segment *BD?*

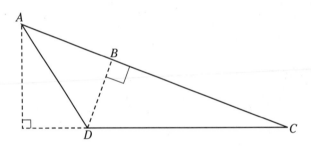

(A) 2

(B) 3

(C) 4

(D) 5

(E) 6

Now check your answers.

4. **E.** Remember that the ratio of the area of similar triangles is the square of the ratio of the lengths. Make sure that you notice the trick here: You're given the ratio of *AB* to *BC*, not *BC* to *AC*. It's easy to figure out the correct ratio, but if you miss that detail, you'll be derailed. *BC:AC* = 2:3, so the area ratio is 4:9. If the smaller triangle has an area of 8, then the larger triangle has an area of 18 (so that the ratio reduces from 8:18 to 4:9). Choice (E) is the one you want.

5. **A.** This one is easy if you know the triangle inequality rule: "The sum of two sides must be greater than the length of the third side." At first glance, all you know is that the third side must be shorter than 3 + 5 = 8 units long, but that fact doesn't narrow down the answer

choices, because none of them are too long. So you have to look for side lengths that are too short. Because you're trying to find something that's too small, start by plugging in Choice (A). If the third side were 2 units long, then 2 + 3 = 5, but the other side is 5 units long, so 2 is not long enough! Choice (A) is correct.

6. **C.** Angles *A* and *C* are equal, meaning that triangle *ABC* is an isosceles triangle. That means that side *AB* is the same length as side *BC*, so the perimeter of the triangle is 4 + 5 + 5 = 14, Choice (C).

7. **C.** The trick to this problem is that you can look at segment *AC* as the base of the triangle and *BD* as the height. After you've got that figured out, you're most of the way to the correct answer. Remember that the area equals $\frac{1}{2}bh$, so you can plug everything into that equation and solve for *h*: $12 = \frac{1}{2}(6)h$, $12 = 3h$, $h = 4$, Choice (C).

Taking a closer look at right triangles

The Greeks weren't the only mathematicians in the ancient world, but they managed to place their "brand" on *geometry,* a word which, by the way, comes from the Greek words for "earth measure." Specifically, a mathematician named Pythagoras wrote the Pythagorean theorem:

$$a^2 + b^2 = c^2$$

You can use this formula to find the sides of any right triangle, in which *a* and *b* are defined as the two legs of the triangle and *c* is the **hypotenuse,** a fancy word for the side opposite the 90° angle. *Note:* This formula — the Pythagorean theorem — appears in the information box on the exam.

A few common right-triangle ratios are frequent fliers on the PSAT/NMSQT, so it's worth memorizing them:

- ✔ **The 3:4:5 triangle:** The sides can be any multiple of these numbers (for example, 15:20:25, with each side multiplied by 5, or 21:28:35, with each side multiplied by 7).

- ✔ **The 5:12:13 triangle:** Strange numbers, huh? But this ratio behaves like any other, so you can multiply each side by 2 and get a 10:24:26 triangle, or multiply by 5 and get a 25:60:65 triangle.

- ✔ **The $s:s:s\sqrt{2}$ triangle:** The *s* stands for a side, and because you have two sides that are equal (both are *s*), this is an **isosceles right triangle,** and the interior angles are 45°, 45°, and 90° *Note:* This formula appears in the information box on the exam.

Although I'm in triangle-land here, I should point out that you can use the information in the preceding bullet to calculate the **diagonal** (a line connecting opposite corners) of a square. If the sides of a square are 65 meters long, the diagonal is $65\sqrt{2}$. You can easily see why this formula works: A square is just two isosceles right triangles glued together, because each side of a square is the same length.

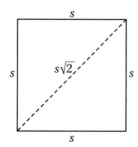

✔ **The $s : s\sqrt{3} : 2s$ triangle:** This one has 30°-60°-90° angles, and for some reason, the exam-writers love it. The hypotenuse (the long side) is double the length of the side opposite the 30° angle. *Note:* This formula appears in the information box on the exam.

If you cut an *equilateral triangle* (one with equal sides) in half, you get two 30°-60°-90° triangles. So if you see a question on the exam about an equilateral triangle, drag out this formula and you'll find the answer in a flash.

Stretch those triangular muscles! Try these problems:

8. An equilateral triangle has a side with a length of x. What is the area of the triangle, in terms of x?

   (A) $\frac{1}{2}x^2$

   (B) $\frac{\sqrt{3}}{4}x^2$

   (C) $\frac{\sqrt{3}}{2}x^2$

   (D) x^2

   (E) $x^2\sqrt{3}$

9. What is the area of the following figure?

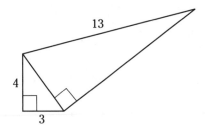

   (A) 6

   (B) 15

   (C) 32

   (D) 36

   (E) 42

10. In the following square, the product of diagonals *AC* and *BD* is 18. What is the perimeter of triangle *ABC*?

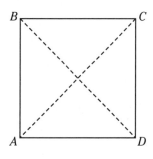

(A) $6 + 3\sqrt{2}$

(B) $9 + 3\sqrt{2}$

(C) 18

(D) 24

(E) 36

Now check your answers.

8. **B.** Always draw a picture if you're having any trouble visualizing a problem:

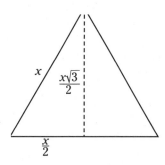

Remember that you can transform all equilateral triangles into a pair of 30°-60°-90° triangles by cutting them in half. That lets you see that the base of one of the smaller triangles is $x/2$, and the height is $\frac{x\sqrt{3}}{2}$, making the area of the whole triangle equal $\frac{1}{2}bh = \frac{1}{2}x\left(\frac{x\sqrt{3}}{2}\right) = \frac{\sqrt{3}}{4}x^2$, Choice (B).

9. **D.** How well do you know your Pythagorean triples? Either way, you can use the Pythagorean theorem to help you solve this problem, or any problem with right triangles. First, look at the small triangle. Its area is $\frac{1}{2}bh = \frac{1}{2}(3)(4) = 6$. Next, you can quickly solve for the hypotenuse using $a^2 + b^2 = c^2$ and determine that it's 5 units long. Pythagorean theorem to the rescue again: $5^2 + b^2 = 13^2$, $b = 12$. That means that the area of the larger triangle is $\frac{1}{2}bh = \frac{1}{2}(12)(5) = 30$. Add those two areas together: 6 + 30 = 36, and you can see that Choice (D) is correct.

10. **A.** Diagonals *AC* and *BD* must be the same length, so they're each $\sqrt{18} = 3\sqrt{2}$ in length. Now you can ignore the square and just pay attention to triangle *ABC,* which is a 45°-45°-90° triangle, with a hypotenuse of $3\sqrt{2}$. Using your knowledge of special triangles (or the formula box), you know that the legs of the triangle must each be 3 units long (because if the leg is *x* units long, the hypotenuse is $x\sqrt{2}$ units long). Therefore, the perimeter of the triangle is $3 + 3 + 3\sqrt{2} = 6 + 3\sqrt{2}$, Choice (A).

Playing with Polygons

A ***polygon*** is a closed, two-dimensional figure with sides made of lines. In other words, a triangle, a square, a rectangle, and any other closed shape you can create by drawing lines is a polygon. Polygons are named according to the number of sides they have: A triangle has three sides (the prefix *tri* means "three"), a ***quadrilateral*** has four, a ***pentagon*** has five, and so on. How high do those numbers go? Well, a ***megagon*** has a million sides, and an ***apeirogon*** has an infinite number of sides. These facts may help you in a trivia contest, but you don't need them for the PSAT/NMSQT. In fact, you don't need vocabulary to handle polygons, just math. In the preceding section I explain triangles. Here I concentrate on polygons with more sides (but no megagons, I promise!). These concepts help you deal with polygons when you encounter them on the exam:

✔ **The sum of the angles inside a four-sided figure equals 360°.** Add up the angles inside a square, rectangle, parallelogram, or any other quadrilateral and you get 360°.

✔ **Squares and rectangles have right angles.** A square has four sides of the same length; a rectangle has two long sides that are equal and two short sides that are equal. Each corner is a right angle (90°). To find the area, multiply length by width. (***Note:*** The area formula is in the information box on the exam.)

✔ **In a parallelogram, the top and bottom sides are parallel and equal, as are the left and right sides.** Technically, squares and rectangles are parallelograms, but you can also have a parallelogram without right angles. Imagine a square or a rectangle slipping sideways (the way furniture does when I try to assemble it). That's a parallelogram. To find the area of a parallelogram, multiply the base by the height. To find the height, measure a perpendicular line from the tallest point to the base, as in this figure:

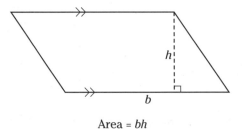

Area = *bh*

Notice that the top and bottom lines in this figure have little double slash marks on them. Those marks tell you that the lines are parallel. When you take the PSAT/NMSQT, don't assume that lines are parallel unless the question tells you so with words or with this symbol.

On the PSAT/NMSQT you may have to find the area of a polygon. (Check the information box if you need help remembering the formulas.) You may also be asked to find the ***perimeter,*** the sum of the lengths of all the sides.

TIP

Often, the easiest way to deal with polygons (especially strangely shaped polygons) is to divide them into triangles, as in this diagram:

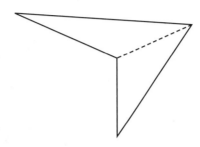

Notice the broken line? It divides this shape into two triangles. Because you know how to figure out the area, perimeter, sides, and angles of a triangle, you can handle whatever you're asked about this figure. (For more information on triangles, see "Conquering the Eternal Triangle" earlier in this chapter.)

TIP

When you divide a polygon into triangles, remember that the sum of the angles in each triangle equals 180°. If you're asked to find the sum of the *interior* (inside) angles of a polygon, multiply the number of triangles by 180°. In the preceding figure, for example, you have two triangles, for a total of 360°.

11. In the following figure, determine the value of $\frac{A+B+C+D+E}{3}$.

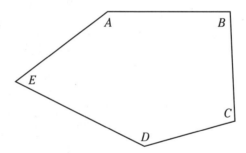

(A) 108°

(B) 120°

(C) 180°

(D) 210°

(E) 540°

12. In parallelogram *ABCD, AB* is parallel to *CD,* and *AB* = *CD* = 6. If the area of parallelogram *ABCD* is 30, how far apart are *AB* and *CD?*

(A) 2.5

(B) 5

(C) 10

(D) 15

(E) 20

13. What is the area of the quadrilateral *ABCD?* Note that sides *AD* and *BC* are parallel.

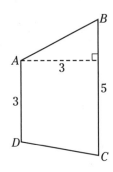

(A) 9

(B) 10

(C) 11

(D) 12

(E) 13

Now check your answers.

11. **C.** You know that there are 180° in a triangle, so pick a corner of the polygon and draw lines to divide it into triangles.

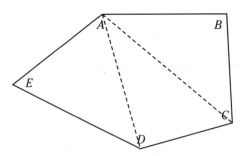

Now it's easy to see that you have three triangles, meaning that the angles add up to $3 \times 180° = 540°$. You want to know what the sum of the angles divided by 3 is, so you're back at 180°, Choice (C).

12. **B.** Draw a picture! After you have your picture, it's easy to see that the distance between *AB* and *CD* is really the height of the parallelogram. To find the area of a parallelogram, you multiply the base by the height, and you already know the area and the base! $A = bh$, $30 = 6h$, $h = 5$, Choice (B).

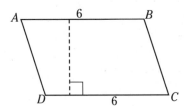

13. **D.** If you happen to know the formula for the area of a trapezoid, you're all set. (It's $\frac{b_1 + b_2}{2} h$, if you were wondering.) If not, you can think of the polygon as a rectangle inserted into a triangle, as deconstructed here:

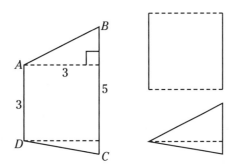

The area of the square is $3 \times 3 = 9$, and the triangle has a base of $5 - 3 = 2$ and a height of 3, making an area of $\frac{1}{2}(2)(3) = 3$. Add those areas together and you get $9 + 3 = 12$, Choice (D).

Going Around in Circles

It's no accident that English contains so many references to circles: *circle* of friends, water *circling* the drain, coming full *circle,* and so forth. Circles are everywhere, especially on the PSAT/NMSQT. When you hit a circle question, remember these facts:

- ✔ **The radius is a straight line from the center of the circle to its edge.** In a test question, the radius is represented by the letter *r.*

- ✔ **The diameter is a straight line from one edge of the circle to another, passing through the center of the circle.** The diameter equals twice the radius.

- ✔ **The circumference of a circle is the distance around its edge.** The formula for circumference is $2\pi r$. The strange symbol is *pi* and equals approximately ²²/₇ or approximately 3.14. Generally, when you're asked to figure out a question with π in it, the answer choices are expressed with π also. You don't need to multiply by ²²/₇ or 3.14 or use the π button on your calculator. *Note:* This formula appears in the information box on the exam.

- ✔ **An arc is any portion of the circumference.** You may be asked to find the length of an arc. No sweat! First, calculate the entire circumference. Next, figure out the ***degree-measure*** of the arc. That's the angle formed when you draw lines from each end of the arc to the center of the circle. Usually, the diagram accompanying the question tells you the degree-measure of the arc, as in this figure:

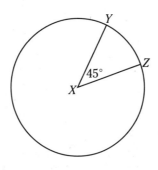

The degree-measure of arc *YZ* is 45°. (If you're not told the degree-measure, the diagram will contain another clue — a triangle or perhaps a vertical angle that allows you to compute the degree-measure. For more information on angles, read "Playing Every Angle" earlier in this chapter.) Don't confuse degree-measure with length. You can have a pizza big enough to fill Times Square or one small enough to fit on a child's plate. A slice of each of those pies may have the same degree-measure, even though you get indigestion after eating the first and hunger pangs after gobbling the second.

Divide the degree-measure by 360. Now you know what fraction of the entire circumference the arc represents. In the preceding figure, divide 45 by 360, which gives you ⅛. Now multiply the circumference by ⅛, and you know how long arc *YZ* is.

You may not be able to determine the circumference of the circle in normal, how-many-feet-of-carpeting-do-I-need numbers. The circumference you calculate may turn out to be 320π, for example. Then, in the preceding example, the arc measures ⅛ of that number, or 40π.

✔ **The area of a circle is** πr^2. In other words, square the radius and multiply the result by π. *Note:* This formula appears in the information box on the exam. You may be asked to find the area of a **sector,** a wedge cut out of the circle like a piece of pie. This kind of problem is as easy as, well, pie. Just find the total area of the circle, divide the degree-measure of the sector by 360, and then multiply the total area of the circle by the result. In the preceding figure, for example, imagine that you had enough information to calculate a total area of 800 square feet. The area of the sector *XYZ* is 800 × ⅛, or 100 square feet. Or, your answer choice may be $\frac{1}{8}\pi r^2$.

Sometimes the PSAT/NMSQT presents you with one shape inside another. Then you have to determine something odd — the area of the shaded portion, perhaps. Don't panic. The question *always* contains enough information to give you an answer. First deal with each shape separately and then figure out how the shapes are related.

Workout time! Try these problems:

14. The area of a circle is 50π. What is the diameter of the circle?

 (A) 5

 (B) $5\sqrt{2}$

 (C) 10

 (D) $10\sqrt{2}$

 (E) 50

15. A wire can be formed into a circle or a square. What is the ratio of the area of the circle to the area of the square?

 (A) 1:4

 (B) 1:3

 (C) 2:π

 (D) 4:π

 (E) 8:π

16. A 14 inch diameter pizza is cut into slices with 30° central angles. Which answer is closest to the combined area of two slices of pizza?

   (A) 8 square inches

   (B) 13 square inches

   (C) 16 square inches

   (D) 19 square inches

   (E) 26 square inches

17. A circle of radius 1 is removed from an equilateral triangle with side lengths of 6. What is the remaining area?

   (A) $9\sqrt{3} - \pi$

   (B) $9\sqrt{3} - \pi/4$

   (C) $9\sqrt{3}$

   (D) $18\sqrt{3} - \pi$

   (E) 24

   Now check your answers.

14. **D.** Remember that the area of a circle is πr^2, so you can solve for the radius: $50\pi = \pi r^2$, $50 = r^2, r = \sqrt{50} = 5\sqrt{2}$. Don't be tricked by Choice (B); remember that you want the diameter, which is twice as long as the radius, or $10\sqrt{2}$, Choice (D).

15. **D.** This is one of those problems that's so much easier if you plug in a number; in this case pick a length for the wire — 4, perhaps. If the wire is 4 units long, then the square it forms is 1 unit long on each side and has an area of 1. Bend the 4 unit long wire into a circle, and the circle's circumference is 4 units. Now you can discover the radius using $C = 2\pi r$, $4 = 2\pi r$, $r = \frac{2}{\pi}$. The area of that circle is $A = \pi r^2 = \pi\left(\frac{2}{\pi}\right)^2 = \frac{4}{\pi}$. The ratio of the area of the circle to the square is $\frac{4}{\pi} : 1$, but that's not an option. Multiply both sides by π, and you get Choice (D).

16. **E.** The pizza's total area has to be $A = \pi r^2$, and the radius is 7 inches (half of the diameter). That means that the area is $\pi(7)^2 = 49\pi \approx 154$ square inches. 30° is $\frac{1}{12}$ of 360°, so the area of one slice is $\frac{1}{12}$ of 154, or about 12.8 square inches. You want the area of two slices, so don't be fooled by Choice (B): 2×12.8 is approximately 25.6 inches, or 26 inches, Choice (E).

17. **A.** First step: Draw a picture.

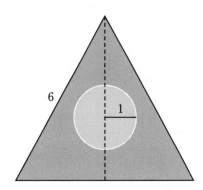

You know the area of the circle is $\pi r^2 = \pi(1)^2 = \pi$, so you subtract π from the area of the triangle, making Choices (A) and (D) seem likely. Now you want to find the area of the equilateral triangle. You know that you can split an equilateral triangle into two 30°-60°-90° triangles, with the height (shown in the diagram as a dashed line) equaling $\sqrt{3}$ multiplied by half of the hypotenuse; $3\sqrt{3}$ in this case. The area of the triangle is $\frac{1}{2}bh = \frac{1}{2}(6)(3\sqrt{3}) = 9\sqrt{3}$.

And you've got it! The area of the remnants of the equilateral triangle is $9\sqrt{3} - \pi$, Choice (A).

On Solid Ground: Answering Volume Questions

Not a lot of solid geometry — generally questions dealing with the volume of three-dimensional, solid shapes — appears on the PSAT/NMSQT. You may run into a question about a cube, a rectangular solid, or a cylinder. Here's what you need to know to ace these problems:

✔ **To find the volume of a cube or a rectangular solid, multiply length by width by height.** Rectangular solids are boxes, and a cube is a box with equal sides and height. You can find the volume of a cube, of course, by computing s^3, where s represents the length of a side. But why bother memorizing an extra fact? Whatever kind of box you have, remember $l \times w \times h$. **Note:** This formula, with the multiplication signs removed, appears in the information box on the exam: $V = lwh$.

✔ **To find the volume of a cylinder, calculate $\pi r^2 h$.** The h in this formula stands for *height*. The r represents *radius*. Remember that the top and bottom of a cylinder are circles, so what you're really doing is calculating the area of one of those circles. Now multiply the result by the height, and you have the volume. **Note:** This formula appears in the information box at the beginning of the math section of the exam.

Very infrequently, you may be asked to calculate the surface area of a cube or other rectangular solid. Just find the area of each side and add them up. Bingo: There's your surface area.

You guessed it. Here's your chance to practice solid geometry:

18. A can of soup contains 300 cubic centimeters of soup. If the can is 10 centimeters tall, what is the approximate radius of the lid?

(A) 3 centimeters

(B) 6 centimeters

(C) 10 centimeters

(D) 15 centimeters

(E) 30 centimeters

19. A shoe box has a base that's 12 inches by 6 inches and is 5 inches deep. If you have a bunch of sugar cubes that are ½ inch long on each side, how many sugar cubes can you fit in the shoe box?

(A) 90

(B) 180

(C) 360

(D) 1,440

(E) 2,880

20. A cardboard pyramid is formed by attaching four equilateral triangles to a square base and leaning them together. What is the minimum area of cardboard needed to make a pyramid that has a base that's 6 inches long on each side?

    (A) $36\sqrt{2}+12$

    (B) $36\sqrt{3}+12$

    (C) $36\sqrt{2}+36$

    (D) $36\sqrt{3}+36$

    (E) $73\sqrt{3}+36$

    Now check your answers.

18. **A.** You know that the volume of a cylinder is $V = \pi r^2 h$, so you can just plug in to solve this problem: $300 = \pi r^2(10)$, $30 = \pi r^2$, $r^2 = \dfrac{30}{\pi}$, so $r = \sqrt{\dfrac{30}{\pi}} \approx 3.09$, Choice (A).

19. **E.** First, find the volume of the shoe box: $V = lwh = (12)(6)(5) = 360$ cubic inches. Each sugar cube has a volume of $\left(\frac{1}{2}\right)^3 = \frac{1}{8}$ of a cubic inch, so 8 sugar cubes fit in every cubic inch of space. That means that you can fit $360 \times 8 = 2{,}880$ sugar cubes in the box — that's a lot of sugar! Choice (E) is correct.

20. **D.** It's great if you can sketch this one, but don't stress out if three dimensions are tricky for you.

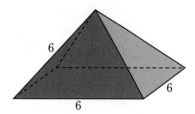

    You know that the base of the pyramid is a square with a side of length 6; therefore, the area of the square must be 36. Each equilateral triangle has a height of $3\sqrt{3}$ (remember the relationship between 30°-60°-90° triangles and equilateral triangles!), so the area of each equilateral triangle is $\frac{1}{2}bh = \frac{1}{2}(6)(3\sqrt{3}) = 9\sqrt{3}$. You have four of those triangles, so together they have an area of $4(9\sqrt{3}) = 36\sqrt{3}$, and the entire figure's surface area is $36\sqrt{3} + 36$, Choice (D).

Chapter 10

Against All Odds: Probability and Statistics

Have you ever bought a lottery ticket? One ***sage*** (wise) fellow said that a lottery ticket is a tax on people who are bad at math, because the odds against winning are ***gargantuan*** (super-sized). You're not bad at math, I'm sure, but you may need to brush up on *probability* — the branch of mathematics that deals with the likelihood that a particular event will occur. In this chapter you can also dust off your knowledge of statistics and data analysis, so you can make sense of those questions on the exam.

What Are the Odds? Determining Probability

Calculating the *probability* that something will happen — also described as the *odds* that it will happen — is simple. Remember this formula:

$$\text{probability of one event} = \frac{\text{number of ways the event can occur}}{\text{total number of possible outcomes}}$$

Imagine that you have (as I do) a jumble of unmatched socks in your drawer. You have 12 yellow socks, 4 orange socks (you were going through a Halloween phase), and 8 green socks. You stick your hand in the drawer. What's the probability that you'll grab an orange sock? Plug in the numbers:

$$\text{probability of grabbing orange sock} = \frac{4 \text{ orange socks}}{12 + 4 + 8 = 24 \text{ socks}}$$

Now reduce the fraction, ¼₄, to ⅙. The probability that you'll grab an orange sock is 1 in 6. Written another way, the odds that your fingers will land on an orange sock are 1 in 6. Still another way to say the same thing: You have a 16.6% chance of ending up with an orange sock. (How did I get that percentage? I divided 1 by 6 and then moved the decimal point two places to the right. For more on calculating percentages, see Chapter 7.)

If you're onto a sure thing — such as the odds that you'll take the PSAT/NMSQT at some point in your life — the probability is 1. For something impossible (that you'll *love* taking the exam), the probability is 0. In other words, all probability (expressed as a fraction) falls between 1 and 0. If you're talking about percents, the highest probability is 100% and the lowest, 0%. Negative probability isn't possible. (The probability of negative probability = 0.)

You may also have to solve questions about the probability that multiple events will occur. For example, say you throw a Halloween party because you need an excuse to wear those orange socks. In your closet you have 5 pirate shirts in different colors and 2 eye patches (1 green and 1 black). How many different combinations of shirts and patches can you make? With multiple events (grabbing a shirt is an event, as is selecting an eye patch), all you need to do is multiply (5×2). There you go: You have 10 possible combinations.

Multiple probability isn't limited to two events. You may have three or many more events. Just multiply all of them and you're on your way to the answer.

One more type of probability involves (gasp!) geometry. (Chapter 9 tells you everything you need to know about geometry.) In geometric probability, the test-makers may ask you to determine the likelihood that a point (or a sky-dive or a home run or whatever) may fall in a given area. Here's an example:

A pitch is a strike if it zooms into the following rectangle. Slugger McGaw hits it out of the park when the ball passes through the shaded area, but he can't hit the ball when it's within the strike zone but *not* inside the shaded area. What is the probability that Slugger will *not* hit the ball if the pitch is a strike?

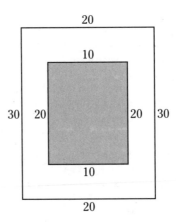

(A) 33%

(B) 40%

(C) 60%

(D) 67%

(E) 75%

Solving this one is easier than hitting Major League pitches. Compute the area of the two rectangles using this formula: area of a rectangle = length × width. The bigger one is 20 x 30 (600 square inches) and the smaller is 10 x 20 (200 square inches). Subtract (600 – 200) to find that the can't-hit zone is 400 square inches. Okay, the entire area (hittable and not-hittable) is 600, so 400/600, or ⅔ of the area, is a no-hit zone. Therefore, the probability that Slugger won't hit the ball is 67%, Choice (D).

To sum up, remember these key facts when solving probability questions:

- ✔ **The likelihood that something will happen:** Use the formula I explained at the beginning of this section.

- ✔ **The likelihood that something will *not* happen:** Use the formula, and then subtract your answer from 1 (if your answer is a fraction or a decimal) or from 100 (if your answer is a percent).

✔ **The number of possible outcomes with multiple events:** Multiply the number of possible events.

✔ **The likelihood that a point is in a geometric form:** Use your knowledge of geometry to compute the area(s), and then calculate the percent.

You'll have better odds of getting probability questions right if you practice. Try these!

1. A game is played with a 10-sided die, where the sides are numbered with odd numbers from 3 through 21. A player wins by rolling a prime number. What is the probability that a player wins?

   (A) 30%

   (B) 40%

   (C) 50%

   (D) 60%

   (E) 70%

2. When Billy gets dressed in the morning, he chooses from among 3 pairs of pants, 2 pairs of shorts, and 8 shirts. How many different outfits can Billy select?

   (A) 13

   (B) 19

   (C) 26

   (D) 40

   (E) 48

3. The following figure shows a dart board consisting of a dark circle inside a light circle. If the diameter of the dark circle is 4 inches and the distance between the dark circle and the edge of the dart board is 3 inches, what is the probability that a dart hits the board and lands in the dark circle?

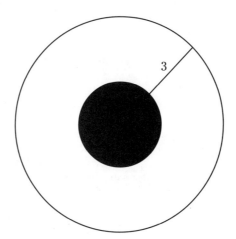

   (A) 16%

   (B) 33%

   (C) 44%

   (D) 57%

   (E) 66%

Now check your answers:

1. **E.** This problem is most easily solved if you write out all the possible outcomes — 3, 5, 7, 9, 11, 13, 15, 17, 19, 21 — and then mark which ones are prime. (Remember: If a number is prime, it can be divided only by itself and 1.) The list contains seven prime numbers: 3, 5, 7, 11, 13, 17, and 19. A player can win in 7 ways, out of 10 possible outcomes, so the probability of winning is $\frac{7}{10}$, or 70%, Choice (E).

2. **D.** Billy isn't going to wear shorts and pants at the same time, so he's really picking from among 3 + 2 = 5 things to wear over his legs. Now just use the formula for multiple events and multiply the number of things he can wear on his legs by the number of things he can wear on his top (8 shirts): $5 \times 8 = 40$ different outfits, so Choice (D) is a winner.

3. **A.** You want to compare the areas of the two circles, so bust out the formula for the area of a circle (or look for it at the beginning of each math section): $A = \pi r^2$. The inner circle has a diameter of 4, and therefore a radius of 2, meaning that the area is $\pi(2)^2 = 4\pi$. The outer circle has a radius of 3 + 2 = 5, so it has an area of $\pi(5)^2 = 25\pi$. All that's left to do is divide the area of the inner circle by the area of the outer circle: $\frac{4\pi}{25\pi} = 0.16 = 16\%$, which brings you to Choice (A).

Munching M and M and M Questions

Hungry? I have some M and M and Ms for you — not candy, but mean, median, and mode problems. They should fill you right up (with knowledge), and then you can chow down on some real food.

The ***mean*** of a group of numbers is just an average. You probably figure out your average every time you take a test or a quiz, or you may keep track of your favorite baseball players' batting averages. You add up the numbers and divide the total by the number of numbers you added. On the PSAT/NMSQT, the test-makers always place the phrase *arithmetic mean* in parenthesis after they ask about an average. Here's a mean question:

> Charles, despite studying for 15 hours without a break, scored 72 on his most recent math test. His previous math grades were 85, 17 (week-old sushi for supper), and 97. What is Charles's average (arithmetic mean) grade?

To solve this problem, add up the grades (72 + 85 + 17 + 97 = 271) and divide by 4, which gives you 67.75.

The test-writers may also tell you the average and ask something else:

> Charles has an average (arithmetic mean) of 70 on his first four math tests. What score must Charles achieve on his next exam to raise his grade above 75?

Okay, you know that the first four grades added together and divided by 4 equal 70. Set up an equation, calling the four added-together grades *x*:

$$\frac{x}{4} = 70$$

Now multiply both sides by 4 and you get *x* = 280. Set up the new equation, this time with a new grade (*y*) which you add to the sum of the four other grades (280) and divide by 5:

$$\frac{280 + y}{5} = 75$$

Multiply by 5 this time and you have 280 + y = 375. Subtract 280 from each side of the equation, which gives you y = 95. Charles has to score a 95 to raise his average to 75 and avoid being grounded for the rest of the school year.

The **median** tells you to put all the numbers in order and find the middle. You aren't calculating an average; you're finding the spot where half of the numbers are bigger and half are smaller. Imagine that Charles's English grades are 75, 32 (that sushi again), 80, 90, and 76. Put them in order:

   32 75 76 80 90

The middle number is 76, which is the median. What happens if the teacher, kindhearted as she is, drops the lowest grade? That gives Charles grades of 75, 76, 80, and 90. Now you can't go to a middle number, so instead you go to the middle *pair* and average them. Add 76 and 80, which gives you 156. Divide 156 by 2, and you find a median of 78.

Sometimes mean and median appear in the same problem. Keep the definitions in mind as you work the problem. For example, you may be told that the average (arithmetic mean) of x, x, y, z, and z is 40 and the median is 30, when $x < y < z$. Then you have to find the value of $x + z$. Okay, because 30 is the median, $y = 30$. Now you have $(2x + 30 + 2z)$ divided by 5 = 40. In equation form that looks like $\frac{2x + 30 + 2z}{5} = 40$. Multiply both sides by 5 and then subtract 30: $2x + 2z = 200 - 30 = 170$. You can rewrite the left side of that equation with a 2 factored out — $2(x + z) = 170$ — and when you divide by 2, you see that $x + z = 85$.

One more "M": **mode.** The mode is simply the number that occurs most frequently. (*Mode* is another word for *fashion*. When something is in fashion, it shows up more than any other style — just like the mathematical mode.) Here are Charles's science grades: 90, 77, 80, 77, 12 (can't stop eating leftover sushi!), 88. The mode is 77 because that number appears twice and the other grades appear only once each.

Try your hand at these practice problems.

4. Find the median of the union of sets A and B if A = {1, 3, 5, 7, 9, 11} and B = {1, 4, 9, 16, 25}

   (A) 5

   (B) 7

   (C) 8

   (D) 9

   (E) 11

5. Crystal polled her family and collected the ages of all her cousins: 3, 7, 9, 9, 10, 12, 13, 13, 13, 16, and 20. What age is the mode?

   (A) 9

   (B) 10

   (C) 11

   (D) 12

   (E) 13

6. Mr. Beta accidentally deleted Sam's test grade from his grade book. Mr. Beta knows that the average (arithmetic mean) test grade was 86. What was Sam's grade?

Name:	Test Grade:
Alyssa	100
Ben	74
Betty	88
Charles	63
Nicholas	95
Sam	
Tomas	88
Average	**86**

(A) 82

(B) 86

(C) 90

(D) 94

(E) 98

Now check your answers:

4. **B.** Your first step should be to find the union of the two sets; remember that the *union* includes all the numbers from either set, and you eliminate only numbers that are repeated. The union of A and B is {1, 3, 4, 5, 7, 9, 11, 16, 25}. Now you can see that the median is 7, the number in the middle, or Choice (B).

5. **E.** The mode is the number that shows up most frequently, so among Crystal's cousins, the mode must be 13, or Choice (E).

6. **D.** Your first step in answering this question is to determine what all seven students' grades added to; you can do that by multiplying the average by 7 (because the average was calculated by adding up all the grades and dividing by 7). So, $86 \times 7 = 602$. Now, add up all the grades that you know: $100 + 74 + 88 + 63 + 95 + 88 = 508$. Sam's grade is the difference between 508 and 602, or 94, Choice (D).

In Graphic Detail: Reading Graphs

As you work your way through the PSAT/NMSQT math problems, you'll run across (*not* stumble over, because you're preparing now!) some questions that ask you to interpret information presented in graphs or charts — sometimes in pairs, and sometimes one of each. These questions are easy, so long as you read the graph or chart carefully and focus on what the question wants you to find.

You may see bar, circle (also known as pie), or two-axes line graphs. Here's the same information — what people do after they complete the PSAT/NMSQT — presented first in a chart and then in a circle graph:

Post-PSAT/NMSQT Activities, 2011-2012

Year	Nail-biting	Yoga	Watching Reality TV	Counting Old Bubble Gum Blobs
2011	10%	30%	40%	20%
2012	8%	36%	44%	12%

Circle Graph
Post-PSAT/NMSQT Activities, 2012

Notice that the activities, whether presented in a chart or a circle graph, always add up to 100%, because the parts are expressed as percents. (For more information on percents, turn to Chapter 7.) If the parts are expressed as fractions or decimals, they add up to 1.

In some graphs, you may see quantities that don't represent parts of a whole. Then the numbers may add up to any sum. Here's a bar graph illustrating the (fake) percentage of students who participated in four post-PSAT/NMSQT activities in 2011 and 2012.

Bar Graph

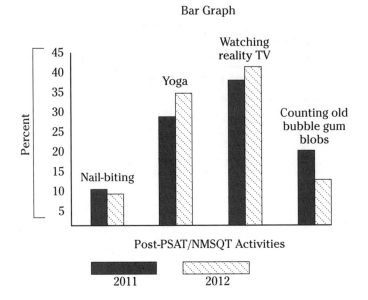

Now take a look at this line graph, which tracks two other post-PSAT/NMSQT activities, fish scaling and vacuuming.

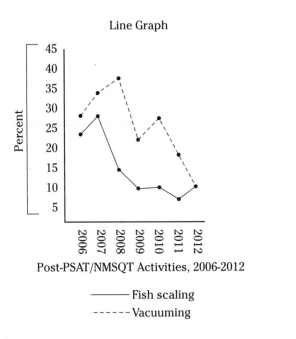

 Are you up for some practice? Use the preceding graphs and charts about post-PSAT/ NMSQT activities to answer these questions. These questions are grid-ins because you don't have five choices listed. Instead, you solve the problem and grid-in the answer, as I explain in Chapter 6. (Note: All the numbers and activities are completely imaginary.)

7. In 2011, 5,000 students took the PSAT/NMSQT in one school district. The students relaxed after the exam in several different ways. According to the earlier chart, how many more students watched reality TV shows than bit their nails?

8. According to the earlier line graph, from 2006 to 2012, in what year was the difference between the percent of students vacuuming and fish-scaling the greatest?

9. Use the line and bar graphs for this question: In 2012, 7,500 students took the PSAT/NMSQT in the Sunnydale district. A survey found that 20% of those students chose fish scaling or vacuuming as their after-test activity, and the remaining 80% selected yoga, reality TV, bubble gum counting, or nail-biting. If one of the 7,500 students is chosen at random, what is the probability that she was either fish-scaling or nail-biting after the exam?

Now check your answers:

7. **1,500.** To solve this problem, multiply 5,000 by 40% (.40 or .4), which gives you 2,000 reality TV watchers. Also multiply 5,000 by 10% (.1), which gives you 500 nail biters. You aren't done yet! Subtract 500 from 2,000 to give you **1,500,** which represents how many more students watched reality TV shows.

8. **2008.** You're looking for the year where the two data points are farthest apart. The years 2008 and 2010 have the biggest looking differences, so focus on those two. In 2008, it looks like 40% of students vacuumed and 15% scaled fish, for a difference of 40 − 15 = 25%. In 2010, 30% vacuumed and 10% scaled fish, for a difference of 30 − 10 = 20%. The year **2008** has the biggest difference.

9. **8.4%.** Take this question one step at a time. First, 20% of 7,500 students is 1,500 students who answered "fish scaling" or "vacuuming" in the survey. Moving on, 10% of those students said that they were scaling fish, so 150 students were scaling fish. Now, of the remaining 80%, or 6,000 students, 8% said that they were biting their nails, or 0.08 × 6,000 = 480 nail biters. Add together your fish scalers and nail biters: 150 + 480 = 630 students. Now divide by the total number of students in the district: 630 ÷ 7,500 = 0.084 = **8.4%** of the students were scaling fish or biting their nails after the exam.

The PSAT/NMSQT sometimes includes *pictograms,* bar graphs with little symbols, each with the same value. The pictogram may be a tiny computer, for example, with a note explaining that each little computer represents 100,000 Angry Birds players. On the "New York City" line you may see 5 little computers (judging from the number of people I see playing the game). Another city may be represented by one complete little computer and then a half computer, representing 150,000 Angry Birds players.

In the following pictogram, each bubble gum blob represents the same number of old gum blobs stuck to the bottom of the desks in each type of classroom. In other words, one gum blob pictogram equals a fixed amount of discarded gum.

Pictogram
Bubble Gum Blobs Found Under Desks - PS 12, District 13

Try this question, based on the pictogram:

10. According to the pictogram, if 250 old bubble gum blobs were stuck to the bottom of the desks in history classrooms, how many old bubble gum blobs were stuck under the desks in English classrooms?

Now check your answer:

10. **125.** To solve this one, take a look at the history line. Notice that you have 5 gum blobs. If 5 gum blob pictograms represent 250 actual blobs, each pictogram represents $\frac{250}{5}$, or 50 blobs. Now check out the English line. You see 2½ pictograms, giving you **125** actual gum blobs as your answer.

Part IV
Practice Makes Perfect: Practice Exams

The 5th Wave   By Rich Tennant

©RICHTENNANT

"The math portion of that test was so easy. I figure I've got a 7 in 5 chance of acing it."

In this part . . .

How's your math? Can you compute how long it will take you to do all four practice tests in this part? Here's the answer: Each PSAT/NMSQT gobbles up 130 minutes of your life, and four of them take 520 minutes, for a grand total of 8 hours and 40 minutes. And that doesn't include setting up, a five-minute bathroom break during each exam, and some additional hours for checking your work.

Here's another question for you: How many migraine headaches will you have while working in this part? The answer: It depends. If you work through this part properly, the answer is zero. If you go about it the wrong way, the number of migraines could skyrocket. So maybe I should explain the proper way to approach these practice exams. Don't even *think* about doing more than one exam in a single day. However, when you begin an exam, be sure to finish it. (Check out the beginning of Chapter 11 for exam timing and procedures.) If possible, score your test on a different day, so your mind is fresh and ready to absorb the explanations I provide for every answer.

Off you go! Good luck!

Chapter 11

Practice Test 1

● ●

𝓑roadway stars sometimes talk about the hum of nervous energy they feel just before they step onto the stage. I bet you're feeling some of that anxiety too, as you contemplate your first stab at the PSAT/NMSQT. The secret is that instead of attempting to banish your nerves, you can ride the energy to a top score. With practice — and this chapter is all about practice! — you can remind yourself that you're smart, prepared, and ready for whatever the test-maker throws at you.

As you work through this exam, you should *simulate* (create a pretend version) a real testing situation. Here's what you need:

- ✔ **A quiet spot where you won't be interrupted:** Your room, with the door shut and a sign saying "KEEP OUT," is a perfect place. Or you can take the test at a quiet library table or a study room at your school. Even a park could work, if weather permits.

- ✔ **A timer:** Use your phone or a watch or sit facing a clock. If the device allows you to do so, set the timer to beep after the allotted number of minutes has passed. If you don't have a timer, write the ending time when you begin a section. In the heat of battle (and taking the exam *is* a battle), you may not remember the time you're supposed to stop.

- ✔ **No helpers:** I include computer searches, shout-outs (by phone or in person), and any devices the College Board *prohibits* (bans) in this category. You may use a calculator, but not one with a raised keyboard.

- ✔ **A couple of number two pencils:** Just as on the real exam, you should bubble your answers with the right kind of pencil.

- ✔ **This book!:** Tear out the bubble-filled answer sheet. (Sounds like fun, right? Too bad the PSAT is not a bubble bath.) Don't turn the page to peek at the test until it's time to start.

- ✔ **A stretch of free time:** Two hours and ten minutes, to be exact. After you begin, don't stop between sections because you won't be able to do so on PSAT-day.

Okay, now you're ready to begin. After you complete this practice test, do something fun to reward yourself. Then check your work by comparing your answers to those in Chapter 12.

Answer Sheet

For the questions in Sections 1 through 5, use the ovals and grid-ins to record your answers.

Section 1: Critical Reading

1. Ⓐ Ⓑ Ⓒ Ⓓ Ⓔ   7. Ⓐ Ⓑ Ⓒ Ⓓ Ⓔ   13. Ⓐ Ⓑ Ⓒ Ⓓ Ⓔ   19. Ⓐ Ⓑ Ⓒ Ⓓ Ⓔ
2. Ⓐ Ⓑ Ⓒ Ⓓ Ⓔ   8. Ⓐ Ⓑ Ⓒ Ⓓ Ⓔ   14. Ⓐ Ⓑ Ⓒ Ⓓ Ⓔ   20. Ⓐ Ⓑ Ⓒ Ⓓ Ⓔ
3. Ⓐ Ⓑ Ⓒ Ⓓ Ⓔ   9. Ⓐ Ⓑ Ⓒ Ⓓ Ⓔ   15. Ⓐ Ⓑ Ⓒ Ⓓ Ⓔ   21. Ⓐ Ⓑ Ⓒ Ⓓ Ⓔ
4. Ⓐ Ⓑ Ⓒ Ⓓ Ⓔ   10. Ⓐ Ⓑ Ⓒ Ⓓ Ⓔ   16. Ⓐ Ⓑ Ⓒ Ⓓ Ⓔ   22. Ⓐ Ⓑ Ⓒ Ⓓ Ⓔ
5. Ⓐ Ⓑ Ⓒ Ⓓ Ⓔ   11. Ⓐ Ⓑ Ⓒ Ⓓ Ⓔ   17. Ⓐ Ⓑ Ⓒ Ⓓ Ⓔ   23. Ⓐ Ⓑ Ⓒ Ⓓ Ⓔ
6. Ⓐ Ⓑ Ⓒ Ⓓ Ⓔ   12. Ⓐ Ⓑ Ⓒ Ⓓ Ⓔ   18. Ⓐ Ⓑ Ⓒ Ⓓ Ⓔ   24. Ⓐ Ⓑ Ⓒ Ⓓ Ⓔ

Section 2: Mathematics

1. Ⓐ Ⓑ Ⓒ Ⓓ Ⓔ   6. Ⓐ Ⓑ Ⓒ Ⓓ Ⓔ   11. Ⓐ Ⓑ Ⓒ Ⓓ Ⓔ   16. Ⓐ Ⓑ Ⓒ Ⓓ Ⓔ
2. Ⓐ Ⓑ Ⓒ Ⓓ Ⓔ   7. Ⓐ Ⓑ Ⓒ Ⓓ Ⓔ   12. Ⓐ Ⓑ Ⓒ Ⓓ Ⓔ   17. Ⓐ Ⓑ Ⓒ Ⓓ Ⓔ
3. Ⓐ Ⓑ Ⓒ Ⓓ Ⓔ   8. Ⓐ Ⓑ Ⓒ Ⓓ Ⓔ   13. Ⓐ Ⓑ Ⓒ Ⓓ Ⓔ   18. Ⓐ Ⓑ Ⓒ Ⓓ Ⓔ
4. Ⓐ Ⓑ Ⓒ Ⓓ Ⓔ   9. Ⓐ Ⓑ Ⓒ Ⓓ Ⓔ   14. Ⓐ Ⓑ Ⓒ Ⓓ Ⓔ   19. Ⓐ Ⓑ Ⓒ Ⓓ Ⓔ
5. Ⓐ Ⓑ Ⓒ Ⓓ Ⓔ   10. Ⓐ Ⓑ Ⓒ Ⓓ Ⓔ   15. Ⓐ Ⓑ Ⓒ Ⓓ Ⓔ   20. Ⓐ Ⓑ Ⓒ Ⓓ Ⓔ

Section 3: Critical Reading

25. Ⓐ Ⓑ Ⓒ Ⓓ Ⓔ   31. Ⓐ Ⓑ Ⓒ Ⓓ Ⓔ   37. Ⓐ Ⓑ Ⓒ Ⓓ Ⓔ   43. Ⓐ Ⓑ Ⓒ Ⓓ Ⓔ
26. Ⓐ Ⓑ Ⓒ Ⓓ Ⓔ   32. Ⓐ Ⓑ Ⓒ Ⓓ Ⓔ   38. Ⓐ Ⓑ Ⓒ Ⓓ Ⓔ   44. Ⓐ Ⓑ Ⓒ Ⓓ Ⓔ
27. Ⓐ Ⓑ Ⓒ Ⓓ Ⓔ   33. Ⓐ Ⓑ Ⓒ Ⓓ Ⓔ   39. Ⓐ Ⓑ Ⓒ Ⓓ Ⓔ   45. Ⓐ Ⓑ Ⓒ Ⓓ Ⓔ
28. Ⓐ Ⓑ Ⓒ Ⓓ Ⓔ   34. Ⓐ Ⓑ Ⓒ Ⓓ Ⓔ   40. Ⓐ Ⓑ Ⓒ Ⓓ Ⓔ   46. Ⓐ Ⓑ Ⓒ Ⓓ Ⓔ
29. Ⓐ Ⓑ Ⓒ Ⓓ Ⓔ   35. Ⓐ Ⓑ Ⓒ Ⓓ Ⓔ   41. Ⓐ Ⓑ Ⓒ Ⓓ Ⓔ   47. Ⓐ Ⓑ Ⓒ Ⓓ Ⓔ
30. Ⓐ Ⓑ Ⓒ Ⓓ Ⓔ   36. Ⓐ Ⓑ Ⓒ Ⓓ Ⓔ   42. Ⓐ Ⓑ Ⓒ Ⓓ Ⓔ   48. Ⓐ Ⓑ Ⓒ Ⓓ Ⓔ

Section 4: Mathematics

21. Ⓐ Ⓑ Ⓒ Ⓓ Ⓔ   25. Ⓐ Ⓑ Ⓒ Ⓓ Ⓔ
22. Ⓐ Ⓑ Ⓒ Ⓓ Ⓔ   26. Ⓐ Ⓑ Ⓒ Ⓓ Ⓔ
23. Ⓐ Ⓑ Ⓒ Ⓓ Ⓔ   27. Ⓐ Ⓑ Ⓒ Ⓓ Ⓔ
24. Ⓐ Ⓑ Ⓒ Ⓓ Ⓔ   28. Ⓐ Ⓑ Ⓒ Ⓓ Ⓔ

29. 30. 31. 32. 33.

34. 35. 36. 37. 38.

Section 5: Writing

1. Ⓐ Ⓑ Ⓒ Ⓓ Ⓔ   9. Ⓐ Ⓑ Ⓒ Ⓓ Ⓔ   17. Ⓐ Ⓑ Ⓒ Ⓓ Ⓔ   25. Ⓐ Ⓑ Ⓒ Ⓓ Ⓔ   33. Ⓐ Ⓑ Ⓒ Ⓓ Ⓔ
2. Ⓐ Ⓑ Ⓒ Ⓓ Ⓔ   10. Ⓐ Ⓑ Ⓒ Ⓓ Ⓔ   18. Ⓐ Ⓑ Ⓒ Ⓓ Ⓔ   26. Ⓐ Ⓑ Ⓒ Ⓓ Ⓔ   34. Ⓐ Ⓑ Ⓒ Ⓓ Ⓔ
3. Ⓐ Ⓑ Ⓒ Ⓓ Ⓔ   11. Ⓐ Ⓑ Ⓒ Ⓓ Ⓔ   19. Ⓐ Ⓑ Ⓒ Ⓓ Ⓔ   27. Ⓐ Ⓑ Ⓒ Ⓓ Ⓔ   35. Ⓐ Ⓑ Ⓒ Ⓓ Ⓔ
4. Ⓐ Ⓑ Ⓒ Ⓓ Ⓔ   12. Ⓐ Ⓑ Ⓒ Ⓓ Ⓔ   20. Ⓐ Ⓑ Ⓒ Ⓓ Ⓔ   28. Ⓐ Ⓑ Ⓒ Ⓓ Ⓔ   36. Ⓐ Ⓑ Ⓒ Ⓓ Ⓔ
5. Ⓐ Ⓑ Ⓒ Ⓓ Ⓔ   13. Ⓐ Ⓑ Ⓒ Ⓓ Ⓔ   21. Ⓐ Ⓑ Ⓒ Ⓓ Ⓔ   29. Ⓐ Ⓑ Ⓒ Ⓓ Ⓔ   37. Ⓐ Ⓑ Ⓒ Ⓓ Ⓔ
6. Ⓐ Ⓑ Ⓒ Ⓓ Ⓔ   14. Ⓐ Ⓑ Ⓒ Ⓓ Ⓔ   22. Ⓐ Ⓑ Ⓒ Ⓓ Ⓔ   30. Ⓐ Ⓑ Ⓒ Ⓓ Ⓔ   38. Ⓐ Ⓑ Ⓒ Ⓓ Ⓔ
7. Ⓐ Ⓑ Ⓒ Ⓓ Ⓔ   15. Ⓐ Ⓑ Ⓒ Ⓓ Ⓔ   23. Ⓐ Ⓑ Ⓒ Ⓓ Ⓔ   31. Ⓐ Ⓑ Ⓒ Ⓓ Ⓔ   39. Ⓐ Ⓑ Ⓒ Ⓓ Ⓔ
8. Ⓐ Ⓑ Ⓒ Ⓓ Ⓔ   16. Ⓐ Ⓑ Ⓒ Ⓓ Ⓔ   24. Ⓐ Ⓑ Ⓒ Ⓓ Ⓔ   32. Ⓐ Ⓑ Ⓒ Ⓓ Ⓔ

Section 1

Critical Reading

Time: 25 minutes for 24 questions

Directions: Choose the *best* answer to each question. Mark the corresponding oval on your answer sheet.

Directions for Questions 1–8: Choose the word or words that best fit the meaning of each sentence.

Example: After work, Edith always _____ home as quickly as possible.

(A) rambled

(B) wandered

(C) avoided

(D) meandered

(E) ran

The answer is Choice (E).

1. Because of its _____ client base, the company sought only candidates without a _____ attitude.

    (A) limited . . . changeable

    (B) homogeneous . . . quaint

    (C) growing . . . prudent

    (D) diverse . . . tolerant

    (E) broad . . . provincial

2. King Arthur's _____ knights have been the subject of many legends, most of which emphasize the knights' power and determination.

    (A) pathetic

    (B) redoubtable

    (C) infamous

    (D) superannuated

    (E) improbable

3. Behind _____ glass, the children appeared as _____ shadows.

    (A) frosted . . . vague

    (B) transparent . . . unclear

    (C) stained . . . monochrome

    (D) opaque . . . distinct

    (E) fragile . . . elongated

4. In contrast to the actor, who spoke for hours, the agent issued a _____ statement.

    (A) loquacious

    (B) temperate

    (C) redundant

    (D) stoic

    (E) terse

5. The famous model _____ in front of the mirror while her lowly servant _____ fearfully after discovering that the bracelet was missing.

    (A) primped . . . strutted

    (B) ducked . . . pranced

    (C) hid . . . rebelled

    (D) preened . . . cowered

    (E) paraded . . . orated

6. Because the publicity director had made extensive use of billboards, the orchestra's posters seemed _____ to everyone who drove on that highway.

    (A) dogmatic

    (B) ubiquitous

    (C) eclectic

    (D) ambiguous

    (E) aesthetic

Go on to next page

7. The _____ effects of the potion were _____ when Eleanor fainted after drinking it.

   (A) varied . . . deliberate

   (B) pristine . . . harmful

   (C) powerful . . . subtle

   (D) beneficial . . . evident

   (E) deleterious . . . obvious

8. The animal's _____ movements revealed its fear of approaching the camp openly.

   (A) blatant

   (B) unanticipated

   (C) overt

   (D) furtive

   (E) direct

Directions for Questions 9–12: Read these two passages and answer the questions that follow each passage based on what is stated or implied in the passage.

Questions 9 and 10 are based on the following passage, an excerpt from AbleTrend, *by John Wang and Grace Wang (Wiley).*

Line   I was still a scientist, and the more I became interested in trading the markets, the more my scientific sensibilities were offended by the arbitrary statements and predictions of the market
(05) gurus. From TV to radio, from magazines to newspapers, from websites to books, investment experts talk about "what the market should be doing." They say things like, "The Dow Jones index should go up 10 percent by the end of this
(10) year." Or, "The target price for this stock should be $78 per share in 12 months." The opinions never stop. In fact, there is no such thing as "should" or "would" or "could" in the trading world. What people tell you has no value. If you
(15) want to win, there is only one way to go: Act on what the market is telling you.

9. Based on the opinions expressed in this passage, with which statement might the author agree?

   (A) Successful investing is impossible.

   (B) True experts understand the market, but the general public does not.

   (C) Let the market guide your investments.

   (D) Science can predict market trends.

   (E) The stock market should be regulated more strictly.

10. The author most likely begins with the statement "I was still a scientist" in order to

   (A) disclaim any expert knowledge of the stock market

   (B) establish that scientific observation of the market is helpful

   (C) show that the market and science can benefit each other

   (D) win support for scientific research

   (E) intrigue readers who are interested in science

Questions 11 and 12 are based on the following passage, an excerpt from Ethical Decision Making in Fund Raising, *by Marilyn Fischer (Wiley).*

     Gifts come with strings attached.   Line
Communities are formed by strings; we want them, but sometimes we resent them. Ralph Waldo Emerson was keenly aware of the rub between independence and interdependence. In   (05)
his essay on gifts, he says, "The law of benefits is a difficult channel, which requires careful sailing, or rude boats. It is not the office of a man to receive gifts. How dare you give them? We wish to be self-sustained. We do not quite forgive a   (10)
giver. The hand that feeds us is in some danger of being bitten."

Go on to next page

11. Which statement best expresses the meaning of "Communities are formed by strings"?

   (A) Gifts should be chosen carefully.

   (B) No gift is ever completely unwelcome.

   (C) Generosity is dangerous.

   (D) Most gifts are unsolicited and unwanted.

   (E) Mutual obligations bind people together.

12. In the context of Line 7, which of the following is the best definition of "channel"?

   (A) station

   (B) guide

   (C) transmitter

   (D) passage

   (E) control

Directions for Questions 13–24: The following two passages discuss London. Read them carefully and answer the questions that follow based on what is stated or implied in the passages.

The first passage is from Collins' Illustrated Guide to London, *and the second is from* Old and New London, *by Walter Thornbury.*

Passage 1

Line   With regard to the origin of London — or *Llyn-Din,* "the town on the lake" — we may mention that the Romans, after conquering its ancient British inhabitants, about AD 61, finally
(05) rebuilt and walled Londinium in about AD 301; from which time it became, in such excellent hands, a place of not a little importance. Roman remains, such as fine pavements, bronzes, weapons, pottery, and coins, are not seldom turned
(10) up by the spade of our sturdy excavators while digging below the foundations of houses; and a few scanty fragments of the old Roman Wall, which was rather more than three miles round, are still to be seen. London, in the Anglo-Norman
(15) times, though confined originally by the said

wall, grew up a dense mass of brick and wooden Line
houses, ill arranged, unclean, close, and for the
most part terribly insalubrious. Pestilence was
the natural consequence. Up to the great plague
of 1664–5, which destroyed 68,596, some say   (20)
100,000 persons — there were, dating from the
pestilence of 1348, no fewer than some nine visitations of widely spreading epidemics in Old
London. When, in 1666, the great fire, which
burnt 13,200 houses, spread its ruins over 436   (25)
acres, and laid waste 400 streets, came to force
the Cockneys to mend their ways somewhat, and
open out their over-cramped habitations, some
good was effected. But, unfortunately, during the
rebuilding of the City, Sir Christopher Wren's   (30)
plans for laying its streets out on a more regular
plan were poorly attended to: hence the still
incongruous condition of older London when
compared, in many instances, with the results of
modern architecture, with reference to air, light,   (35)
and sanitary arrangements. On account of the
rubbish left by the fire and other casualties, the
City stands from twelve to sixteen feet higher
than it did in the early part of its history — the
roadways of Roman London, for example, being   (40)
found on, or even below, the level of the cellars
of the present houses.

From being a city hemmed within a wall,
London expanded in all directions, and thus
gradually formed a connection with various clus-   (45)
ters of dwellings in the neighborhood. It has, in
fact, absorbed towns and villages to a considerable distance around: the chief of these being
the city of Westminster. By means of bridges, it
has also absorbed Southwark and Bermondsey,   (50)
Lambeth and Vauxhall, on the south side of the
Thames, besides many hamlets and villages
beyond the river.

By these extensions London proper, by
which we mean the *City,* has gradually assumed,   (55)
if we may so speak, the conditions of an existence like that of a kernel in a thickly surrounding and ever-growing mass.

Passage II

Writing the history of a vast city like London
is like writing a history of the ocean — the area   (60)
is so vast, its inhabitants are so multifarious, the
treasures that lie in its depths so countless.
What aspect of the great chameleon city should
one select? For, as Boswell, with more than his
usual sense, once remarked, "London is to the   (65)
politician merely a seat of government, to the

Go on to next page ⟩

Line grazier a cattle market, to the merchant a huge
exchange, to the dramatic enthusiast a collection
of theatres, to the man of pleasure an assem-
(70) blage of taverns." If we follow one path alone, we
must neglect other roads equally important; let
us, then, consider the metropolis as a whole, for,
as Boswell well says, "The intellectual man is
struck with London as comprehending the whole
(75) of human life in all its variety, the contemplation
of which is inexhaustible." In histories, in biogra-
phies, in scientific records, and in chronicles of
the past, however humble, let us gather materials for a record of the great and the wise, the
(80) base and the noble, the odd and the witty, who
have inhabited London and left their names
upon its walls. Wherever the glimmer of the
cross of St. Paul's can be seen we shall wander
from street to alley, from alley to street, noting
(85) almost every event of interest that has taken
place there since London was a city.

    The houses of old London are encrusted as
thick with anecdotes, legends, and traditions as
an old ship is with barnacles. Strange stories
(90) about strange men grow like moss in every crev-
ice of the bricks. Let us, then, roll together like a
great snowball the mass of information that time
and our predecessors have accumulated, and
reduce it to some shape and form. Old London is
(95) passing away even as we dip our pen in the ink,
and we would fain erect quickly our itinerant photographic machine, and secure some views of it
before it passes. Roman London, Saxon London,
Norman London, Elizabethan London, Stuart
(100) London, Queen Anne's London, we shall in turn
rifle to fill our museum, on whose shelves the
Roman lamp and the vessel full of tears will stand
side by side with Vanessa's fan; the sword-knot of
Rochester by the note-book of Goldsmith. The his-
(105) tory of London is an epitome of the history of
England. Few great men indeed that England has
produced but have some associations that connect them with London. To be able to recall these
associations in a London walk is a pleasure per-
(110) petually renewing, and to all intents inexhaustible.

13. The reference to "Llyn-Din" (Line 2)

    (A) explains where London is situated

    (B) connects the modern name of the city
with its ancient origins

    (C) contrasts the Roman name for the city
with a Cockney term

    (D) hints at the mysterious origin of London

    (E) reveals that geographical features are
always important

14. The "excellent hands" (Lines 6–7) imply that

    (A) the Romans were good administrators
of the city

    (B) Londoners knew how to do manual
labor

    (C) Londoners worked hard

    (D) Romans built many things

    (E) the inhabitants of London were known
for their bronze weapons

15. In the context of Line 17, which is the best
definition of "close"?

    (A) shut

    (B) nearby

    (C) sealed

    (D) crowded

    (E) secure

16. The details of epidemics and fire in Lines
19–29 serve to illustrate the

    (A) fragility of human life

    (B) vulnerability of great cities

    (C) possible consequences of density in a
city

    (D) reasons why city-dwellers live shorter
lives

    (E) need for proper medical care

17. According to Passage I, London grew

    (A) because of access to a river

    (B) by building tall, multistory houses

    (C) by incorporating towns near its borders

    (D) only within a fortified wall

    (E) because the Cockneys behaved better

18. With which statement would the authors of
Passages I and II agree?

    (A) The history of London has never been
told accurately.

    (B) London has a rich and varied history.

    (C) The city needs access to an ocean.

    (D) The Roman wall around London should
have been preserved.

    (E) London is too large.

Go on to next page

19. The author of Passage II quotes Boswell (Lines 65–70 and 73–76) in order to

    (A) explain who wrote the history of London

    (B) provide an example of an important person who lived in London

    (C) contradict the view that London is "vast" (Line 59)

    (D) introduce an expert opinion

    (E) emphasize the many different ways people relate to London

20. The "barnacles" mentioned in Line 89 may best be understood as

    (A) sea creatures

    (B) human stories and culture

    (C) erosion

    (D) new construction

    (E) odd structures

21. The "Roman lamp" (Line 102), "Vanessa's fan" (Line 103), the "sword-knot of Rochester" (Lines 103–104), and the "note-book of Goldsmith" (Line 104) may best be defined by what phrase from Passage II?

    (A) "the whole of human life in all its variety" (Lines 74–75)

    (B) "histories" (Line 76)

    (C) "scientific records" (Line 77)

    (D) "names upon its walls" (Lines 81–82)

    (E) "some views of it" (Line 97)

22. In contrast to the author of Passage II, the author of Passage I is

    (A) more positive about the benefits of city life

    (B) less aware of the city's history

    (C) more open about the disadvantages of city living

    (D) more optimistic about public institutions

    (E) less interested in the past

23. In the context of Line 80, which is the best definition of "base"?

    (A) bottom

    (B) foundation

    (C) support

    (D) low-class

    (E) commonplace

24. In contrast to Passage I, Passage II is

    (A) more historical

    (B) less abstract

    (C) less positive

    (D) less poetic

    (E) more general

STOP YOU MAY CHECK YOUR WORK ON THIS SECTION ONLY. DO NOT GO BACK TO ANY PREVIOUS SECTION.

Section 2

Mathematics

Time: 25 minutes for 20 questions

Directions: Find the correct answer to each question and fill in the corresponding oval on the answer sheet.

Notes:

✔ You may use a calculator.

✔ All numbers used in this exam are real numbers.

✔ All figures lie in a plane.

✔ You may assume that all figures are to scale unless the problem specifically indicates otherwise.

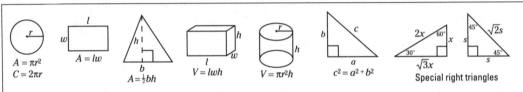

$A = \pi r^2$
$C = 2\pi r$
$A = lw$
$A = \frac{1}{2}bh$
$V = lwh$
$V = \pi r^2 h$
$c^2 = a^2 + b^2$
Special right triangles

There are 360 degrees of arc in a circle.

There are 180 degrees in a straight line.

There are 180 degrees in the sum of the interior angles of a triangle.

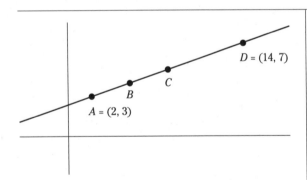

1. On the line shown in this figure, *C* is the midpoint of *AD,* and *B* is the midpoint of *AC.* What are the coordinates of point *B?*

(A) (4, 4)

(B) (4, 5)

(C) (5, 4)

(D) (6, 4)

(E) (8, 5)

2. Let the symbol & be defined as follows: $a \& b = 2a - b^2$. Which expression is equivalent to $3 \& 2$?

(A) 2 & 1

(B) 2 & 3

(C) 3 & –2

(D) 4 & 3

(E) 6 & –3

Go on to next page

3. In rectangle *ABCD,* the coordinates are *A* (1, 3), *B* (6, 3), and *C* (6, –1). What are the coordinates of point *D?*

    (A) (1, –3)

    (B) (1, –1)

    (C) (3, –1)

    (D) (3, 1)

    (E) (6, –1)

6. Which of the following expressions has a value of –2 if $f(x) = 3x^2 - 5$?

    (A) $f(-4)$

    (B) $f(-2)$

    (C) $f(0)$

    (D) $f(1)$

    (E) $f(3)$

4. For which set is the median less than the mode?

    (A) {1, 2, 3, 3, 4}

    (B) {2, 2, 2, 3}

    (C) {1, 1, 2, 5, 6}

    (D) {1, 2, 4, 5, 5, 6}

    (E) {4, 4, 5, 6}

7. If $x = -5$, then $|2x - 3| =$

    (A) –13

    (B) –7

    (C) 2

    (D) 7

    (E) 13

5. If $\sqrt{3-x} = 2$, $x^2 + 2 = $?

    (A) –1

    (B) 0

    (C) 1

    (D) 2

    (E) 3

8. Suppose set A = {1, 2, 7, 8} and set B = {2, 3, 4, 5}. Which of the following numbers is included in the intersection of A and B?

    (A) 1

    (B) 2

    (C) 3

    (D) 5

    (E) 7

Go on to next page

9. The ratio of red fish to blue fish in an aquarium is 1:2. Which of the following could be the total number of fish in the aquarium?

(A) 4

(B) 12

(C) 16

(D) 20

(E) 22

10. Where do $2x + y = 3$ and $x - y = 6$ intersect?

(A) $(1, -1)$

(B) $(2, -2)$

(C) $(2, 2)$

(D) $(3, -3)$

(E) $(3, 3)$

11. If p is an odd integer, which of the following expressions represents an even integer?

(A) $p + 3$

(B) $2p - 1$

(C) $2p + 1$

(D) $3p + 4$

(E) $p^2 + 2$

12. Suppose $p = a^2 b^{-3}$ and $q = a^3 b^2$. Which expression represents $\frac{p}{q}$?

(A) $\frac{1}{a^2 b^3}$

(B) $\frac{b^{-3}}{ab^2}$

(C) $\frac{a}{a^2 b^4}$

(D) $\frac{ab^{-3}}{b^2}$

(E) $a^5 b$

13. Which of the following is a solution of $y = x^2 - 3x + 2$?

(A) $(0, 0)$

(B) $(0, 1)$

(C) $(1, 0)$

(D) $(2, 2)$

(E) $(3, 0)$

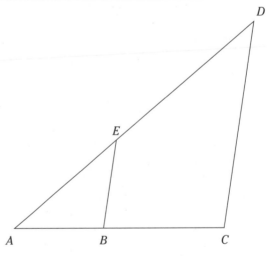

Not drawn to scale

14. In this triangle, $AB = 5$, $BC = 10$, $AE = 6$, and BE is parallel to CD. Determine the ratio of $BE:CD$.

(A) 1:2

(B) 1:3

(C) 1:4

(D) 1:5

(E) 2:1

Go on to next page

15. Which of the following is the equation of the line passing through the point $\left(\frac{5}{6}, \frac{1}{3}\right)$ and the origin?

(A) $y - 1 = \frac{2}{5}x$

(B) $y = \frac{1}{3}x$

(C) $y = \frac{2}{5}x$

(D) $y + 1 = \frac{2}{5}x$

(E) $y + 1 = \frac{5}{6}x$

16. If $g(x) = x^2 - 2x + 4$, which expression represents $g(2x)$?

(A) $4x^2 - 4x + 4$

(B) $4x^2 - 4x$

(C) $2x^2 - 4x + 4$

(D) $2x^2 + 2x - 4$

(E) $x^2 - x + 1$

17. AD is a diameter of circle O. If angle AOB is $70°$ and AD is 3 units long, how long is arc BCD?

(A) $\frac{6}{7}\pi$

(B) $\frac{7}{6}\pi$

(C) $\frac{7}{12}\pi$

(D) $\frac{11}{12}\pi$

(E) $\frac{11}{16}\pi$

18. The volume of a cylinder is 64π cubic inches. If the radius of the cylinder is 4 inches, the height of the cylinder is

(A) 2

(B) $\frac{4}{\pi}$

(C) 4

(D) 4π

(E) 16

19. If p is divisible by $2q$, q is divisible by $3r$, and p, q, and r are positive integers, then p must be divisible by

(A) 5

(B) 6

(C) 7

(D) 8

(E) 9

20. If $2^{a+4} = 4^{a-1}$, what is the value of $3^{a/2}$?

(A) 1

(B) 3

(C) 6

(D) 9

(E) 27

STOP YOU MAY CHECK YOUR WORK ON THIS SECTION ONLY. DO NOT GO BACK TO ANY PREVIOUS SECTION.

Section 3
Critical Reading

Time: 25 minutes for 24 questions

Directions: Choose the *best* answer to each question. Mark the corresponding oval on your answer sheet.

Directions for Questions 25–48: In the following sentences, choose the word or words that, when placed in the blanks, best fit the meaning of the sentence.

Example: After work, Edith always _____ home as quickly as possible.

(A) rambled

(B) wandered

(C) avoided

(D) meandered

(E) ran

The answer is Choice (E).

25. When the chef learned that health inspectors had arrived, she scurried to scrub every work surface in order to obtain a _____ report.

(A) sympathetic

(B) considerate

(C) timely

(D) favorable

(E) consequential

26. Because reservations were not required, the event organizers prepared for a(an) _____ number of guests.

(A) indeterminate

(B) inconclusive

(C) intangible

(D) hospitable

(E) convenient

27. Alan's broken leg _____ his participation in the championship match.

(A) disables

(B) precludes

(C) repels

(D) resists

(E) facilitates

28. The _____ scene in which the guide dog was wounded aroused the viewers' _____.

(A) plausible . . . incredulity

(B) pivotal . . . ennui

(C) judicious . . . emotions

(D) lucid . . . caution

(E) poignant . . . sympathy

29. James urged the witness to stick to the facts and not _____ the truth.

(A) efface

(B) disparage

(C) embellish

(D) compose

(E) compile

Go on to next page

Directions for Questions 30–33: Read these two passages, both adapted from etiquette books, and answer the questions that follow based on what is stated or implied in the passages.

Passage 1

Line Man was not intended to live like a bear or a hermit, apart from others of his own nature; instead, man was born for sociability and finds his true delight in society. *Society* is a word capa-
(05) ble of many meanings: a group of the highest level; the little set of friends to which man is bound by early ties; the companionship of current friends or relatives. Even society with one dear companion is a pleasant state for a man to
(10) be in. This society, composed of many varying elements, is where each individual must submit and merge his own identity into the universal whole if he wishes to glide down the current of polite life, smoothly and pleasantly.

Passage 11

(15)   The customs of social life need frequent restating and adaptation to new needs. They are customs because they are the best rules of conduct that have been garnered from the experiences of many generations living under common
(20) conditions. To know these customs, to catch their spirit, and to follow them in an intelligent way, without slavish exactitude but with careful observance, make one skillful in the art of social interaction and at home in any society. Etiquette
(25) will not take the place of good moral character, nor will it replace an accurate knowledge of human nature and the arts of practical life. However, good manners will unlock to any man or woman the doors of success and profit,
(30) which, without proper etiquette, would have remained forever closed.

30. Both authors would agree that society

   (A) is defined by those in the highest class
   (B) flows from instinctive behavior
   (C) should follow established rules of etiquette
   (D) is in need of reform
   (E) is in conflict with individual liberty

31. All the following would be included in the definition of "society" given in Passage I EXCEPT

   (A) childhood companions
   (B) family
   (C) people seen every day
   (D) fellow citizens
   (E) celebrities

32. According to Passage II, the primary reason to learn etiquette is to

   (A) achieve happiness
   (B) honor one's ancestors
   (C) rise to a higher socio-economic level
   (D) adapt to new circumstances
   (E) smooth social encounters

33. Compared to the author of Passage II, the author of Passage I

   (A) places more emphasis on happiness
   (B) values social hierarchy more
   (C) concentrates less on the benefits of etiquette
   (D) advocates closer attention to rules
   (E) focuses primarily on children

Go on to next page

Directions for Questions 34–41: Read the following passage and answer the questions that follow based on what is stated or implied in the passage.

This passage is excerpted from an introductory essay in Sacred Fire: The QBR 100 Essential Black Books *(Wiley).*

Community and identity are two of the most important criteria used to evaluate the humanity, potential, and spiritual worth of a people. Despite the political, economic, and social (05) oppression that has plagued us since our forced introduction to these shores, our troubled march toward full equality in the face of overwhelming odds has been nurtured by our faith in our worth as individuals and our connection to (10) each other. When protesters during the bloody southern civil rights campaigns of the mid-sixties carried signs reading I AM A MAN, every black person in America knew exactly what was being said. At that moment, we snatched back the (15) power to define ourselves.

It was our sense of community, our blood-tie forged by ancestral love and mutual history, that provided us with the backbone to withstand our often brutal lives with an eye on the promised (20) land of tomorrow. Our sense of a collective identity prevented us from completely falling victim to the powerful negative stereotypes and myths manufactured by the pro-slavery establishment. Our entrenched self-knowledge prevented us (25) from buckling under the flood of pseudoscientific theories concocted to reduce our status to that of a childlike, primitive beast of burden. We never really believed that.

If you were not entirely human, how could (30) you love your woman or children? How could you maintain a family? How could you appreciate the lush harmonies of music or admire the breathtaking beauty of a flower in full bloom? Or create anything of lasting wonder from your lim-(35) ited powers of reason and imagination?

We never really bought their theories about us. If we had, we would no longer exist. We knew the truth. We knew how it felt to face indignity and injustice on a daily basis; we knew how it felt to be wounded on a spirit level; we knew what it (40) meant to be an outsider. Yet we found ways to sustain ourselves. The mission of African-American writers under these maddening circumstances has often been to use words as weapons in the war for self-definition, the war (45) waged for the demise of Topsy, Sambo, and Uncle Tom — the stereotypical roles that presumed to represent us.

What is celebrated in the words and images of the writers in this section of *Sacred Fire* is (50) individual freedom and the collective power of the alienated, the disinherited, the marginal. These writers wrote to survive, to avoid total assimilation and annihilation, to maintain a power of choice in their daily lives not guaran-(55) teed by the ballot box. Style and soul, along with smarts, were essential weaponry in these outsiders' arsenal. These elements of our identity and community were the unique things that set us apart aesthetically from all others, isolated us (60) artistically from the Western tradition, separated us spiritually from the American experience.

Yet we always knew who we were, and we spoke up when it was time for us to tell them who we were. Without this wisdom, without this (65) knowledge gained from the many obstacles overcome, we would be a people devoid of strength, a people to be pitied. These writers on the front lines knew that and produced enduring works with this axiom in mind, ever trumpeting the tri-(70) umphs of the past, ever respectful of the steep losses along the way, ever vigilant of the dangers ahead.

34. Which phrase best describes this passage?

(A) definition of literary works

(B) presentation of factual evidence

(C) explanation of historical events

(D) argument for a point of view

(E) personal narrative

Go on to next page →

35. The "forced introduction to these shores" (Lines 5–6) is most likely a reference to

    (A) slavery

    (B) immigration

    (C) assimilation

    (D) adaptation

    (E) emigration

36. In the context of this passage, which of the following represents the most likely extension of the statement, "I AM A MAN" (Line 12)?

    (A) I am male.

    (B) I do not conform to the stereotypes.

    (C) I possess qualities traditionally associated with men.

    (D) I have a group identity.

    (E) I do not belong to a group.

37. The series of questions in Paragraph 3 (Lines 29–35) serve to

    (A) define "our entrenched self-knowledge" (Line 24)

    (B) list the author's doubts

    (C) intrigue the reader by provoking an argument

    (D) show how ridiculous the "pseudo-scientific theories" (Lines 25–26) are

    (E) mirror the reader's doubts about the author's ideas

38. The "power of choice in their daily lives not guaranteed by the ballot box" (Lines 55–56) most likely refers to

    (A) decisions about family

    (B) candidacy for political office

    (C) freedom to define oneself

    (D) selection of public officials

    (E) career paths

39. With which statement would the author of this passage most likely agree?

    (A) When writers are suffering, they can't express themselves.

    (B) Scientists don't understand literature.

    (C) Writers don't learn from their experiences.

    (D) Works by important white American writers form a separate literary tradition.

    (E) African-American writers have little in common with one another.

40. In the context of this passage, the reference to "words as weapons" (Lines 44–45) implies that

    (A) literature has the potential to make social change

    (B) words can be misunderstood

    (C) authors should defend themselves

    (D) writers can't affect social views

    (E) writers must choose their words carefully

41. In the context of this passage, what is the "axiom" referred to in Line 70?

    (A) Be positive.

    (B) Identity comes partly from past experiences.

    (C) Overcome all obstacles.

    (D) Artistic freedom is crucial for a writer.

    (E) Be aware of danger.

Go on to next page

Directions for Questions 42–48: Read this passage and answer the questions that follow based on what is stated or implied in the passage.

This passage is an excerpt from The Promised Land, *an autobiography by Mary Antin.*

Line   I did not, like my sister, earn my bread in those days; but let us say that I earned my salt by sweeping, scrubbing, and scouring on Saturdays, when there was no school. My moth-
(05) er's housekeeping was necessarily irregular, as she was pretty constantly occupied in the store; so there was enough for us children to do to keep the bare rooms shining. Even here Frieda did the lion's share; it used to take me all
(10) Saturday to accomplish what Frieda would do with half a dozen turns of her capable hands. I did not like housework, but I loved order; so I polished windows with a will, and even got some fun out of scrubbing by laying out the floor in
(15) patterns and tracing them all around the room in a lively flurry of soapsuds.

There is a joy that comes from doing common things well, especially if they seem hard to us. When I faced a day's housework I was half
(20) paralyzed with a sense of inability, and I wasted precious minutes walking around it, to see what a very hard task I had. But having pitched in and conquered, it gave me an exquisite pleasure to survey my work. My hair tousled and my dress
(25) tucked up, streaked arms bare to the elbow, I would step on my heels over the damp, clean boards, and pass my hand over chair rounds and table legs to prove that no dust was left. I could not wait to put my dress in order before running
(30) out into the street to see how my windows shone. Every workman has these moments of keen delight in the product of his drudgery. Men of genius, likewise, in their hours of relaxation from their loftier tasks, prove this universal rule.
(35) I know a man who fills a chair at a great univer-sity. I have seen him hold a roomful of otherwise restless youths spellbound for an hour. And I have seen this scholar, his ponderous tomes shelved for a space, turning over and over with
(40) cherishing hands a letter box that he had made

out of cardboard and paste and exhibiting it   Line proudly to his friends. For the hand was the first instrument of labor, and a respect for the work of the hand survives as an instinct in all of us.

The stretch of weeks from June to   (45) September, when the schools were closed, would have been hard to fill in had it not been for the public library. At first I made myself a cal-endar of the vacation months, and every morn-ing I tore off a day and comforted myself with the   (50) decreasing number of vacation days. But after I discovered the public library I was not impatient for the reopening of school. The library did not open till one o'clock in the afternoon, and each reader was allowed to take out only one book at   (55) a time. Long before one o'clock I was to be seen on the library steps, waiting for the door of para-dise to open. I spent hours in the reading room, pleased with the atmosphere of books, with the order and quiet of the place, so unlike anything   (60) on Arlington Street. The sense of these things permeated my consciousness even when I was absorbed in a book, just as the rustle of pages turned and the tiptoe tread of the librarian reached my ear, without distracting my atten-   (65) tion. Anything so wonderful as a library had never been in my life. It was even better than school in some ways. One could read and read, and learn and learn, as fast as one knew how, without being obliged to stop for stupid little   (70) girls and inattentive little boys to catch up with the lesson. When I went home from the library I had a book under my arm; and I would finish it before the library opened next day, no matter till what hours of the night I burned my little lamp.   (75)

42.   The comparison between Frieda and the narrator in Paragraph 1 (Lines 1–16) implies that

(A) the narrator does more housework than Frieda

(B) the narrator likes housework more than Frieda

(C) Frieda is more efficient at housework than the narrator

(D) the narrator avoids housework by con-vincing Frieda to do additional chores

(E) the narrator uses salt as a cleaning product

Go on to next page

43. In the context of Line 13, what is the best definition of "will"?

    (A) enthusiasm

    (B) self-control

    (C) boredom

    (D) testament

    (E) restraint

44. In the context of Line 35, "chair" may best be defined as

    (A) an item of furniture

    (B) a teaching job

    (C) leadership

    (D) management

    (E) a position of the body

45. The anecdote about "a man who fills a chair at a great university" is intended to

    (A) portray intellectual work as more satis-fying than physical work

    (B) contrast the "restless youths" with the narrator

    (C) show that art is important

    (D) provide an example of genius

    (E) emphasize the rewards of manual labor

46. The narrator's description of the calendar (Lines 45–48) implies that she

    (A) can't fill her days

    (B) enjoys keeping track of time

    (C) has a busy schedule

    (D) is waiting for school to begin

    (E) does not know when the library is open

47. Which of the following is a common ele-ment in the narrator's attitude about housework and the library?

    (A) an appreciation for manual labor

    (B) impatience with everyday tasks

    (C) distaste for physical work

    (D) a love of order

    (E) a need to be active

48. The tone of this passage may best be described as

    (A) regretful

    (B) nostalgic

    (C) argumentative

    (D) defiant

    (E) patronizing

STOP YOU MAY CHECK YOUR WORK ON THIS SECTION ONLY.
DO NOT GO BACK TO ANY PREVIOUS SECTION.

Section 4
Mathematics

Time: 25 minutes for 18 questions

Directions: This section contains two different types of questions. For Questions 21–28, choose the *best* answer to each question. Mark the corresponding oval on the answer sheet. For Questions 29–38, follow the separate directions provided before those questions.

Notes:

✔ You may use a calculator.

✔ All numbers used in this exam are real numbers.

✔ All figures lie in a plane.

✔ You may assume that all figures are to scale unless the problem specifically indicates otherwise.

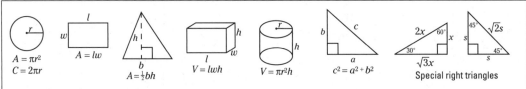

$A = \pi r^2$
$C = 2\pi r$

$A = lw$

$A = \frac{1}{2}bh$

$V = lwh$

$V = \pi r^2 h$

$c^2 = a^2 + b^2$

Special right triangles

There are 360 degrees of arc in a circle.

There are 180 degrees in a straight line.

There are 180 degrees in the sum of the interior angles of a triangle.

21. A number is tripled, and the result is squared. The square is divided by 4 and then reduced by 5. If the result is 4, what could the original number have been?

(A) 1

(B) 2

(C) 3

(D) 4

(E) 5

22. If *d* represents the average (arithmetic mean) of a set of 7 numbers, what can you determine about the numbers?

I.   the sum of the numbers

II. the median number

III. the largest number

(A) I only

(B) II only

(C) III only

(D) I and II

(E) I and III

Go on to next page

23. What is the next number in this sequence of numbers?

    −4, 12, −36, 108, . . .

    (A) −432

    (B) −324

    (C) 144

    (D) 216

    (E) 324

24. The volume of a cube is 27. What is the perimeter of one of the faces of the cube?

    (A) 3

    (B) 9

    (C) 12

    (D) 16

    (E) 36

4

4

25. Determine the area of the shaded region of this figure.

    (A) 16

    (B) 16π

    (C) $16 - 4\pi$

    (D) $16 - 16\pi$

    (E) 64

26. A jar contains red, yellow, and blue marbles. Fifteen percent of the marbles are red, 24 marbles are yellow, and 10 marbles are blue. If a marble is randomly drawn from the jar, what is the probability that it's a blue marble?

    (A) 15%

    (B) 20%

    (C) 25%

    (D) 30%

    (E) 35%

27. If $2a + b = 5$ and $4a^2 - b^2 = -15$, then what is the value of $2a - b$?

    (A) −4

    (B) −3

    (C) −2

    (D) −1

    (E) 0

28. Line *l* passes through the points (1, 4) and (−2, 10). Which of the following is an equation of a line that is perpendicular to line *l*?

    (A) $y = -x + 4$

    (B) $y = 2x + 4$

    (C) $y = -2x + 6$

    (D) $y = -\frac{x}{2} + 6$

    (E) $y = \frac{x}{2} + 2$

Go on to next page

Directions for student-produced response Questions 29–38: Solve the problem and then write your answer in the boxes on the answer sheet. Then mark the ovals corresponding to your answer, as shown in the following example. Note the fraction line and the decimal points.

Answer: $^7/_2$

Answer: 3.25

Answer: 853

Write your answer in the box. You may start your answer in any column.

Although you don't have to write the solutions in the boxes, you do have to blacken the corresponding ovals. You should fill in the boxes to avoid confusion. Only the blackened ovals are scored. The numbers in the boxes aren't read.

There are no negative answers.

You may grid in mixed numbers, such as 3½, as a decimal (3.5) or as a fraction (⅞). Don't grid in 3½; it will be read as ³¹⁄₂.

Grid in a decimal as far as possible. Don't round your answer and leave some boxes empty.

A question may have more than one answer. Grid in one answer only.

29. If 27 is 15% of *x*, then what is 55% of *x?*

30. A machine manufactures 3 cutting boards every 2 minutes. How many cutting boards can it manufacture during an 8-hour work shift?

31. *p, 3p,* and *5p* represent the measures of the angles in a triangle. What is the degree measure of the largest angle of the triangle?

32. A group of 8 friends goes out to dinner. Each person orders either pasta or chicken. The pasta dish costs $12.15, and the chicken dish costs $14.75. If the total cost of the dishes was $105.00, how many people ordered the chicken?

Go on to next page

33. What is the value of $x^{3/2}y^{2/3}$ if $x = 9$ and $y = 8$?

36. A sporting event attracts 3,500 spectators. If 10% of the spectators are over 65 and 54% of the spectators are between 21 and 65, inclusive, then how many of the spectators are younger than 21?

34. If $2x^2 - 6 = x$, what is one possible value for x?

Pull-ups per Day	Number of Days
1	3
2	4
3	4
4	3
5	2

37. Denise is challenging herself to average 3 pull-ups per day over 20 days. So far she has completed 16 days of her workout; her data is shown in this table. What is the average number of pull-ups per day Denise must complete over the next 4 days in order to reach her goal?

35. Triangle ABC is isosceles, with A (1, 3), B (–1, 7), and C (k, 7). What is the value of k?

38. Washington High School has 400 students. Each student has the option of studying French, Spanish, both French and Spanish, or neither language. Fifty students have elected not to study either language, and among students who study only one language, 80 more study Spanish than French. If 380 French and Spanish textbooks were distributed at the beginning of the year, how many students are studying only French?

STOP YOU MAY CHECK YOUR WORK ON THIS SECTION ONLY. DO NOT GO BACK TO ANY PREVIOUS SECTION.

Section 5

Writing

Time: 30 minutes for 39 questions

Directions: Choose the *best* answer to each question. Mark the corresponding oval on your answer sheet.

Directions for Questions 1–20: Read the following sentences carefully. Part or all of each sentence is underlined. Beneath each sentence are five choices. Choice (A) is the original, and the other choices represent different ways of expressing the same meaning. If the sentence is grammatically correct and effectively worded, select Choice (A). If one of the other choices would improve the sentence, select that answer.

Example: Henry wanted to be an architect and that he would have a happy family.

(A) that he would have a happy family

(B) that his family would be happy

(C) to have a happy family

(D) his family should be happy

(E) happiness for his family

The answer is Choice (C).

1. As more and more people read with electronic devices, making sales of paper books decline.

    (A) making sales of paper books decline

    (B) paper book sales decline

    (C) it makes that paper book sales decline

    (D) making sales of paper books, which are declining

    (E) paper books with declining sales

2. My best friend wrote me a letter and explained about how she was considering running for mayor.

    (A) and explained about how she was considering

    (B) having explained that she was considering

    (C) which explained how her consideration was about

    (D) explaining that she was considering

    (E) that had explained her consideration about

3. The ruins of the Parthenon, an ancient temple in Greece, are more popular than any site in that country, which has a rich archaeological heritage.

    (A) are more popular than any site in that country

    (B) have been more popular than any site in that country

    (C) are more popular than any other site in that country

    (D) is more popular than any site there

    (E) are popularer than any other site

Go on to next page

4. Because of the drought, the government has ordered that <u>leaky pipes must be repaired by you in order that water be conserved</u>.

    (A) leaky pipes must be repaired by you in order that water be conserved

    (B) you must repair leaky pipes in order to conserve water

    (C) a person must repair leaky pipes so that you conserve water

    (D) leaky pipes must be repaired and water will be conserved by you

    (E) repairing leaky pipes is what you must do so that water will be conserved

5. Both of Alexander's parents are doctors, so it's not surprising <u>that Alexander wants to study it</u>.

    (A) that Alexander wants to study it

    (B) about Alexander wanting to study it

    (C) that Alexander wants to study medicine

    (D) about Alexander wanting to study it

    (E) knowing that Alexander wants to study medicine

6. When the clock struck twelve, <u>it was while the party guests, intent on welcoming the new year, were</u> cheering and dancing.

    (A) it was while the party guests, intent on welcoming the new year, were

    (B) while the party guests, intent on welcoming the new year, were

    (C) the party guests, intent on welcoming the new year, they were

    (D) the party guests, intent on welcoming the new year, were

    (E) the party guests were intent on welcoming the new year, and had been

7. When writing an essay or a research paper, <u>be sure to credit all the sources you consult</u>.

    (A) be sure to credit all the sources you consult

    (B) crediting all your sources

    (C) credit all the sources consulted by you

    (D) ensuring credit to all your sources

    (E) be sure to credit all the sources having been consulted

8. Sojourner Truth worked tirelessly to end slavery and to achieve equal rights for women, <u>being the reason why her role in American history is important</u>.

    (A) being the reason why her role in American history is important

    (B) therefore her role in American history is important

    (C) the reason why her role in American history is important

    (D) and therefore she played an important role in American history

    (E) but she played an important role in American history

9. Despite the fact that the budget for band uniforms is larger this year than in any previous year, either the band members or the principal <u>has to raise</u> additional money.

    (A) has to raise

    (B) have to raise

    (C) having to raise

    (D) has raising

    (E) will have raised

Go on to next page

10. <u>Everyone whom we believe is interested in running</u> for club president has already submitted a nominating petition.

    (A) Everyone whom we believe is interested in running

    (B) Everyone who we believe is interested in running

    (C) Everyone, whom we believe is interested in running,

    (D) All those whom we believe is interested in running

    (E) All those who we believe is interested

11. <u>Irregardless of the fact that</u> dragons never existed, many legends and folk tales feature these creatures.

    (A) Irregardless of the fact that

    (B) Although

    (C) Despite being a fact that

    (D) While having been a fact that

    (E) Regarding the fact that

12. Shakespeare's villain Macbeth is a complex <u>character, Macbeth descends into evil.</u>

    (A) character, Macbeth descends into evil

    (B) character, Macbeth descended into evil

    (C) character, and Macbeth descends into evil

    (D) character who descends into evil

    (E) character, descending into evil

13. The distinguished law firm, Peabody and Sommes, <u>were established in Boston but soon opened</u> branch offices in several other major cities.

    (A) were established in Boston but soon opened

    (B) established in Boston, but soon opened

    (C) was established in Boston but soon opened

    (D) established in Boston, soon it was opening

    (E) it was established in Boston but soon it opened

14. While scientists are testing a hypothesis, they create <u>an experiment, and then they check the results of the experiment</u>.

    (A) an experiment, and then they check the results of the experiment

    (B) an experiment, which they then check to see the results of it

    (C) an experiment and check the results

    (D) and check the results of an experiment they had done

    (E) and experiment and check the results of it

15. If the city council president <u>would have known about the new law, she would not have</u> criticized the police in her speech.

    (A) would have known about the new law, she would not have

    (B) had known about the new law, she would not have

    (C) knew about the new law, she would not have

    (D) were to have known about the new law, she had not

    (E) was knowing about the new law, she would not have

16. In his statement to the press, <u>the artist explained that because a triangle had three sides</u>, he chose that symbol to represent the three branches of government.

    (A) the artist explained that because a triangle had three sides

    (B) the artist explained that because a triangle will have three sides

    (C) the artist explained that a triangle has three sides

    (D) the artist explained that because a triangle has three sides

    (E) the artist, explaining that because a triangle had three sides

Go on to next page

17. David was annoyed when he heard that the committee had chosen another candidate <u>because he felt equally as qualified</u> when compared to the winner.

    (A) because he felt equally as qualified

    (B) feeling equally as qualified

    (C) feeling that he was equally as qualified

    (D) having felt qualified equally

    (E) because he felt equally qualified

18. The cake batter, which contained butter, several cups of cream, and chocolate chips, <u>were ready to be poured</u> into the pan.

    (A) were ready to be poured

    (B) had been ready to be poured

    (C) was ready to be poured

    (D) it being ready, were poured

    (E) was ready being poured

19. Having studied for days, <u>the exam was found to be easy by Keisha, who was always well prepared</u>.

    (A) the exam was found to be easy by Keisha, who was always well prepared

    (B) Keisha, who was always well prepared, found the exam easy

    (C) Keisha, having always been well prepared and finding the exam easy

    (D) the exam, being found easy by Keisha, always well prepared

    (E) the exam had been found easy by Keisha, always well prepared

20. In the first scene of Shakespeare's *Hamlet,* a ghost <u>appears but refuses to speak</u>, even though the other characters on stage are eager to listen.

    (A) appears but refuses to speak

    (B) had appeared but refuses to speak

    (C) having appeared, but it refuses to speak

    (D) appeared, but is refusing to speak

    (E) appearing but refusing to speak

Directions for Questions 21–34: Read the following sentences carefully. Four portions of each sentence are underlined. Some sentences are correct, and some contain one error. If the sentence is correct, bubble Choice (E) for "no error." If an underlined portion of the sentence contains an error, bubble that letter.

Example:

<u>On the day</u> of the <u>prom, Martin</u> and his
  A   B

friends <u>had gone</u> to the mall <u>to rent</u> tuxedos.
       C   D

<u>No error</u>.
  E

The answer is Choice (C).

21. Having completed <u>several volumes of his</u>
                         A

    <u>biography</u> of Lyndon Johnson, <u>historian</u>
       B   B

    Robert Caro <u>had begun</u> research on
                   C

    <u>Johnson's</u> White House years. <u>No error</u>.
      D   E

22. Please <u>distribute the questionnaires</u>
                  A

    <u>about housing and income</u> <u>to whomever</u>
            B   C

    <u>has requested</u> one. <u>No error</u>.
       D   E

23. <u>Preparing for his upcoming trip</u> to
                 A

    <u>London, Arthur</u> <u>has seldom been</u>
         B   C

    <u>more happier</u> than now, as he selects the
       D

    best guidebook and plans trips to

    important landmarks. <u>No error</u>.
                            E

24. Gil Shaham, <u>a world-famous violinist,</u>
                      A

    <u>began studying</u> the violin <u>while still</u>
       B   C

    <u>a young child</u> <u>and played his first</u>
                         D

    <u>important concert</u> as a teenager.

    <u>No error</u>.
      E

Go on to next page

25. The low-lying areas <u>along the</u>
    A
    <u>Mississippi River are</u> <u>in danger of</u>
    B
    <u>flooding as</u> the storm picks up strength
    <u>and speed, but</u> residents <u>had begun</u>
    C   D
    to place sandbags on the river banks.
    <u>No error.</u>
    E

26. Researchers <u>found that taking</u> "quick
    A
    bites" of a subject — <u>studying for a few</u>
    B
    minutes at a time — <u>are</u> more effective
    C
    <u>than studying</u> for several hours without
    D
    a break. <u>No error.</u>
    E

27. In most cultures, <u>during the dark winter</u>
    A
    months <u>there is</u> usually a few holidays
    B
    <u>that center upon</u> the symbol of light in
    C
    the form of stars, <u>lamps, or other</u> illumi-
    D
    nations. <u>No error.</u>
    E

28. <u>Evelyn and myself</u> plan to prepare
    A
    <u>at least</u> five dozen cookies for the
    B
    bake sale, <u>even though</u> we have
    C
    <u>only a few spare hours</u>. <u>No error.</u>
    D   E

29. <u>For several centuries</u>, artifacts <u>were</u>
    A   B
    <u>taken</u> from that site <u>without regard</u>
    C
    <u>of their</u> historical or symbolic value.
    D
    <u>No error.</u>
    E

30. Samuel Clemens, <u>better known as Mark</u>
    A
    <u>Twain, lived</u> <u>for a short time in</u>
    B   C
    Hartford, where he entertained guests,
    raised his children, and <u>that he wrote</u>
    D
    <u>several novels there</u>. <u>No error.</u>
    E

31. <u>The new bicycle lanes are painted</u> bright
    A
    green <u>so that</u> drivers <u>can distinguish</u> them
    B   C
    more easily <u>from lanes</u> of a neutral color.
    D
    <u>No error.</u>
    E

32. <u>When you compare</u> the price of a new
    A
    telephone <u>with</u> the price of a new
    B
    <u>computer, the telephone</u> may be
    C
    <u>cheapest</u>. <u>No error.</u>
    D   E

33. <u>Shared</u> <u>between the dog groomer and I</u>,
    A   B
    the work <u>of preparing the animals</u> for
    C
    competition <u>was completed</u> quickly.
    D
    <u>No error.</u>
    E

34. <u>Alarmed by the smoke</u> <u>having poured</u>
    A   B
    underneath the door, the council <u>soon put</u>
    C
    an end to discussion <u>and exited</u> the room.
    D
    <u>No error.</u>
    E

Go on to next page

Directions for Questions 35–39: Following is a first draft of a student essay. The essay needs revision. Read the essay and the questions that follow and choose the best answer to each question.

[1] Lately, it seems impossible to turn on the television or click on a website without encountering a discussion of food and beverages. [2] What should be in school lunches and which diet leads to weight loss are popular topics. [3] The health value of processed or fast foods is an issue too.

[4] In a recent study mice were divided into three groups. [5] One group of mice lived in a bare cage and ate normal dry pet food every day. [6] The second group lived in a cage that was a "mouse paradise." [7] The mice received tasty, varied food. [8] They had many toys to play with. [9] Their water was even flavored! [10] The last group had everything like the second group, but they also had an exercise wheel. [11] After many weeks, scientists tested the mice. [12] The second group was happy. [13] They were no smarter than at the beginning of the experiment. [14] The group that exercised became smarter. [15] They performed better on tests that measure intelligence, and scans of their brains showed that their brains had actually changed. [16] Exercise made the difference.

35. Which of the following is the best version of Paragraph 1?

(A) NO CHANGE

(B) Delete Sentence 1.

(C) Delete Sentence 2.

(D) Insert this sentence between Sentences 1 and 2: "More and more Americans are overweight or obese."

(E) Add this sentence after Sentence 3: "Perhaps the most intriguing question is whether food affects intelligence."

36. Which of the following is the best revision of Sentences 7, 8, and 9?

(A) NO CHANGE

(B) The mice received tasty, varied food and even flavored water. They also had many toys to play with.

(C) The mice received tasty, varied food, and they had many toys to play with, and their water was even flavored!

(D) Receiving tasty, varied food, the water was even flavored. They had many toys to play with.

(E) With many toys to play with, the mice received tasty, varied food, their water was even flavored.

37. What change, if any, should occur between Sentences 11 and 12?

(A) NO CHANGE

(B) Insert a sentence describing the tests.

(C) Insert a sentence specifying how many weeks had passed before the mice were tested.

(D) Insert a sentence explaining how the first group responded to the tests.

(E) Insert a sentence describing the behavior of the mice in the second group.

38. How should Sentences 12 and 13 be revised?

(A) NO CHANGE

(B) The second group was happy, but they were no smarter than at the beginning of the experiment.

(C) The second group, being happy, they were no smarter than at the beginning of the experiment.

(D) No smarter than at the beginning of the experiment, the second group had been found to be happy.

(E) Irregardless of being happy, the second group was no smarter than at the beginning of the experiment.

Go on to next page

39. Which sentence, if any, would be best as a concluding statement following Sentence 16?

    (A) NO CHANGE

    (B) If mice exercise, they actually increase their intelligence.

    (C) Yes, mice are not human, but they may show the way to increased intelligence.

    (D) Someday scientists may discover that human brains also improve with exercise.

    (E) It is important for mice to exercise, not just eat.

Chapter 12

Practice Test 1: Answers and Explanations

⬤ ⬤

*T*hink of this chapter — answers to the first practice test in Chapter 11 — as a detective's magnifying glass. Here you behave like a crime scene investigator. (The crime, of course, is that you have to waste more than two hours taking a test.) A detective looks for clues, and you do too: clues to areas on the PSAT/NMSQT where you may need more practice. So run your magnifying glass over the answers you wrote. If you (gasp) find a wrong answer, mark it with an X. If you skipped a question, circle the question number. After you know how many right, wrong, and skipped questions you have, turn to the appendix, where you'll find a scoring grid to help you convert those raw scores into a PSAT/NMSQT score for critical reading, math, and writing.

But wait! As they say on late-night TV commercials, there's more. Before you move on to another practice test, take a few minutes to read the explanations in this chapter. You may be tempted to read only the explanations for the questions you got wrong. Bad idea! I've tucked extra vocabulary words, tips, and strategies into all the explanations, so you may learn something even from the questions you answered correctly. If you're short on time, turn to the end of this chapter to find an abbreviated answer key.

Section 1: Critical Reading

1. **E.** The word "because" tells you right away that you're looking for cause-and-effect answers. Another key word is "without." Remember that the successful candidate will *not* have the quality described in the second blank. You can cross out Choice (A) because the word pair doesn't have a cause-and-effect relationship. Choice (B) is out too, because a **quaint** attitude is old-fashioned, and that word doesn't have much to do with the first blank. (**Homogeneous** means "of the same type or kind.") Choice (C) washes out because, regardless of what's happening to the client base, you wouldn't dump someone who's **prudent** (sensible, keeps things within limits). Choice (D) doesn't work because someone who isn't **tolerant** (accepting of differences) can't deal with a **diverse** (varied) population. Okay, you're left with Choice (E). If the client base is "broad," you want someone with international or diverse experience. **Provincial** means "with a limited perspective, or narrow." Choice (E) is your answer.

2. **B.** The knights have "power and determination," so you're looking for something positive. Dump Choices (A), (C), and (D), because **pathetic** means "deserving of pity," **infamous** means "famous, but for bad reasons, like a bank robber," and **superannuated** is, like your grandparents, "old." Choice (E) doesn't fit, because the sentence doesn't suggest that the knights couldn't have existed. The positive answer is Choice (B), because **redoubtable** means "deserving of respect or honor," an excellent quality in a knight.

3. **A.** Real-world experience helps you here. Picture a window. If it's "frosted," everything you see is a little fuzzy, so Choice (A) is the answer. You can rule out Choice (B) because *transparent* glass lets you see through it perfectly; therefore, the children's image wouldn't be "unclear." Choice (C) is a dud because "stained" glass has colors, and *monochrome* means "all one color." Choice (D) is similar to Choice (B): You can't see through *opaque* glass, and the children wouldn't be *distinct* — "revealing differences." Choice (E) is from another planet because the tendency of the glass to break has nothing to do with what you see. Yup, Choice (A) is the answer you seek.

4. **E.** The key to this question appears at the beginning of the sentence: "contrast" — a word that signals an opposite. If the actor "spoke for hours," you know the agent didn't. Someone who is *terse* uses few words, so Choice (E) is the answer. The other choices don't fit. Choice (A), *loquacious,* is out because that word means "talkative." Choice (B), *temperate,* means "moderate" — where you are if you fall in the middle of two extremes. Choice (C), *redundant,* means "repetitive," and Choice (D), *stoic,* means "seeming indifferent to pain or hardship." Yes, Choice (E) is the answer.

5. **D.** The sentence is almost a tiny film script — the model, the maid, and the difference in their attitudes make a great scene. Use your real-world experience to imagine a famous model's favorite action in front of a mirror. You can drop Choices (B) and (C) because the model will look, not duck, and you can't hide in front of a mirror. The first half of each remaining answer works, so it's time to consider the second blank. What does a servant do "fearfully"? Not show off, which is implied by Choices (A) and (E). To *strut* is to walk proudly, and to *orate* is to speak as if you had an audience of millions. To *cower,* on the other hand, is "to crouch in fear," making Choice (D) your answer.

6. **B.** This one is pure vocabulary. If you know the meaning of the word choices, you're fine. If not, you're sunk. Here are the definitions: *dogmatic* means "rigid," *ubiquitous* is "appearing everywhere," *eclectic* refers to material "from many sources," *ambiguous* means "open to interpretation," and *aesthetic* is "conforming to good taste." Lots of billboards means lots of posters, so Choice (B) is the best answer.

7. **E.** This one's easier if you concentrate on the second half of the sentence. If Eleanor faints, you know something went wrong. The fact that *you know* means that the "effects of the potion" were easy to see. Okay, now you've narrowed your options to Choices (D) and (E). Fainting isn't a good thing, so *beneficial* (advantageous) isn't the proper choice for the first blank. *Deleterious* (causing harm) works perfectly. Just to round out the vocabulary lesson, *pristine* means "pure," and *subtle* is "not obvious."

8. **D.** Another little scene for the film in your head: an animal, afraid, can't come to the camp "openly." Okay, what describes the animal's movements? Sneaky, probably, but that's not one of your choices. *Furtive* is a choice, though, and it means "sneaky." Can you stand a little more vocabulary? *Blatant* and *overt* are right out in the open, with the first word having a hint of "Yeah, so?" in it. Yes, Choice (D) is the one you want here.

9. **C.** The passage criticizes "market gurus" (Line 4) and instead advises the reader, "Act on what the market is telling you." In other words, the market should be your guide, as Choice (C) states. The author is "offended" (Line 3) by "predictions of the market gurus" (Line 4), so Choice (B) is out. Line 14 says, "If you want to win," implying that a way to "win" is possible, so Choice (A) doesn't work. The passage contains no evidence to support Choices (D) or (E). Choice (C) is definitely the one you want.

10. **B.** The author doesn't like "arbitrary statements and predictions" (Line 4) and says that "should," "would," and "could" (Line 13) have no place in investing. Furthermore, the author suggests that you must "Act on what the market is telling you" (Line 15). Okay, you have to observe the market and then throw money at it. Sounds like Choice (B) to me!

11. **E.** The *metaphor* (imaginative comparison) expresses how a community is structured by saying that it's "formed by strings." The rest of the passage talks about giving and receiving, as well as "independence and interdependence" (Line 5). Clearly, the strings are obligations — what people owe to each other. Choice (E) fits perfectly.

12. **D.** The word "channel" is followed by a reference to "sailing" (Line 7) and "boats" (Line 8). Okay, you're on the water, trying to navigate a passage. (Think of the English Channel, a narrow strip of water that separates Britain from France.)

As you see in Question 12, more than one answer fits the meaning of "channel," but only one is appropriate for the sentence the word appears in. Don't jump at the first meaning! Check the context before you select an answer.

13. **B.** Line 1 refers to "the origin of London," so you know you're in early times. True, the term is defined as "the town on the lake" (Line 2), but you can't tell exactly where London is situated, as Choice (A) implies, because the world contains a lot of lakes. Line 5 implies that the Romans called London "Londinium," so Choice (C) is out. Choice (D) is on another planet, because the passage has no mystery in it at all, and Choice (E) is way too general. Choice (B), the correct answer, refers to an early name for what is now London, clearly linking London and Llyn-Din. (If you say the word in your head, you notice that the two names sound similar.)

14. **A.** Passage I explains that under the Romans, London became "a place of not a little importance" (Line 7). In other words, the Romans made the city an important place. Okay, Choice (A) says the same thing, because an administrator runs things, and if you make something important, you probably run it well.

15. **D.** Passage I refers to London as a "dense mass of brick and wooden houses" (Lines 16–17) that are "close" (Line 17). As usual in a vocabulary-in-context question, every answer is a possible definition of "close," but only one, Choice (D), fits the sentence, because "dense" and "close" are synonyms.

16. **C.** The two best possibilities here are Choices (B) and (C), because the lines from Passage I telling you about "pestilence" (Line 22) and "fire" (Line 24) describe dangers. (**Pestilence,** by the way, means "disease.") Of those two answers, Choice (C) is more specific, and therefore better. Why? Well, a city may be vulnerable for many reasons — air pollution because of too many cars, for example. But the author of Passage I talks about the "dense mass" (Line 16) that is "insalubrious" (unhealthful). So the vulnerability of London to pestilence and fire arose from density, as Choice (C) states.

17. **C.** Westminster, Southwark, Bermondsey, Lambeth, and Vauxhall (Lines 49–51) are some of the cities that London "absorbed" (Line 50). Therefore, Choice (C) works nicely.

18. **B.** Passage I refers to a "kernel in a thickly surrounding and ever-growing mass" (Lines 57–58) and moves from pre-Roman to Roman to Anglo-Norman times, and even beyond. Passage II begins with the idea that writing the history of London is "like writing a history of the ocean" (Line 60) because the people who live there are so **multifarious** (diverse) and the city's treasures are "countless" (Line 62). Sounds like a "rich and varied history" — the words in Choice (B) — to me!

19. **E.** Passage II tells you nothing about Boswell, who was a famous biographer, so you can rule out Choices (A), (B), and (D). Boswell's words, on the other hand, tell you that no one London exists — that the city appears different to different people, a sentiment expressed by Choice (E). Choice (C) isn't supported by Boswell's words. Choice (E) is your answer.

20. **B.** The "barnacles" form part of a **simile,** a description created by a comparison. Barnacles are, in fact, tiny animals that live underwater. (If you live anywhere near a boat, chances are you've seen barnacles attached to the boat's sides or bottom.) In Passage II, however, barnacles are there just to tell you about London's houses, which have picked up, over time, a ton of stories from the people who lived in them ("anecdotes, legends, and traditions" — Line 88). Bingo: Choice (B) is your answer.

21. **E.** Just before the list of items the question refers to, the author of Passage II says that old London "is passing away" (Lines 94–95). The author expresses the need to set up a "photographic machine" (Lines 96–97) to "secure some views of it" (Line 97) before London changes. Okay, the objects, which are in a museum (Line 101), are part of the history of London — the "views" that may all too quickly pass away. Choice (E) is the best answer.

22. **C.** Passage I spends a lot of time with pestilence (including plague) and fire. Passage II is much rosier, with an appreciation for the variety of people who have lived in London throughout its history. Though Passage II does mention "base" and "odd" inhabitants (Line 80), no details appear, and those negative terms are balanced by "noble" (Line 80) and "witty" (Line 80). Therefore, the author of Passage I is less positive and more upfront about the disadvantages of London, making Choice (C) the answer.

23. **D.** The "base" people are placed as opposites to the "noble" (Line 80), so they must be "low-class," as Choice (D) states.

24. **E.** Passage II uses many imaginative comparisons; the city is like "an ocean" (Line 60), where all sorts of people have "left their names upon its walls" (Lines 81–82). The author sees the city as "passing away even as we dip our pen in the ink" (Line 95). Passage I, on the other hand, provides names and dates, even listing the cities that London merged with. Yup, Passage II is definitely more general than Passage I, making Choice (E) your answer.

Section 2: Mathematics

1. **C.** To solve this problem, first determine the coordinates of point C by using the midpoint formula, averaging the x-values and y-values of A and D: $\left(\frac{2+14}{2}, \frac{3+7}{2}\right) = (8, 5)$. Now that you have point C, you can use the same idea to find the coordinates of point B: $\left(\frac{2+8}{2}, \frac{3+5}{2}\right) = (5, 4)$.

2. **C.** If you're really clever, you'll see that $a \& b$ relies on b being squared, so the sign of the number in b's position doesn't affect the answer. Always be on the lookout for shortcuts resulting from squaring the variables. Because Choice (C) is the same as the original 3 & 2, except the 2 is negative, you get the same result. If you don't have the good luck of noticing that nifty trick, you can just plug in each of the choices. According to the formula, $3 \& 2 = 2(3) - (2)^2 = 6 - 4 = 2$. Checking each choice: (A) $2 \& 1 = 3$, (B) $2 \& 3 = -5$, you know (C) is 2, (D) $4 \& 3 = -1$, and (E) $6 \& -3 = 3$.

3. **B.** The best way to solve this is to sketch out a coordinate plane where points A, B, and C are, as shown in the following figure.

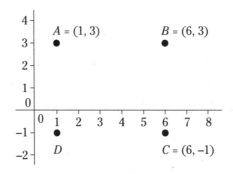

After you have that all set, you can easily see where point D needs to go to make a rectangle — below A and to the left of C. D shares an x-coordinate with A and a y-coordinate with C.

4. **D.** Recall that the *median* of a set is the number that's in the middle if the numbers are arranged in order, or, for an even number of numbers, the median is the average of the two middle numbers. The *mode* of a set is the number that appears most often. Choice (A) has a median and mode of 3, Choice (B) has a median and mode of 2, Choice (C) has a median of 2 and mode of 1, Choice (D) has a median of 4.5 and mode of 5 (the only answer choice with a median less than mode!), and Choice (E) has a median of 4.5 and mode of 4.

5. **E.** The first thing you want to do is solve for x using the first equation. If you square both sides, you see that $3 - x = 4$, so x is -1. Then it's easy to plug x in to the expression $x^2 + 2 = (-1)^2 + 2 = 3$.

6. **D.** For this problem, the easiest thing is to try out the answer choices. The first one you want to check is Choice (C) because it's easy to plug 0 in for x: $f(0) = 3(0)^2 - 5 = -5$. You want a number that's a little bit bigger, so Choice (D) is a good one to test out next. Plugging in: $f(1) = 3(1)^2 - 5 = 3 - 5 = -2$, the number you're looking for. After you get there, you can stop checking, but just in case you want to check your math, $f(-4) = 43$, $f(-2) = 7$, and $f(3) = 22$.

7. **E.** Remember to complete all the calculations inside of the absolute value sign before applying the absolute value! In this case, $2(-5) - 3 = -10 - 3 = -13$, and then $|-13| = 13$, or Choice (E).

8. **B.** This question is really checking to see whether you remember that the intersection of two sets is the elements that the sets have in common. Because 2 is the only number appearing in both set A and set B, 2 is in the intersection of those sets.

9. **B.** The key here is to think that for every red fish you have 2 blue fish, so the fish in the tank will come in multiples of 3. Choice (B) is the only answer that's a multiple of 3, so it's the correct answer.

10. **D.** The key here is substitution. If you can solve one of the equations for one of the variables, then you can substitute that value in to the other equation. One way to do that is to solve the first equation for y: $y = 3 - 2x$. Then you can plug this into the second equation: $x - (3 - 2x) = 6$, and solve for x. $x - 3 + 2x = 6$, $3x - 3 = 6$, $3x = 9$, $x = 3$. You've got it narrowed down to Choices (D) and (E), and can figure out which one by plugging your newfound x value into either equation: $2(3) + y = 3$ and solving for y: $y = -3$.

11. **A.** If you can't remember the rules for odd and even numbers, you can simply pick your favorite odd number and see which of the answer choices works out to be even (remember *plugging in* from Chapter 7?). As it turns out, the very first one, Choice (A), works! Odd + Odd = Even.

12. **B.** Do you remember your exponent rules? A quick hint: A negative exponent is really a reciprocal, so $b^{-3} = \dfrac{1}{b^3}$. In this case, $\dfrac{p}{q} = \dfrac{a^2 b^{-3}}{a^3 b^2} = \dfrac{a^2}{a^3 b^2 b^3} = \dfrac{1}{ab^5}$. Now the trick is to figure out which of the answer choices is equivalent to that. Choices (A), (C), and (E) all have b in the wrong place or raised to the wrong exponent, so you can eliminate those three. Choice (D) has a in the numerator instead of the denominator, so you're left with Choice (B).

13. **C.** This question requires you to plug in the answer choices to see whether they work in the equation. Recall that the first coordinate in an ordered pair represents an x-value, and the second represents a y-value. If you plug 0 in for x, y must equal 2, so that eliminates Choices (A) and (B). Next, try plugging in 1 for x: $(1)^2 - 3(1) + 2 = 0$, so $(1, 0)$ is an ordered pair that works in this equation, and you found your answer!

14. **B.** Similar triangles are the heart of this question. First, you can prove that the triangles are similar by finding that they have two angles in common. They share angle A, so you have one angle. Also, BE and CD are parallel with transversal AC, so angles ABE and ACD must be congruent because they're corresponding angles. Now that you know triangles ABE and ACD are similar, you can compare corresponding sides. Side AB is 5, and AC is 15, so $AB{:}AC = 5{:}15$ or $1{:}3$. All other corresponding sides in the similar triangles will have the same similarity ratio, making Choice (B) the right one.

15. **C.** Because the line passes through the origin $(0, 0)$, you know that the y-intercept is 0. This means you can eliminate any equation that has any addition or subtraction in it. (The right equation has only a slope.) Right away, Choices (A), (D), and (E) are gone. Next, remember that slope is change in y over change in x, or, as some people say, "rise over run." The y-value changes from 0 (at the origin) to $\dfrac{1}{3}$, and the x-values change from 0 to $\dfrac{5}{6}$. Put those results into a change-in-y-over-change-in-x fraction, and remember to multiply by

the reciprocal of the denominator to simplify: $\dfrac{\frac{1}{3}}{\frac{5}{6}} = \dfrac{1}{3} * \dfrac{6}{5} = \dfrac{6}{15} = \dfrac{2}{5}$. Choice (C) is the only one left that has a slope of $\dfrac{2}{5}$.

16. **A.** Substitution is the key to this problem. Wherever you see an x in the original function, you should replace it with $2x$ and simplify: $g(2x) = (2x)^2 - 2(2x) + 4 = 4x^2 - 4x + 4$.

17. **D.** The first thing you want to do in this problem is figure out the measure of angle *BOD*. You know that angle *AOB* and *BOD* must add up to 180°, so angle *BOD* = 180° − 70° = 110°. Next, determine the circumference of the circle using either circumference formula, $2\pi r$ or πd. The problem gives you the diameter (3 units), so the circumference is 3π. Now, set up a proportion: $\dfrac{part}{whole} = \dfrac{part}{whole}$, or $\dfrac{110°}{360°} = \dfrac{x}{3\pi}$, if x is the arc length you're looking for. Solving for x and reducing, you get $x = \dfrac{11}{12}\pi$, Choice (D).

18. **C.** Recall that the volume of a cylinder is $V = \pi r^2 h$. (This formula is at the beginning of each math section, in case you don't remember it.) You know that $V = 64\pi$ and that $r = 4$, so you can plug those into the equation: $64\pi = \pi(4)^2 h = 16\pi h$. Divide both sides by 16π, and you see that the height is 4.

19. **B.** Because q is divisible by $3r$, any number divisible by q must be divisible by 3. You know that p is divisible by $2q$, so p is divisible by both 2 and 3, making it divisible by 6.

20. **E.** The key to this problem is remembering that $4 = 2^2$ and substituting that into the right side of the equation: $4^{a-1} = \left(2^2\right)^{a-1} = 2^{2(a-1)} = 2^{2a-2}$. Now that both sides of the equation have the same base (2), you can set the exponents equal to each other to solve for a: $a + 4 = 2a - 2$, so $a = 6$. But wait! Don't let Choice (C) fool you! The problem asks for the value of $3^{a/2}$, not of a. $3^{6/2} = 3^3 = 27$, or Choice (E).

Section 3: Critical Reading

25. **D.** Logic takes you to the correct answer here. The chef needs to stay in business, and pleasing the health inspector is essential. If something is **favorable**, it is "advantageous" or "helpful." Were you tempted by Choice (A)? **Sympathetic** is a positive word, but it deals with emotions — not the content of health inspections! If you opted for Choice (C), you fell into a trap. True, the chef is pressed for time. The inspector isn't! So the report doesn't have to arrive soon — in a **timely** fashion — it simply has to favor the restaurant.

26. **A.** Before I explain the answer, let me say that reservations should be required. How else will you know how much food to prepare? Okay, now that I've gotten that off my chest, think about what happens when reservations aren't required, the situation in this sentence. Exactly! You have to prepare for an unknown, or **indeterminate**, number of guests — in other words, Choice (A). Choice (B) may have attracted you because **inconclusive** also refers to an unknown. However, "inconclusive" is generally applied to investigations or attempts at problem-solving, not to head counts for a party. The other three choices don't make sense. If something is **intangible**, it can't be seen or touched. (Loyalty, for example, is intangible.) **Hospitable** is the adjective applied to a good host, not to the guests.

27. **B.** Real-world (and hopefully not personal) experience tells you that you can't play sports with a broken leg. Okay, which choice takes Alan out of the match? Choice (A) is tempting, but you don't **disable** participation. You disable machines or people. Choice (C) is a non-starter, because **repel** (to push back with force) isn't what the broken leg is doing. Choice (D) isn't right; people resist, not legs. Choice (E) is the opposite of what you want, because to **facilitate** is "to make easier." Now check out Choice (B). To **preclude** is to make impossible, so Choice (B) is for "best answer."

28. **E.** This sentence has a simple cause-and-effect structure, so you hop to the second blank and check whether the first blank is a possible cause. Choice (E) is an easy fit, because **sympathy** comes from something that moves you emotionally, the exact definition of

poignant, and a wounded guide dog certainly draws sympathy from the audience. The other pairs don't work. *Incredulity* (disbelief) doesn't show up when something seems possible, or *plausible* in SAT vocabulary-land. Nor is *ennui* (boredom) a good partner for a scene that's *pivotal* (referring to the point when everything changes). Emotions aren't a direct result of wise behavior, which the adjective *judicious* describes. Plus, caution can't easily be linked to something that's *lucid* or clear. Choice (E) is the answer you seek.

29. **C.** If you stick to the facts, you present the truth without changing anything. To *embellish* is to add extras — imaginative details or exaggerations. The only other answer remotely in the running is Choice (B), because to *disparage* is to put down, to show no respect for. However, Choice (C) is better because it relates closely to the first part of the sentence. A witness isn't asked whether the truth is a good thing; a witness is asked to tell the truth, the whole truth, and nothing but . . . well, you know the rest. The answer is Choice (C).

30. **C.** In Passage I, the author states that "each individual must submit . . . into the universal whole" (Lines 11–13). To "submit" implies yielding to authority, and authorities make rules. Similarly, Passage II *asserts* (expresses the opinion) that social customs are "the best rules of conduct" (Lines 17–18). Therefore, both authors accept the rules.

31. **D.** Lines 4–8 offer several definitions of "society," including "of the highest level," or Choice (E); the group with "early ties," or Choice (A); and "friends or relatives," Choices (B) and (C). What's left out? The country, also known as Choice (D).

32. **C.** The two main contenders for best answer are Choices (B) and (C). Lines 28–29 states that manners "will unlock to any man or woman doors of success and profit." Sounds like Choice (C) to me! True, the author of Passage II honors age-old customs that are "garnered from the experiences of many generations" (Lines 18–19). However, that line describes what etiquette does, not the reason to learn it. Therefore, Choice (C) is better than Choice (B).

33. **A.** Both authors want good manners, but they give different reasons. Passage II zeroes in on "success and profit" (Line 29), while Passage I praises "the current of polite life" (Lines 13–14) which flows "smoothly and pleasantly" (Line 14) when the individual "submit[s]" (Line 11). The word "pleasantly" is key. The author of the passage values happiness, as Choice (A) states.

34. **D.** The passage makes a point about African-American writers and their work in the very first sentence: "Community and identity are two of the most important criteria used to evaluate the humanity, potential, and spiritual worth of a people" (Lines 1–3). That sentence is a thesis statement, which the rest of the passage supports. Like all thesis statements, this one can be challenged, so the passage is an argument for the author's point of view. Choice (D) is thus the best answer. The other options don't fit. The passage doesn't mention any specific literary works, facts, or historical events, so Choices (A), (B), and (C) are out. Nor do you hear an individual's story, so Choice (E) is wrong. You're left with Choice (D), the correct answer.

35. **A.** Your knowledge of history helps you with this question because the passage discusses African-American writers, and slavery involved involuntary, or "forced," movement from Africa to America. Even if you slept through American history class (and I hope you didn't!), the reference to the "pro-slavery establishment" (Line 23) is a dead giveaway. Before you move on to the next question, add a few vocabulary words to your personal dictionary. *Immigration* and *emigration* are opposites; immigration takes you into a country, and emigration takes you out of one. *Assimilation* is the slow process of blending in with the majority culture, and *adaptation* is "changing to suit new circumstances."

36. **B.** Line 22 refers to the "powerful negative stereotypes and myths manufactured by the pro-slavery establishment." Clearly, the protest signs dispute the stereotypes, some of which "reduce our status to that of a childlike, primitive beast of burden" (Lines 26–27). The gender isn't an issue, as the passage contains no other references to male or female roles. Yes, the passage argues for identification with a group, but Choice (D) takes the concept too far, and Choice (E) is inaccurate. Choice (B) stands for "best" here.

37. **D.** These questions aren't meant to be answered. In fact, the author knows that each has only one possible answer: a loud "no" to the "pseudoscientific theories concocted to reduce our status to that of a . . . beast of burden" (Lines 25–27). Therefore, Choice (D) is the best choice here.

38. **C.** The "power of choice" statement shows up in a discussion of "words and images" (Line 49) used by African-American writers "to survive, to avoid total assimilation and annihilation" (Lines 53–54). It follows a paragraph about "self-definition" (Line 45) in the face of stereotypical roles (Line 47). Therefore, the power is that of self-definition, or "the freedom to define oneself," also known as Choice (C).

39. **D.** Line 60 states that African-American writers, the "us" of the passage, are "isolated artistically from the Western tradition." It's logical to conclude that the "Western tradition" is largely white, so Choice (D) makes sense. The other choices actually contradict the author's statements in the passage.

40. **A.** The cited paragraphs contain references to a "mission" (Line 42), the "war for self-definition" (Line 45), and the "war waged for the demise of Topsy" (Lines 45–46) and other stereotypes of African Americans. Therefore, the words are weapons in the fight against stereotypes, a social change. The correct answer is Choice (A).

41. **B.** The last paragraph (Lines 63–73) talks about the knowledge acquired "from the many obstacles overcome" (Lines 66–67), so you may have jumped at Choice (C). However, the "obstacles" are part of the history of African Americans. Also, the last sentence tells more of the story, referring to "the triumphs of the past" (Lines 70–71) and the "steep losses along the way" (Lines 71–72). The writer says that "without this wisdom" (Line 65), "we would be a people devoid of strength" (Line 67). No doubt about it, the author is speaking about identity in relation to experience. Choice (B) is the answer you want.

42. **C.** The narrator contrasts her work with that of her sister (Line 1) and says that Frieda "did the lion's share" (Line 9), which is the largest portion. The narrator also says that Frieda got more done "with a half a dozen turns of her capable hands" (Line 11) than the narrator could do in "all Saturday" (Lines 9–10). Therefore, Frieda is more efficient, as Choice (C) states.

43. **A.** I wish this author would come to my house on cleaning days! She certainly throws herself into the task. Take a look at what she says. The narrator "polished windows with a will" (Line 13) because she "loved order" (Line 12), and she even went outside to see "how my windows shone" (Lines 30–31). Okay, the task wasn't fun by itself, but it was satisfying, so "enthusiasm" is the best answer here.

44. **B.** A "chair" may be an honor — and a job — given to some professors. Even if you're not familiar with academic terminology, the narrator goes on to describe the man as a teacher and a scholar. Choice (B) fits perfectly.

45. **E.** The professor may work at a "great university" (Lines 35–36), but he is proudest of something he made with his hands, a "letter box" (Line 40). The *anecdote* (short account of something that happened) ends with a positive statement about the hand and labor, making Choice (E) an excellent answer.

46. **D.** Unlike me (vacation? I can't wait!), the narrator says that "the stretch of weeks" (Line 45) of summer "would have been hard to fill" (Line 47) without the public library. Because she is "comforted . . . with the decreasing number of vacation days" (Lines 50–51), you know that she loves school and is waiting for school to begin, as Choice (D) states.

47. **D.** The key here is to find an answer that works for *both* housework and the library. Reading carefully, you see that the narrator "loved order" (Line 12) even though she wasn't wild about beginning her household chores. She also says that she "spent hours in the reading room, pleased . . . with the order and quiet of the place" (Lines 58–60). No doubt about it, Choice (D) is the answer.

Don't be fooled by answers that *almost* fit. In the preceding question, you may have jumped at Choice (A) because the narrator does praise manual labor. However, she doesn't mention manual labor when she's speaking about the library, so that answer is wrong.

48. **B.** The narrator is talking about her past, and though she didn't actually live in paradise (don't forget the household chores!), she isn't whining about how much she suffered. In fact, she mentions several positive things — her joy in completing housework, her time in the library (which she enters through the "door of paradise" — Line 57), and her love of schoolwork. Clearly she is remembering a fairly happy time, so ***nostalgic,*** a word referring to fond reflection on the past, works nicely here. As long as I'm in vocabulary mode, I should mention that ***patronizing*** implies that the narrator is looking down on the reader — not the case here.

Section 4: Mathematics

21. **B.** If you don't want to try to turn this paragraph into an algebraic expression, you can just work backwards. The result is 4, and that number comes from reducing something by 5: The previous result was $4 + 5 = 9$. Nine was the result of dividing a number by 4, so that number was $9 \times 4 = 36$. Thirty-six came from squaring a number, so the original number may have been 6 (–6 is also possible, but all the answer choices are positive, so you're probably safe to ignore that solution). Six was the result of tripling a number (multiplying by 3), so the original number must have been 2, Choice (B). If you want to check the algebraic expression you came up with instead of working backwards (with x as the unknown number): $\frac{(3x)^2}{4} - 5 = 4$.

22. **A.** You get the average of a set of numbers by adding up all the numbers and then dividing by the number of numbers (in this case, 7). If you multiply the average by 7, you'll know what the numbers added up to (option I). To determine the median number, you need to know the actual numbers you're working with so that you can line them up in order and find the middle, so option II is out. Similarly, you can't determine what the largest number is without knowing more than just the sum of a set of numbers, so option III is out.

23. **B.** Each number in the sequence switches sign, so you know that the next term will be negative: Choice (A) or (B). Each number is also 3 times larger than the previous one, so the next number is $-3 \times 108 = -324$.

24. **C.** If the length of a side of a cube is x, then the volume of the cube is $V = x^3$. You know that the volume is 27, so you can deduce that x is 3. Each face (side) of the cube is made up of a square with side lengths of 3, so the perimeter of a face of the cube is $3 \times 4 = 12$, or Choice (C).

25. **C.** The shaded area is the result of subtracting the area of a quarter of a circle from the area of a square. The area of the square is $4 \times 4 = 16$, and the area of the quarter circle is $\frac{1}{4}\pi r^2 = \frac{1}{4}\pi(4)^2 = 4\pi$. This means that the area of the shaded region is $16 - 4\pi$.

26. **C.** If 15% of the marbles are red, then 85% of the marbles are not red. You know that there are $24 + 10 = 34$ not-red marbles. To determine what percent of the not-red marbles are blue, you can set up a proportion of blue marbles over all not-red marbles: $\frac{b}{85\%} = \frac{10}{34}$. If you cross-multiply and solve for b, $b = 25\%$, or Choice (C).

27. **B.** The key to solving this problem is recognizing the difference of perfect squares. Recall that $(x+y)(x-y) = x^2 - y^2$, so whenever you see an equation with the difference of perfect squares, remember that you can easily factor. In this case, you can rewrite the expression so that the squares are easier to see: $4a^2 - b^2 = (2a)^2 - b^2$. Now it's clear that it will factor into $(2a+b)(2a-b)$. Using substitution, you know that $(5)(2a-b) = -15$, so $2a - b = -3$.

28. **E.** Perpendicular lines have opposite reciprocal slopes, meaning that the slopes multiply to –1. So the first thing you need to do is find the slope of the line through the two points given. Slope $= \frac{\Delta y}{\Delta x} = \frac{10-4}{-2-1} = \frac{6}{-3} = -2$. The opposite reciprocal of –2 is $\frac{1}{2}$, so you want to find an equation that has a slope of $\frac{1}{2}$. The only equation that fits that requirement is Choice (E).

29. **99.** For this question, you don't even need to figure out what x is; you can just set up a proportion: $\frac{a}{27} = \frac{55\%}{15\%}$. After you cross-multiply to solve for a, you determine that a is 99.

30. **720.** If the machine makes 3 boards in 2 minutes, you can deduce that it can make $3 \times 30 = 90$ boards in one hour, because there are 30 two-minute sections in an hour. Multiply the hourly rate by 8 hours, and you get $90 \times 8 = 720$ cutting boards.

31. **100.** A triangle has 180°, so you know that $p + 3p + 5p = 180°$, so $9p = 180°$ and $p = 20°$. You want to find the biggest angle, represented by $5p = 5(20°) = 100°$.

32. **3.** Let x be the number of people in the group that ordered chicken. That means that $8 - x$ people ordered pasta. Multiply the number of people ordering each dish by the price of the dish to get the following equation: $x(14.75) + (8 - x)(12.15) = 105$. You can simplify this equation: $14.75x + 8(12.15) - 12.15x = 105$; $2.6x + 97.2 = 105$; $2.6x = 7.8$, so $x = 3$. Three people ordered the chicken.

33. **108.** When you have rational (fraction) exponents, it's important to remember that the numerator is the number of times you're multiplying a number by itself, and the denominator is the root you're taking. If the denominator is 2, you take the square root; if it's 3, you take the cube root; and so on. If $x = 9$, then $x^{3/2} = 9^{3/2} = \left(\sqrt{9}\right)^3 = 3^3 = 27$; and if $y = 8$, then $y^{2/3} = 8^{2/3} = \left(\sqrt[3]{8}\right)^2 = 2^2 = 4$. Substituting back into the original: $x^{3/2}y^{2/3} = (27)(4) = 108$.

34. **2.** The best way to solve a quadratic equation (and this equation is **quadratic** because it has an x^2 term) is to move everything to one side of the equation and then factor: $2x^2 - x - 6 = 0$; $(2x + 3)(x - 2) = 0$. Then set each of the factors equal to zero and solve for x: $x = -\frac{3}{2}$ or $x = 2$. Grid-in questions don't allow negative answers, so your answer here is 2.

35. **3 or 4.** You definitely want to draw a picture for this problem. The most straightforward way to see this problem is that side AB is one of the two sides that are congruent in the isosceles triangle, so point C is as far from A as B is but on the other side of the vertical line passing through A. This (labeled $C1$ on the diagram) results in $k = 3$. The other way to see the triangle is with side AB as the base, with AC and BC as the congruent sides. In this case, you need the altitude of the triangle to be perpendicular to AB and passing through the line $y = 7$ (this intersection is labeled $C2$), resulting in $k = 4$.

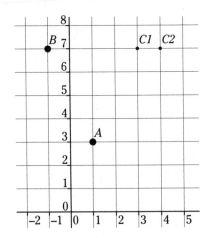

36. **1,260.** You know that $10\% + 54\% = 64\%$ of the spectators are 21 years old or older, meaning that 36% of the spectators are under 21. To determine how many people that is, simply multiply: $(0.36)(3,500) = 1260$ people are under 21 years old.

37. **¹⁵⁄₄ or 3.75.** The first thing you want to do is determine how many pull-ups Denise has already done over the past 16 days. Multiply the number of pull-ups by the number of

days, and add all those products together: $(1)(3) + (2)(4) + (3)(4) + (4)(3) + (5)(2) = 45$ pull-ups. If Denise wants an average of 3 pull-ups per day over 20 days, she needs to have completed $(20)(3) = 60$ pull-ups by the end of the 20 days. That means that over the next 4 days, Denise must do $60 – 45 = 15$ pull-ups, for an average rate of ¹⁵⁄₄ pull-ups per day.

38. **120.** This is a problem best solved with a Venn diagram.

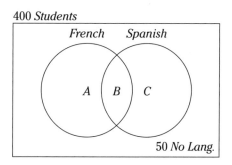

A is the number of students taking only French class, *B* is the number of students taking both French and Spanish, and *C* is the number of students taking only Spanish. You know that $400 – 50 = 350$ students are enrolled in one or both of the language courses, so $A+B+C = 350$. You also know that 380 textbooks were given out: $(A+B)+(B+C) = 380$, so 30 students must be taking both languages ($B = 30$). You can now write $A+30+C = 350$, or $A+C = 320$. You know that $A+80 = C$ because 80 more students study just Spanish than just French. Using substitution: $A+(A+80) = 320$, so $A = 120$.

Section 5: Writing

1. **B.** The original "sentence" is actually a sentence fragment, lacking one complete thought. The first statement ("As more and more people read with electronic devices") leaves you hanging; you're waiting for more information. The second portion of the original supplies a verb, "making," but no subject. Choice (B) gives a complete thought and has a good subject/verb combo ("sales decline"). Add Choice (B) to the beginning of the sentence, and you're all set. None of the other choices create a complete thought except Choice (C), which has unnecessary words.

2. **D.** The original sentence isn't terrible, but it is wordy and awkward, as is Choice (C). Choice (D) gets the same information across in fewer words. Choices (B) and (E) are in the wrong tense.

3. **C.** When you compare, you must be logical. The sentence tells you that the Parthenon is in Greece, so it can't be more famous than any structure in Greece, because it can't be more famous than itself. Add "other" and you're all set. Choice (B) is in the wrong tense, and Choice (D) incorrectly uses the singular verb "is," which doesn't match the plural subject "ruins." Choice (E) has an improper comparison, "popularer."

4. **B.** Okay, the original isn't completely terrible, but passive voice ("must be repaired by you") isn't necessary. Choice (B) switches to active ("you must repair"), always a better choice unless you don't know who did the action or you *do* know but are trying to avoid responsibility. Choice (C) pairs a third-person noun ("a person") with a second-person pronoun ("you") — penalty box. Stay in third person or in second, but don't shift between them. Choice (D) is out because of a passive verb, and Choice (E) piles on way too many words. Yup, go with Choice (B).

5. **C.** The problem with the original sentence is the pronoun "it." What does "it" refer to? Absolutely nothing, according to the sentence. You need to insert a noun ("medicine"). Both Choices (C) and (E) do so, but Choice (E) adds "knowing," which doesn't fit the sentence. Go for Choice (C), the correct answer.

6. **D.** The original sentence needs to go on a diet. Some of its words — "it was while" — aren't needed. Choice (D) is slim but does the job. Choices (A) and (C) also contain unnecessary words. Choice (B) creates a sentence fragment, and Choice (E) has a tense error.

When you're working on sentence improvement, check for extra words. The torturers (oops, I mean test-writers) want to see trim sentences that express the same idea as the original, wordy version.

7. **A.** Gasp! I actually placed a correct sentence in this section, as does the College Board from time to time. The other choices prune words, but they don't improve the sentence. Choices (B) and (D) are fragments. Choices (C) and (E) move to passive voice, which is seldom a better place to be! Go for Choice (A).

8. **D.** In the original sentence, the underlined portion is a description (a participle, in case you're into English-teacher lingo). However, the description has nothing to hang on; it's just sitting there. The same situation occurs in Choice (C), where an **appositive** (a definition of a noun or pronoun stated earlier in the sentence) is also drifting without an anchor. Choice (B) creates a run-on sentence because "therefore" isn't a **conjunction** (a joining word). Choice (D) takes care of the problem by using "and" (which _is_ a conjunction) in front of "therefore." Choice (E) changes the meaning of the sentence. Choice (D) is the right answer.

9. **A.** Yup, I hit you with another correct sentence. You need present tense to match the present-tense verb in the first part of the sentence ("is"), so Choice (E) is out. You also need a singular verb, because in a sentence with two subjects joined by "either/or" or "neither/nor," the verb matches the closest subject, which in this sentence is "principal." The singular verb "has" is what you want, so Choice (B) flops. Choices (C) and (D) aren't correct forms in _any_ sentence. You're left with Choice (A), the right answer.

10. **B.** A _who/whom_ question. Time to run for the lifeboats, right? Wrong. The selection of _who_ or _whom_ is actually easy. All you need to know is that _who_ is for subjects and _whom_ for objects. If you're able to pair every verb with a subject, the proper word is probably _whom_. If you have a verb with no subject, chances are you need _who_ to act as the subject. (I say "probably" and "chances are" because one rare exception exists, a subject complement. You won't find anything so complicated on the PSAT, though.) In this sentence, "we believe" is one subject/verb pair and "Everyone has submitted" is another. Okay, what about the verb "is"? You need a subject, and "who" does the job. Now you know that Choices (B) and (E) are possibilities. Choice (E) is wrong because "All those" is plural, and "is" is singular. In the grammar world, singular and plural don't mix, so Choice (B) is your answer.

11. **B.** "Irregardless" looks like an important word, but it isn't actually a word at all. Go for "although" (Choice B), because it's simple and correct.

12. **D.** Choice (A), the original, is a run-on sentence — a grammatical felony. Something other than a comma has to link the statement "Macbeth descends into evil" to the rest of the sentence. Okay, Choice (C) adds "and." The conjunction "and" makes the sentence correct, but it lacks style. Choice (D) joins the ideas with the pronoun "who" — a more stylish and a completely correct answer.

13. **C.** The subject, "law firm," is singular and requires a singular verb. (Pairing singular subjects and plural verbs is like sprinkling tuna salad on vanilla ice cream: _not_ a good idea.) You can rule out Choice (A) because of its plural verb, "were."

14. **C.** The original sentence isn't wrong, but it is wordy. Choice (C) gets the job done more efficiently and is the best answer.

15. **B.** Question 15 presents a situation grammarians call "condition contrary to fact" — a hypothetical statement that requires a subjunctive verb. Don't worry about the terminology. Just remember that when you have an "if" statement that talks about something that isn't true, use "had" or "were," never "would." The "would" belongs in the second part of the sentence, the consequences or situation that would result *if* the hypothetical situation were true. In Question 15, two choices are possible: Choice (B), which uses the helping verb "had," and Choice (D). Choice (D) has the wrong verb tense. Go for Choice (B).

16. **D.** A triangle doesn't change, so the appropriate verb to describe it must be in present tense. Therefore, now you know that you're looking for an answer with "has," not "had." If you insert Choice (C) into the sentence, you end up with a run-on sentence. Choice (D), on the other hand, works perfectly and is the answer you want.

17. **E.** "Equally as qualified"? I don't think so! No such expression exists in standard English. Opt for "equally qualified" — Choice (E) — and you're all set.

18. **C.** Were you fooled by the "butter, several cups of cream, and chocolate chips"? I'm not talking about calorie count (though that cake sounds a bit rich!). I'm talking about those words that may distract you from the true subject of this sentence ("batter"), which is singular. A singular subject needs a singular verb — "was." Choices (C) and (E) are in the running, but Choice (E) drops out because "ready being poured" isn't standard English. Choice (C) is correct.

19. **B.** The sentence begins with a descriptive verb form ("Having studied for days"). The rule is that introductory descriptive verb forms *must* describe the subject. In the original sentence, therefore, "the exam" studied for days. Nope. "Keisha" has to be the subject of the sentence. Choices (B) and (C) are both fine in that respect, but Choice (C) creates a fragment, not a complete sentence. Choice (B) is the best answer in this one.

20. **A.** Yes! A correct sentence! When you write about literature, present tense is best, and the original sentence properly employs two present-tense verbs, "appears" and "refuses." The other choices mix and match tenses, which is frequently a bad idea and downright wrong when you have no valid reason to switch from one tense to another.

21. **C.** The introductory verb form ("Having completed") places that action in the past, prior to another action. The main verb of the sentence, therefore, should be in simple past tense ("began") or perhaps present progressive tense ("is beginning"). The verb "had begun" doesn't fit because the "had" places an action in the past, before another past action. As written, the sentence gives you two actions that are supposed to precede another action — which doesn't exist!

22. **C.** The verb "has requested" requires a subject, and "whomever" can't function as a subject. That pronoun is reserved for objects. The correct pronoun would be "whoever," so Choice (C) is your answer.

Were you fooled by the word "to"? It's a preposition, and a preposition needs an object. However, the verb "has requested" needs a subject. Object, subject — what's a worried test-taker to do? Easy! Opt for the subject, because verbs *always* need subjects. By the way, the object of the preposition isn't one word but rather a few: "whoever has requested one." (For the grammar experts, the object of the preposition is a clause.)

23. **D.** "Happier" creates a comparison all by itself; the "more" is overkill.

24. **E.** Everything is in place here: the commas surrounding "a world famous violinist" (which serves as an appositive to the subject, in case you care), the compound verbs ("began" and "played"), and the extra information stated in "while still a young child." The words "he was" or "Gil was" are implied, but that's okay because the subject that's stated ("Gil Shaham") matches the implied subject. Yup, no error here.

25. **D.** The helping verb "had" places an action further in the past than another action. In this sentence, you have two present-tense verbs ("are" and "picks"), so "had" isn't justified. (The proper expression is "have begun.")

26. **C.** The verb "are" is plural, but its subject ("taking quick bites") is singular. You need a singular verb, "is."

Did the dashes in Question 26 confuse you? Dashes plop extra information into a sentence. Think of them as handles; lift out the words they enclose, and you should see the basics of the sentence more clearly.

27. **B.** The word "there" can never be a subject. Look after the verb to find the subject, which in this sentence is "holidays." Because "holidays" is a plural noun, you need "there are," not "there is."

28. **A.** The pronoun "myself" (or any of the "-self" or "-selves" pronouns) should appear only when the action doubles back on the subject ("I told myself not to worry") or, in rare cases, for emphasis ("I myself will take the PSAT"). The correct expression is "Evelyn and I."

29. **D.** In standard English, the expression is "regard for," not "regard of."

30. **D.** When you see a list in a sentence, check that every item in the list has the same grammatical identity. (Don't worry about terminology. Just "hear" the words in your head. If they sound like they match, they probably do.) In Sentence 30, "entertained," "raised," and "wrote" match, but "that he wrote" breaks the pattern. There's your error!

31. **D.** The standard English expression is "more easily than," not "more easily from."

32. **D.** Comparing two things calls for "cheaper," not "cheapest," the proper form for comparing more than two items.

33. **B.** The preposition "between" calls for an object pronoun, "me," not a subject pronoun, "I."

34. **B.** The smoke and the alarm are simultaneous, give or take a nano-second or two, so you shouldn't place the helping verb "having" in front of "drifted." The helping verb places the action of drifting further in the past. The correct expression is "pouring."

35. **E.** The first paragraph mentions several issues centering on food: school lunches, weight loss, and processed or fast food. The second paragraph zeroes in on food and intelligence. What's the connection? Right now, you can't find one, because the author didn't include a transition sentence. Choice (E) solves that problem by linking general food issues to the food/intelligence study.

36. **B.** Putting the food and water together makes sense, followed by the toys. Choice (B) is the smoothest and has no grammar errors. Choice (C) sounds more childlike — too many *ands*. Choice (D) has a dangling modifier (as written, the water is receiving the food), and Choice (E) is a run-on sentence. Yup, go for Choice (B).

37. **D.** The mice were divided into three groups, but Paragraph 2 doesn't tell you how the mice in group one reacted to the tests. The reader is left wondering. Yes, it would be nice to know what kind of tests were given, as Choice (B) states, and how many weeks passed during the study, which is Choice (C), but those details aren't as important as a report on group one. The correct answer is Choice (D).

38. **B.** As originally written, these two sentences are short and choppy. Combining them is a good idea, but only Choice (B) does so in a grammatically correct and efficient fashion.

39. **D.** The essay begins with human beings' search for improved intelligence and then goes into detail on an experiment with mice. A good concluding sentence, therefore, should take the essay full circle, returning to people, as Choice (D) does.

Answer Key for Practice Test 1

Section 1

1. E	7. E	13. B	19. E
2. B	8. D	14. A	20. B
3. A	9. C	15. D	21. E
4. E	10. B	16. C	22. C
5. D	11. E	17. C	23. D
6. B	12. D	18. B	24. E

Section 2

1. C	6. D	11. A	16. A
2. C	7. E	12. B	17. D
3. B	8. B	13. C	18. C
4. D	9. B	14. B	19. B
5. E	10. D	15. C	20. E

Section 3

25. D	31. D	37. D	43. A
26. A	32. C	38. C	44. B
27. B	33. A	39. D	45. E
28. E	34. D	40. A	46. D
29. C	35. A	41. B	47. D
30. C	36. B	42. C	48. B

Section 4

21. B	26. C	31. **100**	36. **1,260**
22. A	27. B	32. **3**	37. **$^{15}\!/_4$ or 3.75**
23. B	28. E	33. **108**	38. **120**
24. C	29. **99**	34. **2**	
25. C	30. **720**	35. **3 or 4**	

Section 5

1. **B**	11. **B**	21. **C**	31. **D**
2. **D**	12. **D**	22. **C**	32. **D**
3. **C**	13. **C**	23. **D**	33. **B**
4. **B**	14. **C**	24. **E**	34. **B**
5. **C**	15. **B**	25. **D**	35. **E**
6. **D**	16. **D**	26. **C**	36. **B**
7. **A**	17. **E**	27. **B**	37. **D**
8. **D**	18. **C**	28. **A**	38. **B**
9. **A**	19. **B**	29. **D**	39. **D**
10. **B**	20. **A**	30. **D**	

Chapter 13

Practice Test 2

. . . .

1 once lived next door to someone who made large batches of meatballs and then froze them for future use. Nothing unusual there, except that she placed the meatballs in a straight line in her freezer. That neighbor had an orderly mind! If you're like her — or a little less obsessive — you probably did Practice Test 1 already. Now you're ready for round two. You know what to do. Set your timer and get started. (Have you blocked out the memories of two hours of annoying test questions that you answered already? I don't blame you a bit. Turn back to Chapter 11 for a refresher.)

If you're less conventional and enjoy skipping around, this may be your first crack at the PSAT/NMSQT. Before you start this exam, check out the beginning of Chapter 11, where you find some general directions. Then turn the page for Practice Test 2. When you're done, treat yourself to a mindless reality TV show or a trip to the mall. Then check your answers with the key in Chapter 14. Read the explanations for all the questions, not just those accompanying the ones you missed. I placed tips and vocabulary builders with the answers, so you may learn something even from questions you answered correctly.

Answer Sheet

For the questions in Sections 1 through 5, use the ovals and grid-ins to record your answers.

Section 1: Critical Reading

1. Ⓐ Ⓑ Ⓒ Ⓓ Ⓔ
2. Ⓐ Ⓑ Ⓒ Ⓓ Ⓔ
3. Ⓐ Ⓑ Ⓒ Ⓓ Ⓔ
4. Ⓐ Ⓑ Ⓒ Ⓓ Ⓔ
5. Ⓐ Ⓑ Ⓒ Ⓓ Ⓔ
6. Ⓐ Ⓑ Ⓒ Ⓓ Ⓔ

7. Ⓐ Ⓑ Ⓒ Ⓓ Ⓔ
8. Ⓐ Ⓑ Ⓒ Ⓓ Ⓔ
9. Ⓐ Ⓑ Ⓒ Ⓓ Ⓔ
10. Ⓐ Ⓑ Ⓒ Ⓓ Ⓔ
11. Ⓐ Ⓑ Ⓒ Ⓓ Ⓔ
12. Ⓐ Ⓑ Ⓒ Ⓓ Ⓔ

13. Ⓐ Ⓑ Ⓒ Ⓓ Ⓔ
14. Ⓐ Ⓑ Ⓒ Ⓓ Ⓔ
15. Ⓐ Ⓑ Ⓒ Ⓓ Ⓔ
16. Ⓐ Ⓑ Ⓒ Ⓓ Ⓔ
17. Ⓐ Ⓑ Ⓒ Ⓓ Ⓔ
18. Ⓐ Ⓑ Ⓒ Ⓓ Ⓔ

19. Ⓐ Ⓑ Ⓒ Ⓓ Ⓔ
20. Ⓐ Ⓑ Ⓒ Ⓓ Ⓔ
21. Ⓐ Ⓑ Ⓒ Ⓓ Ⓔ
22. Ⓐ Ⓑ Ⓒ Ⓓ Ⓔ
23. Ⓐ Ⓑ Ⓒ Ⓓ Ⓔ
24. Ⓐ Ⓑ Ⓒ Ⓓ Ⓔ

Section 2: Mathematics

1. Ⓐ Ⓑ Ⓒ Ⓓ Ⓔ
2. Ⓐ Ⓑ Ⓒ Ⓓ Ⓔ
3. Ⓐ Ⓑ Ⓒ Ⓓ Ⓔ
4. Ⓐ Ⓑ Ⓒ Ⓓ Ⓔ
5. Ⓐ Ⓑ Ⓒ Ⓓ Ⓔ

6. Ⓐ Ⓑ Ⓒ Ⓓ Ⓔ
7. Ⓐ Ⓑ Ⓒ Ⓓ Ⓔ
8. Ⓐ Ⓑ Ⓒ Ⓓ Ⓔ
9. Ⓐ Ⓑ Ⓒ Ⓓ Ⓔ
10. Ⓐ Ⓑ Ⓒ Ⓓ Ⓔ

11. Ⓐ Ⓑ Ⓒ Ⓓ Ⓔ
12. Ⓐ Ⓑ Ⓒ Ⓓ Ⓔ
13. Ⓐ Ⓑ Ⓒ Ⓓ Ⓔ
14. Ⓐ Ⓑ Ⓒ Ⓓ Ⓔ
15. Ⓐ Ⓑ Ⓒ Ⓓ Ⓔ

16. Ⓐ Ⓑ Ⓒ Ⓓ Ⓔ
17. Ⓐ Ⓑ Ⓒ Ⓓ Ⓔ
18. Ⓐ Ⓑ Ⓒ Ⓓ Ⓔ
19. Ⓐ Ⓑ Ⓒ Ⓓ Ⓔ
20. Ⓐ Ⓑ Ⓒ Ⓓ Ⓔ

Section 3: Critical Reading

25. Ⓐ Ⓑ Ⓒ Ⓓ Ⓔ
26. Ⓐ Ⓑ Ⓒ Ⓓ Ⓔ
27. Ⓐ Ⓑ Ⓒ Ⓓ Ⓔ
28. Ⓐ Ⓑ Ⓒ Ⓓ Ⓔ
29. Ⓐ Ⓑ Ⓒ Ⓓ Ⓔ
30. Ⓐ Ⓑ Ⓒ Ⓓ Ⓔ

31. Ⓐ Ⓑ Ⓒ Ⓓ Ⓔ
32. Ⓐ Ⓑ Ⓒ Ⓓ Ⓔ
33. Ⓐ Ⓑ Ⓒ Ⓓ Ⓔ
34. Ⓐ Ⓑ Ⓒ Ⓓ Ⓔ
35. Ⓐ Ⓑ Ⓒ Ⓓ Ⓔ
36. Ⓐ Ⓑ Ⓒ Ⓓ Ⓔ

37. Ⓐ Ⓑ Ⓒ Ⓓ Ⓔ
38. Ⓐ Ⓑ Ⓒ Ⓓ Ⓔ
39. Ⓐ Ⓑ Ⓒ Ⓓ Ⓔ
40. Ⓐ Ⓑ Ⓒ Ⓓ Ⓔ
41. Ⓐ Ⓑ Ⓒ Ⓓ Ⓔ
42. Ⓐ Ⓑ Ⓒ Ⓓ Ⓔ

43. Ⓐ Ⓑ Ⓒ Ⓓ Ⓔ
44. Ⓐ Ⓑ Ⓒ Ⓓ Ⓔ
45. Ⓐ Ⓑ Ⓒ Ⓓ Ⓔ
46. Ⓐ Ⓑ Ⓒ Ⓓ Ⓔ
47. Ⓐ Ⓑ Ⓒ Ⓓ Ⓔ
48. Ⓐ Ⓑ Ⓒ Ⓓ Ⓔ

Section 4: Mathematics

21. Ⓐ Ⓑ Ⓒ Ⓓ Ⓔ   25. Ⓐ Ⓑ Ⓒ Ⓓ Ⓔ
22. Ⓐ Ⓑ Ⓒ Ⓓ Ⓔ   26. Ⓐ Ⓑ Ⓒ Ⓓ Ⓔ
23. Ⓐ Ⓑ Ⓒ Ⓓ Ⓔ   27. Ⓐ Ⓑ Ⓒ Ⓓ Ⓔ
24. Ⓐ Ⓑ Ⓒ Ⓓ Ⓔ   28. Ⓐ Ⓑ Ⓒ Ⓓ Ⓔ

29.   30.   31.   32.   33.

34.   35.   36.   37.   38.

Section 5: Writing

1. Ⓐ Ⓑ Ⓒ Ⓓ Ⓔ   9. Ⓐ Ⓑ Ⓒ Ⓓ Ⓔ   17. Ⓐ Ⓑ Ⓒ Ⓓ Ⓔ   25. Ⓐ Ⓑ Ⓒ Ⓓ Ⓔ   33. Ⓐ Ⓑ Ⓒ Ⓓ Ⓔ
2. Ⓐ Ⓑ Ⓒ Ⓓ Ⓔ   10. Ⓐ Ⓑ Ⓒ Ⓓ Ⓔ   18. Ⓐ Ⓑ Ⓒ Ⓓ Ⓔ   26. Ⓐ Ⓑ Ⓒ Ⓓ Ⓔ   34. Ⓐ Ⓑ Ⓒ Ⓓ Ⓔ
3. Ⓐ Ⓑ Ⓒ Ⓓ Ⓔ   11. Ⓐ Ⓑ Ⓒ Ⓓ Ⓔ   19. Ⓐ Ⓑ Ⓒ Ⓓ Ⓔ   27. Ⓐ Ⓑ Ⓒ Ⓓ Ⓔ   35. Ⓐ Ⓑ Ⓒ Ⓓ Ⓔ
4. Ⓐ Ⓑ Ⓒ Ⓓ Ⓔ   12. Ⓐ Ⓑ Ⓒ Ⓓ Ⓔ   20. Ⓐ Ⓑ Ⓒ Ⓓ Ⓔ   28. Ⓐ Ⓑ Ⓒ Ⓓ Ⓔ   36. Ⓐ Ⓑ Ⓒ Ⓓ Ⓔ
5. Ⓐ Ⓑ Ⓒ Ⓓ Ⓔ   13. Ⓐ Ⓑ Ⓒ Ⓓ Ⓔ   21. Ⓐ Ⓑ Ⓒ Ⓓ Ⓔ   29. Ⓐ Ⓑ Ⓒ Ⓓ Ⓔ   37. Ⓐ Ⓑ Ⓒ Ⓓ Ⓔ
6. Ⓐ Ⓑ Ⓒ Ⓓ Ⓔ   14. Ⓐ Ⓑ Ⓒ Ⓓ Ⓔ   22. Ⓐ Ⓑ Ⓒ Ⓓ Ⓔ   30. Ⓐ Ⓑ Ⓒ Ⓓ Ⓔ   38. Ⓐ Ⓑ Ⓒ Ⓓ Ⓔ
7. Ⓐ Ⓑ Ⓒ Ⓓ Ⓔ   15. Ⓐ Ⓑ Ⓒ Ⓓ Ⓔ   23. Ⓐ Ⓑ Ⓒ Ⓓ Ⓔ   31. Ⓐ Ⓑ Ⓒ Ⓓ Ⓔ   39. Ⓐ Ⓑ Ⓒ Ⓓ Ⓔ
8. Ⓐ Ⓑ Ⓒ Ⓓ Ⓔ   16. Ⓐ Ⓑ Ⓒ Ⓓ Ⓔ   24. Ⓐ Ⓑ Ⓒ Ⓓ Ⓔ   32. Ⓐ Ⓑ Ⓒ Ⓓ Ⓔ

Section 1

Critical Reading

> **Time:** 25 minutes for 24 questions
>
> **Directions:** Choose the *best* answer to each question. Mark the corresponding oval on your answer sheet.

Directions for Questions 1–8: Choose the word or words that best fit the meaning of each sentence.

Example: After work, Edith always _____ home as quickly as possible.

(A) rambled

(B) wandered

(C) avoided

(D) meandered

(E) ran

The answer is Choice (E).

1. United in name only, the partners pursued _____ goals and scarcely spoke to each other.

   (A) unified

   (B) affirmative

   (C) impossible

   (D) incomplete

   (E) disparate

2. Despite his tendency to _____ money, Donald was never in debt because of his generous salary.

   (A) bank

   (B) squander

   (C) amass

   (D) borrow

   (E) invest

3. Decades ago, air travel was a _____ reserved for the wealthy, who expected numerous _____ during the flight.

   (A) privilege . . . drawbacks

   (B) boon . . . inconveniences

   (C) luxury . . . amenities

   (D) commonplace . . . adornments

   (E) value . . . fees

4. Representing 70 countries and every area of expertise, the delegates were a very _____ group.

   (A) eclectic

   (B) eccentric

   (C) gregarious

   (D) philanthropic

   (E) nomadic

5. After _____ experiments, scientists understood the role of these chemicals better than ever before.

   (A) inconclusive

   (B) simplistic

   (C) contentious

   (D) exhaustive

   (E) questionable

6. _____ is an important concept in every culture, often expressed in an epic about a hero and a villain.

   (A) Diversity

   (B) Singularity

   (C) Variety

   (D) Duality

   (E) Multiplicity

Go on to next page

7. To celebrate the end of the war, the victors declared a general _____, offering pardons to those they had conquered.

   (A) amnesty

   (B) truce

   (C) surrender

   (D) emigration

   (E) constitution

8. In any _____ both parties benefit from an _____ judge.

   (A) city . . . urbane

   (B) agreement . . . aggrieved

   (C) trial . . . acquitted

   (D) contract . . . additional

   (E) dispute . . . impartial

Directions for Questions 9–12: Read these two passages and answer the questions that follow each passage based on what is stated or implied in the passage.

Both passages are from Psychiatry, 2nd Edition, *edited by Allan Tasman, Jerald Kay, and Jeffery A. Lieberman (Wiley).*

Passage 1

Line   Addiction is a complex maladaptive behavior produced by repeated exposure to rewarding stimuli. There are two primary features common to both natural and pharmacological stimuli that
(05) elicit addiction. First, the rewarding stimulus associated with the addiction is a compelling motivator of behavior at the expense of behaviors leading to the acquisition of other rewarding stimuli. Thus, individuals come to orient increas-
(10) ing amounts of their daily activity around the acquisition of the rewarding stimulus to which they are addicted. Second, there is a persistence of craving for the addictive stimulus, combined with an inability to regulate the behaviors asso-
(15) ciated with obtaining that stimulus. Thus, years after the last exposure to an addictive stimulus, re-exposure or environmental cues associated with that stimulus will elicit behavior aimed at obtaining the reward.

Passage 11

Line   Many smokers have successfully quit smoking without participating in formal treatment. Although only about 3 to 4 percent are successful during the first year, this success rate
(05) improves with multiple attempts and probable self-learning through trial and error and learning from others. The primary unassisted method is "cold turkey" (immediate and complete cessation), followed by spontaneous strategies to
(10) handle cravings and triggers. Some smokers attempt to limit intake, taper the number of cigarettes smoked, or switch to a reduced tar or nicotine brand. These methods have been shown to be less successful. Self-help literature, Internet resources, and Nicotine Anonymous groups can
(15) be effective.

9. According to Passage I, which of the following, if any, are characteristics of addiction?

   I.   repeated doses of the addictive substance

   II. arranging one's life around the addictive substance

   III. criminal behavior

   (A) I only

   (B) I and II

   (C) II and III

   (D) all of the above

   (E) none of the above

10. Which is the best definition of the "spontaneous strategies" (Line 9) cited in Passage II?

    (A) gradual withdrawal from cigarettes

    (B) advice from a medical professional

    (C) support from others trying to quit

    (D) actions taken when craving a cigarette

    (E) avoidance of cigarette smoke

11. What advice would the author of Passage II most likely give to a smoker trying to quit?

    (A) If at first you don't succeed, try again.

    (B) Smoke fewer cigarettes every day.

    (C) Seek help from your doctor.

    (D) You must join a support group.

    (E) Smoke only in unfamiliar places.

Go on to next page ➡

12. Compared to Passage I, Passage II

    (A) is more general

    (B) places more emphasis on the reasons why people smoke

    (C) contains more information on everyday activities

    (D) focuses more on the nature of addiction

    (E) includes more information on tactics for quitting smoking

Directions for Questions 13–24: Read this passage and answer the questions that follow based on what is stated or implied in the passage.

This passage — in which a young woman, Catherine Morland, accompanies an older friend, Mrs. Allen, to a public gathering place — is from Jane Austen's Northanger Abbey.

Line With more than usual eagerness did Catherine hasten to the pump-room[1] the next day, secure within herself of seeing Mr. Tilney there before the morning were over, and ready
(05) to meet him with a smile; but no smile was demanded — Mr. Tilney did not appear. Every creature in Bath, except himself, was to be seen in the room at different periods of the fashionable hours; crowds of people were every
(10) moment passing in and out, up the steps and down; people whom nobody cared about, and nobody wanted to see; and he only was absent.

    "What a delightful place Bath is," said Mrs. Allen as they sat down, "and how pleasant it
(15) would be if we had any acquaintance here." This sentiment had been uttered so often in vain that Mrs. Allen had no particular reason to hope it would be followed with more advantage now; but we are told to "despair of nothing we would
(20) attain," as "unwearied diligence our point would gain"; and the unwearied diligence with which she had every day wished for the same thing was at length to have its just reward, for hardly had she been seated ten minutes before a lady of
(25) about her own age, who was sitting by her, and had been looking at her attentively for several minutes, addressed her with great complaisance in these words: "I think, madam, I cannot be mistaken; it is a long time since I had the pleasure of
(30) seeing you, but is not your name Allen?" This

question answered, as it readily was, the Line stranger pronounced hers to be Thorpe; and Mrs. Allen immediately recognized the features of a former schoolfellow and intimate, whom she had seen only once since their respective mar- (35) riages, and that many years ago. Their joy on this meeting was very great, as well it might, since they had been contented to know nothing of each other for the last fifteen years. Compliments on good looks now passed; and, (40) after observing how time had slipped away since they were last together, how little they had thought of meeting in Bath, and what a pleasure it was to see an old friend, they proceeded to make inquiries and give intelligence as to their (45) families, sisters, and cousins, talking both together, far more ready to give than to receive information, and each hearing very little of what the other said. Mrs. Thorpe, however, had one great advantage as a talker, over Mrs. Allen, in a (50) family of children; and when she expatiated on the talents of her sons, and the beauty of her daughters, when she related their different situations and views — that John was at Oxford, Edward at Merchant Taylors', and William at (55) sea — and all of them more beloved and respected in their different station than any other three beings ever were, Mrs. Allen had no similar information to give, no similar triumphs to press on the unwilling and unbelieving ear of (60) her friend, and was forced to sit and appear to listen to all these maternal effusions, consoling herself, however, with the discovery, which her keen eye soon made, that the lace on Mrs. Thorpe's pelisse[2] was not half so handsome as (65) that on her own.

    "Here come my dear girls," cried Mrs. Thorpe, pointing at three smart-looking females who, arm in arm, were then moving towards her. The Miss Thorpes were introduced; and Miss (70) Morland, who had been for a short time forgotten, was introduced likewise. The name seemed to strike them all; and, after speaking to her with great civility, the eldest young lady observed aloud to the rest, "How excessively like her (75) brother Miss Morland is!" For a moment Catherine was surprised; but Mrs. Thorpe and her daughters had scarcely begun the history of their acquaintance with Mr. James Morland, before she remembered that her eldest brother (80) had spent the last week of the Christmas vacation with the Thorpe family, near London.

    The whole being explained, many obliging things were said by the Miss Thorpes of their wish of being better acquainted with her; of (85)

Go on to next page

Line being considered as already friends, through the friendship of their brothers, etc., which Catherine heard with pleasure, and answered with all the pretty expressions she could com-
(90) mand; and, as the first proof of amity, she was soon invited to accept an arm of the eldest Miss Thorpe, and take a turn with her about the room. Catherine was delighted with this extension of her Bath acquaintance, and almost forgot Mr.
(95) Tilney while she talked to Miss Thorpe. Friendship is certainly the finest balm for the pangs of disappointed love.

Their conversation turned upon dresses, balls, and flirtations. Miss Thorpe, however,
(100) being four years older than Miss Morland, and at least four years better informed, had a very decided advantage in discussing such points; she could compare the balls of Bath with those of Tunbridge, its fashions with the fashions of
(105) London; could rectify the opinions of her new friend in many articles of tasteful attire; and could discover a flirtation between any gentleman and lady who only smiled on each other. These powers received due admiration from
(110) Catherine, to whom they were entirely new.

1. Social gathering place where water is pumped from wells.

2. A woman's cape.

13. In the context of Paragraph 1 (Lines 1–12), the "people whom nobody cared about, and nobody wanted to see" (Lines 11–12) are most likely

(A) the Thorpes

(B) everyone but Henry Tilney

(C) Mrs. Allen's friends

(D) servants

(E) ill-mannered guests

14. Mrs. Allen's statement, "how pleasant it would be if we had any acquaintance here" (Lines 14–15), is discussed in Lines 15–30 in order to

(A) emphasize Mrs. Allen's appreciation of Bath

(B) show the disadvantages of Bath

(C) reveal tension between Mrs. Allen and Catherine

(D) establish that Mrs. Allen is a newcomer

(E) reveal Mrs. Allen's view of society

15. In the context of Line 23, what is the best definition of "just"?

(A) only

(B) mere

(C) complete

(D) exact

(E) fair

16. The statement that "[t]heir joy on this meeting was very great, as well it might" (Lines 36–37) may be characterized as

(A) mocking

(B) straightforward

(C) irresponsible

(D) argumentative

(E) frank

17. The description of the conversation between Mrs. Allen and Mrs. Thorpe (Lines 40–66) implies that

(A) Mrs. Thorpe is embarrassed by her appearance

(B) both are generous

(C) they are proud of their families

(D) each woman cares more about herself than about the other

(E) both are hard of hearing

18. What is Mrs. Allen's attitude toward the information Mrs. Thorpe conveys about the Thorpe children?

(A) confusion

(B) skepticism

(C) trust

(D) interest

(E) gullibility

19. According to the passage, what is Mrs. Thorpe's "advantage" (Line 50)?

(A) talkativeness

(B) social position

(C) children

(D) elegant clothing

(E) wealth

Go on to next page ➡

20. Which statement best describes the way in which Mrs. Allen is "consoling herself" (Lines 62–63)?

    (A) I am more observant.

    (B) My sons are more talented.

    (C) I have no reason to describe my triumphs.

    (D) Catherine is prettier than Mrs. Thorpe's daughters.

    (E) I am better dressed than Mrs. Thorpe.

21. Paragraph 3 (Lines 67–82) serves to

    (A) illustrate Catherine's poor manners

    (B) establish Mrs. Thorpe's pride in her offspring

    (C) reveal a connection between Catherine and the Thorpes

    (D) display Catherine's forgetful nature

    (E) show Catherine's resentment at being left out of the conversation

22. In the context of Line 83, what is the best definition of "obliging"?

    (A) indebted

    (B) helpful

    (C) condescending

    (D) polite

    (E) required

23. The statement that friendship is "the finest balm for the pangs of disappointed love" is an example of which literary device?

    (A) metaphor

    (B) simile

    (C) understatement

    (D) personification

    (E) hyperbole

24. Which of the following statements best describes the relationship between Catherine and Miss Thorpe?

    (A) Catherine doesn't believe everything that Miss Thorpe says.

    (B) Miss Thorpe acts as Catherine's teacher.

    (C) Catherine is more adept at picking up social cues.

    (D) Miss Thorpe attends social gatherings less frequently than Catherine.

    (E) Miss Thorpe is younger.

STOP YOU MAY CHECK YOUR WORK ON THIS SECTION ONLY. DO NOT GO BACK TO ANY PREVIOUS SECTION.

Section 2

Mathematics

Time: 25 minutes for 20 questions

Directions: Find the correct answer to each question and darken the corresponding oval on the answer sheet.

Notes:

✔ You may use a calculator.

✔ All numbers used in this exam are real numbers.

✔ All figures lie in a plane.

✔ You may assume that all figures are to scale unless the problem specifically indicates otherwise.

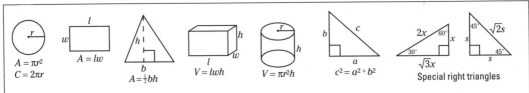

$A = \pi r^2$
$C = 2\pi r$

$A = lw$

$A = \frac{1}{2}bh$

$V = lwh$

$V = \pi r^2 h$

$c^2 = a^2 + b^2$

Special right triangles

There are 360 degrees of arc in a circle.

There are 180 degrees in a straight line.

There are 180 degrees in the sum of the interior angles of a triangle.

1. Suppose p is a prime number greater than 5. Which of the following must be true?

    I. p is divisible by 3

    II. p is odd

    III. $2p$ is even

    (A) I only

    (B) II only

    (C) III only

    (D) I and III

    (E) II and III

2. Which point in the diagram represents the product XY?

    (A) A

    (B) B

    (C) C

    (D) D

    (E) E

Go on to next page

3. Thirty percent of a number is 36. What is 80% of the number?

    (A) 10.4
    (B) 16.25
    (C) 96
    (D) 120
    (E) 150

Questions 4 and 5 both refer to the following bar graph. The graph represents how many dozens of cookies each student made for a bake sale.

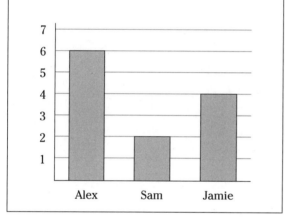

4. How many cookies did the three students make all together?

    (A) 12
    (B) 13
    (C) 84
    (D) 130
    (E) 144

5. How many more cookies did Alex make than Jamie?

    (A) 2
    (B) 4
    (C) 20
    (D) 24
    (E) 48

6. Jenn is twice as old as Henri, and Henri is three years older than Madge. If Jenn is n years old, how old is Madge in terms of n?

    (A) $\frac{n}{2} - 3$
    (B) $\frac{n}{2} + 3$
    (C) $2n + 3$
    (D) $2(n - 3)$
    (E) $2(n + 3)$

7. The set $P = \{-3, -1, 2, 4, 8\}$ and the set $Q = \{-1, 0, 1, 2\}$. How many elements are contained in the union of sets P and Q?

    (A) 2
    (B) 5
    (C) 6
    (D) 7
    (E) 9

8. Line l passes through the points $(-1, 3)$ and $(4, -1)$. The equation of a line parallel to l that passes through the point $(1, 1)$ is:

    (A) $y = -\frac{5}{4}x + \frac{9}{4}$
    (B) $y = -\frac{4}{5}x + \frac{1}{5}$
    (C) $y = -\frac{4}{5}x + \frac{9}{5}$
    (D) $y = \frac{4}{5}x + \frac{1}{5}$
    (E) $y = \frac{5}{4}x - \frac{1}{4}$

Go on to next page

9. What's the length of a diagonal of a piece of paper that's 6 inches wide and 9 inches long?

   (A) $\sqrt{5}$

   (B) $\sqrt{13}$

   (C) $3\sqrt{5}$

   (D) $3\sqrt{13}$

   (E) $9\sqrt{13}$

10. Suppose the operation % is defined so that $a \% b = 2a^b$. Which is equivalent to 2 % 6?

   (A) 3 % 4

   (B) 4 % 3

   (C) 6 % 2

   (D) 6 % 3

   (E) 8 % 3

11. Simplify: $(3x-1)^2 - (3x-2)$

   (A) $3x^2 - 9x + 3$

   (B) $6x^2 - 9x - 1$

   (C) $9x^2 - 9x - 1$

   (D) $9x^2 - 9x + 3$

   (E) $9x^2 - 3x + 3$

12. Suppose $3a - 5b = 2c$ and $2b = a - c$. What is the value of a in terms of c?

   (A) $a = -2c$

   (B) $a = -c$

   (C) $a = -\dfrac{2c}{3}$

   (D) $a = c$

   (E) $a = \dfrac{2c}{3}$

13. What is the range of $f(x) = x^2 - 2x - 3$?

   (A) $f(x) \le -4$

   (B) $f(x) \ge -4$

   (C) $f(x) \ge -3$

   (D) $f(x) \le 1$

   (E) $f(x) \ge 1$

14. In this diagram (not drawn to scale), line BC is parallel to line ED. The measure of angle ABC is represented by $5x$, and the measure of angle BDE is represented by $4x$. What is the measure of angle DBC?

   (A) $20°$

   (B) $40°$

   (C) $80°$

   (D) $100°$

   (E) $160°$

Go on to next page

15. If $f(x) = 2x - \dfrac{3}{x}$, which of the following represents $f\left(-\dfrac{1}{x}\right)$?

    (A) $-2x - \dfrac{3}{x}$

    (B) $-3x - \dfrac{2}{x}$

    (C) $\dfrac{2}{x} - 3x$

    (D) $2x - \dfrac{3}{x}$

    (E) $3x - \dfrac{2}{x}$

16. Solve for x: $x - \sqrt{5 - 4x} = 0$

    (A) $x = -5$

    (B) $x = -1$

    (C) $x = 1$

    (D) $x = 4$

    (E) $x = 5$

17. A square is inscribed in a circle of diameter d. Which expression represents the area of the square?

    (A) $\dfrac{1}{4}d^2$

    (B) $\dfrac{1}{2}d^2$

    (C) d^2

    (D) $2d^2$

    (E) $4d^2$

18. Which answer choice is equivalent to 2^{4x}?

    (A) 4^{2x-2}

    (B) 4^{2x-1}

    (C) $4^{\frac{x}{2}}$

    (D) $8^{\frac{3x}{4}}$

    (E) $8^{\frac{4x}{3}}$

19. Sara went to the store to purchase shirts and pants. Each shirt that she purchased cost $15.50, and each pair of pants cost $19.75. If Sara spent $121.25 and brought home 7 new clothing items, how many shirts did she buy?

    (A) 1

    (B) 2

    (C) 3

    (D) 4

    (E) 5

20. A cylinder has a height of 4 inches and a volume of 36π cubic inches. What is the surface area of the cylinder, in square inches?

    (A) 9π

    (B) $12 + 18\pi$

    (C) $12 + 24\pi$

    (D) 42π

    (E) 60π

STOP YOU MAY CHECK YOUR WORK ON THIS SECTION ONLY.
DO NOT GO BACK TO ANY PREVIOUS SECTION.

Section 3
Critical Reading

Time: 25 minutes for 24 questions

Directions: Choose the *best* answer to each question. Mark the corresponding oval on your answer sheet.

Directions for Questions 25–29: Choose the word or words that best fit the meaning of each sentence.

Example: After work, Edith always _____ home as quickly as possible.

(A) rambled

(B) wandered

(C) avoided

(D) meandered

(E) ran

The answer is Choice (E).

---

25. The painting is _____ by shades of green that overlap and _____ each other.

(A) encrusted . . . reveal

(B) enlivened . . . complement

(C) shadowed . . . agitate

(D) sliced . . . confuse

(E) obscured . . . plagiarize

26. Many believe that vocal talent is _____, present at birth in some lucky children.

(A) prodigious

(B) obdurate

(C) inexorable

(D) determined

(E) innate

27. The executive's request for better _____ was granted in light of the additional responsibility she had been given.

(A) elucidation

(B) compensation

(C) consideration

(D) evaluation

(E) installation

28. A(n) _____ reader understands only basic information and fails to grasp the _____ of the literary work.

(A) subpar . . . promotion

(B) enthusiastic . . . decision

(C) immature . . . nuances

(D) excellent . . . subtlety

(E) accomplished . . . entirety

29. Ignorant of the host's expectations, Jack's snub was not discourteous but rather _____.

(A) deliberate

(B) inadvertent

(C) intuitive

(D) practiced

(E) hostile

Go on to next page

Directions for Questions 30–33: Read these passages and answer the questions that follow each passage based on what is stated or implied in the passage.

Questions 30 and 31 are based on the following passage, excerpted from The Prince, *by Machiavelli.*

Line   Therefore, a prince who has a strong city, and has not made himself hateful, will not be attacked, or if anyone should attack he will only be driven off with disgrace; again, because that
(05) the affairs of this world are so changeable, it is almost impossible to keep an army a whole year in the field without being interfered with. And whoever should reply: If the people have property outside the city, and see it burnt, they will
(10) not remain patient, and the long siege and self-interest will make them forget their prince; to this I answer that a powerful and courageous prince will overcome all such difficulties by giving at one time hope to his subjects that the
(15) evil will not be for long, at another time fear of the cruelty of the enemy, then preserving himself adroitly from those subjects who seem to him to be too bold.

30. According to the passage, which of the following statements is true?

   (A) To protect his city, a prince should keep a standing army in the field.

   (B) The best protection for a prince is the support of his people.

   (C) No ruler can withstand a determined enemy.

   (D) A prince's subjects respond only to fear.

   (E) A prince should negotiate with enemies.

31. Which statement best describes the attitude of the author of this passage?

   (A) Nothing is more important than the people's welfare.

   (B) Armies are always loyal.

   (C) A prince's priority is to maintain his own power.

   (D) War is to be avoided at all costs.

   (E) Trust only those subjects who are bold.

Questions 32 and 33 are based on the following passage, excerpted from How to Live on 24 Hours a Day, *by Arnold Bennett.*

Line   You get into the morning train with your newspaper, and you calmly and majestically give yourself up to your newspaper. You do not hurry. You know you have at least half an hour
(05) of security in front of you. As your glance lingers idly at the advertisements, your air is the air of a leisured man, wealthy in time, of a man from some planet where there are a hundred and twenty-four hours a day instead of twenty-four. I
(10) read five English and two French dailies, and the news-agents alone know how many weeklies, regularly. I am obliged to mention this personal fact lest I should be accused of a prejudice against newspapers when I say that I object to the read-
(15) ing of newspapers in the morning train. Newspapers are produced with rapidity, to be read with rapidity. There is no place in my daily program for newspapers. I read them as I may in odd moments.

32. The author's principal reason for not reading newspapers on the train is that

   (A) only a half hour is available

   (B) the ads are distracting

   (C) he reads too many newspapers

   (D) newspapers don't merit an uninterrupted half hour

   (E) he doesn't think enough attention is paid to newspapers

33. As used in this passage (Line 19), the word "odd" most nearly means

   (A) strange

   (B) uneven

   (C) peculiar

   (D) occasional

   (E) unique

Go on to next page

Line **Directions for Questions 34–41:** Read this passage and answer the questions that follow based on what is stated or implied in the passage.

This passage is an excerpt from Scientific American: Inventions and Discoveries, *by Rodney Carlisle (Wiley).*

Line   The keeping of time by sundial was credited to the Greek scientist Anaximander (610–547 BC), although there is solid evidence that both the Chinese and the Egyptians used such devices

(05) far earlier. The water clock, or clepsydra, was noted in an Egyptian tomb inscription from 1500 BC, and remains of one have been dated to the 14th century BC, in the temple of Amun-Re at Karnak. The Egyptians were the first to divide

(10) the day into 12 equal parts and the night into 12 parts. Near the equator, the slight seasonal variation in the length of the day may have facilitated such a notion of even division. Water clocks were used in China in the 6th century BC,

(15) and the remains of one have been found in Athens from about 350 BC. There were different designs of water clocks. Some would have a float, which would indicate the time as water trickled out through a small passage in the bottom of a

(20) vessel. Others were more elaborate, in which the water would drive small figurines that would ring bells.

     In Europe, mechanical clocks began to appear in the period AD 1321–1335, but Chinese models

(25) preceded them. Mechanical clocks appeared to descend from earlier water clocks. A cosmic engine built in Khafeng China in AD 1090 consisted of a 30-foot-high building, with a geared mechanism that was driven by a waterwheel. On

(30) top, a celestial display showed star and planet position, while dozens of miniature figures announced the time of day or night. The cosmic engine ran for more than 130 years.

     The father of European clockmaking is

(35) Giovanni de Dondi (1318–1389), although his father, Jacopo de Dondi, built a town clock at Padua. Giovanni's major contribution was similar to the Chinese cosmic engine. Known as an *astratrium,* it took 16 years to build and began opera-

(40) tion in 1364. It showed the movements in the sky of the Sun, the Moon, and the five known planets and presented the cycle of religious holidays as well as daily time. To allow for the elliptical orbits of the Moon and Mercury, according to

(45) the current Ptolemaic view, he made elliptical

gears, and he provided for the irregular orbit of   Line Venus. It was the most complicated machine known to exist since the construction of the Antikythera computer, a geared device built in ancient Greece to represent the motions of the   (50) planets. De Dondi's clock operated for some years after his death but was "retired" as beyond repair in 1530. De Dondi's clock was by no means the first in Europe, where the first to strike an hour is said to have been built in Milan in 1335.   (55)

     In the 14th century, weights rather than waterpower drove European town clocks in public bell towers. Surviving examples of town clocks in St. Albans Abbey in England, in Prague, Bern, and Munich all were characterized by   (60) astronomical representations and figurines. Most of the large town clocks had iron gears. Springs replaced weights as the driving force in smaller clocks in the late 1430s, apparently derived from the contemporary use of springs in locks and fire-   (65) arms. Peter Henlein, a German locksmith, began making small spring-driven clocks about 1500. In the 17th century, pendulum clocks and balance springs were introduced. The 18th century development of the chronometer was a crucial addi-   (70) tion to the tool kit of the ocean navigator.

     The psychological and social effects of advances in timekeeping are subjects of interesting speculation. Even the ancient Greeks noted that lawyers and playwrights seemed wedded   (75) to the clepsydra. The development of town clocks in the 14th century in Europe may have allowed for more regulation of daily business, and the development of more precision in later timekeeping certainly assisted scientists in   (80) recording chemical and physical phenomena. But whether the town clock led to a more regulated daily life, or the regulation of daily life created a marked need that the town clock filled, is open to discussion.   (85)

34. The purpose of Paragraph 1 (Lines 1–22) is to

    (A) emphasize the importance of timekeeping

    (B) create a timeline for the development of clocks

    (C) show that ancient cultures created timepieces

    (D) illustrate that historical accounts are often wrong

    (E) explain why Egyptian clocks were superior to Chinese clocks

Go on to next page ➡

35. According to Lines 11–13 ("Near the equator . . . even division"), the Egyptians are responsible for

   (A) understanding the importance of timekeeping

   (B) taking credit away from ancient Greek inventors

   (C) relating the sun to timekeeping

   (D) dividing day from night

   (E) the concept of a 24-hour day

36. According to the passage, water clocks may tell time by

   (A) emptying a container

   (B) floating objects with bells

   (C) mechanical means

   (D) reflecting the sun off a wet surface

   (E) measuring the motion of waves

37. The clock described in Paragraph 2 was called a "cosmic engine" (Lines 26–27) probably because

   (A) it relied on water

   (B) its design was universal

   (C) it measured time for more than a century

   (D) it displayed the position of stars and planets

   (E) it was extremely tall

38. Giovanni de Dondi is called the "father of European clockmaking" because

   (A) the astratrium was the first technically complex clock in Europe

   (B) his clocks were similar to Chinese clocks

   (C) his astratrium was the first clock to strike the hour

   (D) clockmaking was a family tradition

   (E) his son also made clocks

39. The reference to "springs" (Line 62) implies that

   (A) mechanical clocks were very heavy

   (B) advances in other fields were adopted by clockmakers

   (C) seasons of the year influenced timekeeping

   (D) the best clocks rely on springs

   (E) navigation was made possible by spring-driven clocks

40. Clocks in England, Prague, Bern, and Munich featured "astronomical representations" (Line 61) most likely because

   (A) clockmakers in these cities copied one another's designs

   (B) clocks from that era relied on the movement of the sun to tell time

   (C) Europeans were interested in astronomy

   (D) timekeeping is related to the movement of stars and planets

   (E) a plentiful supply of iron was available

41. In relation to the rest of the passage, the last paragraph (Lines 72–85)

   (A) shifts from general to specific

   (B) summarizes information stated earlier

   (C) considers the significance of advancements in timekeeping

   (D) introduces a new topic

   (E) extends the timeline covered in the passage

Go on to next page

Directions for Questions 42–48: Read these two passages, both of which discuss the identity of Shakespeare. Answer the questions that follow based on what is stated or implied in these passages.

Passage 1

Line   The likeness of Shakespeare in the Folio of 1623 has frequently been called "an abominable libel on humanity." And yet its fidelity is certified by Ben Jonson[1] in laudatory lines. If there was a
(05)   better likeness of Shakespeare in existence, why was it not reproduced in that famous Folio? The same ugly engraving reappeared in all the later editions up to 1685.

    The bust on the monument at Stratford was
(10)   first noticed in 1623. It was not taken from life, and is unlike any picture of Shakespeare. It presents him in the act of composition, and, says Boaden, "it is hardly a stretch of fancy to suppose him in the actual creation of Falstaff[2] him-
(15)   self." More likely, we should say, Falstaff was Shakespeare — Fall-staff, Shake-spear.

    The most familiar pictures of Shakespeare are very different from either of these, and generally far more intellectual and refined. They are
(20)   pretended copies of what is called the Chandos portrait, but are not much like it. The Chandos picture was painted by an unknown artist and has been altered by a later hand. It is said to have been owned by Sir William Davenant, who
(25)   died in 1668; and he is said to have obtained it from an actor named Joseph Taylor, who died about 1653 at the age of 70.

1. A playwright and contemporary of Shakespeare.
2. A comic character in three Shakespearean plays.

Line Passage II

    There is one point above all others which bears strongly against the theory that William
(30)   Shakespeare, of Stratford-on-Avon, was the author of the so-called Shakespeare's Plays, and that is the audacious doggerel[3] which has been found on his tombstone. William Shakespeare, after a disreputable youth, marrying at 17 or 18 a
(35)   woman many years older than himself, was the son of a father who could not write his name, who was in debt and difficulty and had been within the clutches of the law. The son of this father found his native place too hot to hold him,
(40)   and if the universal tradition on the subject is

worth anything, having a warrant out against him Line for poaching,[4] "flitted" to London, became a stage-player, went in for speculation in building a theatre, bought a house in his native place, another in London, retired, died, and was buried   (45) in Stratford in 1616.

    His epitaph[5] was inscribed at his request upon his tomb. He appears to have been in the habit of writing or quoting such lines, and got the credit for this sort of poetry from his com-   (50) panions. It is plain that in those years it was the custom in London churches to put verses of questionable merit on monuments and tombs, that it was usual to "crib" or copy them from others and use them as their own. The epitaph   (55) on the stone over Shakespeare's grave has been pressed into the service by a believer in his writings to prove — first, that he "curst those who should move his bones," because he was fearful that when his renown was acknowledged, his   (60) bones would be moved from their last resting-place in the Stratford that he loved, to find a grave in Westminster Abbey,[6] and secondly, by a non-believer, that when the imposture was found out, they would be exhumed and cast out to the   (65) four winds of heaven!

3. Poorly written verse.
4. The crime of hunting on private land without permission.
5. Inscription on a tombstone.
6. A church in London where many famous writers are buried.

42. In the context of Passage I, which is the best definition of "abominable libel on humanity" (Lines 2–3)?

 (A) too beautiful to be true

 (B) animalistic portrait

 (C) dangerous monster

 (D) an insult to all human beings

 (E) a lie

43. The question in Passage I (Lines 4–6) implies that

 (A) no earlier picture of Shakespeare exists

 (B) the image of Shakespeare in the Folio of 1623 is an accurate portrayal

 (C) the Chandos portrait of Shakespeare bears a stronger resemblance to Shakespeare

 (D) better images of Shakespeare existed in 1623

 (E) no images of Shakespeare are realistic

Go on to next page ➡

44. In the context of Line 13, what is the best definition of "fancy"?

    (A) overdecorated

    (B) wish

    (C) imagination

    (D) plain

    (E) luxurious

45. The author of Passage I implies that most portraits of Shakespeare are "far more intellectual and refined" (Line 19) than the one printed in the Folio of 1623 because

    (A) no one knows what Shakespeare really looked like

    (B) artists were jealous of Shakespeare's accomplishments

    (C) artists imagined that Shakespeare's appearance reflected intelligence and culture

    (D) early artists were cruder

    (E) later artists were more accurate

46. The information about Shakespeare and his father (Lines 33–38) is intended to

    (A) portray Shakespeare's background negatively

    (B) establish that the writer came from a good family

    (C) show that Shakespeare and his father were similar

    (D) emphasize the importance of Stratford in Shakespeare's life

    (E) summarize all the known facts of Shakespeare's life

47. The statement in Passage II — "if the universal tradition on the subject is worth anything" (Line 40) — implies that

    (A) breaking with tradition is risky

    (B) the story about poaching is probably true

    (C) Shakespeare was not a poacher

    (D) following tradition is seldom a good idea

    (E) Shakespeare followed traditional ways

48. Which of the following statements about the authors of Passages I and II is true?

    (A) Neither believes that the man called Shakespeare wrote the plays attributed to him.

    (B) Both believe that the man called Shakespeare wrote the plays.

    (C) The author of Passage II includes more factual information than the author of Passage I.

    (D) The author of Passage I doesn't directly address whether Shakespeare wrote the plays, as the author of Passage II does.

    (E) The author of Passage II relies more on historical data than the author of Passage I.

STOP YOU MAY CHECK YOUR WORK ON THIS SECTION ONLY. DO NOT GO BACK TO ANY PREVIOUS SECTION.

Section 4

Mathematics

Time: 25 minutes for 18 questions

Directions: This section contains two different types of questions. For Questions 21–28, choose the *best* answer to each question. Mark the corresponding oval on the answer sheet. For Questions 29–38, follow the separate directions provided before those questions.

Notes:

✔ You may use a calculator.

✔ All numbers used in this exam are real numbers.

✔ All figures lie in a plane.

✔ You may assume that all figures are to scale unless the problem specifically indicates otherwise.

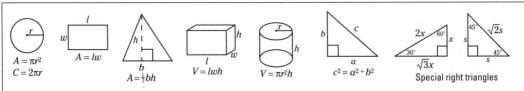

There are 360 degrees of arc in a circle.

There are 180 degrees in a straight line.

There are 180 degrees in the sum of the interior angles of a triangle.

21. A warehouse has two types of computers: laptop and desktop. The computers are in a laptop-to-desktop ratio of 4:7. Which of the following is a possible number of computers that the warehouse has?

(A) 14

(B) 25

(C) 61

(D) 77

(E) 95

22. A menu has 6 appetizers, 8 main dishes, and 3 desserts. If a meal consists of 1 appetizer, 1 main dish, and 1 dessert, how many different meals could you order?

(A) 17

(B) 48

(C) 51

(D) 144

(E) 432

Go on to next page

23. A number is doubled, then increased by 12, and then divided by 3 for a result of 2. What was the original number?

    (A) –12

    (B) –6

    (C) –3

    (D) 3

    (E) 9

24. Which value is not in the domain of $g(x) = \sqrt{9 - x^2}$?

    (A) –3

    (B) –1

    (C) 0

    (D) 2

    (E) 4

25. Where will the lines $y = 2x + 9$ and $y = -\frac{1}{2}x + 4$ intersect?

    (A) (–5, –1)

    (B) (–2, 3)

    (C) (–2, 5)

    (D) (–2, 13)

    (E) (2, 13)

26. Solve for x: $|3x + 5| \leq 4$

    (A) $-3 \leq x \leq -\frac{1}{3}$

    (B) $-3 \leq x \leq \frac{1}{3}$

    (C) $-\frac{1}{3} \leq x \leq -\frac{1}{3}$

    (D) $-\frac{1}{3} \leq x \leq 3$

    (E) $\frac{1}{3} \leq x \leq 3$

27. Solve for x: $x^2 - x < 6$

    (A) $-3 < x < 2$

    (B) $x < -2$

    (C) $-2 < x < 3$

    (D) $x < 2$

    (E) $x < 3$

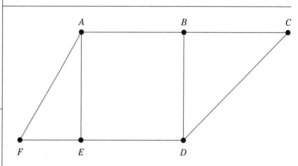

28. In this figure, angle F is 60°, angle C is 45°, and $ABDE$ is a square. Determine the perimeter of quadrilateral $ACDF$ if EF is 5 units long.

    (A) $15 + 20\sqrt{3}$

    (B) $15 + 15\sqrt{3} + 5\sqrt{6}$

    (C) $20 + 15\sqrt{3} + 5\sqrt{6}$

    (D) $25 + 15\sqrt{3}$

    (E) $25 + 20\sqrt{3}$

Go on to next page

Directions for student-produced response Questions 29–38: Solve the problem and then write your answer in the boxes on the answer sheet. Then mark the ovals corresponding to your answer, as shown in the following example. Note the fraction line and the decimal points.

Answer: $^7\!/_2$

Answer: 3.25

Answer: 853

Write your answer in the box. You may start your answer in any column.

Although you don't have to write the solutions in the boxes, you do have to blacken the corresponding ovals. You should fill in the boxes to avoid confusion. Only the blackened ovals will be scored. The numbers in the boxes won't be read.

There are no negative answers.

You may grid in mixed numbers, such as 3½, as a decimal (3.5) or as a fraction (½). Don't grid in 3½; it will be read as $^3\!/_2$.

Grid in a decimal as far as possible. Don't round your answer and leave some boxes empty.

A question may have more than one answer. Grid in one answer only.

---

29. If a, b, and c are the sides of a triangle, where $a = 10$ and $b = 2$, what is a possible value of c if c must be an integer?

30. Jim lives 10 miles due north of Ian, and Mariano lives 24 miles due east of Jim. How many miles apart are Ian's and Mariano's homes?

31. Line k passes through the points (–6, 2) and (6, –8). Determine the product of the slope and the y-intercept of line k.

32. What is the sum of the factors of 36?

Go on to next page

33. A pizza has a diameter of 16 inches. If you want to cut the pizza so that each slice has an area between 15 and 22 square inches, how many slices can you cut the pizza into?

36. Define $a \# b = \frac{2a+b}{2}$. What is the value of $(1\#6)\#(3\#4)$?

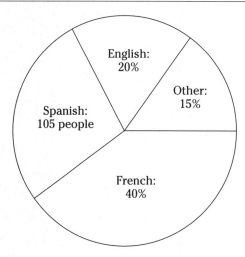

34. This chart represents the results of a survey of the passengers on an airplane. Each passenger was asked what his or her primary language is. How many passengers are on the airplane?

37. Miki's math class has five tests per semester, and all the tests are out of 100 points. On the first three tests she earned a 70, a 95, and an 82. What's the lowest possible grade that Miki can get on either of the two remaining tests if she wants an average test grade of 88?

35. An open-top box with a square base is constructed from exactly 132 square centimeters of cardboard. If the area of the base of the box is 36 square centimeters, what is the volume of the box?

38. A dart is thrown at this circular dartboard, which consists of three circles lined up inside of a fourth circle. If the dart lands on the board, what's the probability that it lands on the shaded portion of the board?

STOP YOU MAY CHECK YOUR WORK ON THIS SECTION ONLY. DO NOT GO BACK TO ANY PREVIOUS SECTION.

Section 5

Writing

Time: 30 minutes for 39 questions

Directions: Choose the *best* answer to each question. Mark the corresponding oval on your answer sheet.

Directions for Questions 1–20: Read the following sentences carefully. Part or all of each sentence is underlined. Beneath each sentence are five choices. Choice (A) is the original, and the other choices represent different ways of expressing the same meaning. If the sentence is grammatically correct and effectively worded, select Choice (A). If one of the other choices would improve the sentence, select that answer.

Example: Henry wanted to be an architect and <u>that he would have a happy family</u>.

(A) that he would have a happy family

(B) that his family would be happy

(C) to have a happy family

(D) his family should be happy

(E) happiness for his family

The answer is Choice (C).

---

1. In his poem "Digging," Seamus Heaney compares <u>the writing of poetry next to his father's work on a farm.</u>

   (A) the writing of poetry next to his father's work on a farm

   (B) the writing of poetry with the way that his father had worked on a farm

   (C) writing poetry and that his father worked on a farm

   (D) poetry with how his father's work was on a farm

   (E) writing poetry with his father's working on a farm

2. <u>Where the school was, a new shopping mall was constructed</u> that covered all traces of the demolished building.

   (A) Where the school was, a new shopping mall was constructed

   (B) Where the school had been, a new shopping mall was constructed

   (C) Where the school has been, a new shopping mall was constructed

   (D) In the place where the school was, a new shopping mall was being constructed

   (E) A new shopping mall was constructed where the school was

Go on to next page

3. Because technology is changing very quick and the price of a device drops when a newer version is manufactured, you may find that older gadgets are cheaper.

(A) Because technology is changing very quick and the price of a device drops

(B) Since technology is changing very quick and the price of a device drops

(C) Because technology is changing very quickly and the price of a device drops

(D) With technology changing very quick and the price of a device dropping

(E) Because technology, which is changing very quickly, and the price of a device drops

4. The reaction to the speech by the committee chair was more extreme among experienced employees than either trainees or job applicants.

(A) among experienced employees than either trainees or job applicants

(B) than either among trainees or job applicants

(C) than among either trainees or job applicants

(D) than it was among either trainees or job applicants

(E) from either trainees or job applicants

5. Baleen whales, growing gigantic by eating only plankton, an extremely small plant form that is becoming scarce.

(A) Baleen whales, growing gigantic by

(B) Baleen whales grow gigantic by

(C) Baleen whales, which grow gigantic by

(D) Growing gigantic, baleen whales which are

(E) Growing gigantic, baleen whales

6. During the first World War, that was when many poets, including Siegfried Sassoon, wrote poetry that chills the reader by describing the horrors of trench warfare.

(A) During the first World War, that was when many poets, including

(B) During the first World War was when many poets, including

(C) Poets, during the first World War, that was when many, including

(D) During the first World War was when many poets, including

(E) During the first World War, many poets, including

7. Instead of fearing multiple births, as some contemporary cultures did, the ancient Greeks celebrated the bonds of loyalty between twins.

(A) the ancient Greeks celebrated

(B) the ancient Greeks had celebrated

(C) the ancient Greeks have celebrated

(D) the ancient Greeks were celebrating

(E) the Greeks that were living in ancient times had celebrated

8. If I would have known about the car accident and subsequent traffic jam, I would have taken an alternate route.

(A) If I would have known about the car accident and subsequent traffic jam

(B) If I had known about the car accident and subsequent traffic jam

(C) Having known about the car accident and subsequent traffic jam

(D) Knowing about the car accident and the traffic jam that was subsequent

(E) If I would have known about the car accident and would have known also about the subsequent traffic jam

Go on to next page

9. Researchers now know that infants understand elementary principles of <u>geometry, and the principles remain</u> with the children as they grow.

    (A) geometry, and the principles remain

    (B) geometry, the principles remaining

    (C) geometry, because the principles remaining

    (D) geometry, which remain

    (E) geometry that the principles remain

10. After a concussion, the brain <u>being more vulnerable</u> to a second injury, so injured athletes should play only after consulting a physician.

    (A) being more vulnerable

    (B) having been more vulnerable

    (C) is more vulnerable

    (D) more vulnerable

    (E) had been more vulnerable

11. <u>Choosing quality ingredients is equally as important as preparing the meal properly.</u>

    (A) Choosing quality ingredients is equally as important as preparing the meal properly.

    (B) Choosing quality ingredients is as equally as important as preparing the meal properly.

    (C) That you should choose quality ingredients is as equally as important as properly preparing the meal.

    (D) Choosing quality ingredients is as important as preparing the meal properly.

    (E) Choosing quality ingredients and preparing the meal properly is equally important.

12. <u>Although few can imagine the national bird as anything other than the bald eagle,</u> Benjamin Franklin favored the wild turkey for that role.

    (A) Although few can imagine the national bird as anything other than the bald eagle

    (B) None imagining the national bird as anything other than the bald eagle

    (C) Although few could have imagined the national bird as anything other than the bald eagle

    (D) The national bird, imagined by few as anything other than the bald eagle

    (E) The bald eagle, imagined by few as anything other than the bald eagle

13. The Supreme <u>Court is located in Washington, D.C., and the court has nine justices who</u> are appointed for life.

    (A) Court is located in Washington, D.C., and the court has nine justices who

    (B) Court, located in Washington, D.C., has nine justices who

    (C) Court is located in Washington, D.C., where it has nine justices who

    (D) Court, that is located in Washington, D.C., and the court has nine justices who

    (E) Court, being located in Washington, D.C., has nine justices who

14. Somebody carried, over long distances <u>and in terrible weather, their</u> precious cargo.

    (A) and in terrible weather, their

    (B) and in terrible weather their

    (C) and in terrible weather, his or her

    (D) being in terrible weather, their

    (E) and carried in terrible weather, their

Go on to next page

15. The drivers of the silver <u>cars — Janice, Arthur, and me — have been asked to lead</u> the parade on Saturday.

    (A) cars — Janice, Arthur, and me — have been asked to lead

    (B) cars — Janice, Arthur, and myself — have been asked to lead

    (C) cars — Janice, Arthur, and me — having been asked to lead

    (D) cars — Janice, Arthur, and I — have been asked to lead

    (E) cars — Janice, Arthur, and I — has been asked to lead

16. Hidden in a corner of the bookshelf, <u>I jumped when a mouse appeared</u>.

    (A) I jumped when a mouse appeared

    (B) I jumped because a mouse appeared

    (C) I jumped with a mouse appearing

    (D) jumping at the mouse's appearance

    (E) the mouse appeared, and I jumped

17. Eleanor Roosevelt, a shy young woman when she married Franklin, was one of the <u>most accomplished First Ladies, later she was</u> an ambassador to the United Nations.

    (A) most accomplished First Ladies, later she was

    (B) most accomplished First Ladies; later she was

    (C) more accomplished First Ladies, later she was

    (D) more accomplished First Ladies, later she had been

    (E) most accomplished First Ladies, but later she was

18. In his mother's eyes, the baby's smile <u>was more cuter than that of</u> any other child.

    (A) was more cuter than that of

    (B) was cuter than that of

    (C) was more cuter than

    (D) was cuter than

    (E) was more cuter than the smile of

19. The heavy box of paper, as well as the shopping bag of pens and <u>crayons, were supposed to be</u> stored in the art supply closet.

    (A) crayons, were supposed to be

    (B) crayons, supposing to be

    (C) crayons, was supposed to be

    (D) crayons that were supposed to be

    (E) crayons, which were supposed to be

20. <u>Wearing dress uniforms, the new police officers saluted as the mayor</u> greeted them.

    (A) Wearing dress uniforms, the new police officers saluted as the mayor

    (B) Having worn dress uniforms, the new police officers saluted as the mayor

    (C) Having been wearing dress uniforms, the new police officers saluted as the mayor

    (D) Wearing dress uniforms, the new police officers saluted the mayor

    (E) Wearing dress uniforms, the mayor saluted the new police officers and

Go on to next page

Directions for Questions 21–34: Read the following sentences carefully. Four portions of each sentence are underlined. Some sentences are correct, and some contain one error. If the sentence is correct, bubble Choice (E) for "no error." If an underlined portion of the sentence contains an error, bubble that letter.

Example:

On the <u>day</u> of the <u>prom, Martin</u> and his
  A   B
friends <u>had gone</u> to the mall <u>to rent</u> tuxedos.
            C   D
<u>No error</u>.
    E

The answer is Choice (C).

---

21. The tornado roaring <u>through the town</u>
    A   B
and <u>destroyed</u> several blocks, disheartening
        C
<u>the inhabitants</u> and threatening the town's
        D
existence. <u>No error</u>.
                    E

22. Jane Goodall <u>and other courageous</u>
                            A
<u>scientists had spent</u> many years
                  B
<u>studying animals</u> in the wild,
        C
<u>documenting the animals' behavior</u>.
                    D
<u>No error</u>.
    E

23. <u>In</u> *The Wizard of Oz,* Dorothy, but not
    A
the Tin Man and the Cowardly Lion,
<u>eventually return</u> to <u>Kansas, where</u> Dorothy
        B   C
<u>is reunited with</u> her family. <u>No error</u>.
        D   E

24. The <u>sales director gave</u> a bonus
        A
<u>to McDonald and myself</u> <u>in order to</u>
        B   C
<u>reward our work</u> on the new product line,

which was <u>introduced</u> in January.
                    D
<u>No error</u>.
    E

25. The <u>announcer declared</u> <u>that the</u> outfielder
            A   B
<u>should of caught</u> the ball, but the outfielder
        C
claimed <u>that he was hampered</u> by a fan's
                    D
interference. <u>No error</u>.
                        E

26. <u>The children chose</u> that dog <u>for their pet</u>
        A   B
<u>because of</u> his energy, friendliness,
        C
<u>and that he loved to play</u>. <u>No error</u>.
                    D   E

27. <u>Diligently filling potholes</u>, the highway
            A
<u>became</u> <u>much safer</u> and the number of
    B   C
accidents decreased <u>sharply</u>.
                              D
<u>No error</u>.
    E

28. The star basketball player <u>was commended</u>
                                              A
<u>for scoring</u> <u>more field goals than</u> <u>anyone on</u>
        B   C   D
his team, which won the championship
three years in a row. <u>No error</u>.
                                E

29. Anyone who <u>is</u> interested <u>in contributing to</u>
                    A   B
the fundraiser <u>deserves</u> praise because
                      C
<u>you have</u> to take care of the less fortunate.
        D
<u>No error</u>.
    E

30. <u>Being that</u> it hasn't rained <u>for three weeks</u>,
        A   B
<u>the ground is extremely dry</u> and the risk of
            C
fire <u>is great</u>. <u>No error</u>.
          D   E

Go on to next page

31. Having sealed the envelope, Peter
    <u>　　　</u>
      A

    <u>was distressed</u> <u>when he realized</u>
      B   C

    <u>that he had not signed</u> the letter.
      D

    <u>No error</u>.
      E

32. <u>Sheila and her mother argued</u>
      A

    <u>for hours</u> <u>about her expensive tastes,</u>
      B   C

    without coming to <u>any meaningful conclu-</u>
                        D

    <u>sion</u>. <u>No error</u>.
      E

33. <u>When you enter the garden, you can't</u>
                  A   B

    <u>hardly believe</u> <u>the sight that meets your</u>
      C

    <u>eyes</u>: an amazing <u>variety of beautiful flowers</u>.
                          D

    <u>No error</u>.
      E

34. The <u>cloth was</u> soft and very
           A

    <u>thin, the tailor</u> <u>struggled to sew it</u> without
      B   C

    <u>tearing or stretching</u> the fabric. <u>No error</u>.
      D   E

Directions for Questions 35–39: Following is a first draft of a student essay. The essay needs revision. Read the essay and the questions that follow and choose the best answer to each question.

---

[1] Some years ago, a major museum exhibited works of art that were forgeries. [2] You may think that the museum was encouraging dishonesty. [3] Well, the point of the exhibition was to draw attention to the fine line between an original work of art and a dishonest forgery. [4] One of the paintings in the show was supposedly by the Spanish artist, who was named Goya. [5] The painting hung in its galleries for many years. [6] Its label proclaimed that Goya was the artist. [7] Then the museum discovered that a 19th century forger made the painting, using elements of works by the real artist but combined in a new way. [8] Was this painting truly dishonest?

[9] In my opinion, I think that the painting was a real work of art. [10] Many people liked that painting when they thought that Goya painted it. [11] I do not think that the name on the canvas matters. [12] If it is a good painting and people like it, the identity of the artist is not important.

[13] The fake Goya disappeared. [14] The gallery where it was now displayed other works by Spanish artists. [15] Some of those paintings, not being as good as the fake Goya.

35. Which of the following, if any, is the best revision of Sentence 3?

    (A) NO CHANGE

    (B) Delete "Well, the point of" and capitalize the next word, "the."

    (C) Change "was" to "had been."

    (D) Change "Well, the point of the exhibition was to draw" to "The exhibition drew."

    (E) Delete "Well, the point of the exhibition was" and capitalize the next word, "to."

36. How may Sentences 5 and 6 best be combined?

    (A) NO CHANGE

    (B) The painting, which hung in its galleries for many years, was proclaimed on its label that Goya was the artist.

    (C) Hanging in its galleries for many years, the painting was labeled as a work by Goya.

    (D) The painting hung in its galleries for many years, with a label which it proclaimed Goya.

    (E) Goya was on the label of the painting, and it hung in the galleries for many years.

37. How may the third paragraph (Sentences 9–12) be improved?

    (A) NO CHANGE

    (B) Delete all first person (*I* and *my* statements).

    (C) Add a sentence about the 19th-century forger.

    (D) Add information about Goya.

    (E) Delete Sentence 12.

Go on to next page

38. What is the best revision, if any, of Sentence 13?

    (A) NO CHANGE

    (B) After the show, the fake Goya disappeared.

    (C) The show ending, the fake Goya disappeared.

    (D) Because the show ended, from which the fake Goya disappeared.

    (E) The fake Goya disappeared, which was when the show ended.

39. How may Sentence 15 be improved?

    (A) NO CHANGE

    (B) Some of those paintings, which were not as good as the fake Goya.

    (C) Some of those paintings were not as good as the fake Goya.

    (D) Some of those paintings, not being as good as the fake Goya, had been displayed anyway.

    (E) Not as good as the fake Goya, some of those paintings had been displayed.

STOP YOU MAY CHECK YOUR WORK ON THIS SECTION ONLY. DO NOT GO BACK TO ANY PREVIOUS SECTION.

Chapter 14

Practice Test 2: Answers and Explanations

• •

*H*ave you ever envied your teacher's right to splash red ink all over your paper? Red looks like the color of revenge, but those red marks are really a way to show you how to improve. I admit, some teachers may use a red pen to get back at you for throwing that spitball or texting during class, but most of us see it as a way to steer you toward greater knowledge. This is the chapter where *you wield* (handle, especially as a weapon or a tool) the red ink. Go over all your answers. Place an X on anything you got wrong. If you skipped a question, circle the question number. After you know how many right, wrong, and skipped questions you have, turn to the appendix, where you'll find a scoring grid to help you convert those raw scores into a PSAT/NMSQT score for critical reading, math, and writing.

Before the ink fades, return to the questions you answered incorrectly or skipped. Try them again. Recheck your answers, and then spend some time going over the explanations in this chapter. You may be tempted to read only the explanations for the questions you got wrong. Resist that temptation. I've tucked extra vocabulary words, tips, and strategies into all the explanations, so you may learn something even from the questions you answered correctly. If you're short on time, turn to the end of this chapter to find an abbreviated answer key.

Section 1: Critical Reading

1. **E.** The sentence tells you that the partners shared nothing but a name. Okay, their goals must be the opposite of "united." Choice (E) swims to the top, because *disparate* means "unlike" or "different." Stretching out the vocabulary lesson, I should tell you that *affirmative* means "positive."

2. **B.** The clue here is "despite," a word that directs you to an unusual pairing of action and result. You know that Donald was "never in debt," so you'd expect him to be the type of person who keeps track of every penny. But the word "despite" sends you to something you *don't* expect. Got it! Donald must *squander* (or waste) money — Choice (B).

3. **C.** The sentence *pivots* (turns) on one crucial point — "the wealthy." What do the wealthy expect? Not *drawbacks* (disadvantages) or inconveniences, so you can rule out Choices (A) and (B). Now look at the first word in the remaining choices. If air travel was "reserved for the wealthy," only the wealthy had access to it. You can axe Choice (D) because something that's *commonplace* is *not* rare and thus not restricted. Choice (E) may tempt you because "the wealthy" can pay "fees," but the first word isn't a good fit, because "value" implies a lack of fees. You're left with Choice (C), which tells you that air travel was a *luxury* (a treat available only rarely, usually because of the price tag). *Amenities* are the little things (hot towels, premium movies, great food) that make you more comfortable, also known as "treats." Yup, Choice (C) is the correct answer.

4. **A.** From all over the world and with lots of different skill sets (*expertise* means "expert knowledge or skill"), these delegates can probably unclog your sink *and* explain the chemical composition of the gunk they removed. They're *eclectic* because they draw "from varied sources." As long as you're in a vocab-building mood, you may as well add these words to your store of knowledge: *eccentric* is "odd," *gregarious* is "sociable or outgoing," *philanthropic* describes a charitable person or action, and *nomadic* means "on the move, having no fixed home." The correct answer is Choice (A).

5. **D.** "Better than ever before," huh? I'm sure that phrase describes you, after you've prepared for the PSAT/NMSQT. Continuing the comparison, I'm sure that you've worked hard and covered every angle. In other words, your preparation for the test has been *exhaustive,* just like the experiments mentioned in the question. Choice (D) is a good match. Choice (A) is the opposite of what you need; *inconclusive* experiments don't yield solid information because no conclusion can be reached. *Simplistic* (too simple), *contentious* (causing disagreement), and *questionable* (open to doubt) don't work. Go for Choice (D) and you're done.

6. **D.** For this question, all you have to do is count. One hero + one victim = two. All right, which answer refers to two? Choice (D), because *duality* refers to two. Choices (A), (C), and (E) also imply more than one, but they're more general. Choice (B) refers to one, so that answer is also a dud. The correct answer is Choice (D).

7. **A.** This question answers itself, as long as you know the definition of *amnesty.* In fact, the definition is "pardons," which is conveniently placed immediately following the blank.

   From time to time the test-makers place a definition after the blank. Keep your eyes open when you see a comma following a blank. You may find a clue there!

8. **E.** Real world experience points you in the right direction here. What kind of judge would "both parties" want? Someone who's *impartial,* or fair. What is a judge involved in? A *dispute,* or disagreement. Yes, I know a judge may also be involved in an "agreement," a "trial," and a "contract." However, those choices fall apart when you examine the second blank. The answer you want is Choice (E).

9. **B.** Passage I tells you that addiction involves "repeated exposure" (Line 2) and that "individuals come to orient increasing amounts of their daily activity" around obtaining the drug. Therefore, I and II are correct. The passage says nothing about crimes or the law, so III is out, making your answer Choice (B).

10. **D.** The best answer is Choice (D) because, if you're *spontaneous,* you're in the moment, acting or reacting instantly, from instinct.

11. **A.** The topic sentence of Passage II explains that the "success rate improves with multiple attempts." True, some of the other choices describe actions that smokers use to kick the habit. However, these strategies are all part of the "multiple attempts" in the first sentence of the passage, so Choice (A) is the best answer.

12. **E.** Passage I concentrates on the nature of addiction in very general terms, and Passage II goes into detail about the ways in which smokers stop smoking. Choice (E) is the best answer to this question.

13. **B.** The first paragraph talks about the "more than usual eagerness" (Line 1) that Catherine feels in the pump-room, where she's scanning the crowd for Henry Tilney, who doesn't appear. Her disappointment is expressed by "people whom nobody cared about, and nobody wanted to see" (Lines 11–12), because she cares only for Henry at that point. Thus, Choice (B) is the right one. You can rule out the other answers easily. The Thorpes don't appear until later in the passage, so Choice (A) doesn't work. Nor is Choice (C) a good answer, because Mrs. Allen says how "pleasant it would be if we had any acquaintance here" (Lines 14–15). The conditional verb, "would be," tells you that she *doesn't* have friends in Bath. Nothing is said about servants or guests, so Choices (D) and (E) don't make the cut.

14. **D.** Mrs. Allen says the same thing over and over to Catherine, not because she dislikes Catherine but because she doesn't have anyone else to talk with — and, probably, not much else to say. (You've met someone like her, right? I know I have!) Therefore, Choice (D) fits nicely.

15. **E.** Many of the choices listed are definitions of "just," but only Choice (E) fits the sentence, in which Mrs. Allen receives a "fair" reward for her efforts.

16. **A.** This question is about tone. To determine the tone of one statement, you may have to look around a bit for clues. The key here is to read a little beyond the quoted words, where you find this gem: "since they had been contented to know nothing of each other for the last fifteen years" (Lines 38–39). So how joyful were they? If they cared so much about each other, they would have kept in touch. Therefore, the statement is mocking the women's behavior.

17. **D.** Competitive talkers, that's what you have here. The women are "far more ready to give than to receive information, each hearing very little of what the other said" (Lines 47–49). The first portion of this quotation rules out Choice (E). *Hearing* isn't the problem; being *willing* to hear is. Yes, they talk about their families, as Line 46 states, but you can't be sure that Mrs. Allen is proud, as only Mrs. Thorpe's details are given. The passage contains no evidence for Choices (A) and (B).

18. **B.** The passage states that Mrs. Allen couldn't trade places with Mrs. Thorpe because Mrs. Allen "had no similar information to . . . press on the unwilling and unbelieving ear" (Lines 58–60) of Mrs. Thorpe. Therefore, Mrs. Allen doesn't trust the accuracy of Mrs. Thorpe's information. ***Skepticism*** means "mistrust," so Choice (B) is your answer.

19. **C.** Mrs. Thorpe talks about "the talents of her sons, and the beauty of her daughters" (Lines 52–53). This statement serves as a definition of her "advantage . . . in a family" (Lines 50–51). Choice (C) is the correct answer.

20. **E.** Mrs. Allen listens to Mrs. Thorpe's ***effusions*** (babbling speech, often about feelings), but Mrs. Allen has no children of her own to brag about. When she sees that "the lace on Mrs. Thorpe's pelisse was not half so handsome as that on her own" (Lines 64–66), Mrs. Allen feels better. Bingo: Mrs. Allen is better dressed, and Choice (E) is your answer.

21. **C.** Paragraph 3 (Lines 67–82) has the "eldest young lady" (Line 74) exclaim that Miss Morland looks like her brother. Immediately after, the Thorpes discuss their acquaintance with James Morland, and Catherine remembers that he visited the Thorpes during his vacation. The two groups are now connected, as Choice (C) states. Did I catch you with Choice (B)? Mrs. Thorpe does exclaim about her "dear girls" (Line 67), but she bragged about them in Paragraph 2, so this line doesn't "establish" her pride.

22. **D.** The things that "were said by the Miss Thorpes" (Line 84) aren't debts or duties; they're pleasant remarks intended to create a bond, a demonstration of good manners. Choice (D) is the right answer.

23. **A.** A ***metaphor*** is an imaginative comparison created without the words "like" or "as." Comparing friendship to a ***balm*** (a soothing cream that heals) is a metaphor. Do you know the other terms? A ***simile*** is the same sort of comparison, this time *with* "like" or "as." ***Understatement*** and ***hyperbole*** are opposites; one says less than is merited and the other more, as in "I have a little homework" (when you're facing three papers, a lab report, and two tests) or "I have a ton of homework" (when your book bag weighs 5 pounds). ***Personification*** attributes human traits to nonhuman objects or beings, such as "cruel wind."

24. **B.** Lines 101–102 explain that Miss Thorpe is "four years better informed" and "had a very decided advantage" in comparing balls, fashions, and other such topics. These ideas were "entirely new" (Line 110) to Catherine, and they inspire respect and even "admiration" (Line 109). Therefore, Miss Thorpe is Catherine's teacher — not of algebra and PSAT prep, but of the really important stuff: social life!

Section 2: Mathematics

1. **E.** Remember that prime numbers are not divisible by anything other than themselves and 1, so it's not possible for a prime number to be divisible by 3 unless the number is 3. Option I is out. All prime numbers other than 2 are odd because all even numbers are divisible by 2, so they have at least one factor besides themselves and 1. You now know that option II must be true. For option III, it's key to remember that when any number is multiplied by 2, the product is even, making option III true as well.

2. **B.** It's a good idea to estimate the numerical values of points X and Y. You can see that X is negative and Y is positive, so you can immediately eliminate Choices (D) and (E). The product of a positive and negative number is always negative. X looks to be about –0.5, and Y looks to be around 1.5. If you multiply those two values together, you get a negative number between –1 and point X, so point B is the one you're looking for.

3. **C.** One way to solve this problem is to figure out what the unknown number is. Let's call it x. You know that 30% of x is 36, which can be expressed algebraically as $0.30x = 36$. Dividing both sides by 0.30 lets you know that x is 120. Finally, figure out what 80% of 120 is by multiplying $0.80(120) = 96$. Done!

4. **E.** This question and the next question are tricky because of the key word "dozen." You may be tempted to think that Alex made 6 cookies instead of 6 dozen cookies: $(6)(12) = 72$ cookies that Alex spent all night baking. After you notice the word "dozen," this problem is much easier. To figure out how many cookies were made, add up how many dozens of cookies each person made: Alex made 6 dozen, Sam 2 dozen, and Jamie 4 dozen, resulting in 12 dozen, or 144 cookies.

5. **D.** Alex made 6 dozen cookies, and Jamie made 4 dozen, so Alex made 2 dozen, or 24, more cookies than Jamie.

6. **A.** After the problem lets you know that n is Jenn's age, reread the question with that fact in mind. If Jenn is twice as old as Henri, then Henri must be $\frac{n}{2}$ years old. Madge is 3 years younger than Henri, so just subtract 3 from Henri's age: $\frac{n}{2} - 3$.

7. **D.** Remember that the union of two sets includes all the members of each of the sets. (FYI: The intersection includes only the members that the sets have in common.) The sets both have –1 and 2, so the union of sets P and Q is {–3, –1, 0, 1, 2, 4, 8}, or a set with 7 elements.

8. **C.** First things first: Figure out the slope of the line between (–1, 3) and (4, –1). The equation for slope is to put "rise over run," or the change in y-values over the change in x-values. Here we go: $\frac{-1-3}{4-(-1)} = \frac{-4}{5}$. Because you're looking for a line parallel to this one, the answer must have the same slope, so you can eliminate all the options besides Choices (B) and (C). Now plug (1, 1) in for x and y to solve for b. Remember the equation $y = mx + b$. Plug in the slope for m and (1, 1) for x and y to solve for b: $1 = \frac{-4}{5}(1) + b$. Solving for b, you get $b = \frac{9}{5}$, Choice (C).

9. **D.** This question is all about my old friend, the Pythagorean theorem. The width and length of the paper are really the legs of a right triangle. Recall that $a^2 + b^2 = c^2$, where a and b are the triangle's legs and c is the hypotenuse. You're looking for the hypotenuse (a diagonal of the paper). $6^2 + 9^2 = c^2$, $c = \sqrt{117}$, but unfortunately that's not one of the answer choices. You can either plug the answer choices into your calculator looking for one that has the same decimal value as $\sqrt{117}$ or notice that 117 is divisible by 9: $\sqrt{117} = \sqrt{(9)(13)} = 3\sqrt{13}$.

10. **B.** First figure out the value of $2 \% 6 : 2(2^6) = 2^1 2^6 = 2^7$. You can see that there's no way 2^7 can be represented as multiples of 3 or 6, eliminating Choices (A), (C), and (D). A longer but surefire way to solve this one is to plug them all into your calculator and see which one matches $2^7 = 128$. Mathematically, $4 \% 3 = 2(4^3) = 2((2^2)^3) = 2(2^6) = 2^7$, your answer. And for the sake of being complete: $8 \% 3 = 2(8^3) = 2((2^3)^3) = 2(2^9) = 2^{10}$.

11. **D.** Remember how to FOIL! $(3x-1)^2 = (3x)^2 - 3x - 3x + 1 = 9x^2 - 6x + 1$. Now you just need to subtract $3x - 2$, without forgetting to distribute the negative: $9x^2 - 6x + 1 - (3x - 2) = 9x^2 - 6x + 1 - 3x + 2 = 9x^2 - 9x + 3$.

12. **B.** Substitution is the key, yet again! Because you want the answer in terms of a's and c's, you want to eliminate the b's. Solve the second equation for b: $b = \frac{a-c}{2}$. You can substitute this result into the first equation, yielding $3a - 5\left(\frac{a-c}{2}\right) = 2c$. If you don't want to deal with fractions, multiply both sides by 2, and then solve for a. $6a - 5(a-c) = 4c$, $6a - 5a + 5c = 4c$, $a = -c$, Choice (B).

13. **B.** The range of a function represents the y-values that the function goes through. The function that you're given is a parabola, so if you can figure out the y-coordinate of the vertex, then you're most of the way to knowing the range, because the vertex is the highest or lowest point in a parabola. Hopefully, you remember that $\frac{-b}{2a}$ can get you the x-coordinate of the vertex of a parabola if you think of the equation as $ax^2 + bx + c$. In this case, b is -2, and a is 1, so the x-coordinate of the vertex is $\frac{-(-2)}{2(1)} = \frac{2}{2} = 1$. You can also get the x-coordinate by factoring the equation into $f(x) = (x+1)(x-3)$ to find the roots at $x = -1$ and $x = 3$. The vertex occurs at their midpoint, 1. Now plug 1 into the equation for x to get the y-coordinate that goes with it: $f(1) = (1)^2 - 2(1) - 3 = -4$. You've narrowed it down to Choices (A) and (B). If you don't remember how to tell whether a parabola is "smiley" or "frowny," you can just plug any other value into the function for x and see if it's bigger or smaller than -4. Zero is always an easy choice, and you'll see that $f(0) = -3$, which is more positive than -4: Choice (B) is your answer.

14. **C.** The angle that you're looking for, *DBC,* is an alternate interior angle to *BDE,* so it also has a measure represented by $4x$. Next you want to notice that angle *ABC* and *DBC* are supplementary, so you know that $5x + 4x = 180°$, so $9x = 180°$ and $x = 20°$. This means that angle *DBC* has a measure of $4x = 4(20°) = 80°$, Choice (C).

15. **E.** This problem is all about substitution. Don't let the fractions mix you up! You want to rewrite the original equation with $-\frac{1}{x}$ wherever there was originally an x: $f\left(-\frac{1}{x}\right) = 2\left(-\frac{1}{x}\right) - \frac{3}{\left(-\frac{1}{x}\right)}$. Remember that you can flip and multiply to get rid of the fraction in the denominator of the second term. Simplifying: $f\left(-\frac{1}{x}\right) = -\frac{2}{x} - 3(-x) = -\frac{2}{x} + 3x$. If you just rearrange the terms, you see that Choice (E) is the one you want.

16. **C.** Because this equation has a square root, you want to isolate the square root first, and then square both sides. Now you have $x^2 = 5 - 4x$; put everything on one side so that one side equals 0, and you've got a factorable quadratic equation: $0 = x^2 + 4x - 5 = (x+5)(x-1)$. Solve for x using the zero product property, and x is 1 or -5. Plug each of those into the original equation, and you see that -5 can't work — the square root of $5 - 4x$ must be a positive number.

17. **B.** A picture is a big help here:

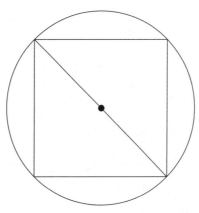

Hopefully you remember that one formula for the area of a quadrilateral is to multiply the lengths of the diagonals and then divide by 2. In case you don't remember that, it's helpful to pick a number for d. Let's say $d = 6$. That means that the radius of the circle is 3. If you cut the square in half along the diagonal, you get a triangle with a base of 6 and a height of 3, or one with an area of $\frac{1}{2}bh = \frac{1}{2}(6)(3) = 9$. Both halves of the square have that same area, so the area of the square is 18. Test the answer choices by plugging in 6 for d, and you want the one that equals 18.

18. **E.** This problem tests your knowledge of exponent rules, and you can easily solve it using substitution. Remember that wherever you see 4, you can replace it with 2^2, and you can replace 8 with 2^3. Going through the options, Choice (A) becomes $\left(2^2\right)^{2x-2} = 2^{4x-4}$, Choice (B) is $\left(2^2\right)^{2x-1} = 2^{4x-2}$, Choice (C) is $\left(2^2\right)^{\frac{x}{2}} = 2^{\frac{2x}{2}} = 2^x$, Choice (D) results in $\left(2^3\right)^{\frac{3x}{4}} = 2^{\frac{9x}{4}}$, and finally, Choice (E) is $\left(2^3\right)^{\frac{4x}{3}} = 2^{\frac{12x}{3}} = 2^{4x}$, the result you're looking for.

19. **D.** A "let statement" will take you far in this problem. Let x be the number of shirts that Sara buys, and y be the number of pairs of pants. You know that $x + y = 7$ and that $15.5x + 19.75y = 121.25$. Solve the first equation for y: $y = 7 - x$. You can now substitute this in for y in the second equation: $15.5x + 19.75(7 - x) = 121.25$. Solve for x, and you see that Sara bought 4 shirts.

20. **D.** This one is tricky! Take it step by step. The volume of a cylinder is $V = \pi r^2 h$, so in this case $36\pi = \pi r^2(4)$. You can solve to find that $r = 3$. The surface area of the cylinder is the area of the two circles plus the area of the cylinder's walls. Each circle has a radius of πr^2, or 9π, so together they account for 18π square inches. The cylinder's walls are really made by taking a rectangle and connecting the ends. The rectangle has a width equal to the height of the cylinder and a length equal to the circumference of the circle. Therefore, the surface area of the cylinder's walls is $lw = (2\pi r)(h) = 2\pi(3)(4) = 24\pi$ square inches. Together, you've got $18\pi + 24\pi = 42\pi$ square inches of surface area.

Section 3: Critical Reading

25. **B.** Picture a picture (sorry, I couldn't resist that phrase!) with several shades of green, overlapping. What happens to the painting? It may be "encrusted," "enlivened," "shadowed," or "sliced" — not literally, of course, but criss-crossed by stripes that seem to slice into the picture. I haven't included Choice (E), "obscured," in my list of possible answers for this sentence, because the green *is* the painting, or at least part of it, so it can't *obscure* or cover it. Now turn to the second blank. Choice (A), ***encrusted*** (covered with a crust), doesn't work well with "reveal." Choice (C) is hard to imagine, because "shadowed" isn't a good match for ***agitate*** (to stir up). Choice (D) is out because colors can't confuse each other, though they may confuse the viewer. You're left with one possibility. Green shades may "work well together" — the meaning of ***complement.*** Choice (B) is the right answer.

26. **E.** Easy sentence, but hard answer choices — that's a typical PSAT/NMSQT pattern. In Question 26, all you have to do is identify the word that means "present at birth," the definition given right after the blanks. Choice (E) is an exact match. Are you willing to cram a few more vocabulary words into your head? ***Prodigious*** means "great in size, force, or influence," and ***obdurate*** is a fancy way of saying "stubborn," as is ***determined.*** If something is ***inexorable,*** it can't be stopped. It's relentless.

27. **B.** You can turn to the real world for help with this one. What do executives request, regardless of their duties? More money — also known as ***compensation,*** or Choice (B). Do you have a moment to learn a new vocabulary word? ***Elucidation*** is "the act of making clear."

28. **C.** Work backwards here to land on the correct answer. Which words may apply to a literary work? All the answer options except Choices (A) and (B). Okay, now look at the first blank. Who can't catch anything more than the "basic information"? Someone who has more to learn. In other words, an *immature* reader. There you go: Choice (C) is your answer.

29. **B.** When you're "ignorant," you don't know what to do, so you may accidentally do the wrong thing. This idea leads you directly to Choice (B), because *inadvertent* means "unintended." The correct answer is Choice (B).

30. **B.** Line 2 tells you that "a prince who . . . has not made himself hateful" is safe from attack, or, if attacked, will see his enemy "driven off in disgrace" (Line 4). If you're not hateful, you have the support of the people, as Choice (B) states.

31. **C.** This passage is from *The Prince,* Machiavelli's famous book about power. Everything in the passage relates to power — how to keep it in the face of enemies or "subjects who seem . . . too bold" (Lines 17–18). Therefore, Choice (C) is a perfect fit.

32. **D.** The author tells you that newspapers "are produced with rapidity, to be read with rapidity" (Lines 16–17) and that he reads them "in odd moments" (Lines 18–19), not in one uninterrupted half hour, as Choice (D) states.

33. **D.** All the choices are definitions of "odd," but only Choice (D) reflects the author's idea that you should read newspapers when you have an occasional free moment, not while you are on the train with a half hour free. Choice (D) is the best answer.

34. **C.** Paragraph 1, Lines 1–22, moves through the ancient world, from Greece to Egypt to China and then back to Greece. Sounds like Choice (C) to me! True, the dates in Paragraph 1 create a timeline, but "the development of clocks" — Choice (B) — continues beyond ancient times, and some of the devices mentioned in the paragraph aren't clocks at all. Also, European clocks from the 14th century are discussed later in the passage. For these reasons, Choice (B) isn't a good option. Nor is Choice (D), which addresses only the first sentence of Paragraph 1, which knocks Anaximander off the "I invented the sundial" throne. The other choices don't appear in Paragraph 1 at all.

35. **E.** The cited line talks about the nearly constant, even division of day and night near the equator, which is where Egypt lies. (In areas more distant from the equator, the days are shorter in winter and longer in summer.) Thus the Egyptians were able to divide the day and night "into 12 equal parts" each (Line 10). Therefore, our current 24-hour day is an Egyptian invention.

36. **A.** Lines 18–20 describe a "vessel" from which "water trickled out." The float probably sank as the water level decreased, presumably lining up with numbers on the side of the container. Choice (A) is the right answer.

37. **D.** If you know the definition of *cosmic* (relating to the universe), you're home free here. Only Choices (B) and (D) refer to the universe, but they do so in different ways. Choice (B) relies on the meaning "common to all," and that definition doesn't fit the context, as many different clock designs are described in the passage. The other relevant meaning is "stars and planets and, well, everything that exists." The fact that the device "showed star and planet position" (Lines 30–31) points you to Choice (D), the correct answer.

38. **A.** This one is tricky because Choices (A), (B), and (D) are true. Being true, though, isn't enough, because you need to find a cause-effect relationship, with the effect being the title "father of European clockmaking." Choice (B) is accurate, but similarity isn't a cause. In fact, it may have been accidental! Choice (D) is also true because you know that Jacopo de Dondi was Giovanni's father and also a clockmaker. So? Having a relative in the business doesn't make you important. Building a device (the astratrium) that "was the most complicated machine" since ancient Greece, or, as Choice (A) puts it, "technically complex," is pretty impressive and reason enough to gain the title.

39. **B.** The passage explains that "[s]prings replaced weights as the driving force in smaller clocks" (Lines 62–63) and that this substitution was "apparently derived from the contemporary use of springs in locks and firearms" (Lines 64–66). Choice (B) is a winning answer.

40. **D.** Stars and planets pop up all over this passage, from the sundial in Line 1 (our sun is a star) to the "motions of the planets" in Lines 50–51. Though the passage doesn't explain exactly how, what's going on in the sky clearly has something to do with timekeeping, making Choice (D) the best one.

41. **C.** When you're writing an essay, you often conclude by answering the "so what?" question, also known as "why are you telling me this?" The last paragraph of this passage is that type of conclusion. It states that town clocks "may have allowed for more regulation of daily business" (Lines 77–78) and "later timekeeping" helped scientists. In other words, Lines 72–85 address the significance of better clocks, also known as Choice (C).

42. **D.** The portrait is later called an "ugly engraving" (Line 7), so you know that this picture of one of the world's most famous authors wouldn't win a beauty contest, shooting down Choice (A). Okay, not beautiful, but nobody mentions animals or monsters either, so Choices (B) and (C) bite the dust. The picture may very well not be accurate, but Line 3 tells you that Ben Jonson "certified" it, so Choice (E) is out. You're left with Choice (D), the right answer. You probably arrived at Choice (D) more quickly if you knew that *abominable* means "hateful" or "unpleasant," and *libel* is the "presentation of false material" to the public. In other words, the portrait showed a man so far from handsome that it badly represented the entire human race!

43. **B.** The first paragraph of Passage I (Lines 1–8) discusses the "likeness of Shakespeare" in the Folio of 1623, an early collection of his work. Although it is apparently an ugly image — "an abominable libel on humanity" (Lines 2–3) — at least one man who lived during Shakespeare's lifetime, Ben Jonson, said it was accurate. (One definition of *fidelity* is "accuracy.") The question emphasizes the main idea of that paragraph, that the "ugly engraving" (Line 7) would have been replaced by something else unless it accurately portrayed Shakespeare, as Choice (B) states.

44. **C.** Line 12 tells you that the bust of Shakespeare shows the playwright "in the act of composition." Boaden thinks that the bust may show Shakespeare in the act of creating a character named "Falstaff." Was Boaden sure? No, but Line 13 says that it is "hardly a stretch of fancy" or imagination, also known as Choice (C).

45. **C.** It's hard to imagine an ugly writer creating beautiful literature, but the author of Passage I, who seems to think that the "ugly engraving" (Line 7) of Shakespeare is the most accurate, can do so. The passage goes on to say that later artists polished Shakespeare's image. They portrayed what they thought a great writer should be — someone who has brain power and upper-class manners. Choice (C) fits well with these ideas.

46. **A.** Not a lot in Lines 33–46 would glorify your family tree. Shakespeare's youth was *disreputable* (of a bad reputation). His father was *illiterate* (couldn't read or write) and had both money and legal troubles. Choice (A) is a good fit. Did I fool you with Choice (E)? These are *not* all the known facts, just some — and some of those are in doubt, also ("if universal tradition on the subject is worth anything" — Lines 40–41 — implies doubt).

47. **B.** The phrase is tucked into a sentence about Shakespeare's life, right before a traditional story about Shakespeare — that he left Stratford because he got caught *poaching,* or hunting without permission. The word "universal" (Line 40) implies that everyone believes the story, so Choice (B) is the answer you seek.

48. **D.** The first passage discusses how Shakespeare looked and stays away from the controversy about whether the historical Shakespeare actually wrote Shakespeare's plays. (For the record, I don't care if a chipmunk wrote them; I love them anyway.) The second passage dives right in, stating that one point "bears strongly against the theory that William Shakespeare" wrote the "so-called Shakespeare's Plays" (Line 31). Therefore, Choice (D) works.

Section 4: Mathematics

21. **D.** The ratio of laptops to desktops is 4:7, which means that the ratio of laptops to computers must be 4:11. So the number of laptops in the warehouse is a multiple of 4, which means that the number of computers is a multiple of 11. Choice (D) is the only option with 11 as a factor.

22. **D.** This problem relies on the multiplication principle. Recall that if you're selecting from independent groups of things, you can multiply the number of items in each group to determine the total number of choices. If you had 2 pairs of pants and 3 shirts, you would have $(3)(2) = 6$ outfits; so to select a meal you have $(6)(8)(3) = 144$ three-course meals.

23. **C.** For this problem your best bet is to work backwards. The final result was 2, which is the number that resulted from dividing something by 3. Therefore, the number before 2 was 3 times bigger, so it must have been 6. Six was the result of increasing a number by 12, so you can subtract 12 from 6 to determine that –6 was the earlier number. Okay, –6 was the result of doubling a number, so if you divide it in half, you know the original number: –3.

24. **E.** The key to this problem is remembering that you aren't allowed to take the square root of a negative number. This means that you're looking for an answer choice that makes the value of $9 - x^2$ negative when you plug the number in for x. You may get tricked by –3, which leads to you taking the square root of 0, but that's allowed: the square root of 0 is 0. Choice (E), 4, is the only one that makes $9 - x^2$ negative, so that's your answer choice.

25. **C.** To find where two lines intersect, you need to solve a system of equations. The easiest way to tackle this one is to set the two equations equal to each other (you're substituting for y). The equation $2x + 9 = -\frac{1}{2}x + 4$ becomes $\frac{5}{2}x = -5$, which becomes $x = (-5)\left(\frac{2}{5}\right) = -2$. Now you can eliminate Choices (A) and (E). Plug $x = -2$ into either of the equations (I'd choose the first one — no fractions!) and solve for y: $y = 2(-2) + 9 = -4 + 9 = 5$.

26. **A.** Recall that the absolute value sign takes whatever is inside and makes it positive. If $3x + 5$ is a positive number, the absolute value sign does nothing, and if $3x + 5$ results in a negative number, the absolute value sign makes it positive. Because the result of this switching is always less than or equal to 4, it's also always greater than or equal to –4. For example, let $3x + 5 = -5$. After the absolute value acts on it, you have positive 5, which is greater than 4. So, you're looking for values of x that make $3x + 5$ less than or equal to 4 and also greater than or equal to –4. You can set that up like this: $-4 \le 3x + 5 \le 4$. Subtract 5 from all sides: $-9 \le 3x \le -1$, and then divide everything by 3: $-3 \le x \le -\frac{1}{3}$, Choice (A).

27. **C.** First, move everything to one side: $x^2 - x - 6 < 0$. Now you have a quadratic that you can factor: $(x - 3)(x + 2) < 0$. The left side equals 0 when x is 3 or –2, so you need to determine which values of x result in the left side's being negative. Pick a number less than –2: if $x = -3$, you get $(-6)(-1) = 6$, which is greater than 0, so you don't want numbers less than –2. Now test a point between –2 and 3. My favorite test point is always 0: $(-3)(2) = -6$, which is less than 0, what you want! For the sake of completeness, also check a number greater than 3. If $x = 4$, you get $(1)(6) = 6$, which is positive, so not something you're interested in. Choice (C) is the one that you want.

28. **B.** This is a tricky one! You want to make sure you remember to use your 30°-60°-90° and 45°-45°-90° triangles. It may help to label the diagram with the angles and sides that you know.

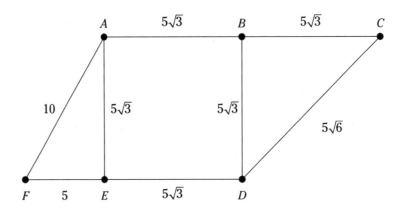

Recall that the hypotenuse in a 30°-60°-90° triangle is always twice as long as the side opposite the 30° angle, meaning that *AF* is 10 units long. Also, the side opposite the 60° angle is equal to the length of the side opposite the 30° angle multiplied by $\sqrt{3}$, so *AE* is $5\sqrt{3}$ long. Because *ABDE* is a square, all four of those sides are $5\sqrt{3}$ units long. Triangle *BDC* is an isosceles right triangle (45°-45°-90°), so *BC* must also be $5\sqrt{3}$ units long. The only side you have left is *CD*. You can use your 45°-45°-90° triangle knowledge to determine its length, or just use the Pythagorean theorem. Either way, it works out to be $5\sqrt{6}$ units long. Add up all the sides (starting at point *A* and going clockwise around the figure) and you get $5\sqrt{3}+5\sqrt{3}+5\sqrt{6}+5\sqrt{3}+5+10=15+15\sqrt{3}+5\sqrt{6}$, Choice (B).

29. **9 or 10 or 11.** This question tests your knowledge of the triangle inequality. Remember that the sum of any two sides must be greater than the length of the third side. If two of the sides of a triangle are 2 and 10, then the third side must be less than 2 + 10 = 12, and must be longer than 10 – 2 = 8. Therefore, any number between 8 and 12 will work.

30. **26.** More fun with triangles! This question is all about the Pythagorean theorem. You can sketch out the relative positions of the homes and see that they form the legs of a right triangle, with the distance you're looking for acting as the hypotenuse.

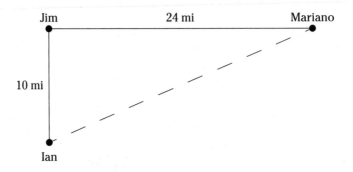

So, substituting into $a^2+b^2=c^2, (10)^2+(24)^2=c^2$, you end up with *c* = 26 miles.

31. **2.5 or $\frac{5}{2}$.** First, find the slope of line *k*. Recall that slope $=\frac{rise}{run}=\frac{(-8)-(2)}{(6)-(-6)}=\frac{-10}{12}=-\frac{5}{6}$. The easiest way to find the *y*-intercept is to set up an equation in $y=mx+b$ form, plug the coordinates of one of the points in for *y* and *x*, and solve for *b*. So far you have $y=-\frac{5}{6}x+b$, and you can use the point (6, –8): $-8=-\frac{5}{6}(6)+b$, which simplifies to $-8=-5+b$, so *b* = –3. Multiplying the slope and *y*-intercept: $\left(-\frac{5}{6}\right)(-3)=\frac{5}{2}$ or 2.5.

32. **91.** Recall that a factor is a number that divides the original number evenly. The factors of 36 are 1, 2, 3, 4, 6, 9, 12, 18, and 36. Just add those up, and you get a sum of 91.

33. **10, 11, 12,** or **13.** If the diameter is 16 inches, then the radius of the pizza is 8 inches. This means that the area of the pizza is $\pi r^2 = \pi(8)^2 = 64\pi$ square inches. If each slice is 15 square inches, you have $\frac{64\pi}{15} \approx 13.4$ slices. If each slice is 22 square inches, then there are $\frac{64\pi}{22} \approx 9.1$ slices. Slices must be whole numbers, so you want to pick a number between 9.1 and 13.4: 10, 11, 12, or 13 slices work well.

34. **420.** First you want to figure out what percent of people speak Spanish as their primary language. English + French + Other = 20 + 40 + 15 = 75%. Now you know that 25% of the people speak Spanish. To determine the total number of people, multiply the number of Spanish speakers by 4 (because 4(25%) = 100%): $4(105) = 420$ passengers.

35. **144.** A quick sketch will probably help you out with this problem. Because you know that the base of the box is a square and that its area is 36 square centimeters, you can deduce that the length of a side of the square is 6 centimeters.

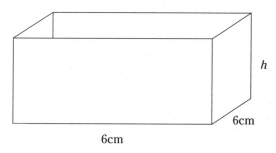

Not drawn to scale

Each of the sides of the box has an area of 6*h,* so the total area of the four sides of the box is 24*h.* You know that the total surface area is 132, so 132 − 36 = 96 square centimeters for the sides. 24*h* = 96, so *h* = 4. The volume of the box is $l \times w \times h = 6 \times 6 \times 4 = 144$ cubic inches.

36. $\frac{13}{2}$ or **6.5.** Take this problem step by step and remember to deal with the parentheses first! Following the rule: $1\#6 = \frac{2(1)+6}{2} = 4$, and $3\#4 = \frac{2(3)+4}{2} = 5$. This means that $(1\#6)\#(3\#4) = 4\#5 = \frac{2(4)+5}{2} = \frac{13}{2}$, or 6.5.

37. **93.** Miki wants an 88 average over 5 tests. Therefore, when you add the scores of the 5 tests together, she needs 5(88) = 440 points. You know that on the first three tests she earned 70 + 95 + 82 = 247 points, meaning that she needs to earn 440 − 247 = 193 more points over two tests. The highest Miki can earn on a test is 100, so the lowest she can earn on a test is 193 − 100 = 93 points.

38. ⅔ or **0.67.** First, you want to pick some numbers. Choose the radius of the white circles to be 1. In that case, the diameter of the black circle is 6 (each white circle has a diameter of 2, and there are 3 white circles stacked up). The area of the big circle is $\pi r^2 = \pi(3)^2 = 9\pi$, and the area of each white circle is $\pi r^2 = \pi(1)^2 = \pi$, so the total area taken up by the white circles is 3π. This means that there's $9\pi - 3\pi = 6\pi$ of shaded area out of a total of 9π, so the probability of landing on the shaded part of the circle is $\frac{6\pi}{9\pi} = \frac{2}{3}$.

Section 5: Writing

1. **E.** When you examine two things, checking for similarities and differences, the expression to use is "compared with." The expression "compared next to" isn't standard English. Also, the things being compared should match grammatically. In other words, a comparison should be parallel. Choice (E) fits both categories.

2. **B.** The sentence has two time frames in it: the existence of the school and the construction of the shopping mall. Both are in the past, but one is farther in the past — the existence of the school, which presumably was torn down before a shopping mall arose in its place. To place something in the past earlier than something else, use "had."

3. **C.** To solve this one you need to know the difference between two words: "quick" (an adjective) and "quickly" (an adverb). Adverbs describe _verbs,_ words that express action or a state of being. In this sentence, "quickly" is needed to describe "is changing." Only two Choices, (C) and (E), include "quickly," but Choice (E) has an illogical change to "which is changing." Go for Choice (C), the correct one.

4. **D.** The sentence contains a comparison, so you know that the terms of the comparison must be parallel. That's grammar lingo for matching. The first portion of the comparison is "The reaction . . . more extreme." You see a subject and a verb in that part of the sentence (reaction was), so you need a subject and a verb in the second part of the comparison, which begins with "than." Only Choice (D) has a subject-verb combo ("it was"), so Choice (D) is your answer.

5. **B.** The original sentence is a fragment because it doesn't have a matching subject-verb combo. "Baleen whales growing" doesn't make sense. "Baleen whales grow," on the other hand, is a good match and points you to Choice (B) as the best answer.

6. **E.** The original sentence has two time clues ("during the first World War" and "that was when"), but only one is needed. Choice (E) eliminates the extra words and gets the job done.

7. **A.** This one has it all — simplicity _and_ proper verb tense (simple past, in case you're curious about names). The sentence is correct, so Choice (A) is your answer.

8. **B.** This sentence expresses what grammarians calls "condition contrary to fact." The "if" portion of this sentence isn't true because the speaker (the _I_) didn't know about the car accident and traffic jam. In that sort of sentence, the untrue portion of the sentence _never_ includes "would." Instead, "had" is what you need here.

   Another way to fix this sentence, not included in the choices, is "If I had known." Same rule applies: Never use "would" to express the untrue idea.

9. **D.** The repetition of "principles of geometry" tells you right away that the sentence can be improved. Slim it down by attaching the information at the end of the sentence with the relative pronoun "which."

   When you find more than one grammatically correct answer choice, opt for the shorter version. Concise writing packs a more powerful punch than wordy, repetitive sentences.

10. **C.** Verb tense is the key here. The second half of the sentence employs a present-tense verb ("should play"), so the first portion should be in present also. You also need a matching subject-verb pair, and the original ("brain being") doesn't work. Go for Choice (C), which offers a good pair ("brain is"), both in present tense.

11. **D.** Everywhere I go these days, I hear "equally as." Nope! Not proper English. Dump the first "as" (not a choice here) or drop the "equally," which is what Choice (D) does. Did I fool you with Choice (E)? The comparison is fine, but the verb should be "are," not "is," because the subject is "choosing" _and_ "preparing" — two things.

12. **A.** I threw in a correct sentence here, just to keep you on your toes. The tense is good, the sentence is complete, the subjects match the verbs — yup, this one is right, so the answer is Choice (A).

13. **B.** Remember that you're looking for a way to improve each sentence. The original sentence is grammatically correct but as clumsy as an ox in a glass factory. Choice (B) reads much more smoothly. Say it aloud to hear the difference! Because Choice (B) improves the sentence, it's the correct answer.

14. **C.** The pronoun "somebody" is singular. (You can't imagine saying, "Somebody are responsible," can you?) Therefore, any pronouns referring to "somebody" must also be singular. Thus "their," a plural pronoun, doesn't work. Go for "his or her," Choice (C), and you're correct.

15. **D.** The "drivers" are defined by the information between dashes. Because "drivers" is a subject, the words between the dashes must be subject material. Oops. The pronoun "me" can't be a subject. (Reserve "me" for objects.) Only "I" can function as a subject. (Use "myself" just for sentences where the action doubles back on the subject, as in "I washed myself.") Now you're down to Choices (D) and (E). Because you're talking about a group, you need a plural verb, which takes you to Choice (D) and the verb "have."

16. **E.** The introductory verb form ("Hidden") must describe the subject. In other words, the description "Hidden in a corner of the bookshelf" must apply to the subject. However, "I" am not "hidden"; "a mouse" is. Therefore, Choices (A), (B), and (C) are out. So is Choice (D), because "jumping" isn't hidden either. Only Choice (E) places the mouse "Hidden in a corner of the bookshelf," and there's your answer.

17. **B.** The original sentence is a run-on, so you have to insert either a semicolon (as Choice (B) does) or a conjunction (as Choice (E) does). The problem with Choice (E) is that "but" doesn't fit the meaning of the sentence. You expect a word that fits the "statement and proof" structure of the sentence, not one that turns it around to a different direction, as "but" does. Go for Choice (B) and you're right.

18. **B.** The underlined portion of the sentence presents you with two problems. The first: How to stop that mother from showing 1,400 baby pictures? Just kidding. The first issue is "more cuter" — an incorrect comparison because "cuter" includes the idea of comparison and makes the "more" unnecessary. The second issue revolves around "than that of." Although it sounds a little odd, it's actually correct. If you dump "that of," you're comparing a baby's smile to other children, not to their smiles. Choice (B) is the best answer.

19. **C.** The subject of this sentence is "box," not "crayons." Why? The "as well as" creates a different clause, so you should ignore everything between the commas when you're matching the subject and the verb. The subject, "box," is singular, and it needs a singular verb, "was." Choice (C) is the only one with a singular verb, and it's your answer.

20. **A.** The introductory verb form, "Wearing dress uniforms," must describe the subject of the sentence. Who saluted? The new police officers. Okay, you can rule out Choice (E). You want the actions to be simultaneous, so "wearing" is better than "having worn" or "having been wearing." Cross out Choices (B) and (C). Now look at Choice (D). If you insert the words from Choice (D), you end up with "saluted the mayor greeted." That doesn't make sense. You're left with Choice (A), the correct response.

21. **A.** The incorrect portion of the sentence is right at the beginning. It should say "tornado roared," not "tornado roaring."

22. **B.** The helping verb "had" places an action in the past before another past-tense action. In this sentence, all three actions (spending time, studying animals, documenting behavior) are more or less *simultaneous* (occurring at the same time), so "had" is unnecessary. One correct form is "have spent," the present perfect tense, which expresses an action begun in the past and continuing in the present. With the verb "have spent," you're saying that the scientists *were* doing all those cool things and are *still* doing them. Another possible correction is "spent," which implies that these actions were all in the past. Either way, "had" is inappropriate, and Choice (B) is your answer.

23. **B.** The subject of the sentence is "Dorothy," a singular noun. In the world of grammar, singular and plural don't mix. The verb should be "returns," not "return."

In general, ignore interruptions that pop up between the subject and the verb when you're choosing between singular and plural verb forms. In particular, pay no attention to "not . . ." and "as well as" or "along with." These grammatical elements have no bearing on the subject-verb combination.

24. **B.** The "-self" pronouns should show up only when the action in the sentence doubles back, as in "she talked to herself because no one else would listen." Here the proper expression is "to McDonald and me."

25. **C.** The expression "should of" (and its close relatives, "would of" and "could of") aren't standard English. The proper expression is "should have," or, when you're using a contraction, "should've."

26. **D.** The list at the end of this sentence — and all lists — must be parallel. Parallelism is an English-teacher term (and a favorite of the PSAT writers). If a sentence is parallel, everything doing the same job in the sentence has the same grammatical identity. The correct expression is "energy, friendliness, and playfulness," because all three are nouns. In the original, though, you have two nouns and "that he loved to play" — a mismatch.

27. **A.** An introductory verb form without a subject *must* describe the subject of the sentence. Therefore, the original sentence has the highway filling potholes. A little hard to imagine, right? A better sentence would begin, "As the road crew diligently filled potholes."

28. **D.** The star is on the team, so how can he score more goals than anyone on the team? Illogical comparisons are a frequent flyer on the PSAT/NMSQT (as well as on the SAT), so pay strict attention when you see a comparison. The correct expression is "anyone else" on the team.

29. **D.** The sentence begins in third person, talking *about* "anyone." The second half of the sentence switches to second person, talking to *you.* Because you have no valid reason to switch, Choice (D) is wrong.

30. **A.** The expression "being that" isn't standard English. Go for "Because."

31. **E.** Everything is in place here: The "having" places the action of sealing before Peter's distress and realization. The "had" places the signing, or what should have been the signing, before the sealing. All the verb forms are in the correct tense, and the sentence is fine.

32. **C.** Whose tastes are we talking about — Sheila's or her mother's? As written, the sentence isn't clear. The "her" must be clarified.

33. **B.** The expression "can't hardly" is a double negative, a no-no (sorry, I couldn't resist the pun) in standard English. The proper expression is "can hardly."

34. **B.** The original sentence is a run-on because two complete thoughts are linked by a comma. Grammatical felony! Use a semicolon or create two separate sentences.

35. **D.** The third sentence needs to go on a diet. The original isn't horrible, but it is bloated. If you say what the exhibition did (drew attention to the fine line . . .), the reader knows that was the point, so you don't have to label it as "the point." In other words, don't over-explain!

36. **C.** The introductory verb form tells you one important piece of information: that the painting was hanging in the museum for many years. The rest of the sentence tells you the other important fact: that Goya's name was on the label. Choice (C) gets all this across concisely.

37. **B.** The third paragraph makes some important points about the nature of art and the identity of the artist. The writer of this essay states these opinions because he or she thinks they're true. The writer doesn't have to say, "In my opinion I think" or "I do not think," because why else would the writer include those ideas?

38. **B.** The third paragraph and the fourth need a transitional idea — something to tie them together. In the original version, you don't know when or why or how the fake disappeared. Choice (B) adds a time clue, telling you that the museum moved on. Choice (C) does the same thing, but with a faulty modifier ("The show ending"). Choice (D) is a fragment, not a complete sentence, and Choice (E) is wordy.

39. **C.** The original sentence isn't actually a sentence; it's a fragment, a grammatical felony. So is Choice (B). Choices (D) and (E) have verb-tense problems, so Choice (C) is the best answer here.

Answer Key for Practice Test 2

Section 1

1. E	7. A	13. B	19. C
2. B	8. E	14. D	20. E
3. C	9. B	15. E	21. C
4. A	10. D	16. A	22. D
5. D	11. A	17. D	23. A
6. D	12. E	18. B	24. B

Section 2

1. E	6. A	11. D	16. C
2. B	7. D	12. B	17. B
3. C	8. C	13. B	18. E
4. E	9. D	14. C	19. D
5. D	10. B	15. E	20. D

Section 3

25. B	31. C	37. D	43. B
26. E	32. D	38. A	44. C
27. B	33. D	39. B	45. C
28. C	34. C	40. D	46. A
29. B	35. E	41. C	47. B
30. B	36. A	42. D	48. D

Section 4

21. D	26. A	31. **2.5 or ⁵⁄₂**	36. **¹³⁄₂ or 6.5**
22. D	27. C	32. **91**	37. **93**
23. C	28. B	33. **10, 11, 12, or 13**	38. **⅔ or .67**
24. E	29. **9 or 10 or 11**	34. **420**	
25. C	30. **26**	35. **144**	

Section 5

1. E	11. D	21. A	31. E
2. B	12. A	22. B	32. C
3. C	13. B	23. B	33. B
4. D	14. C	24. B	34. B
5. B	15. D	25. C	35. D
6. E	16. E	26. D	36. C
7. A	17. B	27. A	37. B
8. B	18. B	28. D	38. B
9. D	19. C	29. D	39. C
10. C	20. A	30. A	

Chapter 15

Practice Test 3

· ·

According to the old saying, three's a crowd, but not when you're practicing for the PSAT/NMSQT. In that context, three is a smart move, because if you've completed two tests already, you're on your way to an excellent score. (I'm assuming you're doing the exams in order, but if you aren't, no worries. Just turn back to Chapter 11 and read the general directions before you begin this test.)

If this *is* your third practice exam, take a close look at what tripped you up on the other two tests so that you know what to work on. Review any unfamiliar concepts by turning to Parts II and III for reading, writing, and math review. You can also consult your school texts or other books. Spend a few moments thinking about timing: Did you run out of minutes at any point? Push yourself to move a little more quickly, so long as you don't sacrifice accuracy. If you can add just one or two more correctly answered questions, your score will benefit.

When you're done, check your answers with the key in Chapter 16. Read the explanations for all the questions, not just those accompanying the ones you missed. I placed tips and vocabulary builders with the answers, so you may learn something by reviewing all the explanations, even those accompanying questions you answered correctly.

Answer Sheet

For the questions in Sections 1 through 5, use the ovals and grid-ins to record your answers.

Section 1: Critical Reading

1. Ⓐ Ⓑ Ⓒ Ⓓ Ⓔ	7. Ⓐ Ⓑ Ⓒ Ⓓ Ⓔ	13. Ⓐ Ⓑ Ⓒ Ⓓ Ⓔ	19. Ⓐ Ⓑ Ⓒ Ⓓ Ⓔ
2. Ⓐ Ⓑ Ⓒ Ⓓ Ⓔ	8. Ⓐ Ⓑ Ⓒ Ⓓ Ⓔ	14. Ⓐ Ⓑ Ⓒ Ⓓ Ⓔ	20. Ⓐ Ⓑ Ⓒ Ⓓ Ⓔ
3. Ⓐ Ⓑ Ⓒ Ⓓ Ⓔ	9. Ⓐ Ⓑ Ⓒ Ⓓ Ⓔ	15. Ⓐ Ⓑ Ⓒ Ⓓ Ⓔ	21. Ⓐ Ⓑ Ⓒ Ⓓ Ⓔ
4. Ⓐ Ⓑ Ⓒ Ⓓ Ⓔ	10. Ⓐ Ⓑ Ⓒ Ⓓ Ⓔ	16. Ⓐ Ⓑ Ⓒ Ⓓ Ⓔ	22. Ⓐ Ⓑ Ⓒ Ⓓ Ⓔ
5. Ⓐ Ⓑ Ⓒ Ⓓ Ⓔ	11. Ⓐ Ⓑ Ⓒ Ⓓ Ⓔ	17. Ⓐ Ⓑ Ⓒ Ⓓ Ⓔ	23. Ⓐ Ⓑ Ⓒ Ⓓ Ⓔ
6. Ⓐ Ⓑ Ⓒ Ⓓ Ⓔ	12. Ⓐ Ⓑ Ⓒ Ⓓ Ⓔ	18. Ⓐ Ⓑ Ⓒ Ⓓ Ⓔ	24. Ⓐ Ⓑ Ⓒ Ⓓ Ⓔ

Section 2: Mathematics

1. Ⓐ Ⓑ Ⓒ Ⓓ Ⓔ	6. Ⓐ Ⓑ Ⓒ Ⓓ Ⓔ	11. Ⓐ Ⓑ Ⓒ Ⓓ Ⓔ	16. Ⓐ Ⓑ Ⓒ Ⓓ Ⓔ
2. Ⓐ Ⓑ Ⓒ Ⓓ Ⓔ	7. Ⓐ Ⓑ Ⓒ Ⓓ Ⓔ	12. Ⓐ Ⓑ Ⓒ Ⓓ Ⓔ	17. Ⓐ Ⓑ Ⓒ Ⓓ Ⓔ
3. Ⓐ Ⓑ Ⓒ Ⓓ Ⓔ	8. Ⓐ Ⓑ Ⓒ Ⓓ Ⓔ	13. Ⓐ Ⓑ Ⓒ Ⓓ Ⓔ	18. Ⓐ Ⓑ Ⓒ Ⓓ Ⓔ
4. Ⓐ Ⓑ Ⓒ Ⓓ Ⓔ	9. Ⓐ Ⓑ Ⓒ Ⓓ Ⓔ	14. Ⓐ Ⓑ Ⓒ Ⓓ Ⓔ	19. Ⓐ Ⓑ Ⓒ Ⓓ Ⓔ
5. Ⓐ Ⓑ Ⓒ Ⓓ Ⓔ	10. Ⓐ Ⓑ Ⓒ Ⓓ Ⓔ	15. Ⓐ Ⓑ Ⓒ Ⓓ Ⓔ	20. Ⓐ Ⓑ Ⓒ Ⓓ Ⓔ

Section 3: Critical Reading

25. Ⓐ Ⓑ Ⓒ Ⓓ Ⓔ	31. Ⓐ Ⓑ Ⓒ Ⓓ Ⓔ	37. Ⓐ Ⓑ Ⓒ Ⓓ Ⓔ	43. Ⓐ Ⓑ Ⓒ Ⓓ Ⓔ
26. Ⓐ Ⓑ Ⓒ Ⓓ Ⓔ	32. Ⓐ Ⓑ Ⓒ Ⓓ Ⓔ	38. Ⓐ Ⓑ Ⓒ Ⓓ Ⓔ	44. Ⓐ Ⓑ Ⓒ Ⓓ Ⓔ
27. Ⓐ Ⓑ Ⓒ Ⓓ Ⓔ	33. Ⓐ Ⓑ Ⓒ Ⓓ Ⓔ	39. Ⓐ Ⓑ Ⓒ Ⓓ Ⓔ	45. Ⓐ Ⓑ Ⓒ Ⓓ Ⓔ
28. Ⓐ Ⓑ Ⓒ Ⓓ Ⓔ	34. Ⓐ Ⓑ Ⓒ Ⓓ Ⓔ	40. Ⓐ Ⓑ Ⓒ Ⓓ Ⓔ	46. Ⓐ Ⓑ Ⓒ Ⓓ Ⓔ
29. Ⓐ Ⓑ Ⓒ Ⓓ Ⓔ	35. Ⓐ Ⓑ Ⓒ Ⓓ Ⓔ	41. Ⓐ Ⓑ Ⓒ Ⓓ Ⓔ	47. Ⓐ Ⓑ Ⓒ Ⓓ Ⓔ
30. Ⓐ Ⓑ Ⓒ Ⓓ Ⓔ	36. Ⓐ Ⓑ Ⓒ Ⓓ Ⓔ	42. Ⓐ Ⓑ Ⓒ Ⓓ Ⓔ	48. Ⓐ Ⓑ Ⓒ Ⓓ Ⓔ

Section 4: Mathematics

21. Ⓐ Ⓑ Ⓒ Ⓓ Ⓔ   25. Ⓐ Ⓑ Ⓒ Ⓓ Ⓔ
22. Ⓐ Ⓑ Ⓒ Ⓓ Ⓔ   26. Ⓐ Ⓑ Ⓒ Ⓓ Ⓔ
23. Ⓐ Ⓑ Ⓒ Ⓓ Ⓔ   27. Ⓐ Ⓑ Ⓒ Ⓓ Ⓔ
24. Ⓐ Ⓑ Ⓒ Ⓓ Ⓔ   28. Ⓐ Ⓑ Ⓒ Ⓓ Ⓔ

29. 30. 31. 32. 33.

34. 35. 36. 37. 38.

Section 5: Writing

1. Ⓐ Ⓑ Ⓒ Ⓓ Ⓔ   9. Ⓐ Ⓑ Ⓒ Ⓓ Ⓔ   17. Ⓐ Ⓑ Ⓒ Ⓓ Ⓔ   25. Ⓐ Ⓑ Ⓒ Ⓓ Ⓔ   33. Ⓐ Ⓑ Ⓒ Ⓓ Ⓔ
2. Ⓐ Ⓑ Ⓒ Ⓓ Ⓔ   10. Ⓐ Ⓑ Ⓒ Ⓓ Ⓔ   18. Ⓐ Ⓑ Ⓒ Ⓓ Ⓔ   26. Ⓐ Ⓑ Ⓒ Ⓓ Ⓔ   34. Ⓐ Ⓑ Ⓒ Ⓓ Ⓔ
3. Ⓐ Ⓑ Ⓒ Ⓓ Ⓔ   11. Ⓐ Ⓑ Ⓒ Ⓓ Ⓔ   19. Ⓐ Ⓑ Ⓒ Ⓓ Ⓔ   27. Ⓐ Ⓑ Ⓒ Ⓓ Ⓔ   35. Ⓐ Ⓑ Ⓒ Ⓓ Ⓔ
4. Ⓐ Ⓑ Ⓒ Ⓓ Ⓔ   12. Ⓐ Ⓑ Ⓒ Ⓓ Ⓔ   20. Ⓐ Ⓑ Ⓒ Ⓓ Ⓔ   28. Ⓐ Ⓑ Ⓒ Ⓓ Ⓔ   36. Ⓐ Ⓑ Ⓒ Ⓓ Ⓔ
5. Ⓐ Ⓑ Ⓒ Ⓓ Ⓔ   13. Ⓐ Ⓑ Ⓒ Ⓓ Ⓔ   21. Ⓐ Ⓑ Ⓒ Ⓓ Ⓔ   29. Ⓐ Ⓑ Ⓒ Ⓓ Ⓔ   37. Ⓐ Ⓑ Ⓒ Ⓓ Ⓔ
6. Ⓐ Ⓑ Ⓒ Ⓓ Ⓔ   14. Ⓐ Ⓑ Ⓒ Ⓓ Ⓔ   22. Ⓐ Ⓑ Ⓒ Ⓓ Ⓔ   30. Ⓐ Ⓑ Ⓒ Ⓓ Ⓔ   38. Ⓐ Ⓑ Ⓒ Ⓓ Ⓔ
7. Ⓐ Ⓑ Ⓒ Ⓓ Ⓔ   15. Ⓐ Ⓑ Ⓒ Ⓓ Ⓔ   23. Ⓐ Ⓑ Ⓒ Ⓓ Ⓔ   31. Ⓐ Ⓑ Ⓒ Ⓓ Ⓔ   39. Ⓐ Ⓑ Ⓒ Ⓓ Ⓔ
8. Ⓐ Ⓑ Ⓒ Ⓓ Ⓔ   16. Ⓐ Ⓑ Ⓒ Ⓓ Ⓔ   24. Ⓐ Ⓑ Ⓒ Ⓓ Ⓔ   32. Ⓐ Ⓑ Ⓒ Ⓓ Ⓔ

Section 1

Critical Reading

Time: 25 minutes for 24 questions

Directions: Choose the *best* answer to each question. Mark the corresponding oval on your answer sheet.

Directions for Questions 1–8: Choose the word or words that best fit the meaning of each sentence.

Example: After work, Edith always _____ home as quickly as possible.

(A) rambled

(B) wandered

(C) avoided

(D) meandered

(E) ran

The answer is Choice (E).

1. _____ in charge, Paul refused to acknowledge that his secretary made all the decisions.

    (A) Actually

    (B) Essentially

    (C) Inevitably

    (D) Obstinately

    (E) Nominally

2. Because safety was a _____, the construction site was _____ by a strict code of conduct.

    (A) necessity . . . supplanted

    (B) priority . . . regulated

    (C) consideration . . . implied

    (D) prerequisite . . . relinquished

    (E) solicitation . . . conceded

3. Entranced by the video game, John _____ the conversation at the gathering.

    (A) studied

    (B) calculated

    (C) ignored

    (D) enhanced

    (E) enriched

4. Although the ambassador had made only _____ comments about the treaty, she recommended that her government accept its terms.

    (A) critical

    (B) positive

    (C) constructive

    (D) explanatory

    (E) illuminating

5. An environmentalist objected to the _____ dining utensils because they could not be reused or recycled.

    (A) enduring

    (B) permanent

    (C) opulent

    (D) disposable

    (E) flimsy

Go on to next page

6. Flower petals, _____ by violent winds, _____ through the town on a mild breeze after the storm ended.

   (A) destroyed . . . sped

   (B) detached . . . wafted

   (C) disintegrated . . . sank

   (D) buoyed . . . sailed

   (E) uprooted . . . plunged

7. Bob's _____ expression and incessant yawns _____ Mary's assertion that, after seeing three films, it was time to go home.

   (A) conciliatory . . . opposed

   (B) defiant . . . upheld

   (C) ambiguous . . . undermined

   (D) bemused . . . contradicted

   (E) jaded . . . supported

8. The building material was an _____, a mixture of several different kinds of plastic.

   (A) amalgam

   (B) artifice

   (C) evasion

   (D) infusion

   (E) inundation

Directions for Questions 9–12: Read these two passages and answer the questions that follow each passage based on what is stated or implied in the passage.

Questions 9 and 10 are based on the following passage, excerpted from Nuclear Energy Encyclopedia, *edited by Steven B. Krivit, Jay H. Lehr, and Thomas B. Kingery (Wiley).*

Passage 1

Line   One billion gallons of oil from 21 disasters have been spilled in the oceans since 1967. In the United States alone, 260 workers have lost their lives in 21 coal-mining accidents since 1970,
(05)   according to the Coal Mine Rescue Association. In Nigeria, on October 18, 1998, a natural gas pipeline explosion took the lives of 1082 people. Members of the public would do well to scrutinize the comparative safety and track record of clean,
(10)   emission-free nuclear energy. They would also

benefit from learning the basic concepts and prin-   Line ciples of nuclear-energy production. The nuclear energy industry would know that the public is never going to believe — nor should it — that nuclear accidents can't happen. However, it   (15) would do well to hear the public's fears and help people understand that nuclear energy has some risks and hazards.

9. The author cites statistics about accidents (Lines 1–7) in order to

   (A) show that natural gas is the most dangerous form of energy

   (B) compare death rates from various types of energy production

   (C) illustrate that nuclear power is not the only dangerous form of energy production

   (D) declare that nuclear power is safe

   (E) assert that nuclear power is too risky

10. Which of the following are true, according to the passage?

    I.   Energy production may lead to accidents.

    II. The public is well-informed about nuclear power.

    III. Nuclear power is relatively safe.

    (A) I only

    (B) I and II

    (C) I and III

    (D) all of the above

    (E) none of the above

Questions 11 and 12 are based on the following passage, excerpted from Psychiatry, *2nd Edition, edited by Allan Tasman, Jerald Kay, and Jeffrey A. Lieberman (Wiley).*

Passage 11

    In North America, important differences   Line have been documented in male and female styles of conversation that for a health professional are relevant to the clinical context. In general, women tend to give more frequent acknowledg-   (05) ments that they are listening to a speaker. They may give signs of assent simply to indicate they are following the conversation. Men tend to be more taciturn and, if they signal assent, it usually means they actually agree with the speaker.   (10)

Go on to next page

These differences in communication style may lead to systematic misunderstandings between men and women that are further aggravated by cultural differences in gender roles and (15) etiquette.

11. The intended audience of this passage is probably

   (A) doctors

   (B) documentary filmmakers

   (C) patients

   (D) women

   (E) men

12. According to the passage, which of the following statements is most likely to be true?

   (A) Gender is reflected only by physical traits.

   (B) Women may appear to agree, even when they do not.

   (C) Men may appear to disagree, even when they do not.

   (D) Etiquette determines speech patterns.

   (E) Doctors generally misunderstand the way in which each gender communicates.

Directions for Questions 13–24: Read these passages and answer the questions that follow based on what is stated or implied.

The first passage is an excerpt from All the Shah's Men, *by Stephen Kinzer (Wiley). The second is from a history of Persia.*

Passage 1

Rising dramatically from the desert of southern Iran, with distant mountains adding to the majesty of the scene, the spectacular ruins of Persepolis testify to the grandeur that was (05) Persia. This was the ceremonial and spiritual capital of a vast empire, built by Cyrus, Darius, and Xerxes, titans whose names still echo through history. Giant statues of winged bulls guard the Gate of All Nations, through which (10) princes from vassal states came once each year to pay homage to their Persian masters. The great Apadana, or Hall of Audience, where these princes knelt together before their dread sovereign, was the length of three football fields. Its (15) roof was supported by thirty-six towering columns, some of which still stand.

Two monumental staircases leading up to the hall are decorated with intricately detailed carvings depicting the annual ritual of obedience. The carvings show rulers of subject states (20) filing past their supreme leader, each bearing gifts symbolizing the wealth of their province. Archaeologists have managed to identify most of them, and the very names of their cultures evoke the richness of antiquity. The warlike Elamites, (25) who lived east of the Tigris River, bring a lion to symbolize their ferocity. Arachosians from Central Asia offer camels and rich furs, Armenians a horse and delicately crafted vases, Ethiopians a giraffe and an elephant's tusk, (30) Somalis an antelope and a chariot, Thracians shields and spears, and Ionians bolts of cloth and ceramic plates. Arabs lead a camel, Assyrians a bull, and Indians a donkey laden with woven baskets. All these tributes were laid (35) before the King of Kings, the monarch who spread Persian power to the edges of the known world.

Migrants from Central Asia and the Indian subcontinent began arriving in this area nearly (40) 4,000 years ago, pushed out by a combination of resource depletion and marauding tribes from the north and east. Among them were the Aryans, from whose name the word Iran is taken. The emperor who united these bands for the (45) first time is Cyrus, one of history's most gifted visionaries and the figure who first conceived of the empire based in the region known as Pars (later Fars).

After rising to power in 559 BC, Cyrus (50) launched a brilliant campaign that brought other leaders on the vast Iranian plateau under his sway. Some he conquered, but many he brought to his side by persuasion and compromise. Today he is remembered for his conquests but (55) also because of the relative gentleness with which he treated his subjects. He understood that this was an even surer way to build a durable empire than the more common means of oppression, terror, and slaughter. (60)

Go on to next page

Passage II

Line   The pillared courts and halls of the vast edifices which monarchs raised at Susa and Persepolis would have had a somewhat bare and cold aspect, if it had not been for their internal
(65) fittings. The floors were paved with stones of various hues and besides were covered in places with carpeting. The spaces between the pillars were filled with magnificent hangings which were fastened with cords of fine linen. The walls of the
(70) apartments were covered with plates of gold. All the furniture was rich and costly. The golden throne of the monarch stood under an embroidered canopy or awning supported by four pillars of gold inlaid with precious stones.

(75)   Excepting the "Seven Princes," no one could approach the royal person unless introduced by a Court usher. The hands of the persons introduced had to be hidden in their sleeves so long as their audience lasted. In crossing the Palace
(80) Courts it was necessary to abstain carefully from touching the carpet which was laid for the king to walk on.

   Etiquette was almost as severe on the monarch himself as on his subjects. He was required
(85) to live chiefly in seclusion; to eat his meals, for the most part, alone; never to go on foot beyond the palace walls; never to revoke an order once given, however much he might regret it; never to draw back from a promise, whatever ill results
(90) he might anticipate from its performance. To maintain the quasi-divine character which attached to him it was necessary that he should seem infallible, immutable, and wholly free from the weakness of repentance.

(95)   As some compensation for the restrictions laid upon him, the Persian king had the sole enjoyment of certain luxuries. The wheat of Assos was sent to the Court to furnish him with bread, and the vines of Helbon were cultivated for the special
(100) purpose of supplying him with wine. Water was conveyed to Susa for his use from distant streams regarded as specially sweet and pure; and in his expeditions he was accompanied by a train of wagons, which were laden with silver flasks, filled
(105) from the clear stream of the Choaspes. The oasis of Ammon contributed the salt with which he seasoned his food. All the delicacies that the Empire anywhere produced were accumulated on his board, for the supply of which each province was
(110) proud to send its best and choicest products.

   Among the more serious occupations of the monarch were the holding of councils, the reviewing of troops, the hearing of complaints, the granting or refusing of redress, the assignment of
(115) rewards, perhaps, in some cases, the trying of causes, and, above all, the general direction of   Line the civil administration and government of the Empire. The concerns of an empire so vast as that of Persia would have given ample employment for the greater part of the day to any monarch who   (120) was determined not only to reign, but to govern.

13. According to Passage I, which statement about Persepolis is true?

   (A) It was located in the mountains.

   (B) It is in relatively the same condition as in ancient times.

   (C) It was an outpost of the Persian empire.

   (D) It was built by the rulers of India.

   (E) It was the capital of Persia.

14. The "Gate of All Nations" (Line 9) probably received its name because

   (A) everyone was equal in Persia

   (B) everyone was allowed to pass through the gate

   (C) the Persian empire included many conquered nations

   (D) Persia was just one of many ancient civilizations

   (E) the city needed protections from other nations

15. In the context of Line 13, what is the best definition of "dread"?

   (A) fearful

   (B) feared

   (C) confident

   (D) anxious

   (E) terrified

16. The items listed in Paragraph 2 of Passage I (Lines 17–38) are similar to those listed in Paragraph 4 of Passage II (Lines 95–110) because both

   (A) illustrate that the ruler merited the best

   (B) reveal the rich natural resources of the Persian empire

   (C) show that the Persian ruler ate well

   (D) enumerate gifts from the ruler's subjects

   (E) display the power and limitations of the ruler

Go on to next page

17. In the context of Line 35, which is the best definition of "tributes"?

    (A) testimonials

    (B) compliments

    (C) taxes

    (D) gratitude

    (E) praise

18. What does the reference to "relative gentleness" (Line 56) imply?

    (A) Cyrus was kind to his family.

    (B) Cyrus was less cruel than other rulers.

    (C) Cyrus's methods were always peaceful.

    (D) Cyrus's subjects were gentle also.

    (E) Cyrus was a good ruler by anyone's standards.

19. With which statement would the author of Passage I probably agree?

    (A) It is best to rule by fear.

    (B) Luxurious palaces are an unjustified expense.

    (C) People often migrate to nations in search of freedom.

    (D) Subjects treated well are more loyal to their ruler.

    (E) A ruler must not reveal weakness.

20. How does the description of the palace differ in these two passages?

    (A) Passage I shows the palace in two time periods, and Passage II concentrates on the present.

    (B) Passage I gives more detail than Passage II.

    (C) Passage I discusses the ruins of the palace, but Passage II describes the palace's decorations as they were in ancient times.

    (D) Passage I explains who lived in the palace, but Passage II does not.

    (E) Passage I gives an overview of the entire palace; Passage II describes only the king's quarters.

21. Which of the following is an example of the "internal fittings" mentioned in Lines 64–65?

    (A) halls

    (B) Palace Courts

    (C) golden throne

    (D) vines of Helbon

    (E) salt from Ammon

22. In the context of Line 83, "severe" may best be defined as

    (A) cruel

    (B) plain

    (C) ruthless

    (D) strict

    (E) important

23. Which of the following actions were forbidden the monarch, according to Passage II?

    (A) changing his orders

    (B) eating in the palace

    (C) conversing with subjects

    (D) drinking impure water

    (E) declaring a holiday

24. In contrast to Passage I, Passage II gives more information about which of the following?

    (A) the wealth of the empire

    (B) the duties of the ruler

    (C) the extent of the empire

    (D) Cyrus and other rulers

    (E) colonies of Persia

STOP YOU MAY CHECK YOUR WORK ON THIS SECTION ONLY. DO NOT GO BACK TO ANY PREVIOUS SECTION.

Section 2

Mathematics

Time: 25 minutes for 20 questions

Directions: Find the correct answer to each question.

Notes:

✔ You may use a calculator.

✔ All numbers used in this exam are real numbers.

✔ All figures lie in a plane.

✔ You may assume that all figures are to scale unless the problem specifically indicates otherwise.

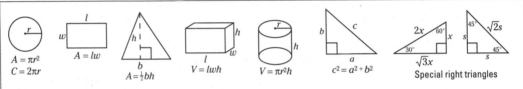

$A = \pi r^2$
$C = 2\pi r$

$A = lw$

$A = \frac{1}{2}bh$

$V = lwh$

$V = \pi r^2 h$

$c^2 = a^2 + b^2$

Special right triangles

There are 360 degrees of arc in a circle.

There are 180 degrees in a straight line.

There are 180 degrees in the sum of the interior angles of a triangle.

---

1. If $a = 3b - 2$, then $-2a + 6b =$

   (A) –4

   (B) –2

   (C) 2

   (D) 4

   (E) 6

2. An odd number is squared and then doubled. When 5 is subtracted from the result, the new number must be

   I. Odd

   II. Even

   III. Prime

   (A) I only

   (B) II only

   (C) III only

   (D) I and III

   (E) none of the above

Go on to next page

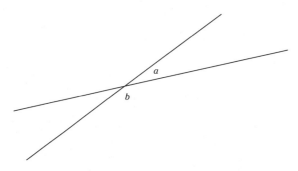

3. The angles a and b are formed by the intersecting lines in this figure. $b - a = 100°$. Determine the measure of angle a.

   (A) $30°$

   (B) $40°$

   (C) $50°$

   (D) $100°$

   (E) $140°$

5. If $-2 < a < -1$ and $0 < b < \frac{1}{3}$, then which of the following choices could be the result of $(ab)^3$?

   (A) -8

   (B) -1

   (C) $-\frac{3}{8}$

   (D) 0

   (E) $\frac{4}{9}$

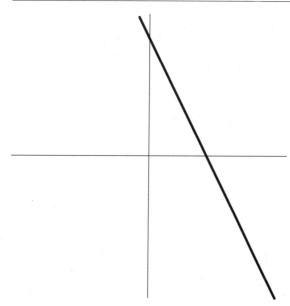

4. What is a possible equation for the line in this figure?

   (A) $y = -2x - 1$

   (B) $y = -2x + 1$

   (C) $y = -\frac{1}{2}x + 3$

   (D) $y = x + 2$

   (E) $y = 2x + 1$

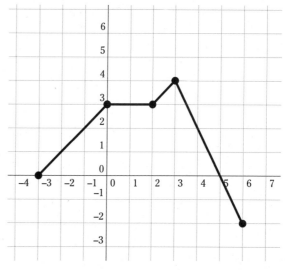

6. The graph of $y = f(x)$ is shown in this figure. Which answer choice represents the graph of $y = -f(x) + 1$?

Go on to next page

(A)

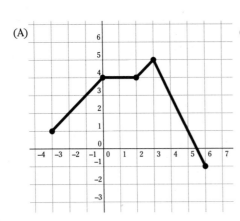

(B)

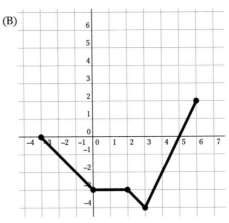

(C)

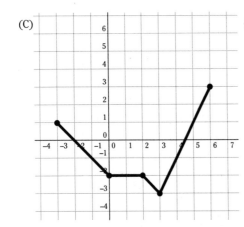

(D)

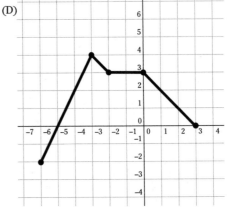

(E)

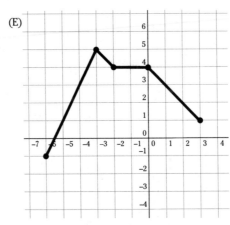

Go on to next page

7. The area of the side of a cube is quadrupled. If the original cube's volume was z, what is the volume now?

    (A) $4z$

    (B) $8z$

    (C) $12z$

    (D) $16z$

    (E) $64z$

10. Solve for x: $-2|3-x| \geq -4$

    (A) $1 \leq x \leq 5$

    (B) $1 < x < 5$

    (C) $x \leq 1$ or $x \geq 5$

    (D) all real numbers

    (E) no solution

8. When five people went to dinner, their total bill, including a 15% tip, was $97.75. If each person ordered the same meal, how much did each meal cost, before tip?

    (A) $9.00

    (B) $12.00

    (C) $16.00

    (D) $17.00

    (E) $22.50

11. A circle has a circumference equal to 10π. What is the area of the circle?

    (A) 5π

    (B) $2\pi\sqrt{10}$

    (C) 20π

    (D) 25π

    (E) 100π

9. You draw a marble from a bag full of them. Fifteen percent of the marbles in the bag are red, 45% are blue, and 24 marbles are yellow. If the marbles in the bag are all either red, blue, or yellow, what is the probability that the marble that you drew from the bag was yellow or red?

    (A) 39%

    (B) 50%

    (C) 55%

    (D) 60%

    (E) 65%

12. A photograph's sides are in a ratio of 3:5. If a frame adds 2 inches to each side of the picture, which expression models the area of the frame?

    (A) $(3x+4)(5x+4)$

    (B) $(3x+2)(5x+2)$

    (C) $(3x+4)\left(\dfrac{5}{3}x+4\right)$

    (D) $4(5x+4)+12x$

    (E) none of the above

Go on to next page

13. What is the equation of a line parallel to $y - 1 = -2(x + 3)$ that passes through $(1, -5)$?

(A) $y = -2x - 5$

(B) $y = 2x - 4$

(C) $y = -x(x + 2) - 1$

(D) $y = -2x - 3$

(E) $y = \dfrac{-4x - 5}{2}$

14. Twice a number is divisible by 4. When 1 is added to the original number, the result is divisible by 5. Which of the following could be the number?

(A) 5

(B) 29

(C) 56

(D) 572

(E) 1,014

15. If $3a + 6y = 2$, and $2x - b = 4$, write $9a + \dfrac{b}{2}$ in terms of x and y.

(A) $-x + 18y + 8$

(B) $x - 18y + 8$

(C) $x - 18y + 4$

(D) $x + 18y + 8$

(E) $4x - 9y$

Questions 16 and 17 both refer to the following figure, a window that is in the shape of a rectangle with a semicircle. The radius of the semicircle is 10 inches, and the height of the rectangle is 30 inches.

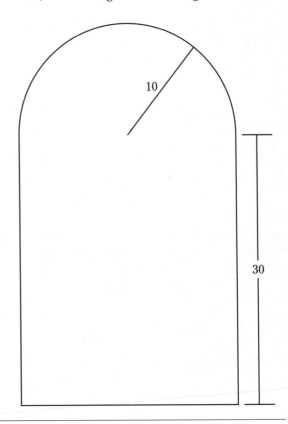

16. What is the area of the window in square inches?

(A) $300 + 50\pi$

(B) 600

(C) $300 + 100\pi$

(D) $600 + 50\pi$

(E) $600 + 100\pi$

17. If window trim costs $2 per inch, how much will it cost to run trim around the perimeter of the window, rounded to the nearest cent?

(A) $111.41

(B) $222.83

(C) $262.83

(D) $285.66

(E) $788.31

Go on to next page

18. A right triangle has an area of 20 square inches. If the length of one of the legs of the triangle is 4 inches, what is the perimeter of the triangle?

    (A) 16

    (B) 24

    (C) $14 + 2\sqrt{29}$

    (D) $14 + 2\sqrt{58}$

    (E) 120

19. What is the product of the solutions to the equation $2x^2 = 5x + 3$?

    (A) $-\frac{3}{2}$

    (B) $-\frac{1}{2}$

    (C) $\frac{5}{2}$

    (D) 3

    (E) 7

20. Determine the shaded area of this figure. The small circles have a radius of 2, the large circle has a radius of 3, and the rectangle is 12 units wide and 8 units tall.

    (A) 17π

    (B) $96 - 17\pi$

    (C) $96 - 14\pi$

    (D) $96 - 13\pi$

    (E) none of the above

STOP YOU MAY CHECK YOUR WORK ON THIS SECTION ONLY. DO NOT GO BACK TO ANY PREVIOUS SECTION.

Section 3
Critical Reading

Time: 25 minutes for 24 questions

Directions: Choose the *best* answer to each question. Mark the corresponding oval on your answer sheet.

Directions for Questions 25–29: Choose the word or words that best fit the meaning of each sentence.

Example: After work, Edith always _____ home as quickly as possible.

(A) rambled

(B) wandered

(C) avoided

(D) meandered

(E) ran

The answer is Choice (E).

---

25. The clerk's account of the accident was _____, but the manager checked the security tapes anyway.

    (A) baffling

    (B) complex

    (C) uncertain

    (D) credible

    (E) puzzling

26. "What a(n) _____ attitude!" exclaimed Ellen as the hardened criminal described his crimes without any remorse.

    (A) magnanimous

    (B) pragmatic

    (C) innocuous

    (D) perplexing

    (E) callous

27. The medicine _____ his symptoms; however, it does not address the underlying cause of the disease.

    (A) redoubles

    (B) augments

    (C) induces

    (D) alleviates

    (E) aggravates

28. The decorations will not _____ the surface of that table if you place a _____ mat underneath them.

    (A) mar . . . protective

    (B) shield . . . decorative

    (C) scratch . . . disparaging

    (D) screen . . . transparent

    (E) malign . . . expensive

29. The _____ students debated the point for hours, with each side hardening its position as the afternoon wore on.

    (A) jocular

    (B) meticulous

    (C) flexible

    (D) flippant

    (E) contentious

Go on to next page

Directions for Questions 30–33: Read these passages and answer the questions that follow based on what is stated or implied in the passages.

The first passage is about Plato, and the second is from a discussion about literature and creativity.

Passage I

Line   Plato, the ancient Greek philosopher, condemned poetry as a "false Siren," likening poetry to the mythological creatures who lured sailors to their deaths by singing beautiful but danger-
(05) ous songs. One critic commented that Plato saw this art as "an ally of all that is low and weak in the soul against that which is high and strong." Yet Plato was open to opposing ideas. He wrote, "We will give her champions, not poets
(10) themselves but poetry-lovers, an opportunity to make her defense in plain prose to show that she is not only sweet — as we well know — but also helpful to society and the life of man, and we will listen in a kindly spirit." Plato further remarked
(15) that "we shall be gainers . . . if this can be proved."

Passage II

Line   Poetry, Marianne Moore tells us in her poem of the same name, is easy to dislike but absolutely necessary to the human experience. She characterizes poetry as an "imaginary garden
(20) with real toads in it," likening it to a fantastical creation that nevertheless expresses truth. Much removed from Moore in form but not spirit is the narrator in Ken Kesey's novel *One Flew Over the Cuckoo's Nest.* A patient in a mental hospital, the
(25) narrator purports to tell readers a story that is true, "even if it didn't happen." To reach what is most real, these authors seem to suggest, one must turn to fantasy.

30. In the context of Passage I, the "low and weak" (Lines 6–7) may best be defined as

(A) mythological creatures

(B) cruelty

(C) musical selections

(D) superficial beauty

(E) disloyalty

31. In the context of Passage I, which of the following are included in the meaning of "this" (Line 15)?

I.   Poetry's contributions to communal life

II. Poetry's ability to ennoble an individual

III. The beauty of poetry

(A) I only

(B) I and II only

(C) II and III only

(D) III only

(E) all of the above

32. Which of the following may be considered the "real toads" referred to in Line 20 of Passage II?

(A) critics of poetry

(B) defenders of poetry

(C) poets

(D) human nature

(E) wildlife

33. Which statement is supported by both Passage I and Passage II?

(A) Poets cannot distinguish between reality and fantasy.

(B) Poetry receives too much attention.

(C) Nature must be protected.

(D) Poetry is imaginative expression.

(E) Reading poetry reveals truth.

Go on to next page

Directions for Questions 34–42: Read the passage and answer the questions that follow based on what is stated or implied in the passage.

This passage is an excerpt from Night and Day, *a novel by Virginia Woolf.*

It was a Sunday evening in October, and in common with many other young ladies of her class, Katharine Hilbery was pouring out tea. Perhaps a fifth part of her mind was thus occupied, and the remaining parts leapt over the little barrier of day which interposed between Monday morning and this rather subdued moment, and played with the things one does voluntarily and normally in the daylight. But although she was silent, she was evidently mistress of a situation which was familiar enough to her, and inclined to let it take its way for the six hundredth time, perhaps, without bringing into play any of her unoccupied faculties. A single glance was enough to show that Mrs. Hilbery, Katharine's mother, was so rich in the gifts which make tea-parties of elderly distinguished people successful, that she scarcely needed any help from Katharine, provided that the tiresome business of teacups and bread and butter was discharged for her.

Considering that the little party had been seated round the tea-table for less than twenty minutes, the animation observable on their faces, and the amount of sound they were producing collectively, were very creditable to the hostess. It suddenly came into Katharine's mind that if someone opened the door at this moment he would think that they were enjoying themselves; he would think, "What an extremely nice house to come into!" and instinctively she laughed, and said something to increase the noise, for the credit of the house presumably, since she herself had not been feeling exhilarated. At the very same moment, rather to her amusement, the door was flung open, and a young man entered the room. Katharine, as she shook hands with him, asked him, in her own mind, "Now, do you think we're enjoying ourselves enormously?" . . . "Mr. Denham, mother,"

she said aloud, for she saw that her mother had forgotten his name.

That fact was perceptible to Mr. Denham also, and increased the awkwardness which inevitably attends the entrance of a stranger into a room full of people much at their ease, and all launched upon sentences. At the same time, it seemed to Mr. Denham as if a thousand softly padded doors had closed between him and the street outside. A fine mist, the etherealized essence of the fog, hung visibly in the wide and rather empty space of the drawing-room, all silver where the candles were grouped on the tea-table, and ruddy again in the firelight. With the omnibuses and cabs still running in his head, and his body still tingling with his quick walk along the streets and in and out of traffic and foot-passengers, this drawing-room seemed very remote and still; and the faces of the elderly people were mellowed, at some distance from each other, and had a bloom on them owing to the fact that the air in the drawing-room was thickened by blue grains of mist. Mr. Denham had come in as Mr. Fortescue, the eminent novelist, reached the middle of a very long sentence. He kept this suspended while the newcomer sat down, and Mrs. Hilbery deftly joined the severed parts by leaning towards him and remarking:

"Now, what would you do if you were married to an engineer, and had to live in Manchester, Mr. Denham?"

"Surely she could learn Persian," broke in a thin, elderly gentleman. "Is there no retired schoolmaster or man of letters in Manchester with whom she could study Persian?"

"A cousin of ours has married and gone to live in Manchester," Katharine explained. Mr. Denham muttered something, which was indeed all that was required of him, and the novelist went on where he had left off. Privately, Mr. Denham cursed himself very sharply for having exchanged the freedom of the street for this sophisticated drawing-room, where, among other disagreeables, he certainly would not appear at his best. He glanced round him, and saw that, save for Katharine, they were all over forty, the only consolation being that Mr. Fortescue was a considerable celebrity, so that tomorrow one might be glad to have met him.

Go on to next page

34. In the context of the passage, what is the best definition of "the little barrier of day" (Lines 5–6)?

    (A) a short period of time

    (B) a stressful moment

    (C) over-scheduled hours

    (D) hours to endure

    (E) sunset

35. Which is the best definition of "faculties" (Line 14) in the context of this passage?

    (A) abilities

    (B) teachers

    (C) creativity

    (D) sensitivity

    (E) learned behavior

36. According to the passage, what does Katharine's mother need from her daughter?

    (A) advice on social issues

    (B) serving of food and drink

    (C) obedience to her mother's commands

    (D) conversation with the guests

    (E) emotional support

37. Katharine probably laughs during the party (Line 32) because

    (A) her mother's party is successful

    (B) she loves parties

    (C) she wants to participate in the party

    (D) the guests amuse her

    (E) appearance and reality differ

38. What adds to the "awkwardness" cited in Line 44?

    (A) The guests do not like Mr. Denham.

    (B) Katharine doesn't know Mr. Denham.

    (C) Mrs. Hilbery is talking when Mr. Denham arrives.

    (D) Mrs. Hilbery can't remember Mr. Denham's name.

    (E) Mr. Denham is late.

39. Which is the most probable explanation for Mr. Denham's feeling "as if a thousand softly padded doors had closed" (Lines 48–49)?

    (A) The guests immediately welcome him.

    (B) He is eager to attend the party.

    (C) The atmosphere at the party contrasts with the lively street.

    (D) The room is warm and inviting.

    (E) The room is silent.

40. What are the "severed parts" (Lines 67–68)?

    (A) daydreams

    (B) stray ideas

    (C) absent members of the family

    (D) social unity

    (E) unfinished refreshments

41. Katharine may best be characterized as

    (A) eager to meet new people

    (B) rebellious

    (C) interested in her guests

    (D) distracted from the conversation

    (E) unwilling to attend the tea party

42. The "disagreeables" (Line 84) include all the following EXCEPT

    (A) Katharine's low social class

    (B) the sophistication of the guests

    (C) the age of the guests

    (D) Mr. Denham's feeling of inferiority

    (E) Mrs. Hilbery's ignorance of Mr. Denham's name

Go on to next page

Directions for Questions 43–48: Read the passage and answer the questions that follow based on what is stated or implied in the passage.

This passage is an excerpt from Shifting the Earth: The Mathematical Quest to Understand the Motion of the Universe, *by Arthur Mazer (Wiley).*

Line   I am the circle. I am the perfect shape, and I boast a list of qualities that no other shape can lay claim to. Every point of my composition is equal. Segments containing midpoints and cor-
(05) ners form the triangle, square, and every other polygon. An ellipse has two points closest to its center and another two points farthest from its center. Only I am composed of points that are all truly equal; that equality defines beauty along
(10) with perfection.

Every line through my center forms a line of reflective symmetry about my center. This infinite set of symmetries expresses itself only through my perfect shape in which every point is
(15) equal. Order the polygons by number of sides. Then, as one indefinitely climbs up the hierarchy and the number of sides increases, the shape of polygons approaches my perfection. I dominate the polygons. As they strive to reach me, they
(20) strive for perfection but can never attain it.

My perfection inspires humans in all their endeavors. For three millennia humans have used me to transport materials across the land whether by horse-powered cart, steam-powered
(25) locomotive, or diesel-powered eighteen wheelers. Circular gears drive mechanical devices; any other shape would cause uneven wear on the equipment. Electric power generators rotate through a circle yielding uncontrollable voltage,
(30) current, and power output.

My symmetry inspires scientists to search for symmetry in nature. They have discovered the cyclic nature of time and stamped its rhythms on a circular clock. In the Northern
(35) Hemisphere, the North Star is a fixed center about which all other stars rotate on a circular pathway. Toss a stone into a lake, and a scientist confirms that waves ripple across the lake in concentric circles. I provide the pattern for the
(40) eye of the hurricane and the rainbow.

Just as mathematicians have discovered an   Line
impressive list of properties I possess, artists
and architects pay homage to my beauty. The
artist adorns figures of religious admiration with
a halo. Light enters a house of worship through a (45)
circular stained-glass window.

As I set the standard of equality, I am the
foundation of many religious and political philos-
ophies. Many religions place all humankind as
equal before God, with people as points of a   (50)
circle and God as the center. Both communism
and democracy strive for the equality of citizens,
one through an equal distribution of goods, and
the other through representative government in
which each citizen has an equal vote in the elec- (55)
toral process.

I am the universal ideal pursued by engi-
neers, scientists, mathematicians, artists, and
philosophers. They pursue me because of my
perfection. But like the polygon's, humankind's (60)
pursuit of perfection is in vain, for perfection is
impossible to attain and so easy to destroy. A
bicycle wheel is never in perfect true. Lay it on
its side and it doesn't rest evenly on the surface.
Even with the naked eye, one can perceive a blip (65)
as it rotates. By adjusting the tension in its
spokes, one can reduce the blip but never eliminate it, and during the course of adjustment, a
new blip always arises. Once close to true, a
small bump in the road perturbs the wheel yet   (70)
farther from perfection.

Human philosophical and social efforts
towards a perfect circle of equality meet with
similar road bumps. A system of privilege blan-
keted the democratic ideals of ancient Athens, as (75)
citizenship was limited to a small select group.
Others had limited or no rights, while some of
the others were no more than the property of
their slave-possessing owners. It is not surprising that my perfect ideal cannot be achieved by (80)
human beings who are endowed with such
imperfect character.

Go on to next page

43. On which literary device is this passage based?

    (A) personification

    (B) metaphor

    (C) simile

    (D) understatement

    (E) hyperbole

44. According to the passage, beauty is based on which quality?

    (A) roundness

    (B) equality

    (C) uniqueness

    (D) number of points

    (E) perspective

45. According to the passage, the circle is involved with all of the following EXCEPT

    (A) timekeeping

    (B) transportation

    (C) health

    (D) government

    (E) religion

46. In the context of Line 63, what is the best definition of "true"?

    (A) factual

    (B) informative

    (C) genuine

    (D) perfectly shaped

    (E) in good condition

47. The author includes the example of a bicycle in order to illustrate

    (A) the importance of relating abstract ideas to real life

    (B) the circle's role in transportation

    (C) that perfection is an unattainable ideal

    (D) a fact about geometry

    (E) how people strive for perfection

48. The "road bumps" (Line 74) are most likely

    (A) inclusive groups

    (B) geometric forms

    (C) privileges given to a few

    (D) unrepaired highways

    (E) human nature

Section 4

Mathematics

Time: 25 minutes for 18 questions

Directions: This section contains two different types of questions. For Questions 21–28, choose the *best* answer to each question. Mark the corresponding oval on the answer sheet. For Questions 29–38, follow the separate directions provided before those questions.

Notes:

✔ You may use a calculator.

✔ All numbers used in this exam are real numbers.

✔ All figures lie in a plane.

✔ You may assume that all figures are to scale unless the problem specifically indicates otherwise.

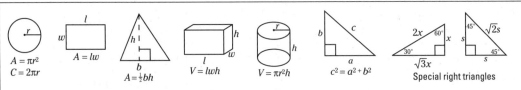

There are 360 degrees of arc in a circle.

There are 180 degrees in a straight line.

There are 180 degrees in the sum of the interior angles of a triangle.

21. Lines l and n are perpendicular and intersect at $(-1, 1)$. If the slope of line l is $\frac{2}{3}$, what is the equation of line n?

(A) $y = -3x - \frac{1}{2}$

(B) $y = -\frac{3}{2}x - \frac{1}{2}$

(C) $y = -\frac{3}{2} + \frac{1}{2}$

(D) $y = \frac{2}{3}x + \frac{5}{3}$

(E) $y = 5x + 3$

22. Julia has 5 pairs of pants, 3 skirts, and 7 shirts. If an outfit consists of a shirt with either a pair of pants or a skirt, how many different outfits could Julia make?

(A) 21

(B) 35

(C) 56

(D) 70

(E) 105

Go on to next page

Questions 23 and 24 both refer to the following chart, which represents how many birds Kat saw each day during five days of observation.

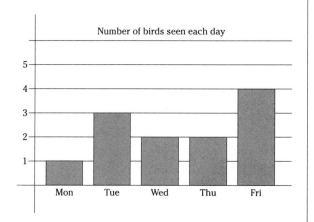

Number of birds seen each day

23. If Kat saw as many birds over the two-day weekend as she did over her initial five days of observation, what was the average number of birds she saw each weekend day?

   (A) 2.4

   (B) 4

   (C) 5

   (D) 6

   (E) 12

24. Which of the following is true about the daily number of birds Kat saw during her initial five-day observation?

   I.   median > mode

   II.   mean > mode

   III. median > mean

   (A) II only

   (B) I and III only

   (C) II and III only

   (D) I, II, and III

   (E) none of the above

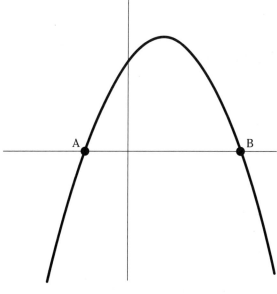

25. Points A and B have coordinates (–2, 0) and (5, 0), respectively. Which equation might represent this graph?

   (A) $y = 2x^2 - 6x - 20$

   (B) $y = x^2 + 4x + 5$

   (C) $y = -x^2 - 3x - 10$

   (D) $y = -2x^2 + 6x + 20$

   (E) $y = -2x^2 - 6x - 20$

26. Which ordered pair represents a solution to the inequalities $y > \frac{1}{2}x - 4$ and $y < 2x + 3$?

   (A) (3, –1)

   (B) (–2, 1)

   (C) (9, 0)

   (D) (2, –4)

   (E) (7, –5)

Go on to next page

27. A can of soup is 5 inches tall and has a radius of 1.5 inches. If the label for the can wraps around the sides, covering them completely, what is the area of the label in square inches?

   (A) 5π

   (B) 7.5π

   (C) 11.25π

   (D) 15π

   (E) 22.5π

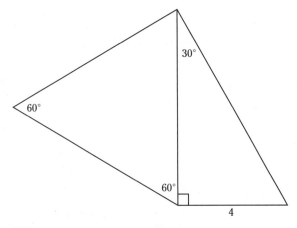

28. What is the perimeter of this figure?

   (A) $4\sqrt{2}+10$

   (B) 20

   (C) $8\sqrt{3}+12$

   (D) $12\sqrt{3}+12$

   (E) 36

Go on to next page

Directions for student-produced response Questions 29–38: Solve the problem and then write your answer in the boxes on the answer sheet. Then mark the ovals corresponding to your answer, as shown in the following example. Note the fraction line and the decimal points.

Answer: $7/2$

Answer: 3.25

Answer: 853

Write your answer in the box. You may start your answer in any column.

Although you don't have to write the solutions in the boxes, you do have to blacken the corresponding ovals. You should fill in the boxes to avoid confusion. Only the blackened ovals will be scored. The numbers in the boxes won't be read.

There are no negative answers.

You may grid in mixed numbers, such as 3½, as a decimal (3.5) or as a fraction (⁷⁄₂). Don't grid in 3½; it will be read as ³¹⁄₂.

Grid in a decimal as far as possible. Don't round your answer and leave some boxes empty.

A question may have more than one answer. Grid in one answer only.

---

29. Simplify. $4 \times 3 + 2 - 10 \div 2$

31. If $f(x) = 3x^2 - 2x - 10$, what is the value of $f(-2) + 3$?

---

30. Triangle ABC is constructed by connecting the points A (5, –2), B (–1, –2), and C (2, 5). What is the area of triangle ABC?

32. What is the sum of the first 8 terms of the following sequence?

$$64, -32, 16, -8, \ldots$$

Go on to next page

33. Mary goes apple picking. She gives half of her apples to Paul, who keeps two thirds of the apples and gives the rest to Kyle. If Kyle has 2 apples remaining after eating 3 of them, how many apples did Mary pick?

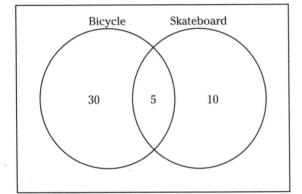

34. This Venn diagram represents the results of a survey of students asking whether they owned a bicycle, skateboard, or both. If 80 students were surveyed, how many students don't own a skateboard?

35. The symbol # is defined so that $a \# b = a^2 b^{-3}$. What is the value of $3 \# 2$?

36. You're trying to decide which of the local swimming pools to join. Waves Pool costs $250 to join and then requires that you pay $5 each time you go to the pool. Splash Pool costs $50 to join, and then you pay $15 each time you go. How many times would you need to go to the pool for the plans to cost the same amount?

37. As a hobby, you create bird feeders. When you sell them for $12 each, you can sell 40 bird feeders. If you double your price, you sell 25% fewer feeders. Your sales drop off linearly as the price increases. How many bird feeders are you likely to sell if each one costs $18?

38. In this figure, a shaded square is inscribed within a circle, which is inscribed within a square, which is inscribed within another circle. If the diameter of the biggest circle is 2, what is the area of the shaded square?

STOP YOU MAY CHECK YOUR WORK ON THIS SECTION ONLY. DO NOT GO BACK TO ANY PREVIOUS SECTION.

Section 5

Writing

> **Time:** 30 minutes for 39 questions
>
> **Directions:** Choose the *best* answer to each question. Mark the corresponding oval on your answer sheet.

> **Directions for Questions 1–20:** Read the following sentences carefully. Part or all of each sentence is underlined. Beneath each sentence are five choices. Choice (A) is the original, and the other choices represent different ways of expressing the same meaning. If the sentence is grammatically correct and effectively worded, select Choice (A). If one of the other choices would improve the sentence, select that answer.
>
> Example: Henry wanted to be an architect and that he would have a happy family.
>
> (A) that he would have a happy family
>
> (B) that his family would be happy
>
> (C) to have a happy family
>
> (D) his family should be happy
>
> (E) happiness for his family
>
> The answer is Choice (C).

1. Dwight D. Eisenhower, <u>after he used to serve as a general</u> in World War II, became President.

   (A) after he used to serve as a general

   (B) serving as a general

   (C) who, as a general

   (D) after he has served as a general

   (E) after serving as a general

2. When the 19th amendment to the Constitution was ratified in 1920, <u>American women were given the right to vote</u>.

   (A) American women were given the right to vote

   (B) American women, being given the right to vote

   (C) the right to vote had been given to American women

   (D) voting as a right of American women was given

   (E) American women was given the right to vote

3. Failure to obtain a permit <u>bars drivers to enter</u> the owners' parking lot.

   (A) bars drivers to enter

   (B) bars drivers from entering

   (C) bars drivers, who wish to enter

   (D) barring drivers from entering

   (E) bars drivers that enter

4. Amy Tan, author of *The Joy Luck Club*, <u>herself also wrote</u> other novels illuminating the lives of Asian-American immigrants and their children.

   (A) herself also wrote

   (B) also wrote, by herself,

   (C) also wrote

   (D) she also wrote

   (E) who also wrote

Go on to next page

5. In order to allow historians around the world to study fragile specimens, scientists make casts, or models, <u>many artists find these replicas valuable as well</u>.

    (A) many artists find these replicas valuable as well

    (B) because many artists find these replicas valuable as well

    (C) and many artists find these replicas valuable as well

    (D) even though many artists find these replicas valuable as well

    (E) which many artists find valuable as well

6. Anyone who cares about the <u>environment, if they want to make a difference</u>, should conserve and recycle as much as possible.

    (A) environment, if they want to make a difference

    (B) environment and wants to make a difference

    (C) environment, if it is that they want to make a difference

    (D) environment, wanting to have made a difference

    (E) environment, and they want to make a difference

7. <u>If Matthew Brady, a famous 19th century photographer, would not have documented</u> the Civil War, historians would not have access to an important resource.

    (A) If Matthew Brady, a famous 19th century photographer, would not have documented

    (B) Had Matthew Brady, a famous 19th century photographer, not documented

    (C) If Matthew Brady, a famous 19th century photographer, did not document

    (D) If Matthew Brady, a famous 19th century photographer, would not had documented

    (E) Undocumented by Matthew Brady, a 19th century photographer, it would have been that

8. The Chimpanzee Project cares for injured and elderly animals <u>with their goal of returning</u> chimpanzees to their natural habitat.

    (A) with their goal of returning

    (B) and they want to return

    (C) because their goal is returning

    (D) with the goal of returning

    (E) with the goal that is to return

9. In the 15th century in the Andes Mountains, the Incas built Machu Picchu, <u>surrounded by valleys that have been continuously cultivated</u> for more than 1,000 years.

    (A) surrounded by valleys that have been continuously cultivated

    (B) surrounded by valleys continuously being cultivated

    (C) which was surrounded by valleys that have been continuously cultivated

    (D) which was surrounded by valleys that continuously had been cultivated

    (E) being surrounded by continuously cultivated valleys

10. The planet Mars, like several others, <u>are named after Roman gods</u>.

    (A) are named after Roman gods

    (B) which are named after Roman gods

    (C) is named after a Roman god

    (D) names a Roman god

    (E) named a Roman god

11. <u>By freezing food in tightly sealed containers, it</u> extends the shelf life by many months.

    (A) By freezing food in tightly sealed containers, it

    (B) If one freezes food in tightly sealed containers, it

    (C) A person freezes food in tightly sealed containers, and it

    (D) Freezing food in tightly sealed containers

    (E) To freeze food in tightly sealed containers is what

Go on to next page

12. <u>Home to 8 million people</u>, the capital city displays architectural, economic, and culinary diversity.

    (A) Home to 8 million people

    (B) Being that it is home to 8 million people

    (C) It is the home of 8 million people

    (D) Eight million people living there

    (E) With it as the home of 8 million people

13. <u>George and his father attended a bicycle race when he was a young man, and now, inspired by that race, he is an Olympic cyclist.</u>

    (A) George and his father attended a bicycle race when he was a young man, and now, inspired by that race, he is an Olympic cyclist.

    (B) As a young man George and his father attended a bicycle race, and now, inspired by that race, he is an Olympic cyclist.

    (C) George and his father attended a bicycle race when George was a young man, and now, inspired by that race, he is an Olympic cyclist.

    (D) Inspired by a bicycle race George attended as a young man with his father, George is now an Olympic cyclist.

    (E) Inspired by a bicycle race George and his father attended when George was a young man, he became an Olympic cyclist.

14. Eagle feathers, especially those of the bald and golden eagles, <u>which are sacred objects</u> in some Native American traditions.

    (A) which are sacred objects

    (B) being sacred objects

    (C) sacred objects

    (D) in that they are sacred objects

    (E) are sacred objects

15. Michelangelo's monumental statue of David is one of the artist's works <u>that has been recognized as a masterpiece</u> of the Italian Renaissance.

    (A) that has been recognized as a masterpiece

    (B) that have been recognized as masterpieces

    (C) recognized as having been like masterpieces

    (D) which is recognized in that it is a masterpiece

    (E) which are recognized in being masterpieces

16. Football, known as soccer in the United States, <u>is more popular in Europe than any sport</u>.

    (A) is more popular in Europe than any sport

    (B) is most popular in Europe than any sport

    (C) is more popular in Europe than any other sport

    (D) which is more popular in Europe than any sport

    (E) that is more popular in Europe than any sport

17. Both <u>the improved machinery and that the employees worked overtime</u> ensured the project's success.

    (A) the improved machinery and that the employees worked overtime

    (B) that the machinery was improved and that the employees worked overtime

    (C) the improved machinery and the employees' overtime work

    (D) the improved machinery and the employees having worked overtime

    (E) the machinery, which improved, and that the employees worked overtime

Go on to next page

18. Unlike birds, their lightweight descendants, most dinosaurs weighed hundreds of tons.

    (A) Unlike birds, their lightweight descendants,

    (B) When you compare them to birds, their lightweight descendants,

    (C) Though birds, which are lightweight and descendants,

    (D) Contrasting dinosaurs and birds by weight, a bird's weight is light and

    (E) Birds, lightweight and descendants of dinosaurs,

19. The Grand Banks lay off the coast of North America and are some of the richest fishing grounds in the world.

    (A) lay off

    (B) are laying off

    (C) lie off

    (D) have lain off

    (E) are off

20. In preparation for the gala, we need someone to order the refreshments, decorate the hall, and the music should be chosen.

    (A) to order the refreshments, decorate the hall, and the music should be chosen

    (B) to order the refreshments, decorate the hall, and to choose the music

    (C) to order the refreshments, decorate the hall, and choose the music

    (D) for ordering refreshments, decorating the hall, and to choose the music

    (E) in the ordering of refreshments and decoration of the hall, with the music being chosen also

Directions for Questions 21–34: Read the following sentences carefully. Four portions of each sentence are underlined. Some sentences are correct, and some contain one error. If the sentence is correct, bubble Choice (E) for "no error." If an underlined portion of the sentence contains an error, bubble that letter.

Example:

On the day of the prom, Martin
A   B

and his friends had gone to the mall
C

to rent tuxedos. No error.
D   E

The answer is Choice (C).

21. You may easy confuse St. John's, a city
         A   B
    in Newfoundland, with St. John, a city in

    New Brunswick, because the only
                              C
    difference in their names is an apostrophe.
                             D
    No error.
    E

22. Scientists have examined not only the cave
              A
    paintings in Lascaux in southwestern
                          B
    France, but also they have studied similar
                         C
    caves in Altamira, near Santander, Spain.
                     D
    No error.
    E

23. Lucille Ball and Desi Arnaz acted in a
                                  A
    long-running television show, I Love Lucy,
                              B
    that brought fame to the actress and he.
    C   D
    No error.
    E

Go on to next page

24. <u>Doctors recommend</u> <u>that on long</u> flights,
    A   B
    a person get up and <u>walk around</u> to
               C
    improve <u>their circulation</u>. <u>No error.</u>
           D   E

25. <u>The number of</u> e-mails <u>the president of that</u>
       A   B
    <u>company receives</u> is <u>equal as</u> the number
            C
    his employees <u>find in their</u> in-boxes every
              D
    day. <u>No error.</u>
        E

26. <u>Until the error was discovered,</u>
             A
    <u>for many years a prominent museum</u>
              B
    <u>displayed the skull of a dinosaur named</u>
              C
    Camarasaurus <u>on the body of another</u>
               D
    dinosaur, Apatosaurus. <u>No error.</u>
               E

27. <u>A stray insect</u> <u>flew into a computer,</u>
       A   B
    <u>which malfunctioned and became</u>
              C
    <u>the basis for the expression</u> "a bug
             D
    in the program." <u>No error.</u>
              E

28. Langston Hughes, <u>whom critics believe</u>
               A
    <u>is one of the most accomplished</u> poets of
              B
    the 20th century, <u>often wrote</u> about
              C
    Harlem, <u>his neighborhood</u>. <u>No error.</u>
           D   E

29. <u>Soaring across the sky</u>, the child watched
              A
    <u>her kite</u>, <u>which she had made</u> <u>herself</u>, with
       B   C   D
    great delight. <u>No error.</u>
             E

30. <u>As</u> she traveled to school <u>every day</u>,
      A   B
    the athlete <u>jumps over</u> trash cans and
             C
    fences to practice <u>her vaulting skills</u>.
              D
    <u>No error.</u>
       E

31. A pedestrian <u>who</u> walks <u>slow on the</u>
           A   B
    <u>streets</u> of Rome <u>will soon find</u> the crowd
             C
    <u>surging</u> around him. <u>No error.</u>
       D   E

32. The student council <u>objected to him</u> get-
              A
    ting an award, <u>as</u> several students <u>claimed</u>
           B   C
    <u>that they</u> <u>had seen him</u> cheat on an exam.
           D
    <u>No error.</u>
       E

33. Sharks, <u>though feared</u> <u>for their deadly</u>
           A   B
    <u>attacks</u>, are in <u>more serious danger</u> from
              C
    humans <u>than humans are</u> from these sea
             D
    creatures. <u>No error.</u>
             E

34. <u>The report was</u> <u>late</u>, so <u>the manager</u>
         A   B   C
    <u>resolved</u> to start <u>more quicker</u> on the next
              D
    assignment. <u>No error.</u>
             E

Go on to next page

Directions for Questions 35–39: Following is a first draft of a student essay. The essay needs revision. Read the essay and the questions that follow and choose the best answer to each question.

[1] The largest creature on earth isn't an elephant or a land animal. [2] It's the blue whale, which can grow to 30 meters, or almost 100 feet, in length. [3] The blue whale is not a fish. [4] It is a mammal. [5] It must breath air in order to survive.

[6] Until this century, you could find many blue whales in every ocean on earth. [7] Now blue whales are not abundant. [8] The whalers killed so many of these magnificent animals that they are considered endangered. [9] A treaty in 1966 protected the whales from hunting.

[10] Although whales are large, the krill that blue whales gather are extremely tiny. [11] Blue whales eat about 40 million krill in a single day! [12] The whale has a strainer in its mouth and swims with its mouth open, sifting water through and leaving the krill behind for the whale to eat.

[13] Whales are protected from hunting, and whales are still not safe. [14] Many dangers, such as collisions with ships and pollution, are problems for whales. [15] More protection is needed for all animals if the earth is to survive.

35. Which of the following is the best way to combine Sentences 3 and 4?

(A) The blue whale is not a fish, but it is a mammal.

(B) Not a fish, the blue whale, it is a mammal.

(C) The blue whale is not a fish but a mammal.

(D) The blue whale is a mammal, it is not a fish.

(E) The blue whale, while not a fish, is a mammal.

36. What, if any, is the best change to Paragraph 2 (Sentences 6–9)?

(A) Add a discussion of the history of whaling.

(B) Delete Sentence 8.

(C) Insert statistics about the blue whale population at various times.

(D) Name the oceans.

(E) Give more information on hunting methods.

37. In context, which of the following sentences should precede Sentence 10, at the beginning of Paragraph 3?

(A) Krill are much smaller than the blue whales.

(B) The treaty protected whales, but not krill.

(C) Though hunted, the blue whale is not a ferocious hunter itself.

(D) Both the blue whale and other animals need a good supply of food.

(E) To protect an animal, you must protect its food supply.

38. Which of the following, if any, is the best change to Sentence 13?

(A) NO CHANGE

(B) Protected from hunting whales are still not safe.

(C) The whales are not safe except from hunting.

(D) Despite that whales have been protected from hunting, whales are still not safe.

(E) The treaty protects them from hunting, but the whales are still not safe.

39. Which of the following, if any, would improve the last paragraph (Sentences 13–15)?

(A) NO CHANGE

(B) Describe a collision between a whale and a boat.

(C) Discuss pollution and how it may be eliminated.

(D) Change Sentence 15 to "More protection is needed for whales if they are to survive."

(E) Insert this sentence between Sentences 14 and 15: "Whales are not the only animals that need protection."

STOP YOU MAY CHECK YOUR WORK ON THIS SECTION ONLY. DO NOT GO BACK TO ANY PREVIOUS SECTION.

Chapter 16

Practice Test 3:
Answers and Explanations

● ●

Have you ever wondered how your teachers feel as they sit behind a desk, watching you sweat over an exam? No, they're not gloating. Instead, they're probably thinking about all that correction — smiling when an answer is right and trying to figure out how to make you understand what you got wrong and why.

Now *you* get to be the teacher, sort of. In this chapter you check your work on Practice Test 3 (Chapter 15). I provide the explanations, though, so you don't have to take on that chore. Just read them carefully, so next time you'll find the correct answer with ease. If you're short on time, turn to the end of this chapter to find an abbreviated answer key.

Section 1: Critical Reading

1. **E.** If the secretary made all the decisions, Paul wasn't really in charge, so he probably has the title but not the power. Therefore, *nominally* (in name only) fits well here. Do you have time for a quick vocabulary builder? *Obstinately* means "stubbornly," and *inevitably* means "bound to happen, unavoidably."

2. **B.** This question may be easier if you start with the second blank. Codes of conduct regulate behavior, so Choice (B) is possible. The other choices aren't good fits: *supplanted* means "replaced by," *implied* means "hinted at but not stated," *relinquished* means "surrendered" or "given up," and *conceded* means "agreed, perhaps after some argument or opposition." Safety is seldom a bad thing, so Choice (B) works well in the first blank also, because a *priority* is something you put first. Take a moment to complete the vocabulary lesson: *prerequisite* is a precondition — something you have to do first, before you do something else. A *solicitation* is a request, the kind a charity makes, for example.

3. **C.** Use your real-life experience here. Picture John, totally involved in the video game to the point where he's "in a trance." What's his role in the conversation? Nada. Nothing. Completely out of it — in other words, Choice (C).

4. **A.** The key word here is "although," which tells you that the sentence contains a change in direction. The second portion of the sentence mentions "recommended," so the ambassador thinks the treaty should be ratified or approved. Okay, the first portion of the sentence has to go in the other direction, toward *critical* (fault-finding) comments. Choice (A) it is!

   Watch out for transition words and phrases — such as "yet," "nevertheless," "despite," and "but" — that send the sentence in another direction.

5. **D.** Save the earth! (I'm not kidding. The PSAT/NMSQT won't do you much good if you have no oxygen to breathe when you're in college.) Back to the question: The utensils can't be "reused or recycled," so they're "made to be thrown away," the definition of *disposable.* The only other possibility is Choice (E), because *flimsy* things are poorly made and break easily. However, you can keep something flimsy if you're careful. Choice (D) is the answer.

6. **B.** The sentence contains two weather conditions — one with "violent winds" and one with a "mild breeze." What is the likely effect of each condition on flower petals? As sometimes happens, you can find the answer more quickly if you start with the second blank. A "mild breeze" probably moved the petals along slowly, and Choice (B), *wafted,* means "drifted" or "floated." The other possibility is Choice (D) because the petals may have *sailed.* The other words imply speed or extreme movement, not what you want with "mild breeze." Now turn to the "violent winds." They most likely *detached,* or separated, the petals, not *buoyed* or raised them.

7. **E.** Three films! I like movies, but that's a lot. No wonder Bob wants to call it a day. Therefore, it's possible that he *upheld* or *supported* Mary's idea about going home. ("Upheld" and "supported" are synonyms.) Choices (B) and (E) make sense only if they're paired with a word that means "tired" or "bored" for the first blank. Bingo: *jaded* is a mixture of those two feelings, so Choice (E) is your answer. Choice (B) doesn't work because *defiant* (opposing forcefully) places Bob in disagreement with Mary, and the "incessant" (nonstop) yawns tell you that he's either tired or bored or both — once again taking you to Choice (E).

8. **A.** This question illustrates the test-writers' occasional urge to define the blank with the words that immediately follow it. An *amalgam* is a mixture. I have to squeeze in a couple of vocabulary extras: *artifice* is a pretense, especially one that's created on purpose. An *evasion* is a dodge, a move to escape. *Infusion* is a mixture, but this word usually refers to liquids. (The peppermint tea I drink is an *infusion.*) *Inundation* is a flood. The correct answer is Choice (A).

9. **C.** The accidents mentioned in the passage involve oil, coal, and gas. After those statistics, the author refers to the "comparative safety and track record" (Line 9) of nuclear power. Choice (C) fits nicely with these statements. True, the number of deaths cited in the passage is largest for gas, but three random accidents, one for each type of power, doesn't justify a blanket statement about the most dangerous form of energy (Choice A) or death rates (Choice B). The author also says that the public "is never going to believe — nor should it" that nuclear power is totally safe, so Choice (D) is a dud. Finally, because the passage says that nuclear energy "has some risks" (Lines 17–18), Choice (E) doesn't work.

10. **C.** The statistics on accidents attributed to oil, coal, and gas tell you that Statement I is true. The author says that the "public would benefit from learning the basic concepts" of nuclear energy, so Statement II is false, because if you don't know the basics, you're not well-informed. The reference in Line 9 to the "comparative safety" of nuclear power places Statement III in the "true column." Because I and III are true, Choice (C) is correct.

11. **A.** Line 4 says that differences in male and female styles of communications "are relevant to the clinical context." A little earlier in the passage you see the phrase "for a health professional" (Line 3). Put these two together and you end up with a passage that's probably geared toward doctors, who work in a clinical context and who are health professionals.

12. **B.** Did you nod your head when you read this passage, despite feeling that the author is totally wrong when it comes to gender and speech styles? If you did so, the author of the passage would guess that you're female, because the passage states that women "may give signs of assent simply to indicate they are following the conversation" (Lines 7–8). Of course, this passage isn't a conversation, and the author may be dead wrong. Whatever: The passage supplies evidence for Choice (B). The runner-up is Choice (D), because the emphasis on "styles" (Line 2) and the reference in Lines 14–15 to "cultural differences in gender roles and etiquette" imply that speech differences are partly determined by society's view of what is proper. However, the passage doesn't make a cause-and-effect statement that's as absolute as Choice (D). Therefore, Choice (B) is better.

13. **E.** The reference in Line 2 to "distant mountains" rules out Choice (A), and the statement about "the ruins of Persepolis" knocks out Choice (B). Because Persepolis is referred to as "the ceremonial and spiritual capital of a vast empire" (Lines 5–6), Choice (C) doesn't work — and Choice (E) does. True, the passage says that people from India came to Persepolis 4,000 years ago, but nothing supports the idea that the rulers of India built the city, so Choice (D) is incorrect.

14. **C.** The Gate of All Nations, according to Line 9, is where "vassal states" (Line 10) entered "to pay homage to their Persian masters" (Line 11). A ***vassal*** is someone who serves a lord — often because the lord conquered the vassal's country. The gifts listed in Paragraph 2 of Passage I (which are homage, the ceremonial show of the vassal's lowly status, and the lord's power over the vassal) come from conquered lands. Put these two ideas together and you have Choice (C).

15. **B.** If you dread something, you fear it. Used as an adjective, ***dread*** refers to what you fear. In Line 13, the "sovereign" is "feared," and Choice (B) is correct.

16. **A.** If you're one of the Persian rulers described in these passages, you don't need to clip coupons or search for sale merchandise. In Passage I, your subjects are bringing their best to your palace, and in Passage II your chef is combing the empire for the tastiest food, wine, and even water. (Sounds like the Upper East Side of Manhattan, where I live and where gourmet shopping is trendy.) Because these two lists include food and nonfood items, Choice (A) works and Choice (C) doesn't. The "cloth and ceramic plates" (Lines 32–33) in Passage I rule out Choice (B) because these items are manufactured, not natural resources. Choice (D) looks good at first glance because the stuff given in Passage I does come from subjects, but you don't know whether the king paid for the food and beverages in Passage II, just that he consumed them. Therefore, Choice (D) isn't necessarily correct. Choice (E) fails because the "limitations of the ruler" don't appear in Passage I and have nothing to do with the list in Passage II. No doubt about it, Choice (A) is correct.

17. **C.** The test-writers love to give you a vocabulary question in which all the answers are definitions of the word, but only one definition fits the sentence. To make your life even more miserable, the correct answer is usually an off-the-wall definition, the kind that seldom appears in ordinary conversation. (I doubt that you'd state that your family paid the government "tributes" last April when they filed their tax returns, even if they wrote big checks to the Feds. See what I mean about an unusual definition?) Anyway, one definition of tributes is ***taxes*** — the goods or services given to rulers or governments. So Choice (C) is correct.

18. **B.** When you're in "relative" territory, you're comparing. If Cyrus showed "relative gentleness" (Line 56), he's being compared to other rulers, who probably used "the more common means of oppression, terror, and slaughter" (Lines 59–60). Choices (C) and (D) may have tempted you, but Cyrus is described as a conqueror, so (C) doesn't fit. Also, the passage doesn't tell you whether Cyrus is being compared to his ***contemporaries*** (rulers living at the same time) or to rulers of any era. Therefore, Choice (E) is too much of a stretch. The best answer is Choice (B).

19. **D.** The passage refers to Cyrus's "relative gentleness" (Line 56) and says that Cyrus "understood that this was an even surer way to build a durable empire" (Lines 57–59). An empire that's durable lasts, so Choice (D) is your answer here. The other statements aren't supported by Passage I.

20. **C.** The first passage relies on a lengthy description of carvings found in the ruins of Persepolis. The second passage describes the interior, including carpeting, hangings, furniture, and even an embroidered canopy. Logic tells you that stuff like that doesn't last long, so the description has to be about ancient times, not the ruin described in Passage I.

21. **C.** You have an easy ride on this one if you know that one definition of "fittings" is "furniture." The only answer that works with this definition is Choice (C), *golden throne*. Never heard the word before? Use logic. The "courts and halls" (Line 61) would be "bare" (Line 63) without the fittings. Furniture fills a room, so Choice (C) makes sense.

22. **D.** Many of the choices are definitions of "severe," but the paragraph talks about the rules the ruler must obey. The preceding paragraph discusses the rules for those visiting the ruler. No one's allowed to throw a spitball or to relax for a minute, so ***strict,*** Choice (D), is what you want here.

23. **A.** Poor king. All that power and nowhere to go. Paragraph 3 of Passage II (Lines 83–94) describes the restrictions (limitations) on his conduct. Because he could "never . . . revoke an order once given" (Lines 87–88), Choice (A) is right.

24. **B.** The first passage is long on the glory of various rulers, including Cyrus, but says very little about Cyrus's obligations. Passage II, on the other hand, tells you that the ruler lived "in seclusion" (isolation) and that he couldn't change his mind or break a promise. Therefore, the ruler's duties are more in focus, and Choice (B) is the answer.

Section 2: Mathematics

1. **D.** Solve the first equation so that a and b are on the same side: $a - 3b = -2$. Notice that $-2a + 6b = -2(a - 3b)$, and you can substitute -2 for $a - 3b$: $-2(-2) = 4$.

2. **A.** Your best bet here is to pick an odd number and test what happens. Three is a good number to test. Three squared is 9, which becomes 18 when doubled. Subtract 5 and the result is 13. You know the result will be odd, and not even, so you're down to Choices (A) or (D). Thirteen is prime, so you should try another starting number, maybe 5. Five squared is 25, which is 50 when doubled. Subtract 5 and you get 45, which is neither even nor prime.

3. **B.** Remember that whenever two lines cross each other, any pair of *adjacent* angles (ones that are next to each other) add to $180°$. This means that $a + b = 180$. From the equation given in the problem, you know that $b = a + 100$, so you can substitute that into the earlier equation: $a + (a + 100) = 180$, so $2a = 80$, so $a = 40°$.

4. **B.** This question is testing your knowledge of slopes and y-intercepts. Remember that in the equation $y = mx + b$, m represents the slope and b represents the y-intercept. The line has a negative slope and a positive y-intercept. The only answers that fit those criteria are Choices (B) and (C). Now look at the slope and decide whether it looks more like -2 or $-\frac{1}{2}$. One good way to decide is to draw in the line $y = -x$, which cuts right through the middle of the axes, to see whether the line in the question is more or less steep. It looks steeper, so -2 is the slope.

5. **C.** You know that a is negative and b is positive, so their product must also be negative. If you cube a negative number, the result is still negative, so Choices (D) and (E) are out. The biggest product you can get using ab would be a little bit smaller than $(-2)\left(\frac{1}{3}\right) = -\frac{2}{3}$, and the smallest product would be a little bit bigger than $(0)(-1) = 0$. The only answer between those values is Choice (C). If that seems a bit tricky, you can also solve this problem by plugging in values and testing them out.

6. **C.** The trick here is to remember that $f(x)$ is just referring to a y value. So you can take points from the original graph, plug in the y-value for $f(x)$, and look for the choice that has that point. Start with $(-3, 0)$. The x value remains the same, and $-(0) + 1 = 1$, so you're looking for an answer choice that contains the point $(-3, 1)$. Choices (A) and (C) are the only ones. Try this with one other point, maybe $(0, 3)$, which after the transformation $(-(3) + 1 = -2)$ gives you the point $(0, -2)$. Choice (C) is the one you're looking for.

7. **B.** You have a cube that you don't know much about. Plug in time! You can assume that each of the edges is 1 unit long, so $z = 1$. That way the volume is 1, and the surface of any side is 1. The new cube has 4 as the area of a side (which is a square), meaning that each side is 2 units long. Because $v = s^3$, you know that the new volume is 8, or $8z$.

8. **D.** This problem is easy if you're willing to use some algebra. You can let x be the cost of each person's dinner. Therefore, the total bill is $5x$ plus the tax, or $5x + 0.15(5x) = 5.75x$. You know that the total was $97.75, so make that equal to $5.75x$ and solve by dividing both sides by 5.75. In the end, you get $x = \$17$, Choice (D).

9. **C.** You know that 15% + 45% = 60% of the marbles are red or blue, so the remainder, 40%, must be yellow. Adding together red and yellow likelihoods: 15% + 40% = 55% probability that the marble is red or yellow.

10. **A.** First, divide everything by –2 (and remember that multiplying or dividing by a negative makes the inequality sign change directions!). $|3-x| \le 2$. This means that $3-x$ is between –2 and 2, so x is between 1 and 5. You can always pick a number in the interval and make sure that it works, if you're not sure of your calculations.

11. **D.** Recall that circumference is $2\pi r$, so in this case the radius must be $\frac{10\pi}{2\pi} = 5$. From here, all you need to do is remember that the area of a circle is $\pi r^2 = \pi(5)^2 = 25\pi$, Choice (D). If you have trouble remembering those formulas, check the beginning of each math section. The test writers place them there for your convenience.

12. **A.** You can label the sides of the drawing you made of the photo (you made a drawing as soon as you saw this problem, right?) with $3x$ and $5x$. Now, draw a rectangle around the photo. Each strip of frame adds 2 inches, so 4 inches are added to each side, making the new outside measurements $3x + 4$ (2 inches on each side), and $5x + 4$. To get the area, just multiply those two expressions together!

13. **D.** Remember that parallel lines have equivalent slopes, so the new line will also have a slope of –2 (recall that the slope is the number that x is multiplied by). From there, the easiest trick is to plug (1, –5) into the equation of a line to determine the y-intercept. $y = mx + b \rightarrow y = -2x + b \rightarrow (-5) = -2(1) + b \rightarrow b = -3$. Choice (D) is the one you want.

14. **E.** For this question, a good approach is to back-solve by trying the numbers. The easiest thing to test is the second statement: If you add 1 to the number, the result is divisible by 5. This is true only with Choices (B) and (E). Now double each number and see whether it's divisible by 4; only Choice (E) works.

15. **C.** This problem is all about substitution! Solve the first equation for $3a$: $3a = 2 - 6y$, and then multiply everything by 3 to get $9a = 6 - 18y$. Next solve the second equation for b: $b = 2x - 4$. Now substitute each of those into the expression: $9a + \frac{b}{2} = (6 - 18y) + \frac{(2x-4)}{2}$. Everything simplifies nicely, and you get $9a + \frac{b}{2} = 6 - 18y + x - 2 = x - 18y + 4$.

16. **D.** Because the top of the window is a semicircle, the width of the window is equal to the diameter of the circle, or 20 inches. The rectangular part of the window has an area of $(20)(30) = 600$ square inches. The area of the semicircle is $\frac{\pi r^2}{2} = \frac{\pi(10)^2}{2} = \frac{100\pi}{2} = 50\pi$ square inches. Together that makes for an area of $600 + 50\pi$ square inches, Choice (D).

17. **B.** You need to determine the perimeter of the window first. The rectangular part only needs trim around the sides and the bottom, so that accounts for 30 + 20 + 30 = 80 inches of perimeter. The perimeter of the semicircle is half of the circumference: $\frac{2\pi r}{2} = \pi r = 10\pi$ inches. This means that the perimeter of the window is $80 + 10\pi$ inches. Multiply that length by the cost per inch, $2, and you get approximately $222.83.

18. **C.** The area of a triangle is $\frac{1}{2}bh$, so you can use the two legs of a right triangle as the base and height (because they meet at a right angle). Call the base 4 inches, so you can set up $A = 20 = \frac{1}{2}(4)h$, which solves to $h = 10$. Now you need the Pythagorean theorem to find the length of the hypotenuse. $a^2 + b^2 = c^2 \rightarrow (4)^2 + (10)^2 = h^2 = 116$, so $h = \sqrt{116} = 2\sqrt{29}$. Adding up the sides of the triangle gets you the perimeter: $4 + 10 + 2\sqrt{29} = 14 + 2\sqrt{29}$.

19. **A.** Whenever you need to solve an equation with an x^2 in it (a quadratic equation), start by moving everything over to one side of the equation. In this case you end up with $2x^2 - 5x - 3 = 0$. You either want to factor this or use the quadratic formula ($x = \frac{-b \pm \sqrt{b^2 - 4ac}}{2a} = \frac{5 \pm \sqrt{25 - 4(2)(-3)}}{2(2)}$). Either way, you end up with x being either 3 or $-\frac{1}{2}$. Multiply those together, and you get $-\frac{3}{2}$.

20. **B.** First, find the area of the rectangle: $(12)(8) = 96$. From 96 you subtract the areas of the three circles. The smaller circles each have an area of $\pi r^2 = 4\pi$, and the larger has an area of $\pi(3)^2 = 9\pi$. This means that the area of the shaded part of the figure is $96 - 2(4\pi) - 9\pi = 96 - 17\pi$, Choice (B).

Section 3: Critical Reading

25. **D.** Two words help you with this question: "but" and "anyway." Both tell you that the manager's actions were a little surprising, given the information in the first part of the sentence. Okay, what would surprise you? Checking a **credible,** or "believable" account.

26. **E.** The criminal has no **remorse** (regret for past actions), so the criminal is **callous,** or "hardened," a clue that appears in the sentence. (You may know someone who has calluses on a hand or foot; the skin is toughened there. The spelling differs, but the meaning is similar.) Time for a few new vocabulary words: **magnanimous** is "generous," **pragmatic** is "practical," **innocuous** is "harmless," and **perplexing** is "puzzling."

27. **D.** The word "however" should shine in your eye like the neon lights of Broadway. When you see that word, you know the sentence is taking a U-turn, moving away from whatever precedes it. The second part of the sentence, everything after "however," talks about *not addressing* (dealing with) the cause of the disease. So if the second part of the sentence is negative, the "however" gives you a hint that the first part of the sentence must state something positive. Choice (D) does so, because if the medicine **alleviates** your symptoms, it eases them. Stop right there! Only a couple of additional minutes will **augment** or **redouble** ("add to" or "double") your vocabulary. To **induce** is "to bring about," and to **aggravate** is "to make worse."

28. **A.** Think about real life for a moment, and you see that mats protect tables. Okay, right away you land on Choice (A), because **protective** is the second term. The first works too: **mar** means "damage." Choice (B) is a close second, because any mat, including a **decorative** one, will **shield** what it covers. But Choice (A) is more precise and therefore the better answer. By the way, **disparaging** means "speaking ill of."

29. **E.** If they're arguing for hours, they like to argue, and **contentious** means "quarrelsome." Do you know the other words? **Jocular** and **flippant** students joke a lot, and **meticulous** people pay attention to tiny details. If you're **flexible,** you bend — physically or intellectually.

30. **D.** Line 12 refers to poetry as "sweet," but poetry is also called a "false Siren" (Line 2). Okay, so far you know that poetry can be sweet but that sweet things (such as the Sirens' songs) can be dangerous. Now check out Line 13, where you see that Plato challenged poetry lovers to show that poetry can be "helpful to society and the life of man." When you put everything together, you have beauty but no substance, also known as Choice (D).

31. **B.** Plato isn't a big poetry fan, but he's willing to hear someone make a case for poetry's role as "helpful to society and the life of man" (Line 13). Statement I is true, because "helpful to society" may be seen as a "contribution to communal life." Statement II also makes the cut, because Plato is also waiting to see that poetry is "helpful" (Line 13) to "the life of man" (Line 13), and if you "ennoble an individual," you improve his or her life. Statement III is a trap. Plato admits that poetry is "sweet" (Line 12) but says that sweetness isn't enough. The argument he wants to hear, which is included in the pronoun "this," goes beyond sweetness. Your answer is Choice (B), because I and II are true, and III is false.

32. **D.** Passage II deals with truth, which, the author **contends** (argues), can be found in imaginative works. The reference to "real toads" is preceded by a statement about "the human experience," so Choice (D) is a perfect fit.

33. **D.** Passage I explains that Plato compared poetry to "mythological creatures," who are clearly not real. Passage II likens poetry to "an imaginary garden" (Line 19). So Choice (D) is **valid** (true) for both passages. Did I catch you with Choice (E)? Passage II certainly comes down on the side of poetry as revealing truth, but Passage I doesn't.

34. **D.** Katharine is pouring tea but thinking about "Monday morning" and "the things one does voluntarily and normally in the daylight" (Lines 8–9). But it's Sunday evening, so she has a while before she can enjoy Monday. She sees that period of time as a "barrier" — an obstacle — a clue that she's not happy about the time she has to spend at the tea party. The only answer that suits Katharine's mood is Choice (D). Choice (A) is tempting, but it's more general than Choice (D) and less supported by the passage because you don't know exactly what "a short period of time" means. When you're taking a test, a short period may be 5 minutes. When you're having fun with your friends, a short period may last 15 hours. Go for Choice (D) and you're done.

35. **A.** Yes, the people who assign homework and tear it apart with red pens are faculty members (teachers), but **faculties** may also be mental abilities or capacity, a definition that works nicely in Line 14. Katharine is going through the motions at the tea party, but her mind is capable of much more, so her "faculties" are unoccupied or unused.

36. **B.** The passage tells you that Mrs. Hilbery was "so rich in the gifts which make tea-parties . . . successful" (Lines 16–18) that "she scarcely needed any help from Katharine" (Lines 18–19) except for the "business of teacups and bread and butter" (Line 20). No doubts here: Mrs. Hilbery needs Katharine for the "serving of food and drink," as Choice (B) states.

37. **E.** Katharine laughs when she imagines the arrival of a guest (Mr. Denham's not there yet). The guest "would think, 'What an extremely nice house to come into!'" (Lines 30–31). The reader knows, however, that Katharine is bored and getting through "the little barrier of day" by thinking about Monday. Therefore, the appearance of a great party differs from Katharine's reality, and Choice (E) is the answer.

38. **D.** Katharine has to tell her mother Mr. Denham's name because "she saw that her mother had forgotten his name" (Lines 41–42), and this fact was **perceptible** (visible) to Mr. Denham, a situation that "increased the awkwardness" (Line 44). Choice (D) is perfect. If you picked Choice (E), don't be discouraged. The test makers often place an answer that's *almost,* but not quite, the best response. Mr. Denham *is* late, but the passage states clearly that it's the mother's forgetfulness, not his late arrival, that adds to the awkwardness.

39. **C.** Sounds like just the thing for post-PSAT/NMSQT relaxation, right? A closed, padded room! Back to the question. The party isn't silent, because the room is "full of people . . . all launched upon sentences" (Lines 46–47). However, Denham has "omnibuses and cabs still running in his head" (Line 55), and he thinks about the "traffic and foot passengers" (Lines 57–58). The party definitely contrasts with "the street outside" (Lines 49–50), making Choice (C) the correct one here.

40. **D.** When Mr. Denham arrives, the guests are discussing a cousin who "has married and gone to live in Manchester" (Lines 76–77). Mr. Denham is left out of the conversation — and the social group — until Mrs. Hilbery draws him in by asking what Denham would do if he were married to an engineer and "had to live in Manchester" (Lines 70–71). Mrs. Hilbery restores the unity of the group and connects the "severed parts," which represent the fractured group.

41. **D.** Katharine isn't rebelling, at least on the outside. She's pouring tea and behaving. In her head, though, she's somewhere else — actually, *sometime* else: Monday. Choice (D) describes her mental absence.

42. **A.** If you're pouring tea for famous novelists, chances are you're *not* in a low social class. But even if you're not sure about Katharine's status, you have evidence in the passage for all the other answers. Mr. Denham refers to the guests' sophistication in Line 83, so Choice (B) bombs. In Line 86, Mr. Denham regrets that the guests are all over 40, and Choice (C) drops out. Mr. Denham curses the fact that "he certainly would not appear at his best" (Lines 84–85) in "this sophisticated drawing room," so down goes Choice (D). The whole "who are you?" moment in Lines 40–42 kills Choice (E). Bingo: Choice (A) is your answer.

43. **A.** When you see "I am the circle" (Line 1), you know you're in personification land. (***Personification*** is the assignment of human qualities — such as the ability to speak — to nonhumans.) You can find some metaphors and similes here and there, but the whole passage is based on the circle's comments. Choice (A) is best.

44. **B.** Line 3 tells you that the circle is composed of equal points and "that equality defines beauty" (Line 9). Clearly, Choice (B) works. True, the passage also equates beauty with perfection, but perfection isn't one of your answer choices.

45. **C.** The passage credits the circle with nearly everything in the universe, but nowhere does the passage mention health. The correct answer is Choice (C).

46. **D.** The wheel is a circle, but if you place the bicycle on its side, something sticks up. It's not a "true" or perfect form.

47. **C.** The bicycle ***anecdote*** (brief story) tells you that the wheel isn't perfect and never can be. Even when you fix it, something else goes wrong. The last paragraph of the passage (Lines 72–82) also describes imperfection, in this case the fact that the ideal of democracy doesn't exist in real life. The dominant idea, then, is that perfection is only for abstract ideas, not real things. Or, as Choice (C) puts it, "perfection is an ***unattainable*** [impossible] ideal."

48. **E.** The bicycle bumps along on wheels that move "yet farther from perfection" (Lines 70–71) when they hit a road bump. That's what you know after you read Paragraph 7 (Lines 57–71). The last paragraph talks about "philosophical and social efforts" (Line 72) to reach equality that never succeed. Why? Well, the last sentence tells you that a "perfect ideal cannot be achieved by human beings . . . with such imperfect character" (Lines 80–82). Therefore, the faults (bumps) lie in human nature, as Choice (E) states.

Section 4: Mathematics

21. **B.** Recall that perpendicular lines have slopes that are opposite reciprocals (or, if it's easier to remember, the slopes have a product of –1). That means that line n has a slope of $-\frac{3}{2}$. You can plug in (–1, 1) for x and y in the slope-intercept equation in order to find the y-intercept. $y = -\frac{3}{2}x + b \rightarrow (1) = -\frac{3}{2}(-1) + b = \frac{3}{2} + b$. Solve for b, $b = -\frac{1}{2}$, so the equation of the line is $y = -\frac{3}{2}x - \frac{1}{2}$, Choice (B).

22. **C.** Julia has 8 choices for bottoms (5 pants + 3 skirts) and 7 shirts for tops. Any one shirt has 8 options to go with it, so she has $(7)(8) = 56$ possible outfits.

23. **D.** Reading the chart you discover that Kat saw 1 bird on Monday, 3 on Tuesday, 2 on Wednesday and Thursday, and 4 on Friday, for a total of $1 + 3 + 2 + 2 + 4 = 12$ birds over those 5 days. If she also wants to see 12 birds over the two-day weekend, she needs to see an average of 6 birds each day.

24. **A.** First, line up the birds in increasing or decreasing order: 1, 2, 2, 3, 4. The median is the middle number, or 2. The mode is the most frequent number, also 2. The mean is the average number: $\frac{12}{5} = 2.4$. This means that I is false (the median and mode are equal), II is true ($2.4 > 2$), and III is false ($2 < 2.6$). Choice (A) is the right one.

25. **D.** The parabola is "frowning" (I would be too if I were in the middle of the PSAT/NMSQT!), so you know that the coefficient for x^2 must be negative, knocking Choices (A) and (B) out of the running. You also know that the y-intercept of the parabola is positive, meaning that the number in the equation without an x in it (the constant term) must be positive. Of the three remaining answers, only Choice (D) has a positive constant term.

26. **A.** The easiest way to answer this question is to plug the answer choices into the inequalities. The answer choice that makes both inequalities true is the one you want. Starting with Choice (A) and the first inequality: $\frac{1}{2}(3) - 4 = -2.5$, which is less than -1. Now check it in the second inequality: $2(3) + 3 = 9$, which is greater than -1. Hey! Your first try was the right answer! If that hadn't worked out, you would just keep checking choices until you found one that worked.

27. **D.** The trick is to realize that if you were to make a vertical slit in the can's wrapper, it would unroll into a rectangle, where the height is the height of the can (5 inches) and the width is the circumference of the top (and bottom): $2\pi r = 3\pi$. Multiply those together, and you've got the area of the paper: $5(3\pi) = 15\pi$ square inches.

28. **C.** You definitely want to mark up the drawing in the test booklet for this one. Also, make sure that you remember your special triangles (or remember to turn back to the beginning of the section, where you'll find them in the formula box).

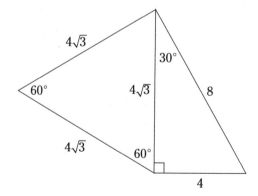

You know that in a 30°-60°-90° triangle, the side opposite the 90° angle is twice as large as the side opposite the 30° angle, so the hypotenuse is 8. The side opposite the 60° angle is equal to the side opposite the 30° angle multiplied by $\sqrt{3}$, so $4\sqrt{3}$ in this case. The triangle on the left is an *equilateral* triangle (all the angles are 60° — that was your tip-off), so the two remaining sides of the perimeter are both $4\sqrt{3}$. Add up all the (exterior) sides and you get $4 + 8 + 4\sqrt{3} + 4\sqrt{3} = 12 + 8\sqrt{3}$.

29. **9.** Remember to use Order of Operations; you may have learned it as PEMDAS or GEMDAS. Either way, you need to multiply and divide first. So, $4 \times 3 = 12$ and $10 \div 2 = 5$. Rewriting the original equation: $12 + 2 - 5 = 14 - 5 = 9$.

30. **21.** The area of a triangle is calculated with $\frac{1}{2}bh$.

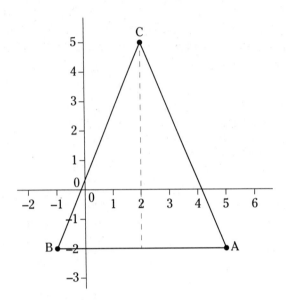

In this case, let AB be the base; it has a length of $5 - (-1) = 6$. You can drop an altitude from point C (shown as a dotted line in this figure) and see that it hits AB at $(2, -2)$. That means that the altitude is $5 - (-2) = 7$ units long. Plug that into the area formula: $A = \frac{1}{2}(6)(7) = 21$.

31. **9.** Substitution is key. Wherever you see an x in the original equation, replace it with a -2 in order to calculate $f(-2)$: $f(-2) = 3(-2)^2 - 2(-2) - 10 = 12 + 4 - 10 = 6$. That's $f(-2)$; now just add 3: $f(-2) + 3 = 6 + 3 = 9$.

32. **42.5.** Begin by writing down the first 8 terms. The pattern is that each number is the result of multiplying the previous number by $-\frac{1}{2}$. Your numbers are: 64, –32, 16, –8, 4, –2, 1, and –0.5. Add those up and you get 42.5.

33. **30.** This problem is easiest if you work backward. Kyle ate 3 apples and had 2 left, meaning that he started with 5 apples. Kyle's 5 apples are one third of Paul's, so Paul had 3(5) = 15 apples. Paul got half of Mary's apples, so Mary must have started with 15(2) = 30 apples.

34. **65.** You can read the Venn diagram to see that 35 students have a bicycle and 15 have a skateboard; 5 of those people have a bicycle and a skateboard. That makes 45 students with wheels. You know that 80 students were surveyed, so 35 of them have neither a bicycle nor a skateboard. To determine how many don't own a skateboard, you want to include the students with neither as well as the students with a bicycle and not a skateboard: 35 + 30 = 65 students.

35. **⁹⁄₈.** Recall that when you have a negative sign in an exponent, you take the reciprocal of the base. For example, $5^{-1} = \frac{1}{5}$. With that in mind, plug 3 and 2 in for a and b in the symbol definition: $3\#2 = 3^2 2^{-3}$. You want to simplify each base and exponent first before multiplying them together: $3^2 = 9$, and $2^{-3} = \frac{1}{2^3} = \frac{1}{8}$. Now you can multiply: $9\left(\frac{1}{8}\right) = \frac{9}{8}$.

36. **20.** Let x be the number of times that you go to the pool. Waves Pool costs you $250 plus $5 for each visit, so the total cost is $250 + 5x$. Splash Pool, with similar calculations, costs $50 + 15x$. Set those two costs equal to each other to determine the number of visits to the pool for the costs to even out: $250 + 5x = 50 + 15x \rightarrow 200 = 10x$, so $x = 20$; you need to go to the pool 20 times for the cost of joining the pools to be the same.

37. **35.** First, you should figure out exactly what's going on if the price is doubled. Doubling the price results in a price of $24 per feeder. That results in 25% fewer sales, or retaining 75% of the sales: $0.75(40) = 30$ feeders sold. You can think of the data points that you're given as points on the coordinate plane. Forty feeders at $12 per feeder would correspond with the point (40, 12), and (30, 24) would be the other data point. Connect those two data points with a line so that you can figure out the number of feeders when they cost $18 each. Slope $= \frac{24-12}{30-40} = \frac{12}{-10} = -\frac{6}{5}$. $y = mx + b = -\frac{6}{5}x + b$. Plug either of your data points in to find b: $24 = -\frac{6}{5}(30) + b$, and $b = 60$, so $y = -\frac{6}{5}x + 60$. You want to know what x (number sold) is when y (cost) is 18, so plug it in: $18 = -\frac{6}{5}x + 60 \rightarrow 42 = \frac{6}{5}x \rightarrow x = 42\left(\frac{5}{6}\right) = 35$ bird feeders.

Another way to see this problem is to notice that 18 is halfway between 12 and 24, so the answer, 35, will be halfway between 40 and 30!

38. **1.** This problem isn't as scary as it looks if you tackle it one step at a time. The outer circle has a diameter of 2, which means that the biggest square's diagonal is 2. Hopefully you recall that the area of a square is half of the product of the diagonals, so the area of the bigger square is $\frac{1}{2}(2)(2) = 2$. This means that one side of the square is $\sqrt{2}$, so the radius of the inner circle is half of that; $\frac{\sqrt{2}}{2}$. That means that the diameter of the inner circle is $\sqrt{2}$, which is a diagonal of the inner square. To find the area of the inner square, you want half of the product of the diagonals: $\frac{1}{2}\left(\sqrt{2}\right)\left(\sqrt{2}\right) = 1$, so the area of the shaded square is 1. You can also work through this problem using 45°-45°-90° triangles to find radii and side lengths.

Section 5: Writing

1. **E.** You have two events in this sentence: Eisenhower's service as a general and his election to the presidency. The original sentence correctly places the military service before the presidency, but "used to serve" hints at a recurring action ("I used to go shopping on Saturdays," for example), not one that continued without a break. Choices (B) and (C) don't work because they make the military and political service *simultaneous* (happening at the same time). Choice (D) includes a present-perfect verb, "has served," which expresses a past action that continues in the present — not the case here. You're left with Choice (E), which places the military service before the political.

2. **A.** The original sentence has everything it needs: good verb tense, proper number (a plural verb matched with a plural subject), and no extra words. Yup, this one's correct as is.

3. **B.** Some of the questions on the PSAT/NMSQT address basic speech and writing patterns, the sort of patterns that can be tricky for those learning English as a second language. Question 3 falls into this category. Why "from entering" and not "to enter"? Mostly custom: You're barred *from* the cafeteria after you fling pudding at the most annoying teacher, and you're not *to enter* the science lab until that dense purple cloud *dissipates* (scatters).

4. **C.** The *-self* pronouns (myself, himself, herself, and so on) should show up in your sentence only when the action doubles back, as in, "I told myself that I'd ace the exam," or when you want to emphasize a point ("Mary herself wrote the speech, with no help from her advisors"). In this sentence, "herself" is unnecessary. The simplest fix, Choice (C), gets the job done.

5. **E.** The original sentence glues two complete thoughts together with a comma. Penalty box! A semicolon or a ***conjunction*** (a joining word) can do the job, but Choices (B) and (D) introduce shades of meaning that don't appear in the original sentence. Choice (C) is possible, but "and" just strings the two thoughts together. Choice (E) is better because it uses "which" to link the casts and the artists with a minimum of fuss.

The PSAT/NMSQT writing section tests more than grammar. Style counts also! If you have two grammatically correct responses, choose the one that flows smoothly and ***conveys*** (transmits) the right meaning.

6. **B.** The pronoun "anyone" is singular, so any pronoun that refers to it must also be singular. In the original sentence, "they" is plural. Mismatch! You can change "they" to "he or she," but none of the choices allow that option. Choices (B) and (D) dump the pronouns entirely, but Choice (D) introduces a different (and wrong) tense. Choice (B) is perfect.

7. **B.** This question tests your knowledge of what grammarians call "condition-contrary-to-fact." In this sort of sentence, one portion expresses something that didn't happen or doesn't exist. The other explains the consequences that would result if the event *had* happened or the state of being *had* existed. The untrue part of the sentence *never* includes the word "would." Never. Ever. To express what didn't happen or doesn't exist, use the subjunctive form of the verb, a fancy term for "had" added to an action verb or "were" for states of being.

8. **D.** The Chimpanzee Project (not a real organization) is singular. (Did you notice that this organization is paired with a singular verb, "cares"?) You can't pair singular and plural in Grammar World, so anything with "their" or "they" is automatically out, because those pronouns are plural. Only Choices (D) and (E) avoid plural pronouns, but Choice (D) gets the job done without extra words and thus is the better answer.

9. **A.** The original sentence correctly describes Machu Picchu with a participle, "surrounded." (Don't worry about the grammar lingo; a ***participle*** is simply a verb form that may be used as a description.) The second verb is in present-perfect tense, which joins an action from the past to the present. Because the valleys were and still are being cultivated, present-perfect tense is, well, perfect in this sentence.

10. **C.** The subject of this sentence is "Mars," a singular noun that must be paired with a singular verb, "is." The prepositional phrase "like several others" *appears* to make the subject plural, but don't be fooled. It's just a distraction.

11. **D.** The original sentence has a pronoun, "it," with no real antecedent. (An ***antecedent*** is the word the pronoun refers to.) Dumping the "it" leaves Choices (D) and (E) as possible answers, but Choice (D) is more concise and therefore better.

12. **A.** The original sentence has everything it needs: a subject ("capital city") and a matching verb ("displays"). The underlined portion is an ***appositive*** (grammar-speak for a word that acts as the equivalent of another word in the sentence). Choice (A) is your answer.

13. **D.** The problem with the original sentence is that you have two males, George and his father, and some pronouns that are ***ambiguous*** (having two possible meanings). Who is in the Olympics? Probably George, because he's younger, but these days you never know. Even older people are star athletes! Choice (D) ***clarifies*** (makes clear) all the pronouns and is the best answer.

14. **E.** The original sentence isn't actually a sentence because it doesn't contain a complete thought. The "which" introduces a description, and no verb is paired with the subject, "feathers." Omit the "which" and "are" now pairs with the subject. Problem solved, and Choice (E) is correct.

15. **B.** In this sentence the key word is the pronoun "that." Before you can choose a verb to pair with "that," you have to decide whether the pronoun is singular or plural. To do so, use your reading comprehension skills. The statement beginning with "that" (a clause, in grammar terminology) talks about recognition as a masterpiece of the Italian Renaissance. According to the sentence, how many of Michelangelo's works fall into the masterpiece categories — one or more than one? Clearly, more than one. So now you know that the pronoun "that" refers to "works," a plural noun. Because "works" is plural, "that" is plural also, and it needs a plural verb — "have been recognized." Choice (B) is correct.

Sentences with the pattern "the only one of the . . . " usually take a singular verb. Look back at Question 15. Suppose it read, ". . . the only one of his works." Now the pronoun "that" would refer to "one" (the statue of David) — a singular element that takes a singular verb such as "has."

16. **C.** Football, soccer — whatever you call it when tens of thousands of fans scream in support of their team — is clearly a sport. The original sentence, though, says that it's "more popular than any sport," an illogical statement because it implies that football *isn't* a sport. Insert "other" and you're all set. Choice (C) is correct.

17. **C.** Most **conjunctions** (joining words) — *and, but, nor, or,* and the like — fly solo. Occasionally conjunctions show up in pairs, as in this sentence, in which "both . . . and" form one link. Here's the deal with paired conjunctions: They have to link similar grammatical elements. In the original sentence you have one noun ("machinery") and one subject/verb combo ("employees worked"). Nope. Only Choice (C) links two nouns ("machinery" and "overtime"), so it's your answer.

18. **A.** The original sentence gets its message across **concisely** (without extra words) and clearly. No problems, so Choice (A) is correct.

19. **C.** "Lie" and "lay" are such annoying verbs that you probably need to lie down after you puzzle out this sentence. First, the difference between the two verbs. "To lie" is "to occupy a position" (or, in another sort of sentence, "to rest or recline"). "To lay" is "to place something in a position." Now that you know the definitions, check out the sentence. The Grand Banks "lie," because they occupy territory near the coast. Before I send you on to the next question, though, I should mention that these devilish verbs have another complication: The past tense of "to lie" is "lay." (See what I mean about having to lie down after figuring out the answer?) The Grand Banks haven't left their position, so past tense isn't an issue. Go for "lie," as Choice (C) is the proper one.

20. **C.** If you see a list, "say" it aloud in your head. (Not with your voice! Then the proctor will send you away!) You should hear matching items, because proper English calls for parallel structure, the idea that everything in a list should have the same grammatical identity. Only Choice (C) fills that role, because "order," "decorate," and "choose" match. You probably noticed that Choice (B) is nearly the same as Choice (C). The difference matters, though. In Choice (B), the first and third items have "to" in front, and the second doesn't. Nope! In Choice (C), the first "to" works as an introduction for all the other items, so you're fine.

21. **A.** "Easy" is an adjective, and by the rules of grammar (carved in stone on my front door), adjectives may describe only nouns or pronouns. Here you need "easily," an adverb, to describe the verb "may confuse."

22. **C.** The paired conjunctions "not only . . . but also" must link similar grammatical elements. After "not only" you have a noun ("paintings"), but after "but also" you have a subject/verb combo ("they have studied"). One of those two has to change, so go for the one that's underlined, Choice (C).

23. **D.** The preposition "to" needs an object, and in this sentence it has two: "actress" and "he." However, "he" is a subject pronoun, not an object pronoun. The correct version is "to the actress and him."

24. **D.** A "person" is singular, and "their" is plural. Singular and plural don't play well together in Grammar Land. Change "their" to "his or her" and you've solved the problem.

25. **C.** You (and anyone or anything) can be "equal to" but not "equal as."

26. **E.** It's fitting, isn't it, that a sentence about an error doesn't actually have an error? This one's fine.

27. **E.** Everything works here — verb tense, subject-verb agreement, and all the elements of a good sentence. Choice (E) is your answer.

28. **A.** The pronoun "whom" works as an object, but in this sentence you need a subject for the verb "is," so "who" is the proper word, not "whom."

29. **A.** The introductory verb form must, in proper English, describe the subject of the sentence, which in this case is "child." Common sense tells you that the kite is soaring, not the kid, so Choice (A) is wrong.

30. **C.** The sentence begins in past tense (traveled), but "jumps" is a present-tense verb. Because you have no reason to change tenses, Choice (C) is wrong. The proper verb is "jumped," to match "traveled."

31. **B.** The adjective "slow" isn't a good descriptor for the verb "walks." You need the adverb, "slowly."

32. **A.** The council didn't object to "him." They objected to "his getting an award." The possessive pronoun "his" places the emphasis on "getting an award," where it belongs.

33. **E.** Everything is in order here — singulars and plurals are properly sorted out, the comparison works, and the verb tense is correct. No error!

34. **D.** The comparative form is "quicker," not "more quicker."

35. **C.** To combine sentences, look for concise connections of ideas. Choice (C) does the job in very few words.

36. **C.** Paragraph 2 is all about numbers — when whales were **_abundant_** (plentiful) and when their population decreased because of hunting. However, the paragraph contains no numbers at all! To show the rise and fall (and, I hope, the rise again after the treaty) of the blue whale, you need statistics.

37. **C.** The first sentence of a paragraph is usually a good spot for a **_transition_** (a movement from one subject to another). Paragraph 2 discusses the hunting of whales, and Paragraph 3 deals with the whales' food supply. Choice (C) connects these ideas and therefore serves as a bridge between one topic and another.

38. **E.** Sentence 13 links two ideas with "and." The sentence is grammatically correct, but "and" doesn't add much to the ideas in the sentence. Choice (E) introduces the "yes, but" pattern that **_concedes_** (gives in on) an idea while still introducing an objection.

39. **D.** The last paragraph generally isn't the best place to introduce new information. Instead, it can sum up the argument you've made earlier in your essay. The original Sentence 15 moves from whales to all animals. I have no objection to protecting all animals (with the possible exception of creepy-crawlies), but such a general statement tacked onto an essay about whales is out of place. Choice (D) broadens the scope of the essay while still keeping the focus on whales.

Answer Key for Practice Test 3

Section 1

1. E	7. E	13. E	19. D
2. B	8. A	14. C	20. C
3. C	9. C	15. B	21. C
4. A	10. C	16. A	22. D
5. D	11. A	17. C	23. A
6. B	12. B	18. B	24. B

Section 2

1. D	6. C	11. D	16. D
2. A	7. B	12. A	17. B
3. B	8. D	13. D	18. C
4. B	9. C	14. E	19. A
5. C	10. A	15. C	20. B

Section 3

25. D	31. B	37. E	43. A
26. E	32. D	38. D	44. B
27. D	33. D	39. C	45. C
28. A	34. D	40. D	46. D
29. E	35. A	41. D	47. C
30. D	36. B	42. A	48. E

Section 4

21. B	26. A	31. **9**	36. **20**
22. C	27. D	32. **42.5**	37. **35**
23. D	28. C	33. **30**	38. **1**
24. A	29. **9**	34. **65**	
25. D	30. **21**	35. **⅜**	

Section 5

1. **E**	11. **D**	21. **A**	31. **B**
2. **A**	12. **A**	22. **C**	32. **A**
3. **B**	13. **D**	23. **D**	33. **E**
4. **C**	14. **E**	24. **D**	34. **D**
5. **E**	15. **B**	25. **C**	35. **C**
6. **B**	16. **C**	26. **E**	36. **C**
7. **B**	17. **C**	27. **E**	37. **C**
8. **D**	18. **A**	28. **A**	38. **E**
9. **A**	19. **C**	29. **A**	39. **D**
10. **C**	20. **C**	30. **C**	

Chapter 17

Practice Test 4

. . . .

Did you know that a tiny plant, the four-leaf clover, is supposed to bring good luck? Consider this practice test, your fourth if you're working through them in order, as your own four-leaf clover, because by the time you finish taking this test, you'll have the skills to ace the exam, even if you arrive at the testing center after walking under a ladder, spilling salt, crossing paths with a black cat . . . whatever brings bad luck! (If you're not doing the exams in order, turn back to Chapter 11 and read the general directions before you begin this test.)

If this *is* your fourth practice exam, don't forget to analyze your performance on the other tests before beginning this one. As always, review any unfamiliar concepts by turning to Parts II and III, where I explain reading, writing, and math concepts.

When you're done, check your answers with the key in Chapter 18. Read the explanations for all the questions, not just those accompanying the ones you missed. I placed tips and vocabulary builders with the answers, so you may learn something by reviewing questions you answered correctly.

Answer Sheet

For the questions in Sections 1 through 5, use the ovals and grid-ins to record your answers.

Section 1: Critical Reading

1. Ⓐ Ⓑ Ⓒ Ⓓ Ⓔ
2. Ⓐ Ⓑ Ⓒ Ⓓ Ⓔ
3. Ⓐ Ⓑ Ⓒ Ⓓ Ⓔ
4. Ⓐ Ⓑ Ⓒ Ⓓ Ⓔ
5. Ⓐ Ⓑ Ⓒ Ⓓ Ⓔ
6. Ⓐ Ⓑ Ⓒ Ⓓ Ⓔ

7. Ⓐ Ⓑ Ⓒ Ⓓ Ⓔ
8. Ⓐ Ⓑ Ⓒ Ⓓ Ⓔ
9. Ⓐ Ⓑ Ⓒ Ⓓ Ⓔ
10. Ⓐ Ⓑ Ⓒ Ⓓ Ⓔ
11. Ⓐ Ⓑ Ⓒ Ⓓ Ⓔ
12. Ⓐ Ⓑ Ⓒ Ⓓ Ⓔ

13. Ⓐ Ⓑ Ⓒ Ⓓ Ⓔ
14. Ⓐ Ⓑ Ⓒ Ⓓ Ⓔ
15. Ⓐ Ⓑ Ⓒ Ⓓ Ⓔ
16. Ⓐ Ⓑ Ⓒ Ⓓ Ⓔ
17. Ⓐ Ⓑ Ⓒ Ⓓ Ⓔ
18. Ⓐ Ⓑ Ⓒ Ⓓ Ⓔ

19. Ⓐ Ⓑ Ⓒ Ⓓ Ⓔ
20. Ⓐ Ⓑ Ⓒ Ⓓ Ⓔ
21. Ⓐ Ⓑ Ⓒ Ⓓ Ⓔ
22. Ⓐ Ⓑ Ⓒ Ⓓ Ⓔ
23. Ⓐ Ⓑ Ⓒ Ⓓ Ⓔ
24. Ⓐ Ⓑ Ⓒ Ⓓ Ⓔ

Section 2: Mathematics

1. Ⓐ Ⓑ Ⓒ Ⓓ Ⓔ
2. Ⓐ Ⓑ Ⓒ Ⓓ Ⓔ
3. Ⓐ Ⓑ Ⓒ Ⓓ Ⓔ
4. Ⓐ Ⓑ Ⓒ Ⓓ Ⓔ
5. Ⓐ Ⓑ Ⓒ Ⓓ Ⓔ

6. Ⓐ Ⓑ Ⓒ Ⓓ Ⓔ
7. Ⓐ Ⓑ Ⓒ Ⓓ Ⓔ
8. Ⓐ Ⓑ Ⓒ Ⓓ Ⓔ
9. Ⓐ Ⓑ Ⓒ Ⓓ Ⓔ
10. Ⓐ Ⓑ Ⓒ Ⓓ Ⓔ

11. Ⓐ Ⓑ Ⓒ Ⓓ Ⓔ
12. Ⓐ Ⓑ Ⓒ Ⓓ Ⓔ
13. Ⓐ Ⓑ Ⓒ Ⓓ Ⓔ
14. Ⓐ Ⓑ Ⓒ Ⓓ Ⓔ
15. Ⓐ Ⓑ Ⓒ Ⓓ Ⓔ

16. Ⓐ Ⓑ Ⓒ Ⓓ Ⓔ
17. Ⓐ Ⓑ Ⓒ Ⓓ Ⓔ
18. Ⓐ Ⓑ Ⓒ Ⓓ Ⓔ
19. Ⓐ Ⓑ Ⓒ Ⓓ Ⓔ
20. Ⓐ Ⓑ Ⓒ Ⓓ Ⓔ

Section 3: Critical Reading

25. Ⓐ Ⓑ Ⓒ Ⓓ Ⓔ
26. Ⓐ Ⓑ Ⓒ Ⓓ Ⓔ
27. Ⓐ Ⓑ Ⓒ Ⓓ Ⓔ
28. Ⓐ Ⓑ Ⓒ Ⓓ Ⓔ
29. Ⓐ Ⓑ Ⓒ Ⓓ Ⓔ
30. Ⓐ Ⓑ Ⓒ Ⓓ Ⓔ

31. Ⓐ Ⓑ Ⓒ Ⓓ Ⓔ
32. Ⓐ Ⓑ Ⓒ Ⓓ Ⓔ
33. Ⓐ Ⓑ Ⓒ Ⓓ Ⓔ
34. Ⓐ Ⓑ Ⓒ Ⓓ Ⓔ
35. Ⓐ Ⓑ Ⓒ Ⓓ Ⓔ
36. Ⓐ Ⓑ Ⓒ Ⓓ Ⓔ

37. Ⓐ Ⓑ Ⓒ Ⓓ Ⓔ
38. Ⓐ Ⓑ Ⓒ Ⓓ Ⓔ
39. Ⓐ Ⓑ Ⓒ Ⓓ Ⓔ
40. Ⓐ Ⓑ Ⓒ Ⓓ Ⓔ
41. Ⓐ Ⓑ Ⓒ Ⓓ Ⓔ
42. Ⓐ Ⓑ Ⓒ Ⓓ Ⓔ

43. Ⓐ Ⓑ Ⓒ Ⓓ Ⓔ
44. Ⓐ Ⓑ Ⓒ Ⓓ Ⓔ
45. Ⓐ Ⓑ Ⓒ Ⓓ Ⓔ
46. Ⓐ Ⓑ Ⓒ Ⓓ Ⓔ
47. Ⓐ Ⓑ Ⓒ Ⓓ Ⓔ
48. Ⓐ Ⓑ Ⓒ Ⓓ Ⓔ

Section 4: Mathematics

21. Ⓐ Ⓑ Ⓒ Ⓓ Ⓔ   25. Ⓐ Ⓑ Ⓒ Ⓓ Ⓔ
22. Ⓐ Ⓑ Ⓒ Ⓓ Ⓔ   26. Ⓐ Ⓑ Ⓒ Ⓓ Ⓔ
23. Ⓐ Ⓑ Ⓒ Ⓓ Ⓔ   27. Ⓐ Ⓑ Ⓒ Ⓓ Ⓔ
24. Ⓐ Ⓑ Ⓒ Ⓓ Ⓔ   28. Ⓐ Ⓑ Ⓒ Ⓓ Ⓔ

29.   30.   31.   32.   33.

34.   35.   36.   37.   38.

Section 5: Writing

1. Ⓐ Ⓑ Ⓒ Ⓓ Ⓔ   9. Ⓐ Ⓑ Ⓒ Ⓓ Ⓔ   17. Ⓐ Ⓑ Ⓒ Ⓓ Ⓔ   25. Ⓐ Ⓑ Ⓒ Ⓓ Ⓔ   33. Ⓐ Ⓑ Ⓒ Ⓓ Ⓔ
2. Ⓐ Ⓑ Ⓒ Ⓓ Ⓔ   10. Ⓐ Ⓑ Ⓒ Ⓓ Ⓔ   18. Ⓐ Ⓑ Ⓒ Ⓓ Ⓔ   26. Ⓐ Ⓑ Ⓒ Ⓓ Ⓔ   34. Ⓐ Ⓑ Ⓒ Ⓓ Ⓔ
3. Ⓐ Ⓑ Ⓒ Ⓓ Ⓔ   11. Ⓐ Ⓑ Ⓒ Ⓓ Ⓔ   19. Ⓐ Ⓑ Ⓒ Ⓓ Ⓔ   27. Ⓐ Ⓑ Ⓒ Ⓓ Ⓔ   35. Ⓐ Ⓑ Ⓒ Ⓓ Ⓔ
4. Ⓐ Ⓑ Ⓒ Ⓓ Ⓔ   12. Ⓐ Ⓑ Ⓒ Ⓓ Ⓔ   20. Ⓐ Ⓑ Ⓒ Ⓓ Ⓔ   28. Ⓐ Ⓑ Ⓒ Ⓓ Ⓔ   36. Ⓐ Ⓑ Ⓒ Ⓓ Ⓔ
5. Ⓐ Ⓑ Ⓒ Ⓓ Ⓔ   13. Ⓐ Ⓑ Ⓒ Ⓓ Ⓔ   21. Ⓐ Ⓑ Ⓒ Ⓓ Ⓔ   29. Ⓐ Ⓑ Ⓒ Ⓓ Ⓔ   37. Ⓐ Ⓑ Ⓒ Ⓓ Ⓔ
6. Ⓐ Ⓑ Ⓒ Ⓓ Ⓔ   14. Ⓐ Ⓑ Ⓒ Ⓓ Ⓔ   22. Ⓐ Ⓑ Ⓒ Ⓓ Ⓔ   30. Ⓐ Ⓑ Ⓒ Ⓓ Ⓔ   38. Ⓐ Ⓑ Ⓒ Ⓓ Ⓔ
7. Ⓐ Ⓑ Ⓒ Ⓓ Ⓔ   15. Ⓐ Ⓑ Ⓒ Ⓓ Ⓔ   23. Ⓐ Ⓑ Ⓒ Ⓓ Ⓔ   31. Ⓐ Ⓑ Ⓒ Ⓓ Ⓔ   39. Ⓐ Ⓑ Ⓒ Ⓓ Ⓔ
8. Ⓐ Ⓑ Ⓒ Ⓓ Ⓔ   16. Ⓐ Ⓑ Ⓒ Ⓓ Ⓔ   24. Ⓐ Ⓑ Ⓒ Ⓓ Ⓔ   32. Ⓐ Ⓑ Ⓒ Ⓓ Ⓔ

Section 1

Critical Reading

Time: 25 minutes for 24 questions

Directions: Choose the *best* answer to each question. Mark the corresponding oval on your answer sheet.

Directions for Questions 1–8: Choose the word or words that best fit the meaning of each sentence.

Example: After work, Edith always _____ home as quickly as possible.

(A) rambled

(B) wandered

(C) avoided

(D) meandered

(E) ran

The answer is Choice (E).

1. Madeline wanted to _____ from her social duties, but, bound by etiquette, she _____ the unexpected guests.

    (A) retreat . . . welcomed

    (B) rest . . . rejected

    (C) withdraw . . . spurned

    (D) recoil . . . identified

    (E) shrink . . . delegated

2. The _____ of the photograph gave viewers a chance to examine the smallest details of the scene.

    (A) mystery

    (B) rigor

    (C) capacity

    (D) opacity

    (E) clarity

3. Although she had just joined the club, Miranda refused to be _____ and commented frequently during the meeting instead of simply listening to the older students' ideas.

    (A) trivialized

    (B) convinced

    (C) marginalized

    (D) compared

    (E) acknowledged

4. By taking the speaker's words out of context, the reporter _____ the message and gave a false impression of the speaker's position.

    (A) identified

    (B) mischaracterized

    (C) recognized

    (D) examined

    (E) asserted

5. Jeff was not uninterested, but his schedule was so busy that he could participate only _____.

    (A) continuously

    (B) capriciously

    (C) surreptitiously

    (D) sporadically

    (E) constantly

Go on to next page

6. _____ in a tight situation, the spy quickly _____ an explanation for being in a private area.

    (A) Credible . . . imagined

    (B) Resourceful . . . fabricated

    (C) Empathetic . . . renounced

    (D) Flagrant . . . exonerated

    (E) Overt . . . indicted

7. _____ swords, the fencers faced each other and prepared to fight.

    (A) Relinquishing

    (B) Brandishing

    (C) Distending

    (D) Opposing

    (E) Requiring

8. After _____ research, the doctor published a paper that no one could _____.

    (A) exhaustive . . . refute

    (B) scanty . . . misunderstand

    (C) diligent . . . respect

    (D) required . . . quell

    (E) laudatory . . . confuse

Directions for Questions 9–12: Read these passages and answer the questions that follow each passage based on what is stated or implied in the passage.

Questions 9 and 10 are based on the following passage, excerpted from Social Media Marketing, _by Dave Evans (Wiley)._

Line The arrival of spam[1] — _on a communications channel that recipients had control over_ — shattered a peaceful coexistence that had been in place for 30 years. Viewers had accepted
(05) commercial interruptions more or less without complaint as the "price" they had to pay for free TV (and amazingly, but to a lesser extent, on for-pay cable stations as well). Even if they objected, short of changing channels there was little they
(10) could do. The Internet, and in particular an e-mail inbox, was different. First, it was "my" inbox and I presumably had the "right" to decide

what landed in it. Second, spam, unlike TV ads, could actually clog my mailbox, slow down the Net, and generally degrade "my" experience. (15) People took offense to that on a _collective_ scale. Spam had awakened a giant, and that giant has been pushing back on intrusive ads ever since.

1. Unasked for e-mail, often to sell a product.

9. In Line 6, "price" is placed in quotation marks probably because

    (A) the author doesn't like TV commercials

    (B) the author is quoting an expert on marketing

    (C) TV viewers don't pay money for free TV

    (D) cable TV has changed the pricing system of commercials

    (E) commercials are very expensive for advertisers

10. In the context of the passage, what is the most likely definition of "a giant" (Line 17)?

    (A) unified opposition

    (B) an Internet site

    (C) a large advertising firm

    (D) an influential computer programmer

    (E) TV viewers

Questions 11 and 12 are based on the following passage, excerpted from The Natural History of Cage Birds.

Line An artificial song is one borrowed from a bird that the young ones have heard singing in the room. Nearly all birds, when young, will learn some strains or airs whistled or played to them regularly every day; but only those whose (05) memory is capable of retaining these will abandon their natural song, and adopt fluently the air that has been taught them. Thus, a young goldfinch learns, it is true, some part of the melody sung by a bullfinch, but the goldfinch will never (10) be able to repeat it as perfectly, a difference not caused by the bird's anatomy, but rather by the superiority of memory in one species over that of the other.

Go on to next page

11. In the context of this passage, what is the best definition of "airs" (Line 4)?

    (A) breezes

    (B) behavior

    (C) stresses

    (D) songs

    (E) musical instruments

12. According to the passage, which of the following statements, if any, are true?

    I.   Birdsong may be learned.

    II. Birdsong is an inherited characteristic.

    III. Birds can't learn songs that don't suit their body's structure.

    (A) I only

    (B) I and II

    (C) II and III

    (D) I, II, and III

    (E) none of the above

Directions for Questions 13–24: Read these passages and answer the questions that follow based on what is stated or implied.

The first passage is an excerpt from Social Psychology, *by Catherine A. Sanderson (Wiley). The second is an editorial.*

Passage 1

Line   Another factor that can lead to stereotyping is perceptual confirmation, meaning the tendency to see things in line with one's expectations. Perceptual confirmation occurs in part
(05) because we interpret ambiguous information as supporting our stereotypes, and therefore see the same behavior in a very different way depending on our expectations. Perceptual confirmation leads people to see mental patients'
(10) behavior as abnormal, view other athletic teams as more unfairly aggressive than their own, and underestimate 11-month-old girl infants' crawling ability and overestimate such behavior in boys.

Because stereotypes lead people to recall
(15) certain information about a person that is consistent with their expectations, they interpret (Line) and encode that information in distinct (stereotypical) ways. In one study, all participants saw a video about a child, Hannah, who was from either a poor background or a rich background. Half of (20) the participants were also given additional information by watching her answer a series of academic problems in an inconsistent way (she got some right and some wrong). Then all participants rated Hannah's academic ability. Although (25) those who did not watch Hannah's academic performance seemed reluctant to judge her ability simply on the basis of her socioeconomic status, those who saw the video of her academic performance readily judged her ability, even though the (30) video provided ambiguous information. Specifically, those with negative expectations (those who thought Hannah was poor), rated her lower on work habits, motivation, and cognitive skills than those who had not seen the video. (35) Those with positive expectations (those who thought Hannah was rich) rated Hannah somewhat higher if they had seen the video. In this case, stereotypes did not have a direct effect on performance expectations, but clearly made sub- (40) jects more willing to see irrelevant information to interpret behavior in line with their stereotype.

We also require fewer examples to confirm our beliefs about a trait that is highly stereotypical of a person in a given group. For example, if a (45) young person misplaces his or her keys, we assume that the person is just being forgetful. But if an older person misplaces his or her keys, we assume that person may be experiencing serious memory loss. (50)

Similarly, confirmation bias describes the tendency to search for information that supports one's initial view. When people have expectations about a particular person, they address few questions to that person and hence acquire rela- (55) tively little information that could disprove their assumptions. People may also ask questions designed to confirm their expectations, which prevents them from obtaining and using disconfirming information. So, if you are meeting a (60) person from Canada for the first time, you might ask him about his love of ice hockey and cold weather, whereas if you are meeting a person from Mexico for the first time, you might ask him or her about his or her love of spicy food and (65) festive music.

Go on to next page

Passage II

Line   When I was called for jury duty recently,
I answered questions from attorneys on both
sides of several cases to see whether I was suit-
(70) able to serve. Some questions were obvious:
Did I know anyone involved in the case? Had I
been the victim of a similar crime? Other questions, though, seemed odd. Where did I get
information — from the radio, the newspaper,
(75) TV, the Internet? What sort of job did I hold? I
was never chosen for a jury, and I was never told
why I was "excused" from a particular case. I was
left wondering why my answers — I tend to read
news articles online, and I work for a major cor-
(80) poration — disqualified me in the eyes of one
side or the other. Which leads me to the next
logical question: Was I the object of stereotyping? Did one attorney assume that my age or
news source would guarantee a verdict against
(85) his client? If so, why was I bumped from two
nearly identical drug cases, first by the defense
and then by the prosecution?
       The same thoughts arise when I log onto a
website for a bit of shopping. The site conve-
(90) niently suggests that "I might like" other products, based on what customers with my
browsing or purchasing history bought. And
sometimes I actually do enjoy looking at these
suggestions, but then again, why would I want to
(95) have the same clothing or books or perfume as
everyone else in my category? And that's the
bottom line: I don't want to be in a category. I
want to be an individual. And I am not alone,
either. A major clothing chain recently experi-
(100) mented with personalized marketing. Women
who logged on were shown only women's clothing. Surprisingly, many women were annoyed;
they wanted to see men's clothing and other
gear. Sales dropped sharply until the website
(105) returned to its original configuration.
       Targeted marketing, as well as my jury expe-
rience, leads me to still another worry. Surveys
show that Americans increasingly live surrounded by people with similar political views
(110) and values. Moreover, a recent study found that
people listen more attentively to a speaker who
agrees with the listeners' opinions. We literally
tune out the opposition. To remain with one's
own group may be comforting, but I worry about
(115) the long-term effects on democracy. Isn't the
goal an exchange of ideas, not solely a reaffirmation? Don't we all benefit from being challenged
and, at the very least, having to defend our
ideas? Yet the soft cloud of sameness wafts
(120) around us, even as we insist on our uniqueness.

13. According to Passage I, which statement
about expectations is true?

(A) Expectations can never be confirmed.

(B) People interpret all behavior in a way
that confirms their expectations.

(C) Expectations may distort one's percep-
tion of events.

(D) Expectations have no effect on
behavior.

(E) People are unaware of their own
expectations.

14. The "we" in Passage I is most likely

(A) scientists

(B) readers

(C) the writer and her sources

(D) young people

(E) all human beings

15. The author of Passage I includes references
to mental patients, sports participants, and
male or female infants (Lines 9–12) because
those groups

(A) are commonly subject to stereotypes

(B) have been studied extensively

(C) include a broad range of expectations

(D) are familiar to everyone

(E) frequently need counseling

16. In Passage I, the reference to infants' ability
to crawl (Lines 12–13) implies that

(A) most people know very little about
infants' ability to crawl

(B) male infants crawl more skillfully than
female infants of the same age

(C) crawling ability is gender-related

(D) female infants are often seen as less
athletic

(E) female infants crawl more than male
infants

Go on to next page

17. According to Passage I, which group would rate Hannah's academic ability the highest?

    (A) those who thought she was wealthy but did not see the video

    (B) those who thought she was wealthy and saw the video

    (C) those who thought she was poor but did not see the video

    (D) those who thought she was poor and saw the video

    (E) those who were acquainted with Hannah

18. The author of Passage I implies that socio-economic status

    (A) is related to academic ability

    (B) is not related to academic ability

    (C) has no relation to academic ability

    (D) is subject to stereotyping

    (E) can't be determined without seeing a video

19. In the context of Line 77 in Passage II, which of the following best defines "excused"?

    (A) released from obligation

    (B) pardoned

    (C) immune to prosecution

    (D) denied bail

    (E) exonerated

20. In Passage II, the "identical drug cases" (Line 86) serve to

    (A) show how juries function

    (B) illustrate the inaccuracy of stereotyping

    (C) highlight problems with the judicial system

    (D) emphasize that defense attorneys and prosecutors ask inappropriate questions

    (E) reveal the nature of bias

21. Passage II implies that personalized marketing is unsuccessful because

    (A) some women wear men's clothing

    (B) women and men shop together

    (C) women resent being narrowly defined

    (D) sales rise when women shop

    (E) retailers don't understand women

22. With which statement would the author of Passage II most likely agree?

    (A) Challenging others' views is impolite.

    (B) Listening to opposing views is helpful.

    (C) Neighborhoods should be comfortable places.

    (D) Americans should move more often.

    (E) Americans should talk about their political views and values.

23. The "soft cloud of sameness" (Line 119) in Passage II is an example of

    (A) simile

    (B) metaphor

    (C) personification

    (D) symbolism

    (E) understatement

24. With which statement would the authors of Passage I and Passage II probably agree?

    (A) Stereotypes are prevalent.

    (B) Lacking solid information, people tend to apply stereotypes.

    (C) People seek greater understanding of one another.

    (D) Living with people who share your views is comforting.

    (E) Diversity of viewpoints is important.

STOP YOU MAY CHECK YOUR WORK ON THIS SECTION ONLY. DO NOT GO BACK TO ANY PREVIOUS SECTION.

Section 2

Mathematics

Time: 25 minutes for 20 questions

Directions: Find the correct answer to each question and mark the corresponding oval on the answer sheet.

Notes:

- ✔ You may use a calculator.
- ✔ All numbers used in this exam are real numbers.
- ✔ All figures lie in a plane.
- ✔ You may assume that all figures are to scale unless the problem specifically indicates otherwise.

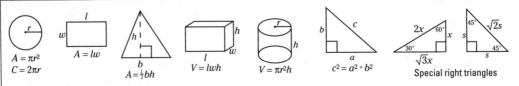

$A = \pi r^2$
$C = 2\pi r$

$A = lw$

$A = \frac{1}{2}bh$

$V = lwh$

$V = \pi r^2 h$

$c^2 = a^2 + b^2$

Special right triangles

There are 360 degrees of arc in a circle.

There are 180 degrees in a straight line.

There are 180 degrees in the sum of the interior angles of a triangle.

1. The expression $2 + 5^2 - (3 - 4)$ equals

    (A) 18

    (B) 20

    (C) 21

    (D) 26

    (E) 28

2. Which line is perpendicular to $\frac{y}{2} + 3 = x - 4$?

    (A) $y = -2x - 5$

    (B) $y = -\frac{1}{2}x + 1$

    (C) $y = \frac{1}{2}x + 6$

    (D) $y = 2x - 4$

    (E) $y = 4x + 3$

Go on to next page

3. Set P contains all multiples of 2, and set Q contains all multiples of 3. Which of the sets described represents the intersection of P and Q?

   (A) all positive integers

   (B) all multiples of 2

   (C) all multiples of 3

   (D) all multiples of 5

   (E) all multiples of 6

5. Jen has 3 times as many shirts as pairs of pants, 5 fewer dresses than shirts, and 6 hats. If x represents the number of pairs of pants that Jen has, write an expression that represents the total number of shirts, pants, dresses, and hats that Jen has.

   (A) $5x + 1$

   (B) $7x + 1$

   (C) $8x - 4$

   (D) $11x - 11$

   (E) $13x + 1$

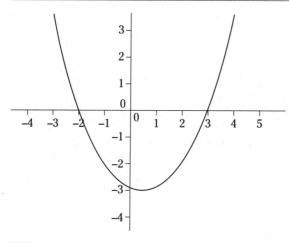

6. Which of the following is not equivalent to $2\sqrt{20}$?

   (A) $\sqrt{2} \times \sqrt{40}$

   (B) $\sqrt{2} \times \sqrt{40}$

   (C) $\sqrt{80}$

   (D) $4\sqrt{5}$

   (E) $8\sqrt{5}$

4. $f(x)$ is shown in this figure. What is the solution to $f(x) \le 0$?

   (A) $x < -2$ or $x > 3$

   (B) $x \le -2$ or $x \ge 3$

   (C) $-2 < x < 3$

   (D) $-2 \le x \le 3$

   (E) $x < 3$

7. Solve for x: $\dfrac{3x+2}{x+2} = \dfrac{1}{3}$

   (A) $x = -2$

   (B) $x = -1$

   (C) $x = -\dfrac{1}{2}$

   (D) $x = \dfrac{1}{2}$

   (E) $x = 2$

Go on to next page

8. If o is an odd number and e is an even number, then $o^2 - e^2$ must be

   I.   odd

   II. even

   III. prime

   (A) I only

   (B) II only

   (C) III only

   (D) I and III only

   (E) none of the above

9. How many miles should Joe run on Friday if he wants his median run for the 5-day period to be 10 miles?

   (A) 9

   (B) 11

   (C) 13

   (D) 15

   (E) 17

10. How many miles should Joe run on Friday if he wants his average (arithmetic mean) distance over the 5 days to be 12 miles?

    (A) 8

    (B) 10

    (C) 12

    (D) 14

    (E) 16

Questions 9 and 10 both refer to the following figure, a chart that represents how many miles Joe ran during the first four days of the week.

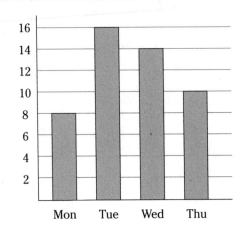

Go on to next page

B C

$4\sqrt{2}$

A D

11. In this square, what is the area of triangle *ABC?*

(A) 4

(B) 6

(C) 8

(D) $8\sqrt{2}$

(E) 16

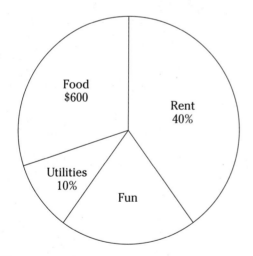

Monthly Spending

Food $600

Rent 40%

Utilities 10%

Fun

12. Jim's monthly spending is shown in this chart. If Jim spends 30% of his money on food, how much money does he spend on fun?

(A) $200

(B) $400

(C) $500

(D) $1,000

(E) $2,000

13. If $x = 7a$, $y = -5a$, and $3x + 5y = 6$, what does *a* equal?

(A) –3

(B) –1.5

(C) 0.75

(D) 1

(E) 1.5

14. What is the equation of a line parallel to the line $y = 2x + 13$ that passes through the point $(a, 7)$?

(A) $y = 2x - 2a + 7$

(B) $y = 2x - 2a - 7$

(C) $y = 2x + 2a + 7$

(D) $y = 2x + a - 14$

(E) $y = 2x - a + 14$

15. A circular pond has 250 feet of shoreline. If the pond is 10 feet deep, what is the approximate volume of the lake, in cubic feet?

(A) 8,000

(B) 25,000

(C) 50,000

(D) 250,000

(E) 500,000

Go on to next page

16. $\dfrac{a^{2x} \cdot a^{x+4}}{a^x} =$

   (A) $\left(a^{x+2}\right)^2$

   (B) $\left(a^{x+4}\right)^2$

   (C) a^{2x+2}

   (D) $2a^{3x+4}$

   (E) $3a^{2x+4}$

17. Define $a \sim b$ so that $a \sim b = a^2b - ab^2$. Which expression is equivalent to $(x \sim y) - (y \sim x)$?

   (A) 0

   (B) $x^2y - xy^2$

   (C) $2x^2y - 2xy^2$

   (D) $2xy^2$

   (E) $2x^2y$

18. The ratio of eggs to lemons in a restaurant refrigerator is 7:2. A dozen eggs are added to the refrigerator, changing the ratio to 15:4. How many lemons are in the refrigerator?

   (A) 4

   (B) 12

   (C) 48

   (D) 60

   (E) 112

19. A car rental company charges a flat rate of $35.75 per day, and then an additional 5 cents for every mile driven. Which expression represents the cost of renting a car for 6 days and driving it for a total of m miles?

   (A) $35.75 + 0.05m$

   (B) $35.75 + 5m$

   (C) $143 + 0.5m$

   (D) $214.5 + 0.05m$

   (E) $214.5 + 5m$

20. A cylindrical water tower is 8 feet tall and has a radius of 5 feet. The water is currently 6 inches deep. If water is added to the water tower at a rate of 80 cubic feet per hour, in approximately how many hours will the tank be 75% full?

   (A) 5.2 hours

   (B) 5.4 hours

   (C) 5.6 hours

   (D) 5.8 hours

   (E) 6 hours

STOP YOU MAY CHECK YOUR WORK ON THIS SECTION ONLY. DO NOT GO BACK TO ANY PREVIOUS SECTION.

Section 3

Critical Reading

Time: 25 minutes for 24 questions

Directions: Choose the *best* answer to each question. Mark the corresponding oval on your answer sheet.

Directions for Questions 25–29: Choose the word or words that best fit the meaning of each sentence.

Example: After work, Edith always _____ home as quickly as possible.

(A) rambled

(B) wandered

(C) avoided

(D) meandered

(E) ran

The answer is Choice (E).

---

25. The failure of the laboratory's freezer _____ the specimens stored there.

    (A) eased

    (B) compromised

    (C) completed

    (D) erased

    (E) checked

26. Alex's enthusiasm for the outing _____ when he discovered that he had to pay double for tickets to the concert.

    (A) waned

    (B) waxed

    (C) increased

    (D) conflated

    (E) swelled

27. The drawing appeared ancient; however, its age could not be _____ even with the most advanced tests.

    (A) reconciled

    (B) ameliorated

    (C) pinpointed

    (D) induced

    (E) adjusted

28. Because Elizabeth is both _____ and _____, she has many friends and an active social life.

    (A) reclusive . . . introverted

    (B) erratic . . . indecisive

    (C) incompatible . . . disarming

    (D) antagonistic . . . energetic

    (E) affable . . . extroverted

29. The grieving crowd wept during the _____, a traditional song played during funerals in that region.

    (A) dearth

    (B) dirge

    (C) fallacy

    (D) vignette

    (E) eulogy

Go on to next page

Directions for Questions 30–33: Read these passages and answer the questions that follow based on what is stated or implied in the passages.

The first passage is an excerpt from A Chemical History Tour, *by Arthur Greenberg (Wiley). The second is a portion of* The Autobiography of Benjamin Franklin.

Passage 1

Line   Benjamin Wilson was appointed by the Duke of York to succeed William Hogarth as Sergeant-Painter in 1764. He speculated in stocks and was declared a defaulter on the Stock Exchange in
(05) 1766. During the 1740s he also developed an interest in electricity and later engaged in a highly charged public debate with Benjamin Franklin on the shape of lightning rods. (Wilson had painted a portrait of Franklin in 1759.)
(10) Franklin argued for a sharp point, and Wilson correctly argued for a rounded point that would not actually attract lightning. He won the debate but his arguments were so excessive that he was criticized for "shameful discord and dissensions"
(15) that continued for years "to the great detriment of science."

Passage II

    The publication of my paper offended an able experimenter, who had formed and published a theory of electricity, which then had
(20) general approval. He could not at first believe that such a work came from America, and said it must have been fabricated by his enemies in Paris. Afterwards he wrote and published a volume of Letters, chiefly addressed to me,
(25) defending his theory and denying the truthfulness of my experiments and of the positions deduced from them. I once purposed answering him, and actually began the answer; but, on consideration that my writings contained a descrip-
(30) tion of experiments which anyone might repeat and verify, and if not to be verified, could not be defended, I did not.

30. According to Passage I, what was the basis of the dispute between Wilson and Franklin?

(A) Wilson treated Franklin with disrespect.

(B) Wilson had painted a portrait of Franklin.

(C) Franklin and Wilson both studied lightning.

(D) Wilson favored a different design for lightning rods.

(E) Franklin won a debate with Wilson.

31. What is the most likely reason that the scientist described in Passage II "could not at first believe" (Line 20) that Franklin's paper was written by an American?

(A) The scientist assumed that the work was wrong.

(B) The scientist assumed that American scientific work differed from European scientific work.

(C) The scientist had many enemies.

(D) The paper offended the scientist.

(E) The scientist could not repeat the experiment.

32. According to Passage II, why didn't Franklin respond to the man who criticized his paper?

(A) Franklin was too offended.

(B) Franklin thought that the experiments could not be verified.

(C) The other scientist had great scientific ability.

(D) The experiment Franklin described could be tested by others.

(E) The other scientist had disproved Franklin's ideas.

33. Both Passage I and Passage II

(A) assume that scientific experiments are risky

(B) show that disagreement is part of science

(C) imply that scientists make enemies easily

(D) believe experiments can't be verified

(E) criticize the scientific method

Go on to next page

Directions for Questions 34–40: Read this passage and answer the questions that follow based on what is stated or implied in the passage.

This passage is an excerpt from Who Goes There? The Story of a Spy in the Civil War, *by B. K. Benson.*

Line

The feature most attractive to me in school work was the debating class. As a sort of *ex-officio* president of this club was one of our tutors, whom none of the boys seemed greatly to like.
(05) He was called Professor Khayme — pronounced Ki-me. Sometimes the principal addressed him as Doctor. He certainly was a very learned and intelligent man; for although the boys disliked him, there was much evidence of the respect he com-
(10) manded from better judges than schoolboys. He seemed, at various times, of different ages. He might be anywhere between thirty and fifty. He was small of stature, not more than five feet tall, and was exceedingly quick and energetic in his
(15) movements, while his face and attitude, no matter what was going on, expressed always complete self-control, if not indifference. I rarely saw him off duty without a peculiar black pipe in his mouth, which he smoked in an unusual way,
(20) emitting the smoke at very long intervals.

I became a frequent visitor at the Doctor's, and gradually learned more and more of this remarkable man. His little daughter told me much that I could never have guessed. She was a
(25) very serious child, perhaps of eleven years, and not very attractive. In fact, she was ugly, but her gravity seemed somehow to suit her that I could by no means dislike her. Her father was very fond of her; of an evening the three of us would
(30) sit in the west room; the Doctor would smoke and read; I would read some special material — usually on philosophy — selected by my tutor; Lydia would sit silently, engaged in sewing or knitting, and absorbed seemingly in her own
(35) thoughts. Lydia at one time said some words which I could not exactly catch, and which made me doubt the seeming poverty of her father, but I attributed her speech to the natural pride of a child who thinks its father great in every way. I
(40) was not greatly interested, moreover, in the

domestic affairs of the household, and never thought of asking for information that seemed withheld. I learned from the child's talk, at odd times when the Doctor would be absent from the
(45) room, that they were foreigners — a fact which I had already taken for granted — but I was never made to know the land of their birth. It was certain that Dr. Khayme could speak German and French, and I could frequently see him reading in
(50) books printed in characters unknown to me. Several times I have happened to come unexpectedly into the presence of the father and daughter when they were conversing in a language which I was sure I had never heard.

(55) The Doctor had no companions. He was at home or at school, or else on the way from the one to the other. No visitor ever showed himself when I was at the cottage. Lydia attended the convent school. I understood from remarks dropped
(60) incidentally, as well as from seeing the books she had, that she mainly studied languages, and I had strong evidence that, young as she was, her proficiency in French and German was excellent.

By degrees I learned that the Doctor was
(65) deeply interested in what we would call speculative philosophy. I say by degrees, for the experience I am now writing down embraces the winters of five or six years. Most of the books that composed his library concerned metaphys-
(70) ics, philosophy, and religion. I believe that in his collection could be found the Bible of every religious faith.

He seldom spoke of the past, but he seemed strangely interested in the political condition of
(75) every civilized nation. The future of the human race was a subject to which he undoubtedly gave much thought. I have heard him more than once declare, with emphasis, that the outlook for the advancement of America was not auspicious. In
(80) regard to the sectional discord in the United States, he showed a strange unconcern. I knew that he believed it a matter of indifference whether secession[1], of which we were beginning again to hear some mutterings, was a constitu-
(85) tional right; but on the question of slavery his interest was intense. He believed that slavery could not endure, whether secession be attempted or abandoned, whether secession fail or succeed.

1. Withdrawal from an organized group, in this case, the withdrawal by eleven states from the United States, which led to the Civil War.

Go on to next page ⟹

34. The narrator of this passage probably

    (A) believes that his classmates are immature

    (B) wants to become president of the debating club

    (C) opposes slavery

    (D) struggles with his schoolwork

    (E) lacks curiosity

35. Which of the following statements about Professor Khayme are true, if any, according to the passage?

    I. He is not a learned man.

    II. He is a strict teacher.

    III. He values privacy.

    (A) I only

    (B) II only

    (C) III only

    (D) I and II

    (E) I, II, and III

36. In the context of Line 27, which is the best meaning of "gravity"?

    (A) seriousness

    (B) force

    (C) heaviness

    (D) enormity

    (E) appearance

37. The narrator implies that Professor Khayme's home was

    (A) luxurious

    (B) ideal for social occasions

    (C) somewhat shabby

    (D) large

    (E) staffed by domestic servants

38. The narrator's relationship with Professor Khayme

    (A) was essential to the narrator's education

    (B) drew resentment from Lydia

    (C) was ruined by arguments about slavery

    (D) was interrupted by the Civil War

    (E) lasted several years

39. According to the passage, Professor Khayme's interests include all the following EXCEPT

    (A) religion

    (B) the issue of slavery

    (C) America's future

    (D) economics

    (E) philosophy

40. According to the passage, the professor's views on secession may be characterized as

    (A) indifferent

    (B) committed

    (C) antagonistic

    (D) controversial

    (E) undeveloped

Directions for Questions 41–48: Read this passage and answer the questions that follow based on what is stated or implied in the passage.

This passage is an excerpt from Frommer's Cape Cod, Nantucket & Martha's Vineyard, *by Laura M. Reckford (Wiley).*

Cape Cod is a curving peninsula only 70 miles long, encompassing hundreds of miles of beaches and more freshwater ponds than there are days in the year. The ocean's many moods rule this thin spit of land, and in summer it has a (05) very sunny disposition indeed. The arm of the Cape has beckoned wayfarers since pre-Colonial times. These days more than five million visitors flock from around the world to enjoy nature's nonstop carnival, a combination of torrid sun (10) and cool, salty air.

On the Cape, days have a way of unfurling aimlessly but pleasantly, with a round of inviolable rituals. First and foremost is a long, restful stint at the beach (you can opt for either the (15) warmer, gently lapping waters of Cape Cod Bay or the pounding Atlantic surf). The beach is generally followed by a stroll through the shops of the nearest town and an obligatory ice cream stop. After a desalinating shower and perhaps a (20)

Go on to next page

Line nap (the pristine air has a way of inspiring snoozes), it's time for a fabulous dinner. There are few experiences quite so blissful as sitting at the picnic table overlooking a bustling harbor
(25) and feasting on a just-caught, butter-dripping, boiled lobster.

Be forewarned, however, that the Cape can be a bit *too* popular at full swing. European settlers waited nearly three centuries to go splash-
(30) ing in the surf, but ever since Victorians donned their bathing costumes, there's been no stopping the waves of sun-, sand-, and sea-worshippers who pour onto this peninsula and the islands beyond every summer.
(35) Experienced travelers are beginning to discover the subtler appeal of the off-season, when the population and prices plummet. For some the prospect of sunbathing with the midsummer crowds on sizzling sand can't hold a candle to
(40) the chance to take long, solitary strolls on a windswept beach, with only the gulls as company. Come Labor Day (or Columbus Day, for stragglers) the crowds clear out, and the whole place hibernates until Memorial Day weekend,
(45) the official start of "the season." It's in this downtime that you're most likely to experience the "real" Cape. For some it may take a little resourcefulness to see the beauty in the wintry, shuttered landscape (even the Pilgrims, who for-
(50) sook this spot for Plymouth, didn't have quite the necessary mettle), but the people who do stick around are an interesting, independent-minded lot worth getting to know.

As alluring as it is on the surface, this region
(55) becomes all the more so as you become intimately acquainted with it. One visit is likely to prompt a follow-up. Although you can see all of the Cape, and the islands as well, in a matter of days, you could spend a lifetime exploring its
(60) facets and still just begin to take it all in. Early Pilgrims saw in this isolated spot an opportunity for religious freedom, whaling merchants the watery road to riches, and artists the path to capturing the brilliance of nature's palette.
(65) Whatever the incursions of commercialism and overdevelopment, the land is infused with spirit, and it attracts seekers still.

41. The intended readers of this passage are most likely

(A) residents of the area

(B) investors

(C) tourists

(D) whalers

(E) artists

42. In the context of Line 5, which of the following is the best definition of "spit"?

(A) saliva

(B) propelled liquid

(C) cooking tool

(D) sputter

(E) thin strip of off-shore beach

43. Which literary device appears in the first paragraph of this passage (Lines 1–11)?

(A) personification

(B) metaphor

(C) symbolism

(D) understatement

(E) rhetorical question

44. The author mentions "European settlers . . . splashing" (Lines 28–30) and Victorians' bathing costumes (Lines 30–31) in order to

(A) show the variety of people who have visited Cape Cod

(B) illustrate the area's history

(C) describe changing attitudes toward beach recreation

(D) emphasize the nearness of the ocean

(E) contrast two vastly different groups

45. According to the passage, which statement about "experienced travelers" is true?

(A) They go to Cape Cod in the summer.

(B) They dislike odd behavior.

(C) They leave Cape Cod on Columbus Day.

(D) They travel only when fares are low.

(E) They are increasingly likely to visit Cape Cod in winter.

Go on to next page

46. The reference to Pilgrims in Line 49 most likely serves to

    (A) emphasize the hardiness of contemporary off-season travelers to this area

    (B) illustrate that Cape Cod doesn't appeal to everyone

    (C) contrast modern and colonial Cape Cod

    (D) criticize the colonists who first arrived in Cape Cod

    (E) spark interest in the area's history

47. The "incursions of commercialism and overdevelopment" referred to in Lines 65–66 imply that Cape Cod

    (A) is a good area for investment

    (B) once had more natural beauty

    (C) offers good shopping opportunities

    (D) has strict zoning laws

    (E) is overpopulated

48. The tone of this passage may be characterized as

    (A) nostalgic

    (B) mocking

    (C) complimentary

    (D) sentimental

    (E) bitter

STOP YOU MAY CHECK YOUR WORK ON THIS SECTION ONLY. DO NOT GO BACK TO ANY PREVIOUS SECTION.

Section 4

Mathematics

Time: 25 minutes for 18 questions

Directions: This section contains two different types of questions. For Questions 21–28, choose the *best* answer to each question. Mark the corresponding oval on the answer sheet. For Questions 29–38, follow the separate directions provided before those questions.

Notes:

✔ You may use a calculator.

✔ All numbers used in this exam are real numbers.

✔ All figures lie in a plane.

✔ You may assume that all figures are to scale unless the problem specifically indicates otherwise.

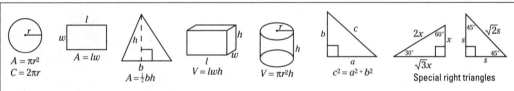

$A = \pi r^2$
$C = 2\pi r$

$A = lw$

$A = \frac{1}{2}bh$

$V = lwh$

$V = \pi r^2 h$

$c^2 = a^2 + b^2$

Special right triangles

There are 360 degrees of arc in a circle.

There are 180 degrees in a straight line.

There are 180 degrees in the sum of the interior angles of a triangle.

21. Which of the following numbers is irrational?

(A) $\sqrt{6}$

(B) $\frac{11}{4}$

(C) 4

(D) $\sqrt{25}$

(E) $2\sqrt{9}$

22. The equation $|2x - 3| = 5$ has the solution(s)

(A) $x = -1$ only

(B) $x = 1$ only

(C) $x = 4$ only

(D) $x = -1$ or $x = 4$

(E) $x = 1$ or $x = 4$

Go on to next page

23. Where do $y = 2x + 5$ and $y = \frac{1}{2}x + \frac{7}{2}$ intersect?

   (A) $(-1, 3)$

   (B) $(1, 3)$

   (C) $(1, 7)$

   (D) $(3, 1)$

   (E) $(6, 7)$

24. Triangle *ABC* is similar to triangle *DEF*. Side *AB* is 3 units long, and side *DE* is 6 units long. If triangle *ABC* has an area of 7 square units, what is the area of triangle *DEF*?

   (A) 7

   (B) 12

   (C) 14

   (D) 28

   (E) 49

25. A concert ticket goes on sale on July 1. On July 3, the price increases by 10%, and on July 5 the new price increases by an additional 10%. If the final ticket price is $5.25 higher than the original ticket price, what was the ticket price on July 1?

   (A) $5

   (B) $20

   (C) $21

   (D) $24

   (E) $25

26. $f(x) = 2x^2 - 3x$. $f(2a) = ?$

   (A) $2a^2 - 6a$

   (B) $4a^2 - 3a$

   (C) $8a^2 - 6a$

   (D) $12a^2 + 6a$

   (E) $16a^2 - 6a$

27. $3^5 \times 2^6 =$

   (A) 6

   (B) 6^5

   (C) 2×6^5

   (D) 5^{11}

   (E) 6^{11}

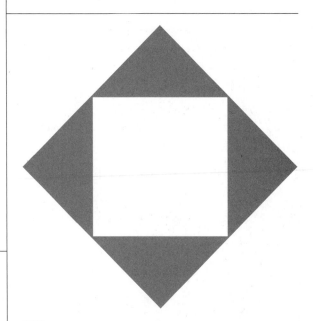

28. A square dartboard is shown in this figure. What is the probability that a randomly thrown dart lands in the shaded area?

   (A) $\frac{1}{4}$

   (B) $\frac{1}{3}$

   (C) $\frac{1}{2}$

   (D) $\frac{3}{5}$

   (E) $\frac{5}{6}$

Go on to next page

Directions for student-produced response Questions 29–38: Solve the problem and then write your answer in the boxes on the answer sheet. Then mark the ovals corresponding to your answer, as shown in the following example. Note the fraction line and the decimal points.

Answer: $^7/_2$

Answer: 3.25

Answer: 853

Write your answer in the box. You may start your answer in any column.

Although you don't have to write the solutions in the boxes, you do have to blacken the corresponding ovals. You should fill in the boxes to avoid confusion. Only the blackened ovals will be scored. The numbers in the boxes won't be read.

There are no negative answers.

You may grid in mixed numbers, such as 3½, as a decimal (3.5) or as a fraction (⁷⁄₂). Don't grid in 3½; it will be read as ³¹⁄₂.

Grid in a decimal as far as possible. Don't round your answer and leave some boxes empty.

A question may have more than one answer. Grid in one answer only.

---

29. Set A contains all single-digit prime numbers, and set B contains all positive multiples of 5 that are less than 16. How many elements are in the union of sets A and B?

31. If $2\sqrt{x} - 7 = -4$, x equals

30. $\left| (3-5)^2 - 45 \div |3-12| \right| =$

32. Gini is 30 years older than Lynn, and Lynn is twice as old as Kevin. If Gini is 33 years older than Kevin, how old is Lynn?

Go on to next page

33. Of the 2,500 people attending a baseball game, 20% ate 1 hot dog, and 6% ate 2 hot dogs. How many hot dogs were consumed at the game?

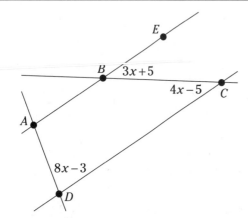

34. In this diagram, line *AB* is parallel to line *DC*. What is the measure of angle *ADC* in degrees?

35. A sports team has a 5:4 ratio of girls to boys. How many people are on the team if there are 12 boys?

36. Arnold sold a pair of sneakers for 30% more than he paid for them. If he sold the shoes for $89.05, how much did he pay for them?

37. If $a^2 - b^2 = 27$ and $a = b + 3$, then $a + b =$?

38. Define $\#a$ to be the sum of the factors of a. For example, $\#4 = 1 + 2 + 4 = 7$. What is $\#12$ equal to?

STOP YOU MAY CHECK YOUR WORK ON THIS SECTION ONLY. DO NOT GO BACK TO ANY PREVIOUS SECTION.

Section 5

Writing

Time: 30 minutes for 39 questions

Directions: Choose the *best* answer to each question. Mark the corresponding oval on your answer sheet.

Directions for Questions 1–20: Read the following sentences carefully. Part or all of each sentence is underlined. Beneath each sentence are five choices. Choice (A) is the original, and the other choices represent different ways of expressing the same meaning. If the sentence is grammatically correct and effectively worded, select Choice (A). If one of the other choices would improve the sentence, select that answer.

Example: Henry wanted to be an architect and <u>that he would have a happy family</u>.

(A) that he would have a happy family

(B) that his family would be happy

(C) to have a happy family

(D) his family should be happy

(E) happiness for his family

The answer is Choice (C).

1. The rent is due on the first day of the month, <u>even where the rent statement is not received</u>.

   (A) even where the rent statement is not received

   (B) even when the rent statement is not received

   (C) even where the rent statement has not been received

   (D) even when the rent statement has not been received

   (E) even not receiving the rent statement

2. The wrestler spoke to many journalists, <u>including he and Ms. Barrows</u>, about the training program.

   (A) including he and Ms. Barrows

   (B) including Ms. Barrows and he

   (C) including Ms. Barrows and him

   (D) which were including Ms. Barrows and him

   (E) Ms. Barrows and him being included

3. The holiday weekend, <u>which begins tomorrow, being</u> a celebration of the nation's independence.

   (A) which begins tomorrow, being

   (B) which begins tomorrow, is

   (C) that begins tomorrow, which is

   (D) beginning tomorrow, that is

   (E) beginning tomorrow, and being

4. Robert <u>was the only one of the many bus riders who weren't</u> texting or speaking on a cellphone.

   (A) was the only one of the many bus riders who weren't

   (B) was the only one of the many bus riders who wasn't

   (C) being the only one of the many bus riders who weren't

   (D) the only one of the many bus riders who weren't

   (E) he was the only one of the many bus riders who weren't

Go on to next page

5. The narrow trunk of the birch tree <u>bent real quick once the boy began to climb</u> above the large branch.

   (A) bent real quick once the boy began to climb

   (B) bent real quick once climbed by the boy

   (C) bent really quickly once the boy began to climb

   (D) bent real quickly once the boy began to climb

   (E) were bent really quickly once the boy begun to climb

6. <u>Where the problem is, Lucy believes, is the lack of planning</u> and inability to complete one task before starting another.

   (A) Where the problem is, Lucy believes, is the lack of planning

   (B) What the problem is, Lucy believes, is the lack of planning

   (C) Lucy believes what the problem is, is the lack of planning

   (D) The problem, Lucy believes, is the lack of planning

   (E) The problem, Lucy believes, is that the lack of planning

7. <u>While shining on his dark glasses, Ellery closed his eyes to shield them from the sun.</u>

   (A) While shining on his dark glasses, Ellery closed his eyes to shield them from the sun.

   (B) While the sun was shining on his dark glasses, Ellery closed his eyes to shield them from the sun.

   (C) Shining on his dark glasses, Ellery closed his eyes to shield them from the sun.

   (D) Shining on his dark glasses, the sun caused Ellery, who was shielding his eyes from the sun, to close them.

   (E) Closing his eyes, Ellery shielded them from the sun shining and the dark glasses.

8. Because technology allows <u>authors to revise as they write</u>, literary scholars can no longer examine early drafts.

   (A) authors to revise as they write

   (B) authors to revise as he or she writes

   (C) revising as the authors are writing

   (D) revision, while they, the authors, are writing

   (E) to revise, authors as they write

9. As the rocket lifted off the launch pad, <u>the crowd cheering and clapping and mission control constantly monitoring</u> every bit of data.

   (A) the crowd cheering and clapping and mission control constantly monitoring

   (B) the crowd cheering and clapping with mission control constantly monitoring

   (C) the crowd cheering and clapping, mission control constantly to monitor

   (D) as the crowd cheering and clapping with mission control constantly monitoring

   (E) the crowd cheered and clapped, and mission control constantly monitored

10. The intricate braids of that region <u>are a visible sign of the inhabitants' reverence</u> for traditional customs.

   (A) are a visible sign of the inhabitants' reverence

   (B) are a visible sign that the inhabitants are reverence

   (C) is a visible sign that the inhabitants feel reverence

   (D) signs visibly of the inhabitants' reverence

   (E) is a visible sign, and the inhabitants feel reverence

Go on to next page

11. When she signed the mortgage documents, the chef celebrated by cooking a feast for her loyal customers.

    (A) When she signed the mortgage documents

    (B) When she was signing the mortgage documents

    (C) Signed the mortgage documents

    (D) When she had signed the mortgage documents

    (E) To sign the mortgage documents

12. The dense, leafy plants covered from view the basement door and hid it.

    (A) covered from view the basement door and hid it

    (B) covering from view the basement door and hid it

    (C) hid the basement door by covering it from view

    (D) covered the basement door and hid it from view

    (E) covering the basement door and hiding it from view

13. Thomas Hart Benton, known for his paintings of working-class Americans, had been born in Missouri to a prominent political family.

    (A) known for his paintings of working-class Americans, had been born

    (B) known for his paintings of working-class Americans, was born

    (C) being known for his paintings of working-class Americans, had been born

    (D) was known for his paintings of working-class Americans and he had been born

    (E) was known for his paintings of working-class Americans, had been born

14. Slabs of bread served as edible plates in the Middle Ages with food piled on top.

    (A) Slabs of bread served as edible plates in the Middle Ages with food piled on top.

    (B) Slabs of bread served as edible plates in the Middle Ages and food piled on top.

    (C) Slabs of bread with food piled on top served as edible plates in the Middle Ages.

    (D) Slabs of bread, serving as edible plates, in the Middle Ages had food piled on top.

    (E) In the Middle Ages, with food piled on top, slabs of bread served as edible plates.

15. Having been elected in 1848, President Zachary Taylor was a member of the Whig Party.

    (A) Having been elected in 1848,

    (B) In 1848, having been elected,

    (C) Being elected in 1848,

    (D) It was in 1848 that he was elected, and

    (E) Elected in 1848,

16. The debaters' words were not as powerful in print than when they were heard aloud.

    (A) as powerful in print than when they were heard

    (B) as powerful in print as when they were heard

    (C) as powerful in print, but when they were heard

    (D) as powerful printed as heard aloud

    (E) powerful in print, but they were more powerful aloud

17. The music and dancing at that performance were subdued, old-fashioned, and they were not well received by the audience.

    (A) and they were not well received by the audience

    (B) and were not well received by the audience

    (C) and not well received by the audience

    (D) and the audience were not receiving them well

    (E) and being not well received by the audience

Go on to next page

18. If Clare would have known about the conference, she would have attended.

    (A) If Clare would have known

    (B) Had Clare known

    (C) If it was that Clare knew

    (D) If Clare knew

    (E) If Clare were knowing

19. The police officer <u>couldn't hardly notice that</u> the car's bumper was dented, so he paid little attention to the complaining driver.

    (A) couldn't hardly notice that

    (B) could hardly notice that

    (C) hardly being able to notice that

    (D) he couldn't notice that

    (E) he couldn't hardly notice

20. <u>Irregardless of the fact that she was blind and deaf</u>, Helen Keller learned to communicate with sign language and became a best-selling author.

    (A) Irregardless of the fact that she was blind and deaf

    (B) Without regard for the fact that she was blind and deaf

    (C) Blind and deaf not being a problem

    (D) Despite being blind and deaf

    (E) Although it was a fact that she was blind and deaf

Directions for Questions 21–34: Read the following sentences carefully. Four portions of each sentence are underlined. Some sentences are correct, and some contain one error. If the sentence is correct, bubble Choice (E) for "no error." If an underlined portion of the sentence contains an error, bubble that letter.

Example:

<u>On the day</u> of the <u>prom, Martin</u> and his
A   B

friends <u>had gone</u> to the mall <u>to rent</u> tuxedos.
   C   D

<u>No error</u>.
E

The answer is Choice (C).

21. <u>In the mid-17th century</u>, <u>New Amsterdam</u>
  A   B

  <u>was</u> a thriving city <u>populated</u>, as New York
          C

  City is now, <u>by people from many nations</u>.
          D

  <u>No error</u>.
   E

22. <u>When he heard the scream</u>, Barney
      A

  <u>ran speedy</u> to the scene, <u>intent on</u> <u>helping</u>
   B   C   D

  the injured. <u>No error</u>.
       E

23. Alan Furst's suspense <u>novels, acclaimed</u>
          A

  <u>by critics, are</u> <u>set in Europe</u> in the years
   B   C

  <u>that lead up to</u> World War II. <u>No error</u>.
   D   E

24. <u>Being that</u> production budgets <u>were low</u>
  A   B

  and lighting expensive, <u>classic films often</u>
          C

  featured <u>shadowy hallways and a limited</u>
        D

  number of sets. <u>No error</u>.
       E

Go on to next page

25. Despite the fact that <u>it was</u> <u>dangerouser to</u>
    _A   _B
    <u>travel</u> by car <u>than by plane</u>, many people
    _C
    are more afraid of <u>flying than driving</u>.
    _D
    <u>No error.</u>
    _E

26. <u>When Baron Pierre de Coubertin created</u>
    _A
    the modern Olympics, <u>he insisted that</u>
    _B
    <u>art competitions be</u> <u>instituted</u>. <u>No error.</u>
    _C   _D   _E

27. Neither the scientists nor their supervisor
    <u>were surprised</u> <u>to see</u> that <u>the experiment,</u>
    _A   _B   _C
    which proved the existence of a subatomic
    particle, <u>was recognized</u> at the awards
    _D
    ceremony. <u>No error.</u>
    _E

28. The corporation <u>does not have</u> a savings
    _A
    <u>account, it relies</u> <u>solely on income from</u>
    _B   _C
    sales <u>to finance research</u> and development
    _D
    of new products. <u>No error.</u>
    _E

29. <u>In the paper it says</u> <u>that fireworks are</u>
    _A   _B
    <u>illegal, and anyone</u> <u>who brings</u> these items
    _C   _D
    to the party will be arrested. <u>No error.</u>
    _E

30. <u>Harvesting fresh herbs from the kitchen</u>
    _A
    <u>garden</u>, the chef <u>he experimented with</u>
    _B
    many combinations <u>before he concluded</u>
    _C
    that oregano and garlic <u>were best</u>.
    _D
    <u>No error.</u>
    _E

31. <u>Nellie Bly was</u> the professional name of
    _A
    Elizabeth Jane Cochran, <u>whom</u>
    _B
    <u>many people believe was</u> one of the best
    _C
    investigative reporters, partly because
    she faked insanity <u>to report on conditions</u>
    _D
    <u>in a mental hospital</u>. <u>No error.</u>
    _E

32. In Jules Verne's novel <u>*Around the World in*</u>
    _A
    <u>*Eighty Days,*</u> a character <u>named</u> Fogg
    _B
    <u>tries to circle</u> the globe <u>by within</u> that time
    _C   _D
    period. <u>No error.</u>
    _E

33. <u>Hawaii is the only state</u> in the nation
    _A
    <u>that is made up</u> of islands, <u>furthermore,</u>
    _B   _C
    Hawaii is the <u>northernmost island chain</u> in
    _D
    Polynesia. <u>No error.</u>
    _E

34. <u>Abandoned animals fill</u> <u>that shelter</u>
    _A   _B
    <u>on the south side</u> of the mountains
    _C
    <u>that were cruelly left</u> by their former
    _D
    owners. <u>No error.</u>
    _E

Go on to next page

Directions for Questions 35–39: Following is a first draft of a student essay. The essay needs revision. Read the essay and the questions that follow and choose the best answer to each question.

[1] World's Fairs have been held around the world for more than 100 years. [2] World's Fairs, or Expos, showcase a country's accomplishments, give a glimpse of the future, and bring tourists. [3] In 1964–1965, for example, visitors from around the world traveled to Queens, New York, to see exhibits from countries, major companies, and other groups. [4] You could see a Michelangelo statue, a demonstration of the latest in computer power, and a swim show for fun. [5] The first World's Fair took place in London, England, in 1851.

[6] In the 21st century, there are fewer world's fairs. [7] With the Internet, one can visit other countries while still at home. [8] To learn about new technology, you can use technology and save money at the same time! [9] World's fairs are expensive. [10] To hold a world's fair costs tens of millions of dollars. [11] When many cities are struggling to maintain basic services, holding a fair appears extravagant. [12] A fair may earn hundreds of millions of dollars though.

[13] In Seattle, Washington, the site of the fair was connected to downtown by a monorail. [14] Fifty years later, it is being used by the city to move tourists to an area of parks and museums. [15] In Montreal, Canada, one exhibit, a dome, became an environmental museum. [16] Pavilions remain from fairs in Japan, Australia, Spain, and many other places.

35. Which of the following, if any, is the best way to improve Paragraph 1 (Sentences 1–5)?

    (A) NO CHANGE

    (B) Delete Sentence 2.

    (C) Delete Sentence 4.

    (D) Combine the information in Sentences 1 and 5.

    (E) Add more information about exhibits in the New York fair.

36. What, if any, is the best change to Sentence 7?

    (A) NO CHANGE

    (B) With the Internet, you can visit other countries while still at home.

    (C) While still at home, the Internet takes you to visit other countries.

    (D) Visiting other countries is easy with the Internet, which we use at home.

    (E) The Internet makes visiting other countries easy, while we are still at home.

37. Which of the following is the best way to combine Sentences 9 and 10?

    (A) World's fairs are expensive, and to hold one costs tens of millions of dollars.

    (B) Costing tens of millions of dollars, world's fairs are expensive.

    (C) World's fairs being expensive, the fairs can cost tens of millions of dollars.

    (D) Because to hold a fair costs tens of millions of dollars, world's fairs are expensive.

    (E) Tens of millions of dollars is what a world's fair costs to hold, and is expensive.

38. Which sentence, if any, should be inserted before Sentence 13?

    (A) NO CHANGE

    (B) World's fairs do not completely disappear when they are officially over.

    (C) Parts of a world's fair can survive.

    (D) Many places still have remnants of their fairs.

    (E) In addition to tourism income, world's fair cities benefit in other ways.

39. Which of the following, if any, would improve the end of this essay?

    (A) NO CHANGE

    (B) List more structures that survive from world's fairs.

    (C) Explain what remains from the earliest world's fairs.

    (D) Discuss future fairs.

    (E) Give the writer's opinion on the value of world's fairs.

Chapter 18

Practice Test 4: Answers and Explanations

● ●

"*P*arting is such sweet sorrow," wrote Shakespeare. I bet you're not sorry to say goodbye to Test 4. (Got the shredder ready, have you?) But don't say "so long" until you check your work and read the explanations in this chapter. Pay special attention, of course, to anything you got wrong, but also *linger* (stay for a while) on questions you answered by guessing. (To guess or not to guess, that is the question. Turn to Chapter 2 to find out.) After you've checked everything, compute your score with help from the charts in the appendix.

If you're short on time, turn to the end of this chapter to find an abbreviated answer key.

Section 1: Critical Reading

1. **A.** This sentence revolves around one word — "but." That little word tells you that the sentence contains a change of direction. Madeline wanted one thing, *but* she did another because of *etiquette* (rules for polite behavior). Okay, look for opposites, and think about the hostess/guest relationship. Almost immediately you see that Choice (A) is the answer, because if you want to retreat, you don't want to welcome guests. In fact, you probably want to lock the door and let the pit bull out. The correct answer is Choice (A).

2. **E.** This is an easy one if you know that *clarity* means "clearness." The only other possibility is Choice (D), because *capacity* is "the amount that can be held or contained." However, the size of the photo doesn't necessarily mean that small details are visible. The "clarity" of the photo does. Before you move on to the next question, add these words to your personal dictionary: *rigor* is "strictness," and *opacity* means "the quality of not reflecting light."

3. **C.** Real-world knowledge helps you with this question. Newcomers generally don't have a lot to say at club meetings. They often sit around the edges, or margins, of the room. The sentence begins with "although," a word that always signals a change in what you expect. Miranda won't be *marginalized,* or pushed to the edge. She'll be a full participant. The correct answer is Choice (C). Did I catch you with Choice (A)? When you *trivialize* something, you treat it as unimportant. The key word in the preceding sentence is "it" — a pronoun used for things or ideas, not for people. Miranda is a person, so Choice (A) isn't appropriate for her.

4. **B.** The last portion of the sentence talks about "a false impression of the speaker's position." Well, if you *mischaracterize* something, you give a false impression. Choice (B) is a perfect match.

5. **D.** Be careful of the double negative that begins this sentence. Jeff's not uninterested, so he's interested. Now look at the "but," which tells you that he can't do what an interested person usually does, which is participate regularly. Finally, look for a word that is the opposite of "regularly," and you arrive at *sporadically*, which means "at irregular intervals." Just a few more words for your vocabulary storehouse: *capriciously* is how you act when sudden thoughts or whims rule, and *surreptitiously* means "in a secret or hidden way."

6. **B.** The spy has to think fast, so he draws on inner talents. In other words, he's *resourceful.* Then he lies, and a fancy word for "lied" is *fabricated.* Take a second to learn these other words: *credible* is "believable," *empathetic* refers to the ability to understand another's feelings, *renounce* is to reject, *flagrant* is "bad, in a very visible way," and *exonerated* means "cleared of wrongdoing." Had enough? Try just two more: *overt* is "out in the open," and *indicted* is what happens to you when you're charged with a crime. Clearly, the only pair that fits is Choice (B).

7. **B.** When you *brandish* a weapon, you wave it around, ready to use it — just the meaning you want for this sentence. *Relinquishing,* or "giving up," doesn't fit. Nor does *distending* (swelling). True, the fencers oppose each other, but the swords don't, so Choice (D) isn't a good answer. Steer clear of Choice (E) also, because if the fencers are "prepared to fight," they already have swords and don't require them. No doubt about it, Choice (B) is the answer.

8. **A.** The doc worked hard, paying attention to every little detail. Thus, his research was *exhaustive* (using all possibilities). It was probably also exhausting, but that word isn't relevant here! Because he checked everything, no one could prove he was wrong, or *refute* his paper. Are you familiar with the other words? *Quell* is "to quiet," and *laudatory* is "praiseworthy."

9. **C.** The passage tells you that commercials are the "price" for "free TV." Huh? If you're paying a price, how can TV be free? Easy. The price isn't money; instead, it's the annoying minute or so of dancing raisins and fancy cars zooming along a highway, the commercials. Because the price isn't really a price, it's in quotation marks. This punctuation is the equivalent of a wink from the writer.

10. **A.** The passage tells you that people "took offense" to spam on a "collective scale" (Line 16). *Collective* means "group." That information is followed by a statement about a giant that "has been pushing back on intrusive ads" (Line 18). So a group has been "pushing back," or opposing, spam. Sounds like "unified opposition" to me! Choice (A) is correct.

11. **D.** The birds learn from "airs" that are "whistled or played to them" (Line 4), so you know you're in musical territory. Don't be fooled by "strains" (Line 4), which usually shows up as "stresses" but in this passage is a synonym for "airs," or musical notes — leading you to Choice (D) as the best answer.

12. **B.** According to the passage, most young birds "will learn" some songs if they hear the songs over and over. Therefore, Statement I is true. The passage also refers to birds' "natural" song, so II is a true statement. Turning to III, you see the exact opposite of what the passage states, that any difference in song is "not caused by the bird's *anatomy* [body structure], but rather by the superiority of memory" (Line 12). Because only I and II are true, Choice (B) is your answer.

13. **C.** At first glance you probably zeroed in on Choices (B) and (C). Passage I tells you that "we interpret ambiguous information" (Line 5) differently, "depending on our expectations" (Line 8). *Ambiguous* behavior has more than one possible meaning, and not all behavior falls into that category. Therefore, Choice (B) is out. Choice (C), on the other hand, fits well with the examples — the behavior of mental patients, sports fans, and babies. Choice (C) is correct.

14. **E.** The pronoun "we" isn't limited by any other statement in the passage. Instead, it's presented as **all-encompassing** (broad enough to include everyone or everything). Therefore, Choice (E) is the answer you seek.

15. **A.** The author discusses these groups in relation to "perceptual confirmation" (Line 8). She says that the behavior of mental patients is more likely to be seen as "abnormal" (Line 10), implying that the mentally ill are stereotyped in this way. (Even a severely ill person can behave normally at times, and the reverse is also true.) Same thing with the kids: Girls are stereotyped as less athletic than boys. The sports example is a little trickier. I tend to see opponents of my beloved Yankees as **inept** (clumsy, incompetent) rather than aggressive, for example. However, the three examples follow the author's statement about stereotypes, so Choice (A) is the best answer.

16. **D.** Nowhere in the passage do you discover how kids *actually* crawl (really well, terribly, backwards, whatever). Therefore, Choices (B), (C), and (E) are out. Choice (A) doesn't work because the accuracy of people's assumptions isn't given. All you know is that people underestimate girls' ability and overestimate boys' ability to crawl. Choice (D) deals with the way in which infants are seen, so it's the only possibility here.

17. **B.** The video was open to interpretation, because Hannah performed well on some questions but not on others. Passage I states that people with "positive expectations [those who thought Hannah was rich] rated Hannah somewhat higher if they had seen the video" (Line 36). Choice (B) is the best answer.

18. **D.** Rich, poor, smart, not-so-smart — the author doesn't tell you anything about *reality,* and reality is key to Choices (A), (B), and (C). Instead, Passage I explains that people who thought Hannah was poor "rated her lower on work habits, motivation, and cognitive skills" (Line 33), while people who thought she was rich did the opposite. Sounds like stereotyping, Choice (D), to me! Choice (E) isn't valid because the video was, according to the passage, open to interpretation. No doubt about it, Choice (D) is the answer.

19. **A.** To be "excused from a particular case" means that the judge says, "You can go now! We don't want you on this case!" The other words relate to legal matters, but only Choice (A) fits the situation in Passage II.

20. **B.** Same crime, same juror, two different views of how that juror will vote on a drug case, based solely on questions about news sources and occupation. You can't get much more **capricious** (unpredictable) than that! Yet stereotyping is all about predicting — what you'll do based on superficial characteristics. Yup, Choice (B) works well here. Did I catch you with Choice (C)? Yes, the judicial system has problems, but that answer is way too general for this question.

21. **C.** In Lines 97–98, the author states, "I don't want to be in a category. I want to be an individual. And I am not alone either." These sentences precede the story about the clothing chain, so it's safe to assume that the problem is being placed in a category — or, as Choice (C) puts it, "being narrowly defined." Were you fooled by Choice (E)? True, some retailers probably don't understand women, but the statement as written is way too broad. Choice (C) works better because the whole editorial is about stereotyping, which Choice (C) specifically addresses.

22. **B.** The third paragraph of Passage II is about democracy, and the author clearly favors "an exchange of ideas, not solely a reaffirmation" (Line 116). Therefore, Choice (B) is your answer. True, at first glance Choice (E) seems possible, because the author favors discussion. However, talking with people who think exactly the same way you do doesn't challenge you. That's bad, according to Line 117 in Passage II, because the author asks a **rhetorical question** (one you aren't supposed to answer but that directs you to a particular response): "Don't we all benefit from being challenged?" Therefore, Choice (E) fails.

23. **B.** A *metaphor* is an implied comparison, when you use one thing to describe another without the words "like" or "as." The "soft cloud of sameness" describes an atmosphere in which everything is comforting because no one ever disagrees or differs from the norm. The answer is Choice (B).

24. **A.** Some of the choices apply to one or the other passage, but only Choice (A) applies to both. Passage I explains how people apply stereotypes, and Passage II discusses occasions in which stereotypes pop up. Hence, Choice (A) works for both.

Section 2: Mathematics

1. **E.** To solve this one, just remember PEMDAS. You have some parentheses, so simplify that first: $3 - 4 = -1$, but you're subtracting that quantity, so your expression simplifies to $2 + 5^2 + 1$. Deal with the exponent, and then add everything up! $2 + 25 + 1 = 28$

2. **B.** The trick here is to realize that y isn't by itself, so you can't deduce anything about the slope of the line yet. Step one is to solve the expression for y by first subtracting 3 from both sides and then multiplying everything by 2: $\frac{y}{2} = x - 7$, $y = 2x - 14$. Now that the equation is in slope-intercept form, you can see that the slope is 2. Perpendicular lines have slopes that are opposite reciprocals, or, you can think of the two slopes having a product of –1. What number do you multiply 2 by to get –1? You're looking for an equation where the slope is $-\frac{1}{2}$, so Choice (B) is the answer.

3. **E.** The first step is to remember that the intersection of two sets contains only the elements that are in both of the original sets, so you're looking for an answer that represents numbers in both sets P and Q. Think about what numbers are multiples of both 2 and of 3, and your answer must be Choice (E), all the multiples of 6.

4. **D.** Remember that $f(x)$ really represents the y-value that results from plugging a particular x into an equation. For this question, you're looking for y-values that are less than or equal to 0, which looks like the y-values that match up with the x-values between –2 and 3. The y-values are negative between those two x-values. The y-values are positive outside of those x-values, so you're looking for an answer that includes the points between –2 and 3; Choices (C) or (D) look good. To decide between them, remember that the question is looking for x-values that give y-values less than *or equal to* 0, so you want to include –2 and 3, as Choice (D) does.

5. **B.** In this problem, you want x to be the number of pairs of pants. If Jen has 3 times as many shirts as pants, that means she has $3x$ shirts. If she has 5 fewer dresses than shirts, then she has $3x - 5$ dresses. Jen has 6 hats, so you don't need to worry about x for the hats. Add all those expressions together for your answer: pants + shirts + dresses + hats = $x + 3x + 3x - 5 + 6 = 7x + 1$.

6. **E.** This problem is testing how well you understand radicals. Remember that you can rewrite 2 as $\sqrt{4}$, so $2\sqrt{20} = \sqrt{4}\sqrt{20}$. You can multiply the numbers inside of the radicals to get $\sqrt{80}$. So you already know that Choice (C) isn't your answer. Now you can see that you can split $\sqrt{80}$ up into other multiples, as in Choices (A) and (B), so neither of those is your answer. You're left with Choices (D) and (E), but if you peek back at Choice (B), you see that you can simplify $\sqrt{16}$ to 4, and therefore rewrite: $\sqrt{5}\sqrt{16} = 4\sqrt{5}$. Choice (E) is the only one that doesn't work!

7. **C.** Cross-multiplying is your friend here: The given equation becomes $3(3x + 2) = 1(x + 2)$ when you cross-multiply, which simplifies to $9x + 6 = x + 2$. Gather the x's on one side and the numbers on the other: $8x = -4$, and then divide to isolate x: $x = -\frac{1}{2}$, Choice (C).

8. **A.** Your best bet here is to just pick some numbers. Let o be 5, and e be 4, and then see what the expression works out to be: $5^2 - 4^2 = 25 - 16 = 9$. Option II is out because 9 is odd, as is option III, because 9 is composite. There you go! Choice (A) it is!

9. **A.** The median of a set of numbers is the number that is in the middle when you line the numbers up in increasing or decreasing order. The numbers given are 8, 16, 14, 10, or, if you put them in increasing order: 8, 10, 14, 16. If Joe wants 10 to be the median, then the fifth number must be less than or equal to 10; Choice (A) fits the bill.

10. **C.** Recall that the mean is the result when you add all the numbers together and then divide by the number of numbers. If you let x represent the number of miles Joe runs on Friday, then the mean would be $\frac{8+16+14+10+x}{5}$. Set that expression equal to 12 (Joe's desired mean), and solve for x: $\frac{48+x}{5} = 12$, $48 + x = 60$, $x = 12$ miles.

11. **C.** One way to solve this problem is to realize that triangle ABC is an isosceles right triangle, or 45°-45°-90° triangle. That means that the length of the hypotenuse is $\sqrt{2}$ times larger than the length of either leg, so in this case the legs are each 4 units long because the hypotenuse is $4\sqrt{2}$ units long. After you figure that out, the rest is easy — just remember (or look in the information box at the beginning of the section) the formula for the area of a triangle and apply it to this problem: $\frac{1}{2}bh = \frac{1}{2}(4)(4) = 8$.

12. **B.** The key is to realize that $600 is 30% of Jim's monthly spending. You can also figure out that rent + food + utilities = 40% + 30% + 10% = 80% of Jim's spending, leaving 20% for fun. You have many ways to determine how much money 20% represents; one way is to see that $200 represents 10% of Jim's spending (divide both numbers for food by 3), so 20% must be $400.

13. **B.** Substitution is your best bet for solving this problem. Use the information given about x and y to rewrite the third equation in terms of a: $3x + 5y = 3(7a) + 5(-5a)$. Simplify: $21a - 25a = 6$, so $-4a = 6$ and $a = -\frac{3}{2}$, Choice (B).

14. **A.** You know that parallel lines have the same slope, so the slope of the line you're creating must also be 2. (Confused? Turn back to Chapter 10 for more information on graphs.) From here, if you happen to know point-slope form for a line, you're all set. Otherwise, use $y = mx + b$. You know that the point $(a, 7)$ is on the line, so you can plug in a for x, 7 for y, and 2 (the slope) for m: $7 = 2(a) + b$ and then solve for b: $b = 7 - 2a$. Plug your value for b back into the original $y = mx + b$ equation, and you're all done: $y = 2x + 7 - 2a$. When you swap the order around a bit, you see that Choice (A) is the answer.

15. **C.** The problem tells you that the pond is a circle and that there are 250 feet of shore, meaning that the circumference of the circle is 250 feet. Recall that $C = 2\pi r$, so you can determine the radius of the pond: $250 = 2\pi r$, $r = \frac{250}{2\pi} \approx 39.8$. Now you can find the surface area of the pond using $\pi r^2 \approx 4976.4$ square feet. Just multiply that area by the depth of the pond (it's shaped like a cylinder) to find the volume, approximately 49,764 cubic feet, which is closest to Choice (C).

16. **A.** How well do you know your exponent rules? If you multiply two exponential expressions with the same base, you add the exponents, and if you divide two exponential expressions with the same base, you subtract the denominator's exponent from the numerator's. You can simplify the numerator first: $a^{2x}a^{x+4} = a^{2x+(x+4)} = a^{3x+4}$. Now deal with the denominator: $\frac{a^{3x+4}}{a^x} = a^{(3x+4)-(x)} = a^{2x+4}$. Unfortunately, that is not one of your answer choices, but luckily it doesn't look anything like Choices (C), (D), or (E), so you can knock those choices out of the running. Now remember another exponent rule: When an exponential expression is raised to an exponent, the exponents are multiplied. So, simplifying Choice (A) results in $a^{2(x+2)} = a^{2x+4}$ (the right answer!).

17. **C.** Just follow the pattern given in the problem, and then simplify. $x \sim y = x^2y - xy^2$, and $y \sim x = y^2x - yx^2 = xy^2 - x^2y$ (you can rearrange the letters if it helps you see patterns). Plugging back into the original expression: $(x \sim y) - (y \sim x) = (x^2y - xy^2) - (xy^2 - x^2y) = 2x^2y - 2xy^2$, Choice (C).

18. **C.** One way to look at this problem is to try to make the ratios look similar; perhaps by making the first one 14:4. That means that adding a dozen eggs changes 14:4 to 15:4, so in 15:4, 15 represents $(15)(12) = 180$ eggs. Set up a proportion to determine the number of lemons: $\frac{4}{15} = \frac{x}{180}$ and then solve for x: $15x = 720$, and $x = 48$.

19. **D.** There are two tricks in this problem. The first is that the car is rented for 6 days, meaning that the flat rate is $6(\$35.75) = \$214.50$. Choices (D) and (E) are looking good. The second trick is that the customer is charged 5 cents per mile, or \$0.05 per mile, so you want to multiply the number of miles by 0.05, as in Choice (D).

20. **B.** One good first step is to determine how much water is already in the tank. You use the formula for the volume of a cylinder, and the depth of the water is 0.5 feet (which is 6 inches). $v = \pi r^2 h = \pi(5)^2(0.5) \approx 39.27$. Hopefully you realized that if the tank is 75% full, then it has a depth of 6 feet $(0.75 \times 8$ feet$)$. That means you want a total of $v = \pi r^2 h = \pi(5)^2(6) \approx 471.24$ cubic feet. You don't need to fill the first 6 inches, so you need a total of $471.24 - 39.27 \approx 431.97$ cubic feet of water. If the water is filling by 80 cubic feet per hour, then it takes $\frac{431.97}{80} \approx 5.4$ hours, or Choice (B).

Section 3: Critical Reading

25. **B.** You may have met the verb *compromise* in another context, perhaps when two sides are trying to hammer out an agreement and each gives a little, compromising to achieve a solution. In this context, though, the word means "to reduce in value." Actually, the two meanings work together, because when you give up a little in a negotiation, you move away from your original, pure position. So too with the lab specimens, which were not the same after the freezer failed.

26. **A.** The tickets are how much? You can almost hear Alex screaming, and you can easily imagine that his enthusiasm decreased. Now all you have to do is find an answer that means "decreased," and Choice (A) is exactly what you want. When something *wanes,* it gets smaller. Choices (B), (C), and (E) are the opposite; they're verbs you use when something gets bigger. Did you stumble on Choice (D)? The verb *inflated* would fit the sentence, but *conflate* means "to merge."

27. **C.** When you *pinpoint* the age, you're sticking a pin in a timeline and saying that you have the correct date. Choice (C) fits the sentence perfectly. Wait! Don't leave until you learn a few vocabulary words. *Reconciled* means "brought into harmony after a dispute" or "accepting one's fate." *Ameliorated* means "improved or made better," and *induced* means "brought about by persuasion."

28. **E.** A little knowledge of vocabulary and the way people relate to each other are the keys to this question. How do you make friends and end up receiving a million invitations? (No, Twitter and Facebook are not answer choices!) You're *affable* (friendly) and *extroverted* (outgoing). Build your vocabulary by learning these words: *reclusive* people stay away from others, and *introverted* people keep their thoughts private. Those who are *erratic* are unpredictable; *indecisive* people can't make decisions. (How do you know someone's indecisive? You ask. If the answer is "well, yes and no," the label fits.) *Incompatible* people are not in harmony with their situation or surroundings, and *disarming* people win you over to their side by charm. If you're *antagonistic,* you're hostile.

29. **B.** A *dirge* is a song played at a funeral, so it's a perfect fit here. The only other funeral word is *eulogy*, which is a speech made in honor of the deceased. Max out your vocab skills: *dearth* is "lack of," a *fallacy* is "a false statement or assumption," and a *vignette* is "a little, pleasing scene or view."

30. **D.** According to Passage I, "Franklin argued for a sharp point" and "Wilson correctly argued for a round point" (Line 10–11). The original cause of the *dispute,* or argument, is the design for lightning rods, as Choice (D) says. True, Wilson was probably disrespectful, as he was scolded for "shameful discord and dissensions" (Line 14), but the *discord* (lack of harmony) and *dissensions* (strong disagreements) came *after* the men differed on the shape of the lightning rod's point and therefore weren't the basis of the dispute.

31. **B.** Choices (B) and (C) are possible here because Passage II says that the scientist "could not at first believe that such a work" (Line 20) came from America and thought it "must have been fabricated" (Line 22) by Parisian enemies. Choice (B) is better because "such a work" implies a judgment. Most likely, the scientist thought the paper was written by Parisians because of its quality or content, implying that he assumed American scientific work is different.

32. **D.** Franklin says that he actually began a response but then realized that his paper "contained a description of experiments which anyone might repeat and verify" (Line 29). He states that if they couldn't be *verified* (proved true), they "could not be defended" (Line 31). In other words, the experiment could be tested by others, not defended by Franklin, as Choice (D) indicates.

33. **B.** In Passage I, Wilson favors a rounded point and Franklin a sharp point for lightning rods, and they argue about how lightning behaves with each design. In Passage II, Franklin explains how he handled disagreement from "an able experimenter" (Line 18). Neither passage implies that disagreement shouldn't occur, though Passage I criticizes Wilson for the way in which he disagreed. Choice (B) is best here.

34. **A.** The narrator says that his professor was disliked by students, but that "better judges than schoolboys" (Line 10) respected Professor Khayme. The narrator implies that his classmates — the schoolboys — are immature. Choice (C) is a trap. The professor thought that slavery "could not endure" (Line 87), but no evidence about the narrator's opinion on the subject appears in the passage. Did I catch you with Choice (D)? Khayme is referred to as a tutor, but tutors can give private instruction to anyone, not just to those who struggle with schoolwork.

35. **C.** You know that the professor speaks many languages and that he teaches philosophy. You also know that he has a wide selection of books and many interests. Therefore, Statement I has no support. Nor does Statement II, because the students may have disliked him for his grading, personal manner, tendency to give a ton of homework, or any number of reasons. Statement III is a winner, because the narrator has to guess about Khayme's origins and economic status and refers to "information that seemed withheld" (Line 42). Because only Statement III can be *verified* (proved true), Choice (C) is the best answer.

36. **A.** Gravity — the force that stops you from floating away from the PSAT/NMSQT (oh, wait, that's your parent!) — can also mean "seriousness," a meaning that Line 25 hints at when Lydia is described as "a very serious child."

37. **C.** Line 35 mentions that Lydia "said some words . . . that made me doubt the seeming poverty of her father." The word "seeming" tells you that you're dealing with appearance, not necessarily reality. Because the narrator is in Khayme's home, you can reasonably assume that it's "somewhat shabby," as Choice (C) says.

38. **E.** The narrator says that he is describing "the winters of five or six years" (Line 68), which fits Choice (E) nicely. The passage contains no evidence for the other choices.

39. **D.** The passage mentions that the professor owned "the Bible of every religious faith" (Line 71) and books on "philosophy" (Line 70), so Choices (A) and (E) are out. The professor's views on slavery and America's future appear in the passage (Lines 85 and 79), so Choices (B) and (C) don't work. You're left with Choice (D), the correct answer.

40. **A.** The professor "showed a strange unconcern" (Line 81) regarding "sectional discord" (disagreements between parts of the country, which of course led to the Civil War). Also, "he believed it a matter of indifference" (Line 82) whether secession was constitutional. Thus, Choice (A) is the best answer.

 You don't need to know anything about the Civil War to answer Question 40, but if you *do* know that the South seceded from the Union and war followed, you may understand the last paragraph of this passage more easily. How do you know the passage is about the Civil War era? The introduction tells you! Always read the introduction!

41. **C.** Everything about this passage screams, "Tourist! Come spend time (and money) in lovely Cape Cod!" The details given all point to a great vacation, including "long, restful stint at the beach" (Line 14) and "a just-caught, butter-dripping lobster" (Line 25). Plus, the last paragraph proclaims that "one visit is likely to prompt a follow-up" (Line 56).

42. **E.** You may never have heard this unusual definition of "spit," but the passage supplies an important clue: The word appears in the phrase "a thin spit of land" (Line 5). Only Choice (E) is a term for land, and it's the right choice here.

43. **A.** The Cape, in this passage, has an "arm" that "has beckoned wayfarers" (Line 7). The Cape also has a "sunny disposition" (Line 6). People have arms and *dispositions* (temperaments), and they beckon. Hence personification (giving human qualities to non-humans) is your answer. Be sure you know the other terms: a *metaphor* and a *simile* make imaginative comparisons by using one thing to describe another. A simile makes the comparison with the words "like" or "as," and a metaphor doesn't. *Symbolism* occurs when something represents a larger idea or theme. A *rhetorical question* is one that the reader (or listener) isn't supposed to answer, because the answer is implied by the context.

44. **C.** The "European settlers waited nearly three centuries to go splashing in the surf" (Line 28), so they weren't exactly beach fans right away. The Victorians wore "bathing costumes" (Line 31). The word "costumes" implies that their beachwear differed from today's bikinis and wet suits. These two groups are mentioned just before a reference to modern beach-goers. Put all that together and you arrive at a change in attitudes toward beach recreation, as Choice (C) states.

45. **E.** The fourth paragraph (Lines 35–53) describes the appeal of Cape Cod in the off-season and remarks that "experienced travelers are beginning to discover the subtler appeal" of the Cape at that time. Because the season is defined as Memorial Day to Labor (or Columbus) Day, Choice (E) fits well here. True, the passage says that "prices plummet" (Line 37) during the off-season, but most of the paragraph is about other benefits of visiting the area. Choice (E) is the best answer.

46. **A.** The Pilgrims, despite sailing for months in a wooden ship across treacherous ocean water, "didn't have quite the necessary *mettle* [character]" (Line 50) to withstand winter at Cape Cod, where the passage says you need "resourcefulness" (Line 48) to appreciate "the beauty in the wintry, shuttered landscape" (Line 48). Because only a chosen few have the strength of character to walk on the beach in January, Choice (A) is the answer here.

47. **B.** An *incursion* is an attack. The phrase in Question 47 appears after the words "[w]hatever the incursions" (Line 65). The phrase also lies between a statement about "the brilliance of nature's palette" (Line 64) and one about the land's being "infused with spirit" (Line 66). Therefore, the author is saying that Cape Cod still has natural beauty, "whatever" or despite, the buildup of homes and businesses. Because it still has natural beauty, you can infer that it once had even more, as Choice (B) says.

48. **C.** In this passage, beach-goers never get bitten by mosquitoes, and no dinner is ever overcooked. Everything in the passage *compliments* (speaks well of) Cape Cod — so much so that I'd like to go there myself. Now. This minute. See you later!

Section 4: Mathematics

21. **A.** Remember that irrational numbers are numbers that can't be written as a fraction of whole numbers. (Numbers that *can* be written as a fraction of whole numbers are called *rational numbers.*) Choices (B) and (C) are both clearly rational, so you can eliminate them. Choice (D) simplifies to 5, and Choice (E) to $2 \times 3 = 6$, so they too are rational and may be eliminated, which leaves you with Choice (A), your answer.

22. **D.** Absolute value takes anything inside of it and makes it become positive. So, $2x - 3$ is either already positive (in which case you can just ignore the absolute value signs and solve for x: $2x - 3 = 5$, $2x = 8$, $x = 4$), or $2x - 3$ is negative, and therefore equal to -5 until the absolute value sign kicks in. In that case you can solve the following equation: $2x - 3 = -5$, $2x = -2$, $x = -1$. Both $x = 4$ and $x = -1$ work, so you want Choice (D). Alternatively, you can simply plug answer choices into the original equation and see which ones work.

23. **A.** Both of the given equations are solved for *y,* so just set them equal to each other: $2x + 5 = \frac{1}{2}x + \frac{7}{2}$. Multiply both sides of the equation by 2 so that you don't have to worry about any fractions: $4x + 10 = x + 7$, and then solve for x: $3x = -3$, $x = -1$. From here plug $x = -1$ into either of the original equations to find the matching *y*-value. But if you're paying attention, you see that Choice (A) is the only one with -1 as the *x*-value, so you have your answer!

24. **D.** Hopefully you remember from your reading of Chapter 9 that "the ratio of the area of similar triangles equals the square of the ratio of their sides." You know the ratio of the side lengths of triangle *ABC* to triangle *DEF* is 3:6 or 1:2, so the ratio of the areas is $1^2 : 2^2$, or 1:4, meaning that triangle *DEF* has 4 times more area than triangle *ABC,* or $4 \times 7 = 28$ square units.

25. **E.** Whenever you work with percentages, everything is easier if you start with 100. So, if the original ticket price were $100, then after the first 10% increase you have $110. Now you want to increase $110 by 10%, which results in $110 + 0.10(110) = 110 + 11 = \$121$ as the final price. Because you were using 100 as the starting price, it's easy to see that the final price is 21% greater than the original price, meaning that $5.25 is equal to 21% of the original ticket price. To find the original price, you just need to know what 100% is $\frac{5.25}{21} = \frac{x}{100}$, and when you solve for *x,* you see that the original ticket price was $25.

26. **C.** This problem is all about substitution. Wherever you see x in the original *f(x)* equation, you want to replace it with $2a$: $f(2a) = 2(2a)^2 - 3(2a)$. Now just apply PEMDAS and you're in the clear, but make sure you apply the square to both 2 and to a: $(2a)^2 = 2^2 a^2 = 4a^2$, $f(2a) = 2(4a^2) - 6a = 8a^2 - 6a$, Choice (C).

27. **C.** This problem is much easier if you can think about exponents as just a short-cut way of writing lots of multiplication. In this problem, think of 3^5 as $3 \cdot 3 \cdot 3 \cdot 3 \cdot 3$, and 2^6 as $2 \cdot 2 \cdot 2 \cdot 2 \cdot 2 \cdot 2$. You can pair up 2's and 3's, and you'll have one extra 2: $(3 \cdot 2)(3 \cdot 2)(3 \cdot 2)(3 \cdot 2)(3 \cdot 2) \cdot 2$, which simplifies to $6 \cdot 6 \cdot 6 \cdot 6 \cdot 6 \cdot 2$, or $6^5 \cdot 2 = 2 \cdot 6^5$, Choice (C).

28. **C.** You aren't given any lengths in this problem, so you can pick whatever numbers you like. One is often a good choice, so make each of the legs of the shaded triangles length 1 (so the outer square has a side length of 2).

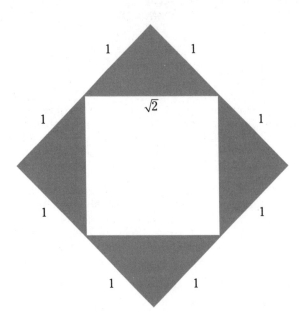

That means that the outer square has an area of $2^2 = 4$. By now you've noticed that each of the shaded triangles is a right triangle, so you can use the Pythagorean theorem to determine the length of the hypotenuse: $1^2 + 1^2 = h^2$, $h = \sqrt{2}$. Now that you know the hypotenuse, you know that the inner square has a side length of $\sqrt{2}$ and an area of $\left(\sqrt{2}\right)^2 = 2$. The outer square's area is 4, and the inner square's area is 2, so the shaded area is equal to $4 - 2 = 2$, and the probability of the dart landing on the shaded area is $\frac{2}{4} = \frac{1}{2}$. One other option is to imagine that the shaded triangles are folded in on the inner square; they fit perfectly! That means that the shaded and unshaded areas are equal, so the probability of hitting the shaded part is $\frac{1}{2}$.

29. **6.** This problem is easiest if you just write down the sets. Set A is $\{2,3,5,7\}$, and Set B is $\{5,10,15\}$. The elements of the union of sets A and B are all the elements in either set, without double-counting (so watch out for 5). That means that the union is $\{2,3,5,7,10,15\}$, a set with 6 elements in it.

30. **1.** PEMDAS to the rescue! Remember that you can treat absolute value signs as parentheses, so you want to simplify $(3 - 5)$ and $|3 - 12|$ first. That simplifies the expression to $\left|(-2)^2 - 45 \div (9)\right|$. Now deal with the exponents and the division, and then simplify: $|4 - 45 \div 9| = |4 - 5| = |-1| = 1$.

31. ¾ or **2.25.** You want to take steps to solve for x, so adding 7 to both sides seems like a good first step: $2\sqrt{x} = 3$. Now divide both sides by 2: $\sqrt{x} = \frac{3}{2}$. To solve for x, you need to square both sides. Take care to make sure you square the numerator and the denominator in the fraction! $x = \left(\frac{3}{2}\right)^2 = \frac{9}{4}$ or 2.25.

Don't forget that you're not allowed to grid in a mixed number. You can grid in ¾, but if you try to grid in 2¼, the scoring machine reads the answer as $\frac{21}{4}$ — and marks you wrong.

32. **6.** You figured out that Kevin is the youngest, I hope, so he's the easiest to represent with a variable; k seems appropriate. We know that Gini, $g = k + 33$, and that Gini is also $g = 2k + 30$ (Lynn is twice as old as Kevin, so you can represent Lynn as $2k$). Set $g = g$ and solve for k: $k + 33 = 2k + 30$, $k = 3$. Kevin is 3 years old, so Lynn is 6 years old.

33. **800.** This question is tricky because of those sports fans who ate 2 hot dogs each. Rather than think of 6% of the people as eating 2 hot dogs, it's easier to pretend that 12% ate 1 hot dog, meaning that 20% + 12% = 32% of the sports fans ate 1 hot dog. Now you just need to determine what 32% of 2,500 is: $0.32(2500) = 800$ hot dogs.

34. **77.** The parallel lines AB and DC are cut by another line (a transversal), BC. That means that the small angles in those intersections are equal, so $3x + 5 = 4x - 5$. You can solve for x easily: $x = 10$. That means that angle ADC has a measure of $8x - 3$, which you now can figure out is equal to $8(10) - 3 = 80 - 3 = 77$ degrees.

35. **27.** There are 12 boys on the team, and their part of the 5:4 ratio is the 4. So if you multiply both parts of 5:4 by 3, you get the actual number of girls and boys: 15:12, making a total of 27 people on the team.

36. **68.5.** Arnold made 30% profit, so he sold the shoes for 130% of the original price, meaning that $89.05 is 130% of the original price. Set up a proportion and determine what 100% of the original price is: $\frac{89.05}{130} = \frac{x}{100}$. Cross-multiply and divide, and you get an original price, x, of $68.50, which you should grid in as 68.5.

37. **9.** This question looks really tricky, but when you know how to look at it, you'll see that you can tackle it without breaking a sweat. First, remember that $a^2 - b^2 = (a+b)(a-b)$ (the difference of perfect squares). You want to know what $a + b$ is, so all you really need to know is the value of $a - b$. But wait! You do know that! If $a = b + 3$, then $a - b = 3$. So, substitute what you know into $a^2 - b^2 = (a+b)(a-b)$: $27 = (a+b)(3)$. Divide both sides by 3, and you get $a + b = 9$.

38. **28.** Recall that the factors of a number are all the whole numbers that divide the number evenly. Think about what numbers you can multiply together to get 12: 1 and 12, 2 and 6, and 3 and 4. Those six numbers are the factors of 12, so to do this problem you just need to add them up: $\#12 = 1 + 12 + 2 + 6 + 3 + 4 = 28$.

Section 5: Writing

1. **D.** The rent statement isn't received in a place, but rather a time ("the first day of the month"), in this sentence. Therefore, "when" is better than "where." Also, the verb tense in the original sentence is off. Because the sentence refers to both the past and present (the period during which the rent statement is sitting under a pile of junk mail in the basement of a post office), the present-perfect verb "has not been received" is better than the present tense ("is not received").

2. **C.** The preposition "including" takes an object pronoun, not a subject pronoun, so you need "him," not "he." That fact rules out Choices (A) and (B). Of the three choices that remain, Choice (C) is the simplest and therefore the most effective.

3. **B.** The original "sentence" is actually a fragment because you don't have a matching subject-verb pair. The *weekend is* fills that requirement, so Choice (B) is best here.

4. **B.** The "who" statement is about not texting or speaking on a cellphone. Using your reading comprehension skills, you see that only one person is in that category — Robert. Therefore, the "who" refers to "Robert," a singular noun, and must be matched with "wasn't," a singular verb.

5. **C.** The action verb "bent" must be described by an adverb (quickly), not an adjective (quick). But, as they say on late-night TV, there's more! The adverb "quickly" must also be described by an adverb (really), not an adjective (real). The only two choices with "really quickly" are Choices (C) and (E), but Choice (E) messes up some perfectly good verbs. Choice (C) is better.

6. **D.** Put your finger over "Lucy believes" and look at the sentence again. You see "What the problem is is the lack of planning." Ouch! Not a good choice. Now cover "Lucy believes" in Choice (D). Here you have "The problem is the lack of planning." Sounds better, right? That's because it *is* right.

When you see "everyone knows" or "I think" or "Lucy believes" (as in Question 6), you should check the sentence with those words removed (temporarily). Sometimes an error becomes visible when you omit opinion statements.

7. **B.** When a sentence begins with a verb form and an implied subject, the grammar authorities decree that the subject that *does* appear in the main portion of the sentence be the same as the omitted subject. Therefore, in the original sentence, "Ellery" should be the subject of both "was shining" (the "was" is also implied) and "closed." "Ellery" can't shine on his own dark glasses, so the first part of the sentence needs revision. Choice (B) takes care of the problem.

8. **A.** Yes! This one has it all. The plural pronoun "they" matches the plural noun "authors," and the verbs are fine too. No changes are necessary, so Choice (A) is your answer.

9. **E.** The original sentence begins with a good subject-verb pair, but the idea isn't complete. "As" creates a dependent clause. Before your head floats right off your neck, calm down and ignore the grammar lingo. Read the sentence again and "hear" it. It's not complete. After the dependent clause, all you have is a subject "the crowd" and descriptive verb forms, "cheering" and "clapping." The original also throws in another subject, "mission control," without a proper verb. The correction pairs each subject with past-tense verbs — perfect!

10. **A.** The subject of the sentence is "braids," a plural noun, so you need the plural verb "are." Now you're down to Choices (A) and (B), the only ones with plural verbs. Choice (B) has a problem, though. The "inhabitants" can't *be* reverence, they can only feel or practice that quality. No doubt here: Choice (A) is the answer.

11. **D.** The signing took place before the celebrating and the cooking, so you need the helping verb "had" to move that event farther in the past.

12. **D.** The original sentence is a bit scrambled. The phrase "from view" should be closer to the verb "hid." Choice (D) solves the problem nicely.

13. **B.** When you're listing events in the past without any reason to put them in order, you don't need "had." (Compare this sentence to Question 11, where the order of events is important.)

14. **C.** The description "with food piled on top" should be close to the word it describes (bread). Choice (C) moves it into proper position.

15. **E.** Simpler, on the PSAT/NMSQT and in life, is often (but not always) better. Choice (E) conveys the information clearly. The participle "elected" matches the tense of the verb "was." Choices (A), (B), (C), and (D) add unnecessary helping verbs or other grammatical elements.

16. **D.** The sentence contains a comparison between written and spoken words. Only Choice (D) expresses this comparison correctly, because only Choice (D) is parallel. In a parallel sentence (don't worry — no math here!), everything doing the same job in the sentence must have the same grammatical identity.

17. **C.** This sentence contains a list, and lists must match. That is, everything on the list should have the same grammatical identity. The original list contains two simple descriptions (subdued, old-fashioned) and a subject-verb combo (they were . . . received). Choice (C) turns the subject-verb combo into a simple description (not well received). Choice (C) is your answer.

18. **B.** This sentence expresses what grammarians call "condition contrary to fact." Clare did *not* know about the conference. Therefore, that portion of the sentence needs a subjunctive verb. (You form the subjunctive by adding a "had" to action verbs or by using "were" for states of being.)

19. **B.** The expression "couldn't hardly" is a double negative and not allowed in proper English. Change "couldn't" to "could" and you're all set.

20. **D.** The word "irregardless" looks long and impressive, but it isn't correct in standard English. Go for the simplest replacement, Choice (D), which conveys the meaning without unneeded words.

21. **E.** Everything is perfect here — verbs, descriptions, shout-out to NYC (my home) — so "no error" is your answer.

22. **B.** The verb "ran" should be described by the adverb "speedily," not by the adjective "speedy."

23. **D.** The verb "lead" is present tense, but World War II is in the past, so the proper expression is "that led up to World War II" — or, if you prefer a description rather than a subject-verb pair, "leading up to World War II."

24. **A.** The expression "being that" isn't standard; go for "because."

25. **B.** Longer words, such as "dangerous," form a comparison with "more" or "less," not with –*er*. The correct expression is "more dangerous."

26. **E.** Surprised? Were you fooled by Choice (C)? The verb "be" is subjunctive, a word you don't have to know. You *do* have to know that when someone insists, commands, or decrees, the verb you need in the second portion of the sentence is the infinitive form, minus the "to." So "to be" loses the "to," and "be" is correct. In fact, the whole sentence is correct!

27. **A.** When the subjects of a sentence are linked by "neither . . . nor" (or "either . . . or"), the subject closest to the verb is in charge. Because "supervisor" is singular, it requires a singular verb (was), not the plural verb (were).

28. **B.** The sentence is a run-on because a comma can't glue one complete thought to another. The sentence needs a semicolon or "because" or another conjunction (joining word) before "it."

29. **A.** The pronoun "it" is meaningless in this sentence because it has nothing to refer to. You can say, "According to the paper, fireworks are. . ." or, "An article in the paper reports that . . ." or something similar, but the "it" has to go.

30. **B.** You have "the chef," so you don't need "he" also.

31. **B.** You need the subject pronoun "who" to pair with the verb "was," not the object pronoun "whom."

32. **D.** The expression should be "within," not "by within."

33. **C.** The word "furthermore" looks very important, but it isn't a legal ***conjunction*** (joining words). You need a semicolon, two separate sentences, or a conjunction to make the sentence correct.

34. **D.** The description "that were cruelly left by their former owners" belongs next to what it describes, "animals."

35. **D.** The first sentence establishes that world's fairs have been around for more than a century. The last sentence also talks about the history of these fairs. Why separate these two? Combine similar ideas, and the paragraph has a more logical structure.

36. **B.** The essay as a whole relies on "you," what grammarians call "second person." Sentence 7 is the only spot with a "third person" pronoun (one). Why switch? You have no good reason, so Choice (B), which stays with second person, is a better sentence than the original. Choices (D) and (E) include "we," so stay away from them. Choice (C) has second person, true, but the wording implies that the *Internet* is still at home, not the person using the Internet. No doubts here: Choice (B) is the only correct choice.

37. **B.** Both sentences say the same thing, with Sentence 9 being the general and Sentence 10 the specific statement. ***Concise*** writing (with no extra words) is strong. Go for Choice B, which gets the job done with a minimum of words.

38. **E.** The second paragraph is about money — the cost of holding a fair offset by the possible income. The third paragraph explains how a city may benefit from structures built for the fair. Choice (E) creates a bridge — what English teachers call a ***transition*** — between Paragraphs 2 and 3 by linking these two advantages of world's fairs.

39. **E.** The essay gives pros and cons of fairs, but then the writer simply stops. The essay lacks a conclusion, which Choice (E) suggests. If the writer is in favor of the fairs, he or she might write about how world's fairs are still valuable, as people learn more by visiting them than they do by looking at a screen. Or, if the writer is against fairs, the last paragraph might discuss the waste of resources on temporary exhibits. Either way, the essay would leave the reader with something to think about.

Answer Key for Practice Test 4

Section 1

1. A	7. B	13. C	19. A
2. E	8. A	14. E	20. B
3. C	9. C	15. A	21. C
4. B	10. A	16. D	22. B
5. D	11. D	17. B	23. B
6. B	12. B	18. D	24. A

Section 2

1. E	6. E	11. C	16. A
2. B	7. C	12. B	17. C
3. E	8. A	13. B	18. C
4. D	9. A	14. A	19. D
5. B	10. C	15. C	20. B

Section 3

25. B	31. B	37. C	43. A
26. A	32. D	38. E	44. C
27. C	33. B	39. D	45. E
28. E	34. A	40. A	46. A
29. B	35. C	41. C	47. B
30. D	36. A	42. E	48. C

Section 4

21. A	26. C	31. ¾ **or 2.25**	36. **68.5**
22. D	27. C	32. **6**	37. **9**
23. A	28. C	33. **800**	38. **28**
24. D	29. **6**	34. **77**	
25. E	30. **1**	35. **27**	

Section 5

1. D	11. D	21. E	31. B
2. C	12. D	22. B	32. D
3. B	13. B	23. D	33. C
4. B	14. C	24. A	34. D
5. C	15. E	25. B	35. D
6. D	16. D	26. E	36. B
7. B	17. C	27. A	37. B
8. A	18. B	28. B	38. E
9. E	19. B	29. A	39. E
10. A	20. D	30. B	

Part V
The Part of Tens

The 5th Wave   By Rich Tennant

"When my parents see the grade I got on the math section, they're going to have a Pythagorean fit."

In this part . . .

Ten fingers, ten toes. That's what humans need for a perfect set of *digits* (the general term for fingers and toes). To have as close to perfect an experience as possible on the PSAT/NMSQT, you also need ten — specifically, the Part of Tens. In this part I explain ten ways to become a better test-taker and ten mistakes to avoid when you take the exam.

Chapter 19

Ten Ways to Improve Your Test-Taking Skills

In This Chapter

▶ Preparing for the test before you take it

▶ Maintaining your focus on test day

The PSAT/NMSQT isn't the only standardized test with the potential to ruin a perfectly good morning. Learning *how* to approach one of these alphabet-soup nightmares (such as the SAT, the ACT, APs, and goodness knows what else) is the best way to ensure that you earn a reward for all your hard work — a scholarship or a leg up on college admissions. To become a better test-taker, read on.

Know the Directions Ahead of Time

The moment you open your test booklet, the stopwatch begins to tick. Yes, you can read the directions during the exam, but why waste time doing so? In this book I explain the directions for sentence completions and passage-based questions in the critical reading section, multiple-choice and grid-in problems in the mathematics section, and sentence-improvement, error-recognition, and paragraph-improvement questions in the writing section. Becoming familiar with the task means less anxiety and more minutes for the actual problems.

That said, I must point out that you should *never* skip the introduction to a critical reading passage. Sometimes you find a useful bit of information there, enough to tip the scale toward one answer and away from another. Also, if you forget a math formula, don't hesitate to peek at the box of formulas at the beginning of each math section.

Go in with a Time Plan

After taking a couple of practice exams from Part IV of this book and examining your performance, you should have a good idea about what kind of question takes you forever and what sort you can complete in a nano-second. Make a time budget before test day, **apportioning** (dividing up and assigning) a reasonable number of minutes for each set of questions. Keep your eye on the clock or on your watch during the exam, and speed up or slow down as needed.

Remember that skipping a question or taking a guess won't kill your score, as long as you follow the guessing strategy I outline in Chapter 2. Your time budget should allow for the fact that you may complete some questions perfectly, guess the answer occasionally, and skip some difficult problems.

Be in the Right Place at the Right Time

Tests bring anxiety, and nervous fingers may turn to the wrong section or enter an answer on the wrong line. (Imagine skipping an answer line and discovering, 20 filled-in lines later, that everything is off by one line!) So talk to yourself, but do so in your head; saying something out loud will land you in the street, your score canceled. Check that you're actually looking at Section 2 when the proctor announces, "Turn to Section 2." Say (silently!), "I am working on Section 2."

As you move from question to question, continue talking, still silently. Say, "The answer to Question 4 is B" as you place your finger on Line 4 and bubble in the oval marked B.

Use the Test Booklet

The exam-writers thoughtfully leave wide margins next to reading passages and surround each math question with a ton of unused space. Use those spots to annotate a passage or calculate the answer to a math problem. When you hand in your question booklet, it should be filled with pencil marks. But — and this is *really* important — nothing in the question booklet counts as an answer. You *must* bubble in your choices to receive points.

Using the test booklet comes with a bonus: It's returned to you when you receive your scores. Then you can go over your errors, following the path you took to the wrong answer. When you take the SAT, you'll be better prepared because you can use the PSAT/NMSQT information to improve your skills.

Avoid Distractions

Make a pact with your friends: You won't stand next to each other in the hallway before πthe test, and you won't even look at them during breaks. Furthermore, you won't instant-message or call each other to discuss the test at any time on the day before the exam. Why? Because when you arrive at test eve or test day, you've done everything you can to prepare. All that's left is to show up in reasonably good shape. Chatting with your friends before the test is a great way to give yourself a nervous breakdown. ***Inevitably*** (unavoidably), someone will say something like "I don't know enough trigonometry," and you'll panic because you didn't review trigonometry. (Good thing, too, because trig isn't on the PSAT/NMSQT.) If you isolate yourself, no one can send you into one of these death spirals.

Eat a Proper Breakfast

The PSAT/NMSQT takes place in the morning, and it lasts nearly three hours. Your mind needs fuel just as much as your body. No matter how much or how little you usually eat for breakfast, prepare for the exam by ***consuming*** (eating) a breakfast that will hold off hunger pangs.

Stay away from sugar, though. Studies show that a sugary meal gives you a **spurt** (quick rush) of energy, followed by a tired spell. Protein lasts longer and provides a steadier supply of power. Try trail mix (nuts and dried fruit), eggs, or whatever you like in the protein-laden category.

Keep Control of Your Eyes and Body

Proctors are required to **eject** (throw out) and report anyone whose behavior is suspect. I'm sure you'd never consider cheating, but you must also take care to avoid the appearance of dishonesty. When you're thinking or relaxing, close your eyes or look up at the ceiling. Don't glance around the room, even if the closest test-taker is 10 feet away.

If you move your body — stretching away tension or working out a cramp — close your eyes while you do so, and stay away from any objects around you. The proctor shouldn't see your hands or feet touching whatever is stowed under your desk (your bag, for example). The only time you can reach for supplies is when the proctor announces a math section and tells you to take out your calculator (which sits under your desk during the critical reading and writing sections).

Answer the Question You're Asked

Do you have to find the prime numbers in a set, or the odd numbers? Are you choosing a statement that doesn't apply to the narrator of a reading passage, or one that does describe him? You can't come up with a correct answer unless you read the question closely and figure out what the test-makers want to know. The prime rule of testing (and of college admissions in general): Give them what they want, when they want it!

The best way to be sure you understand the question is to underline key words or phrases — *more than, less than, purpose, characteristics of,* and so forth.

Focus on the Task at Hand

It's fine to skip around during the exam, answering the questions you're sure of before turning to those that puzzle you. However, hopping all over the place is *not* a good idea. Remember that, except for the passage-based reading and writing questions, everything proceeds from easy to hard, according to statistical evidence the College Board collects. So moving through a section in order is probably best, with some exceptions.

What exceptions? I thought you'd never ask. Because you've brilliantly prepared for the PSAT/NMSQT with this book, you already know where your strengths and weaknesses lie. If you **detest** (hate) geometry because you get many wrong answers, consider leaving those problems for last. If you never met a probability question you didn't like, do every one of those first. You can also skip a reading passage that appears difficult, returning to it later as time permits.

If you have trouble focusing, place your non-writing hand over everything above the question you're working on, and cover everything below with the answer sheet. With only one question visible, maintaining focus is easier.

Learn from Experience

In this book you have a chance to take four practice tests before the big day arrives. Use as many of those chances as possible! Walking into the exam room knowing what to expect is a huge *asset* (advantage). Also, study the explanations that I've provided for each question when you score your practice exams. Before you take the actual PSAT/NMSQT, review the topics that stumped you. Make a list of errors you should avoid — grammar or math facts, perhaps. Read that list from time to time, so you know where you should be extra careful. For instance, suppose you often forgot to check punctuation in error-recognition questions. Place punctuation on your list. You may even write "punctuation!" at the top of the test page to remind yourself to look at commas and semicolons.

Chapter 20

Ten Mistakes to Avoid on the PSAT/NMSQT

In This Chapter

▶ Reading complete passages and paying attention to details

▶ Using math principles to solve math problems

▶ Arriving at the test rested and keeping the test in perspective

I once proctored an exam during which a very nervous student turned green, bent over, and deposited his breakfast all over the answer sheet. Big mistake! I sincerely hope your breakfast stays where it belongs, inside your digestive system. I also hope you avoid these ten critical mistakes when it's your turn to take the PSAT/NMSQT.

Misreading the Diagrams

In the PSAT/NMSQT math sections, plenty of problems come with diagrams — little triangles, lines running up and down, graphs, charts, and so forth. These diagrams are there to help you, but they usually aren't drawn to scale and can be misleading. Don't assume, for example, that one angle is larger than another unless you're told that it is. Just because one section of a circle graph looks the same size as another doesn't mean they're equal.

Bottom line: The diagrams and graphs give you information, but the words and numbers in the problems should be your primary source.

Substituting Memory for Logic

You hit Question 12, an equation. You're supposed to find the value of *x*. Great, you think. Yesterday when I was practicing I found the value of *x* in an equation like this one. All I had to do was subtract 4 from each side and then simplify. So you subtract 4 from each side and simplify — and come up with the wrong answer! That's what happens when you rely on memory, not logic.

When you solve a math problem, use the principles of math that you learned in school and while preparing for the PSAT/NMSQT. Apply those principles, and your answer will be correct.

Working Out of Order

Two *cryptic* (coded) sets of letters help you solve math problems on the PSAT/NMSQT: FOIL and PEMDAS. FOIL tells you the order of operations when you're multiplying two terms by two terms, such as $(x^2 + 8)$ and $(4 - 7x^2)$. You multiply the **F**irst, **O**uter, **I**nner, and **L**ast terms of the problem in that order and then combine like terms for the answer. If you ignore FOIL, you'll be *foiled* (prevented from succeeding) in your quest for a good math score.

Similarly, PEMDAS tells you how to solve a multipart problem. Use the letters to remember that you should work on everything in **P**arentheses, then turn to **E**xponents, then **M**ultiply or **D**ivide moving from left to right, and finally **A**dd or **S**ubtract as you go from left to right. (You may know this as GEMDAS, in which case you begin with **G**roupings and then proceed to the other operations.) Don't mess with PEMDAS (or GEMDAS) or you'll end up with the wrong answer.

Skipping Part of a Critical Reading Passage

If your reading speed is on the slow side, you may be tempted to zero in on the lines referred to in each critical reading question and skip everything else in the passage. This strategy may work occasionally — for a vocabulary-in-context question, for example — but far too often you'll be pulled toward the wrong answer if you don't read the entire selection. Why? Because the test-writers purposely plant some wrong answers that *could* be correct if a statement elsewhere in the paragraph, or in another paragraph, were not present. Instead of skipping sentences to save time, get to work now on increasing your reading speed. (Chapter 4 tells you how.)

Going for a Good, but Not the Best, Answer

The people who create PSAT/NMSQT questions have an annoying habit: They love to hit you with two answer choices that at first glance seem correct. The problem, of course, is that only one is right. Here's what I mean. Suppose you come across a ratio problem concerning high school athletes. You're told that the school has 9 baseball players for every 5 basketball players. You have to determine the total number of athletes in these two sports. One of the answer choices is 28, which represents 18 baseball players and 10 basketball players. That's a good answer if — and only if — the problem asks for the *possible* total number of athletes. But another answer choice, "cannot be determined," is the best, and therefore the correct, answer. Why? Because any 9-to-5 ratio works for this question. The ratio tells you only what *can be* true, not what *is* true.

I used a math example, but similar tricks pop up in critical reading and writing questions also. Don't be an *unwary* (careless) test-taker and jump on a seemingly good answer. Check everything to be sure you've selected the best choice.

Forgetting about Verbs

When you're working through the writing section, don't forget about verbs! Verbs power every sentence: They specify action or state of being, give information about the time period discussed in the sentence, and may even indicate whether something did or did not happen. Verbs, however, are particularly **vulnerable** (exposed) to errors. The test-writers **exploit** (take advantage of) verbs' tendency to stray from proper English by placing many incorrect verbs in the error-recognition and sentence-improvement problems.

Check agreement; a singular subject must pair with a singular verb. Note the tense and be sure it's appropriate. For example, a present perfect verb expresses an action or state of being that began in the past and continues in the present. A present perfect verb doesn't belong in a sentence that talks about something that ended. Look for helping verbs (*would, could, must,* and so forth) and be sure they express the proper shade of meaning. Only when you know that everything is A-OK in Verb Land should you move on to some other aspect of the sentence.

Stubbornly Sticking to Your First Impression

When you work through sentence completions in the critical reading section, you may "hear" an answer in your mind. In fact, you actually should try to fill in the blank with a word of your own before you look at the answer choices. But what happens when none of the answers match what's in your mind? Some people get stuck, unable to free themselves from their first idea. But that road leads to ruin, because one of those answers *must* be correct.

Here's a better way: Check your **initial** (first) impression. If it leads you to an answer choice, go for it. If it doesn't, you must adapt. Try to examine the sentence from a different angle. Opening yourself up to other possibilities may **yield** (produce) a correct answer.

Erasing Incompletely

As you work through the test, you may realize that an answer you initially chose is incorrect. Good for you! But when you record the new choice, don't neglect the old. You don't have to grind a hole in the paper, but incompletely erasing a previous answer automatically earns you a quarter-point deduction, because to the scoring machine, two answers to the same question are always scored as an error. Be sure your number two pencil has a good eraser, and use it carefully.

Shortchanging Sleep Time

Partying — or studying — late into the night before the PSAT/NMSQT is a bad idea. Do you really want to yawn your way through five sections of reading, writing, and arithmetic? I don't think so! Resting, relaxing with a hobby or a dumb TV show, and chatting with friends about anything other than the test are good ideas, as long as you stop at a reasonable hour and start snoring. You can always party *after* the exam. Resolve to arrive at the test with a good night's sleep behind you.

Losing Perspective

Yes, you want to do well on the PSAT/NMSQT. Of course, you should aim for scores that reflect your very best effort, ability, and preparation. But the PSAT/NMSQT is a test. Just a test! Not a permanent solution to war, illness, poverty, or any life or death situation. When you sit down to work on the exam, remember that you're answering questions, not determining the course of your entire life. You'll be calmer and more focused, and the results will be better.

Appendix

Scoring the Exams

• •

In This Appendix

▶ Computing your critical reading score

▶ Figuring out your math score

▶ Calculating your writing score

• •

*F*or any of the four practice exams, use the formulas in this appendix to figure out your PSAT/NMSQT scores for each section of the exam.

Calculating Your Critical Reading Score

First, figure out your raw critical reading score, using the following method.

1. **Count the total number of correct answers in both critical reading sections and place the number on Line 1.**

2. **Multiply the total number of wrong answers in both critical reading sections by ¼ and round to the nearest whole number. Place your answer on Line 2.**

3. **Subtract Line 2 from Line 1 to get your raw critical reading score.**

4. **Convert the raw score by using the following chart.**

Line 1 _____

Line 2 _____

Raw Critical Reading Score _____

Critical Reading Conversion Table

Raw Critical Reading Score	Converted Critical Reading Score
48	80
47	80
46	78
45	75
44	74
43	73
42	71
41	69
40	68
39	67

(continued)

Critical Reading Conversion Table *(continued)*

Raw Critical Reading Score	*Converted Critical Reading Score*
38	66
37	65
36	63
35	62
34	62
33	61
32	60
31	59
30	58
29	57
28	56
27	55
26	54
25	54
24	53
23	52
22	51
21	50
20	49
19	48
18	47
17	46
16	45
15	44
14	43
13	42
12	41
11	40
10	39
9	38
8	37
7	36
6	34
5	33
4	32
3	30
2	29
1	27
0	25
below 0	20

Scoring the Math Sections

How cruel to make you calculate after you've finished calculating answers to PSAT/NMSQT questions! Do it anyway, following these steps:

1. **Count the total number of correct answers in both math sections and place the number on Line 1. Count both multiple-choice and grid-ins for this step.**

2. **Ignore the grid-ins for this step. Multiply the number of wrong answers to everything except the grid-ins by ¼ and round to the nearest whole number. Place your answer on Line 2.**

3. **Subtract Line 2 from Line 1 to get your raw math score.**

4. **Convert the raw score by using the following chart.**

Line 1 _____

Line 2 _____

Raw Math Score _____

Mathematics Conversion Table

Raw Math Score	Converted Math Score
38	80
37	78
36	76
35	72
34	70
33	68
32	66
31	65
30	64
29	62
28	61
27	60
26	59
25	58
24	57
23	55
22	54
21	53
20	52
19	51
18	50
17	48

(continued)

Mathematics Conversion Table *(continued)*

Raw Math Score	Converted Math Score
16	47
15	46
14	45
13	44
12	43
11	42
10	41
9	40
8	39
7	38
6	36
5	35
4	34
3	33
2	32
1	31
0	26
below 0	25 or lower

Determining Your Writing Score

To calculate your writing score, count the number of correct and incorrect answers in the writing section. Then follow these steps:

1. **Place the total number of correct answers on Line 1.**

2. **Multiply the total number of wrong answers by ¼ and round to the nearest whole number. Place your answer on Line 2.**

3. **Subtract Line 2 from Line 1 to get your raw writing score.**

4. **Convert the raw score by using the following chart.**

Line 1 _____

Line 2 _____

Raw Writing Score _____

Writing Conversion Table

Raw Writing Score	Converted Writing Score
39	80
38	80
37	78
36	77
35	76
34	74
33	73
32	71
31	69
30	68
29	66
28	64
27	63
26	60
25	59
24	57
23	56
22	55
21	53
20	52
19	51
18	50
17	49
16	48
15	47
14	46
13	45
12	44
11	42
10	41
9	40
8	38
7	37
6	35
5	34

(continued)

Writing Conversion Table *(continued)*

Raw Writing Score	Converted Writing Score
4	32
3	30
2	28
1	26
0	24
below 0	22 or lower

Index

multiple-choice questions. *See also specific practice tests; specific question types by name*
  guessing strategy for, 26
  mathematics section, 71–72
multiplication
  of algebraic terms, 98–99
  exponents, working with, 97, 319
  in order of operations, 81–83
  of radicals, 83
  symbols for in algebra problems, 95
multiplication principle, 229
myself, use of, 188, 233

• N •

National Achievement Scholarships, 17, 20
National Hispanic Recognition Program, 18
National Merit Scholarship, 16–17, 20
National Merit Scholarship Corporation, 16, 17
National Merit Scholarship Qualifying Test. *See* NMSQT
National Scholarship Service, 17
negative exponents, 97, 179, 278
negative numbers
  general discussion, 80
  in grid-ins, 73
  practice test 2, 224, 229
negative probability, 133
NMSQT (National Merit Scholarship Qualifying Test)
  logistics, 19–26
  overview, 1–6, 9
  versus SAT, 9–10
  scholarships, 16–18
  scoring, 15–16
  sections of, 10–15
  test-taking skills, improving, 333–336
nonstandard expressions
  in error-recognition questions, 61
  in sentence-improvement questions, 59
*n*th term, in sequences, 90
number two pencils
  bringing to exam, 21
  using for practice tests, 145
numbers
  in grid-ins, 72–73
  types of, 79–81

numbers questions. *See also specific practice tests*
  absolute value, 83–84
  distance problems, 88–90
  number types, 79–81
  order of operations, 81–83
  overview, 12, 79
  percentage problems, 84–86
  radicals, 83–84
  rate problems, 88–90
  ratio, 86–87
  sequences, 90–92
  sets, 92–93
  time problems, 88–90
numerator, fractional exponents, 184
numerical coefficient, in algebra, 96

• O •

object
  prepositions, 187
  who/whom, 186
object pronouns, 66–67
odd numbers, 80, 224
odds (probability). *See also specific practice tests*
  general discussion, 133–136
  overview, 12–13
  practice test 2, 231
  practice test 3, 273
  practice test 4, 324
off-topic sentences, paragraph-improvement questions, 63
omitted information, in passage-based questions, 51
open-ended math questions (grid-ins)
  general discussion, 72–73
  graphs, analyzing, 140–142
  overview, 13
  practice test 1 answers and explanations, 184–185
  practice test 1 questions, 166–167
  practice test 2 answers and explanations, 230–231
  practice test 2 questions, 212–213

Notes

Notes

Apple & Mac

iPad For Dummies,
5th Edition
978-1-118-49823-1

iPhone 5 For Dummies,
5th Edition
978-1-118-35201-4

MacBook For Dummies,
4th Edition
978-1-118-20920-2

OS X Mountain Lion
For Dummies
978-1-118-39418-2

Blogging & Social Media

Facebook For Dummies,
4th Edition
978-1-118-09562-1

Mom Blogging
For Dummies
978-1-118-03843-7

Pinterest For Dummies
978-1-118-32800-2

WordPress For Dummies,
5th Edition
978-1-118-38318-6

Business

Commodities For Dummies,
2nd Edition
978-1-118-01687-9

Investing For Dummies,
6th Edition
978-0-470-90545-6

Personal Finance
For Dummies, 7th Edition
978-1-118-11785-9

QuickBooks 2013
For Dummies
978-1-118-35641-8

Small Business Marketing
Kit For Dummies,
3rd Edition
978-1-118-31183-7

Careers

Job Interviews
For Dummies, 4th Edition
978-1-118-11290-8

Job Searching with
Social Media
For Dummies
978-0-470-93072-4

Personal Branding
For Dummies
978-1-118-11792-7

Resumes For Dummies,
6th Edition
978-0-470-87361-8

Success as a Mediator
For Dummies
978-1-118-07862-4

Diet & Nutrition

Belly Fat Diet For Dummies
978-1-118-34585-6

Eating Clean For Dummies
978-1-118-00013-7

Nutrition For Dummies,
5th Edition
978-0-470-93231-5

Digital Photography

Digital Photography
For Dummies,
7th Edition
978-1-118-09203-3

Digital SLR Cameras &
Photography For Dummies,
4th Edition
978-1-118-14489-3

Photoshop Elements 11
For Dummies
978-1-118-40821-6

Gardening

Herb Gardening
For Dummies, 2nd Edition
978-0-470-61778-6

Vegetable Gardening
For Dummies, 2nd Edition
978-0-470-49870-5

Health

Anti-Inflammation Diet
For Dummies
978-1-118-02381-5

Diabetes For Dummies,
3rd Edition
978-0-470-27086-8

Living Paleo For Dummies
978-1-118-29405-5

Hobbies

Beekeeping
For Dummies
978-0-470-43065-1

eBay For Dummies,
7th Edition
978-1-118-09806-6

Raising Chickens
For Dummies
978-0-470-46544-8

Wine For Dummies,
5th Edition
978-1-118-28872-6

Writing Young Adult Fiction
For Dummies
978-0-470-94954-2

Language &
Foreign Language

500 Spanish Verbs
For Dummies
978-1-118-02382-2

English Grammar
For Dummies, 2nd Edition
978-0-470-54664-2

French All-in One
For Dummies
978-1-118-22815-9

German Essentials
For Dummies
978-1-118-18422-6

Italian For Dummies,
2nd Edition
978-1-118-00465-4

Available in print and e-book formats.

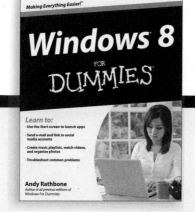

Available wherever books are sold. For more information or to order direct: U.S. customers visit www.Dummies.com or call 1-877-762-2974.
U.K. customers visit www.Wileyeurope.com or call (0) 1243 843291. Canadian customers visit www.Wiley.ca or call 1-800-567-4797.
Connect with us online at www.facebook.com/fordummies or @fordummies

Math & Science

Algebra I For Dummies,
2nd Edition
978-0-470-55964-2

Anatomy and Physiology
For Dummies,
2nd Edition
978-0-470-92326-9

Astronomy For Dummies,
3rd Edition
978-1-118-37697-3

Biology For Dummies,
2nd Edition
978-0-470-59875-7

Chemistry For Dummies,
2nd Edition
978-1-1180-0730-3

Pre-Algebra Essentials
For Dummies
978-0-470-61838-7

Microsoft Office

Excel 2013 For Dummies
978-1-118-51012-4

Office 2013 All-in-One
For Dummies
978-1-118-51636-2

PowerPoint 2013
For Dummies
978-1-118-50253-2

Word 2013 For Dummies
978-1-118-49123-2

Music

Blues Harmonica
For Dummies
978-1-118-25269-7

Guitar For Dummies,
3rd Edition
978-1-118-11554-1

iPod & iTunes
For Dummies,
10th Edition
978-1-118-50864-0

Programming

Android Application
Development For Dummies,
2nd Edition
978-1-118-38710-8

iOS 6 Application
Development For Dummies
978-1-118-50880-0

Java For Dummies,
5th Edition
978-0-470-37173-2

Religion & Inspiration

The Bible For Dummies
978-0-7645-5296-0

Buddhism For Dummies,
2nd Edition
978-1-118-02379-2

Catholicism For Dummies,
2nd Edition
978-1-118-07778-8

Self-Help & Relationships

Bipolar Disorder
For Dummies,
2nd Edition
978-1-118-33882-7

Meditation For Dummies,
3rd Edition
978-1-118-29144-3

Seniors

Computers For Seniors
For Dummies,
3rd Edition
978-1-118-11553-4

iPad For Seniors
For Dummies,
5th Edition
978-1-118-49708-1

Social Security
For Dummies
978-1-118-20573-0

Smartphones & Tablets

Android Phones
For Dummies
978-1-118-16952-0

Kindle Fire HD
For Dummies
978-1-118-42223-6

NOOK HD For Dummies,
Portable Edition
978-1-118-39498-4

Surface For Dummies
978-1-118-49634-3

Test Prep

ACT For Dummies,
5th Edition
978-1-118-01259-8

ASVAB For Dummies,
3rd Edition
978-0-470-63760-9

GRE For Dummies,
7th Edition
978-0-470-88921-3

Officer Candidate Tests,
For Dummies
978-0-470-59876-4

Physician's Assistant Exam
For Dummies
978-1-118-11556-5

Series 7 Exam
For Dummies
978-0-470-09932-2

Windows 8

Windows 8 For Dummies
978-1-118-13461-0

Windows 8 For Dummies,
Book + DVD Bundle
978-1-118-27167-4

Windows 8 All-in-One
For Dummies
978-1-118-11920-4

e Available in print and e-book formats.

Available wherever books are sold. For more information or to order direct: U.S. customers visit www.Dummies.com or call 1-877-762-2974.
U.K. customers visit www.Wileyeurope.com or call (0) 1243 843291. Canadian customers visit www.Wiley.ca or call 1-800-567-4797.
Connect with us online at www.facebook.com/fordummies or @fordummies

Take Dummies with you everywhere you go!

Whether you're excited about e-books, want more from the web, must have your mobile apps, or swept up in social media, Dummies makes everything easier .

Visit Us

Like Us

Follow Us

Watch Us

Join Us

Pin Us

Circle Us

Shop Us

Dummies products make life easier!

- DIY
- Consumer Electronics
- Crafts

- Software
- Cookware
- Hobbies

- Videos
- Music
- Games
- and More!

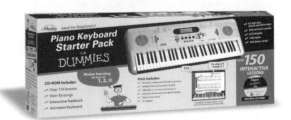

For more information, go to **Dummies.com**® and search the store by categor

For Dummies is a registered trademark of John Wiley & Sons, Inc.

FOR
DUMMIES
A Wiley Branc